murach's
Python
programming

Michael Urban
Joel Murach

BEGINNER TO PRO

murach's
Python
programming

Michael Urban

Joel Murach

MIKE MURACH & ASSOCIATES, INC.

4340 N. Knoll Ave. • Fresno, CA 93722

www.murach.com • murachbooks@murach.com

Editorial team

Authors:	Michael Urban
	Joel Murach
Editors:	Mike Murach
	Elizabeth Drake
Production:	Maria Spera

Books for web developers

Murach's HTML5 and CSS3 (3rd Edition)

Murach's JavaScript and jQuery (3rd Edition)

Murach's PHP and MySQL (3rd Edition)

Murach's Java Servlets and JSP (3rd Edition)

Murach's ASP.NET 4.6 with Web Programming with C# 2015

Murach's ASP.NET Web Programming with VB 2012

Books on core Java, C#, and Visual Basic

Murach's Beginning Java with NetBeans

Murach's Beginning Java with Eclipse

Murach's Java Programming (5th Edition)

Murach's C# 2015

Murach's Visual Basic 2015

Books for database programmers

Murach's MySQL (2nd Edition)

Murach's SQL Server 2016 for Developers

Murach's Oracle SQL and PL/SQL for Developers (2nd Edition)

For more on Murach books, please visit us at www.murach.com

10 9 8 7 6 5 4
ISBN: 978-1-890774-97-4

Content

Expanded contents

Section 2 Other concepts and skills

Chapter 18   **How to build a GUI program**

Appendix A   **How to set up Windows for this book**

Appendix B   **How to set up Mac OS X for this book**

Introduction

If you want to learn how to program but have little or no experience, you've chosen the right *language*. That's because Python has a simple syntax that makes it easier to learn than other programming languages. At the same time, it's a powerful language that provides all of the features that you need to master in *any* programming language. So a foundation in Python makes it easier to add other languages to your resume.

Beyond that, whether you're new to programming or have years of experience, you've chosen the right *book* for learning Python programming. If you're a beginner, our self-paced approach helps you build competence and confidence at every turn of the page. If you're an experienced programmer, this same self-paced approach lets you learn Python faster and more thoroughly than you've ever learned a language before.

Either way, when you're through, you'll have mastered the most important skills that are needed on the job, including those for object-oriented programming, database programming, and GUI programming. At that point, this book becomes a quick reference that you can rely on whenever you need to refresh your memory about coding details or apply a new feature to your work.

What this book does

To make this book as effective as possible, this book is divided into four sections:

- Section 1 presents an eight-chapter course in Python that gets you off to a great start. This section works for both newbies and experienced programmers because it lets you set your own pace. If you're a beginner, you'll move slowly and do all the exercises. If you have experience, you'll move more quickly, skimming through material you already know to focus on skills that are new to you or that you've never mastered.

- Section 2 presents the other Python essentials that every programmer should know. That includes expanding on the skills for working with numbers and strings that were presented in section 1. It also includes new skills like working with dates and times, dictionaries, recursion, and algorithms.

- Section 3 consists of three chapters that show how to design and develop object-oriented programs. This is a critical skillset in today's world, and it complements the procedural skills you learned in section 1. When you complete this section, you'll be able to develop programs that combine the best procedural practices with the best object-oriented practices.

- The focus of section 4 is to show you how all of the skills that you've learned in the first three sections are applied to real-world programs. First, chapter 17 shows you how to use Python for database programming, a must in businesses large and small. Then, chapter 18 shows you how to use Python to develop programs with graphical user interfaces (GUIs).

Why you'll learn faster and better with this book

Like all our books, this one has features that you won't find in competing books. That's why you'll learn faster and better with our book than with any other. Here are a few of those features.

- As you page through this book, you'll see that all of the information is presented in "paired pages," with the essential syntax, guidelines, and examples on the right page and the perspective and extra explanation on the left page. This helps you learn faster by reading less...and this is the ideal reference format when you need to refresh your memory about how to do something.

- To show you how Python works, this book presents 45 complete programs that build from the simple to the complex. We believe that studying the code for complete programs is critical to the learning process... and yet you won't find programs like ours in other Python books.

- Of course, this book also presents hundreds of short examples, so it's easy to find an example that shows what you want to do. Even better, our paired pages make it easier to find the example that you're looking for than it is with traditional books that embed the examples in the text.

- Like all our books, this one has exercises at the end of each chapter that give you hands-on experience practicing what you've learned. These exercises also encourage you to experiment and to apply what you've learned in new ways…just as you'll have to do on the job. Because our exercises start from partial programs that provide the boilerplate code, you get more practice in less time because you can focus on the skills you've just learned.

What software you need

To develop Python programs, you just need to download and install Python. It includes an integrated development environment (IDE) called IDLE that you can use for coding, testing, and debugging your programs. Chapter 1 shows how to use IDLE, and appendixes A and B show how to install Python and IDLE on Windows and Mac OS X systems.

If you're going to develop programs that use a SQLite database as shown in chapter 17, you also need to download and install a program for working with the tables in the database. For that, we recommend *DB Browser for SQLite*, and appendixes A and B also provide the instructions for installing it.

How our downloadable files can help you learn

If you go to our website at www.murach.com, you can download all the files that you need for getting the most from this book. This includes:

- the programs presented in this book
- the starting points for the exercises
- the solutions to the exercises

These files let you test, review, and copy the code. If you have any problems with the exercises, the solutions are there to help you over the learning blocks, an essential part of the learning process. And in some cases, the solutions will show you a more elegant way to handle a problem, even when you've come up with a solution that works. Here again, appendixes A and B show how to download and install these files on Windows and Mac OS X systems.

Support materials for instructors and trainers

If you're a college instructor or corporate trainer who would like to use this book as a course text, we offer a full set of the support materials you need for a turnkey course. That includes:

- instructional objectives that help your students focus on the skills that they need to develop
- dozens of projects that let your students prove how well they have mastered those skills
- test banks that let you measure how well your students have mastered those skills
- a complete set of PowerPoint slides that you can use to review and reinforce the content of the book

Instructors tell us that this is everything they need for a course without all the busywork that you get from other publishers.

To learn more about our instructor's materials, please go to our website at www.murachforinstructors.com if you're an instructor. Or if you're a trainer, please go to www.murach.com and click on the *Courseware for Trainers* link, or contact Kelly at 1-800-221-5528 or kelly@murach.com.

Please remember, though, that the primary component for a successful Python course is this book. Because your students will learn faster and more thoroughly when they use our book, they will have better questions and be more prepared when they come to class. Because our guided exercises start from partial programs, your students will get more and better practice in lab. And because our paired pages are so good for reference, your students will be able to review for tests and do their projects more efficiently.

Please let us know how this book works for you

From the start of this project, we've had two goals for this book. First, we wanted to make this the best-ever book for people with no experience who want to learn how to program. To do that right, we knew we not only had to make the book easy enough for beginners, but also had to teach all of the skills that a programmer needs to know.

Second, we wanted to make this the best-ever book for experienced programmers who want to add Python to their skillsets. To do that right, we've carefully selected the content, organized it from simple to complex in each chapter, and packed the book full of code examples and sample programs. That's why we believe that this book will help experienced programmers learn Python faster and better than ever. And when they're done, this book will be their best-ever on-the-job reference.

Now, we hope we've succeeded. We thank you for buying this book. We wish you all the best with your Python programming. And if you have any comments, we would appreciate hearing from you.

Joel Murach, Author
joel@murach.com

Mike Murach, Publisher
murachbooks@murach.com

Section 1

Essential concepts and skills

The eight chapters in this section get you off to a fast start by presenting a complete subset of the essential concepts and skills that you need for Python programming. First, chapter 1 introduces you to Python and shows you how to use an integrated development environment (IDE) called IDLE to develop and run programs. Then, chapters 2, 3, and 4 present skills that let you develop substantial programs of your own.

At that point, you're going to need to improve your testing and debugging skills, so that's what chapter 5 shows you how to do. Then, chapters 6, 7, and 8 continue your development. When you complete this section, you'll be able to design, code, test, and debug Python programs that can work with data that's stored in files.

1

An introduction to Python programming

This chapter starts by showing why Python is considered by many to be the best language for teaching beginners how to program. Next, this chapter presents the concepts and terms that you need to know before you start programming. Then, it shows how to use an integrated development environment (IDE) called IDLE to develop and test Python programs.

Introduction to Python

The *Python* programming language was developed in the 1990s by Guido van Rossum of the Netherlands. It was intended to be a simple, intuitive language that is as powerful as traditional languages, and it succeeded at that. Guido named the language Python because he was a big fan of "Monty Python's Flying Circus," and he continues to be involved in the development of Python. In fact, some developers in the Python community refer to him as the "Benevolent Dictator for Life (BDFL)".

Why Python works so well as your first programming language

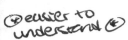

Figure 1-1 summarizes the case for learning Python as your first programming language. Here, you can see a short excerpt from a Java program and an excerpt from a Python program that does the same thing. This shows how much closer to plain English Python is and how much simpler the syntax for Python is. In fact, you'll often be able write a Python program with far less code than the same program would take in C++, Java, C#, or other traditional programming languages. And yet, you can learn most of the concepts and skills that you need for those languages when you learn Python, without getting slowed down by trivial coding details.

Beyond that, Python supports a wide range of applications. It is used by many successful companies. And it is *open source*, which means that its source code is available to the entire Python community.

In short, Python is a powerful programming language that lets you develop programs in less time and with less code than other programming languages. That's why it's a great language for learning how to program. But it's also a great language if you already know how to use another language or two.

In this figure, the Python timeline shows that Python 2 became available in the year 2000. This was replaced by Python 3 in 2008. However, Python 3 isn't *backward compatible*. That means that Python 3 can't run most programs written for Python 2. Conversely, Python 2 isn't *forward compatible*. That means that it can't run most programs written for Python 3.

In this book, you'll learn how to write programs for Python 3, and you'll learn how to use Python 3 to run those programs. As a result, compatibility won't be a problem. That's a great way to learn Python.

Four general-purpose programming languages

```
C++
Java
C#
Python
```

The Python timeline

Year	Month	Release	Description
2000	October	2.0	First release of Python 2
2008	December	3.0	A redesign of Python that isn't backward compatible
2010	July	2.7	Last release of Python 2 with support until 2020
2015	September	3.5	The latest release at this writing

Syntax differences between Python and Java

Some Java code

```java
private static double calculateFutureValue(
    double monthlyInvestment, double monthlyRate, int months)
{
    double futureValue = 0.0;
    for (int i = 1; i <= months; i++) {
        futureValue =
            (futureValue + monthlyInvestment) * (1 + monthlyRate);
    }
    return futureValue;
}
```

Python code that works the same

```python
def calculateFutureValue(monthlyInvestment, monthlyRate, months):
    futureValue = 0.0
    for i in range(months):
        futureValue =
            (futureValue + monthlyInvestment) * (1 + monthlyRate)
    return futureValue
```

Why Python is a great first language

- Python has a simple syntax that's easier to read and use than most other languages.
- Python has most of the features of traditional programming languages. As a result, you can use Python to learn the concepts and skills that apply to those languages too.
- Python supports the development of a wide range of programs, including games, web applications, and system administration.
- Python is used by many successful companies, including Google, IBM, Disney, and EA Games. As a result, knowing Python is a valuable skill.
- Python is *open source*. There are many advantages to being open source.

Figure 1-1   Why Python works so well as your first programming language

Three types of Python applications

An *application*, or *app*, is computer software that performs a task or related set of tasks. However, applications can also be referred to as *programs*, even though one application may actually consist of many related programs. In practice, most people use these terms interchangeably. In this book, we use the term program to refer to the short applications that it presents.

In any event, figure 1-2 shows three types of applications that you can create with Python. The first type is a *console application*. In this type of application, you enter commands at the *command prompt* in the *console* that's available from your operating system.

In this case, a console application is being run on a Windows system. As a result, it uses the Command Prompt window that's available from Windows. On a Mac OS X system, though, a console application runs in the Terminal window. Because console applications are the easiest type of application to develop, you'll work with console applications in the first three sections of this book.

The second type of Python application is a *GUI application*. That's an application that has a *graphical user interface (GUI)*. In this figure, the GUI application performs the same tasks as the console application. In other words, it gets the same input from the user, performs the same calculation, and displays the same result. However, the GUI application is more user-friendly and intuitive. You'll learn how to develop this type of application in the last section of this book.

The third type of application shown in this figure is a *web application*. Unlike a *desktop application*, which runs directly on your computer, a web application can be called by a web browser that's running on a computer or mobile device and can use a server to process or store data. In this figure, the web application performs the same task as the console and GUI applications. Although this book doesn't show how to develop web applications, you should know that Python frameworks are available to help you develop that type of application with Python.

You should also know that you can use Python as a *scripting language* to work with other software applications or to develop system administration programs that perform tasks like automatically backing up a server or rotating log files. Because programs like this usually run in the background, they don't always have a user interface. When you finish this book, though, you will have the skills you need to write this type of program.

A console application

＋ commands prompt in console

A GUI application
- graphical user interface

＊ more user-friendly

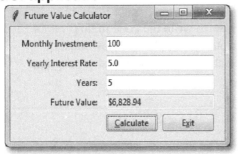

A web application

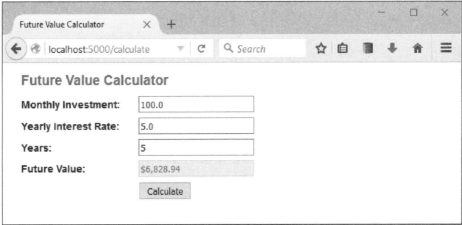

Description

available from operating system

- A *console application* is a desktop application that uses the *console* to interact with the user.

- A *GUI application* is an application that uses a *graphical user interface* (*GUI*) to interact with the user.

- A *web application* typically gets requests from a web browser, processes them on a web server, and returns the responses to the web browser.

Figure 1-2   Three types of Python applications

The source code for a console application

To show you what a Python program looks like, figure 1-3 shows the source code for a console application. This application gets three values from the user: a monthly investment amount, a yearly interest rate, and a number of years. Then, the program takes these entries and calculates the future value of the monthly investments with the interest calculated each month.

For now, just note that the code begins with a line that starts with a hash (#) and a bang (!). This line is commonly called the *shebang line*. It is ignored by Windows, but it's used by Unix-like operating systems, including Mac OS X, to specify the interpreter for the program. In this case, the shebang specifies that this program should be run using Python 3. As a result, you can use this shebang line for all programs in this book.

In the next chapter, you'll start learning how to write the code in this program. Then, by the time you complete chapter 3, you'll know how most of the code in this program works, and you'll be able to write comparable programs of your own.

#! : shebang line

The source code for a console application

```
#!/usr/bin/env python3

import locale

# set the locale for use in currency formatting
result = locale.setlocale(locale.LC_ALL, '')
if result == 'C':
    locale.setlocale(locale.LC_ALL, 'en_US')

# display a welcome message
print("Welcome to the Future Value Calculator")
print()

choice = "y"
while choice.lower() == "y":

    # get input from the user
    monthly_investment = float(input("Enter monthly investment:\t"))
    yearly_interest_rate = float(input("Enter yearly interest rate:\t"))
    years = int(input("Enter number of years:\t\t"))

    # convert yearly values to monthly values
    monthly_interest_rate = yearly_interest_rate / 12 / 100
    months = years * 12

    # calculate the future value
    future_value = 0
    for i in range(months):
        future_value = future_value + monthly_investment
        monthly_interest_amount = future_value * monthly_interest_rate
        future_value = future_value + monthly_interest_amount

    # format and display the result
    print("Future value:\t\t\t" + locale.currency(
        future_value, grouping=True))
    print()

    # see if the user wants to continue
    choice = input("Continue? (y/n): ")
    print()

print("Bye!")
```

(handwritten annotations:) shebang line — program run using Python 3

Discussion

- This application gets three values from the user: monthly investment amount, yearly interest rate, and number of years. Then, it calculates and displays the future value that the investments will grow to.

- The first line in this program is called the *shebang line*, or *shebang*. It specifies the interpreter that should be used to run this program. In this book, all programs should be run by Python 3.

Figure 1-3   The source code for a console application

How Python compiles and runs source code

The code in a program like the one in the last figure can be referred to as Python *source code*. To create the file that contains this source code, the programmer uses a text editor or integrated development environment (IDE), which you'll learn more about in a moment.

However, before the Python source code can be run (or executed) on a computer, the code must be translated into code that the computer can understand, as shown in figure 1-4. Here, you can see that the files that contain the source code have the .py extension. Then, the *Python interpreter* is used to translate (or *compile*) the source code into *bytecode*.

This bytecode can be run by any computer that has the *Python virtual machine* installed on it. This virtual machine translates the bytecode so it can be run by the operating system of the computer.

Since the Python virtual machine is part of the Python interpreter, it is available on all platforms that support Python. In fact, that's why Python is said to be *platform-independent*. In other words, it is the virtual machine that makes it possible for Python to run on a wide variety of operating systems.

Although this compilation process is complicated, it's done automatically with the push of a single key when you're using an IDE to develop your Python programs as shown later in this chapter. For now, all you need to take away from this figure is that Python source code is compiled into bytecode that's run by the computer's operating system.

How Python compiles and runs source code

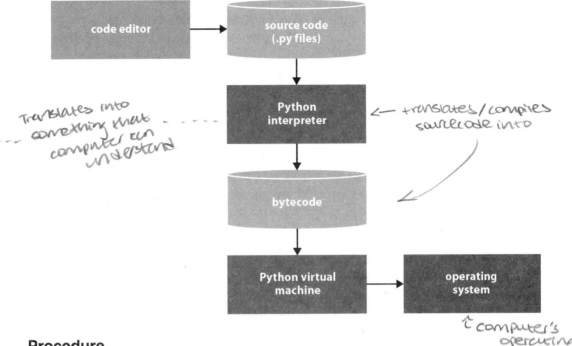

(handwritten note, left:) Translates into something that computer can understand

(handwritten note, right:) ← translates/compiles sourcecode into

(handwritten note, bottom right:) ↑ computer's operating system

Procedure

Step 1 The programmer uses a *text editor* or *IDE* to enter and edit the *source code*. Then, the programmer saves the source code to a file with a .py extension.

Step 2 The source code is *compiled* by the Python *interpreter* into *bytecode*.

Step 3 The bytecode is translated by the Python *virtual machine* into instructions that can interact with the operating system of the computer.

Description

- Although this procedure is complicated, it runs behind the scenes when you're developing Python programs. As a result, it's mostly invisible to the developer.

- Python bytecode can be run on any operating system that has a Python virtual machine. That's why Python is said to be *platform-independent*.

- If the program imports modules, the Python interpreter saves the compiled bytecode for those modules in files that have .pyc or .pyo extensions. This is an import optimization that can improve the startup time for a program.

Figure 1-4   How Python compiles and runs source code

How disk storage and main memory work together

Now that you know how a program is compiled and run, it's worth taking a minute to go over how the main memory of a computer and the disk storage of a computer work together as an application runs. This conceptual background can help you understand what needs to be done when you develop a program that works with data in disk storage. In addition, figure 1-5 presents the terms that you need to be familiar with.

To start, you should know that a computer consists of a *Central Processing Unit* (*CPU*) and *main memory*, which is often referred to as *RAM* (*Random Access Memory*). When an application runs, its bytecode is stored in main memory and its instructions are executed by the CPU. In addition, the data that the application is currently using is stored in main memory. This type of storage is temporary, however, so the data is lost when the application ends.

To store the data of an application, *disk storage* is commonly used. This type of storage remains after the application ends so it is called *persistent data storage*. In chapter 7, you'll learn how to work with persistent data that's stored in a file. Then, in chapter 17, you'll learn how to work with persistent data that's stored in a database.

In general, two types of software are stored on disk. *Systems software* consists of the programs that control the operation of the system. That includes the *operating system* for the computer, like Windows for a PC or OS X for a Mac. In contrast, *application software* consists of the applications that are available on the system. That includes applications such as web browsers, word processors, and spreadsheet programs.

When a computer starts, it loads the operating system from disk storage into main memory. Then, when you start an application, the operating system loads the application from disk storage into main memory, and it runs the application. If the application requires persistent data while it is running, it reads the data from disk storage into main memory and then processes it. If the application updates the data or creates new data, it writes the data from main memory back to disk storage.

The storage capacity of main memory and disk storage is measured in *bytes*. For instance, main memory used to be measured in *megabytes* (*MB*), which is millions of bytes, but now it is usually measured in *gigabytes* (*GB*), which is billions of bytes. For the record, a *byte* consists of eight *binary digits*, or *bits*, and each byte is roughly equivalent to one character of data, like an A or a B.

If you're comfortable with these concepts and terms, you're ready to learn how to use an IDE to create, test, and debug Python programs as shown in the next few figures. Otherwise, it's worth taking a few minutes to review the terms in this figure because they're terms that every programmer should know.

Main memory and disk storage as an application runs

Main memory *CRAM)*

Operating system
The application that's running
The data for the application

(TEMPORARY)

Disk storage – *persistent data storage*

Systems software – *operations of system*
Application software – *applications systems*
Application data

(PERSISTENT)

How disk storage and main memory work together

- When you start the computer, it loads the operating system <u>into</u> main memory. Then, you use the features of the operating system to start an application.

- When you start an application, the operating system loads it into main memory. Then, it runs the application.

- As the application runs, it may read data from disk storage into main memory or write data from main memory to disk storage.

Description

- The *system software* for a computer provides all of the software that is needed for running the applications, including the *operating system*.

- The *applications software* consists of the applications that are available on the system.

- A computer consists of a *CPU* (*Central Processing Unit*) and *main memory*, also known as *RAM* (*Random Access Memory*).

- The data in main memory is lost when an application ends. *Disk storage* is used for *persistent data storage* which remains after an application ends.

- Main memory and disk storage are commonly measured in *megabytes* (*MB*) and *gigabytes* (*GB*), and a *byte* is roughly equivalent to one character of data.

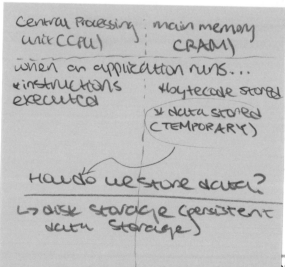

Central Processing : main memory
unit (CPU)   (RAM)

when an application runs...
*instructions   *bytecode stored
executed   *data stored
                    (TEMPORARY)

How do we store data?
↳ disk storage (persistent
  data storage)

Figure ... ork together

How to use IDLE to develop programs

Although you can use a text editor to develop Python programs, most programmers use an *integrated development environment (IDE)* because an IDE usually helps you get more done in less time. One IDE that's popular for Python programming is PyCharm, which is a free, open-source IDE that runs on most operating systems. Another is Eclipse, which is a general-purpose IDE that has a plugin called pyDev for doing Python development.

However, for this book, we recommend using an IDE named *IDLE*. This IDE is included with the Python distributions for Windows and Mac OS X and can be easily installed on Linux. Besides that, it's easy to use. If that's not enough, the name of this IDE is the same as the last name of Eric Idle, a sly reference to one of the founding members of the Monty Python comedy group.

How to use the interactive shell

Figure 1-6 shows how to use IDLE's *interactive shell*. This shell makes it easy to enter and test Python statements without writing full programs. This is another feature that makes Python work so well as a first programming language.

When you start the shell, it displays some version and copyright information followed by its prompt (>>>). At this prompt, you can type any Python code that you want to run. Then, when you press the Enter key, Python runs the code, displays the results if there are any, and displays another prompt.

In this figure, the first prompt executes a print() function that prints "Hello out there!" to the console. This displays the characters coded within the quotation marks immediately after the prompt. Then, the next three prompts evaluate arithmetic expressions and display the result of each expression immediately after the prompt.

The fifth prompt executes another print() function. However, this print() function doesn't include quotation marks around the characters, and those quotation marks are required. As a result, the shell displays an error message for a SyntaxError that says "invalid syntax".

The next two prompts show what happens when you set a variable named x equal to 5 and then add 10 to that variable named x. The result is 15.

The last statement attempts to add 15 to X. This displays a NameError message that says "name 'X' is not defined". That's because variable names are case sensitive so x and X refer to two different variables. The variable named x has been defined earlier in this session, but the variable named X has not been defined yet in this session.

This interactive session shows how the Python shell can help you build your coding skills. That's why this book encourages you to use it whenever you need to experiment with Python code. In fact, one of the exercises at the end of this chapter walks you through your first use of this shell.

Incidentally, when you see a notation like File→Close, it means to pull down the File menu and select the Close command. Similarly, Run→Python Shell means to pull down the Run menu and select the Python Shell command. You'll see this notation throughout the book.

IDLE's interactive shell

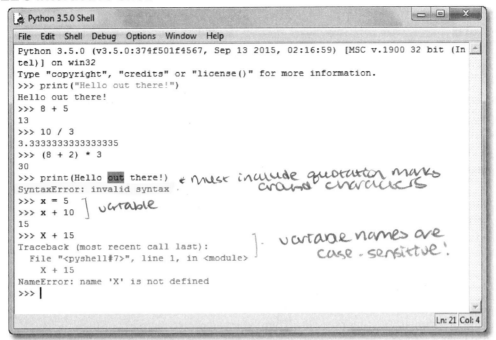

How to open, close, and restart the interactive shell

- To start IDLE, use the features of your operating system. This opens an interactive shell.
- To close the interactive shell, click on its close button or select File→Close.
- To restart an interactive shell, select Run→Python Shell from another IDLE window.

How to use the interactive shell

- Enter Python code after the >>> prompt. Then, press Enter.
- If you enter valid code that produces a result, the shell displays the results.
- If you enter invalid code, the shell displays an error message.

Description

- The *interactive shell* makes it easy to experiment with Python code and view the results right away. This is another feature that makes Python a good first language for beginning programmers.

Figure 1-6   How to use the interactive shell

How to work with source files

Figure 1-7 shows IDLE's editor window. In general, this editor works like a simple word processor. So, to edit the source code for a program, you can use many of the same techniques that you use with your word processor.

On a Windows system, for example, you can use Ctrl+X or Ctrl+C to cut or copy the selected characters, Ctrl+V to paste the characters in a new location, and Ctrl+Z to undo the last change that you made. You can also use Ctrl+Del or Ctrl+Backspace to delete an entire word at a time. And you can right-click on a selection to get a shortcut menu with commands that are appropriate for the selected text.

You can also use the drop-down menus to find the commands that you may want to use. For instance, you can use the commands in the File menu to create, open, save, and close source files. You can use the Window menu to switch between open files. And you can use the Edit and Format menus to edit and format a selection.

If you want to make a copy of a source file that you're working on, you can use the Save As command. This command is useful when you want to experiment with a variation of the same program. It's also useful if you want to start a new program from an existing program. Then, you can delete the parts of the program that you don't want, keep the parts that you do want, and get your program off to a fast start.

ctrl + x : cut
ctrl + c : copy
ctrl + v : paste
ctrl + z : undo
ctrl + delete : delete entire word

IDLE's editor with a source file displayed

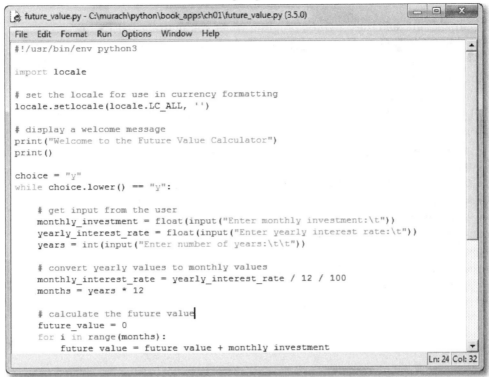

```
future_value.py - C:\murach\python\book_apps\ch01\future_value.py (3.5.0)

File  Edit  Format  Run  Options  Window  Help
#!/usr/bin/env python3

import locale

# set the locale for use in currency formatting
locale.setlocale(locale.LC_ALL, '')

# display a welcome message
print("Welcome to the Future Value Calculator")
print()

choice = "y"
while choice.lower() == "y":

    # get input from the user
    monthly_investment = float(input("Enter monthly investment:\t"))
    yearly_interest_rate = float(input("Enter yearly interest rate:\t"))
    years = int(input("Enter number of years:\t\t"))

    # convert yearly values to monthly values
    monthly_interest_rate = yearly_interest_rate / 12 / 100
    months = years * 12

    # calculate the future value
    future_value = 0
    for i in range(months):
        future_value = future_value + monthly_investment
```

Ln: 24 Col: 32

How to create, open, save, and close source files

- Use the File menu and common techniques for your operating system.

How to switch between a source file window and its shell window

- Use the Window menu. Or, arrange the windows on your screen so both are visible, and then click on the window you want to use.

How to enter and edit Python code

- Use the Edit and Format menus, common editing keystrokes, and context menus.

Description

- Like other programs that you've used, IDLE provides menus for working with files, editing and formatting selected text, and switching from one window to another.

Figure 1-7   How to work with Python source files

How to compile and run a program

To compile and run a Python program when you're using IDLE, you can just press the F5 key. Then, Python compiles the source code into bytecode and runs it. It's that simple. This is summarized in figure 1-8, and you can compare that to the procedure in figure 1-4, which is done automatically by IDLE.

If you're compiling and running a program that works with the console, IDLE uses the interactive shell as the console. This makes it easy to test the program and to switch between the shell and the editor as you do that.

This assumes that the source code doesn't have any errors. However, it's common for source code to have errors. In that case, you need to fix the errors before Python can compile and can run the program. The next figure shows how to do that.

Incidentally, if you're developing a professional program that uses the console, you have to do the final testing by using the real console of a system. However, you don't need to do that when you're learning Python with IDLE. Instead, you can use the IDLE shell as the console for all of your programs.

A console application that's being run in the shell

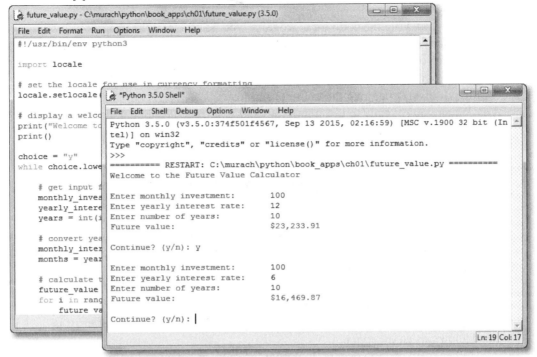

How to compile and run a Python program

- From the editor window, press the F5 key or select Run→Run Module.
- If IDLE displays a dialog box that indicates that you must save the program first, click OK to save it. Then, if the program doesn't have any errors, IDLE runs the program in the interactive shell.

Description

- When you run a program, Python attempts to compile and run the program, as in figure 1-4. If it doesn't detect any errors, it runs the program.
- However, if Python detects any errors, it usually alerts you as shown in the next figure, and it doesn't run the program.
- When you use IDLE to run a console application, it uses the shell as the console.
- On most platforms, IDLE's shell automatically becomes active when you run a console application. If it doesn't, you have to switch to the shell after you run the application.

Figure 1-8   How to compile and run a Python program

How to fix syntax and runtime errors

After you write the code for a program, you need to *test* the program. When you do that, your goal is to find all of the errors (or *bugs*) in the program. Whenever you find a bug, you need to *debug* it by fixing it. Then, you need to test the program again, fix the next bug that's found, and continue this process until you finish debugging the entire program.

When you're ready to test a program and you try to compile and run it, two types of errors are likely to be detected. The first type is a *syntax error*. These are errors that occur because the Python coding rules have been violated. As a result, the program can't be compiled.

The first example in figure 1-9 shows the dialog box that's displayed when a syntax error is detected. In addition, the point at which the error was detected is highlighted in the source code. Keep in mind, though, that the error may not be exactly at that point. In fact, it is likely to be in the previous statement. In this example, the error occurs because the statement before the highlighted statement should end with another right parenthesis.

The other type of error is a *runtime error*. This type occurs after all the code has compiled cleanly and the program is being executed. Then, an error message is displayed that helps you identify the cause of the error. This type of error is also known as an *exception*.

When an exception occurs, the program ends, or "crashes," unless the exceptions are handled by the program. In chapter 8, you'll learn how to *handle* the *exceptions* that occur so your programs won't crash. However, you can often prevent exceptions from occurring in the first place by fixing the code that caused the exception.

The second example in this figure shows a message that's displayed for an exception. Here, the last line of the message says that a NameError has occurred because "year" is not defined. If you look at the first example, you can see that this variable is coded as "years", not "year", which is why the exception occurred. To fix it, you just add the "s" to "year". Although this may not make sense to you right now, it will as soon as you start developing programs of your own.

When you fix the errors for a program, you'll note that IDLE catches just one error each time. As a result, you need to correct an error, try to run the program again, fix the next error, and continue until all of the syntax errors have been fixed. After that, you need to do the same for the runtime errors.

A dialog box for a syntax error

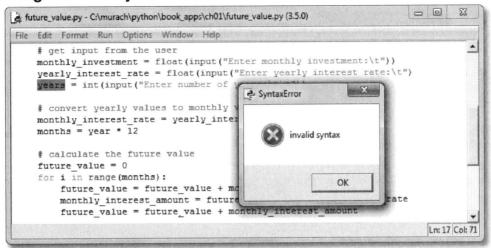

A message that's displayed for a runtime error

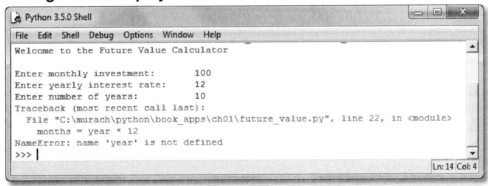

Description

- After you write the code for a Python program, you *test* the program to make sure it works. As part of that process, you will usually find errors (*bugs*) so you will have to *debug* the program.

- A *syntax error* violates one of the rules of Python coding so the source code can't be compiled. In contrast, a *runtime error* occurs when a Python statement can't be executed as the program is running.

- When you try to run a program, IDLE detects one syntax error at a time. For each error, a dialog box is displayed and the point at which the error was detected is highlighted. Then, you close the dialog box, fix the error, and try again.

- When all of the errors have been fixed, the program will run. But here again, only one runtime error is detected at a time. So you have to fix the error, run the program again, and keep going until all of runtime errors have been debugged.

- A runtime error is also known as an *exception*, and how to handle exceptions is one of the critical skills that you'll learn in chapter 8 of this book.

Figure 1-9   How to fix syntax and runtime errors

Perspective

Now that you've finished this chapter, you should understand the concepts and terms that have been presented. You should also be familiar with the way IDLE works. At this point, you're ready to start learning how to program. And that's what you're going to do in the next chapter.

Terms

Python
open source
backward compatible
forward compatible
application
app
program
console application
console
command prompt
GUI application
web application
desktop application
scripting language
shebang line
source code
compile
interpreter
bytecode
virtual machine
platform-independent
CPU (Central Processing Unit)

main memory
RAM (Random Access
    Memory)
disk storage
persistent data storage
systems software
operating system
application software
byte
bit
megabyte (MB)
gigabyte (GB)
integrated development
    environment (IDE)
IDLE
interactive shell
testing
debugging
syntax error
runtime error
exception
exception handling

Summary

- *Python* is a powerful programming language with a simple syntax that's easy to read and understand. That's why it's such a good first language for beginners.

- Python can be used to develop *desktop applications* such as *console applications* and *GUI applications*. Python can also be used to develop *web applications*. And Python can be used as a *scripting language* for purposes such as system administration.

- Before the *source code* for a Python program can be run, it is *compiled* by the Python *interpreter* into *bytecode* that can be run by the Python *virtual machine* for a computer. The bytecode and virtual machine are what makes Python *platform-independent*.

- When a program is being run, the *operating system*, the program, and the program's data are all stored in the *main memory* of the computer.

- *Disk storage* provides *persistent data storage* for the data that's operated upon by a program. Disk storage also stores all of the *systems software* and *applications software* of the system.

- An *integrated development environment (IDE)* like *IDLE* makes it easier to develop Python programs.

- You can use IDLE's *interactive shell* to enter and test Python code such as expressions, functions, and statements. You use its editor to enter and edit Python source code.

- To run a program with IDLE, you can press the F5 key. If the program uses the console, the IDLE shell is used as the console.

- The goal of *testing* is to find all of the errors in a program. The goal of *debugging* is to fix all the errors.

- If a program has *syntax errors*, you need to correct them before the program can be compiled. If a program has *runtime errors*, you need to debug each one until the program runs correctly.

- A runtime error is also known as an *exception*. To make sure that a program doesn't crash, you must learn how to *handle* the *exceptions* that occur.

Before you do the exercises for this chapter

Before you do any of the exercises in this book, you need to install Python. In addition, you need to install the source code for this book from our website (www.murach.com). For details, see the appendix for your operating system.

Exercise 1-1   Experiment with IDLE's interactive shell

This exercise guides you through experimenting with Python's interactive shell.

1. Start IDLE. That should display a window for the interactive shell.

2. Enter the following print() functions and arithmetic expressions into the interactive console:

```
>>> print("The meaning of life")
The meaning of life
>>> print()

>>> 30 + 12
42
>>> 30-12
18
>>> 3 * 4
12
>>> 12/3
4.0
>>> 1 / 3
0.3333333333333333
>>> 3 * 4 + 30
42
>>> 3 * (4 + 30)
102
```

Note that (1) the print() function prints a blank line if you don't code anything between the parentheses, (2) the * is used for multiplication in an arithmetic expression, (3) the spaces before and after arithmetic operators aren't required, and (4) parentheses are used just as they are in algebraic expressions. If you make entry errors, the shell should display appropriate error messages.

3. Try entering these statements to see how they work:

```
var1 = 30
var2 = 25
var1 + 10
var1
var1 + var2
var_2
```

The last one is deliberately incorrect so it should display an error message.

4. Continue experimenting if you like. However, this should make more sense after you read the next chapter and learn how to start writing Python code.

Exercise 1-2   Use IDLE to run programs

This exercise guides you through the process of using IDLE to compile and run three programs.

Run the console version of the Future Value program

1. Start IDLE and open the future_value.py file that should be in this folder:

    murach/python/book_apps/ch01

2. Press F5 to compile and run the program. Then, enter values for monthly investment, yearly interest rate, and years when you're prompted for them. This should display the future value that's calculated from your entries.

3. When you're asked if you want to continue, enter "y" if you want to do another calculation or "n" to exit the program. Then, close the IDLE window for the source code.

Run the GUI version of the Future Value program

4. Open the future_value_gui.py file that should be in the same folder as the future_value.py file.

5. Select Run→Run Module to compile and run the program. Then, enter values for the first three text boxes, and click the Calculate button to view the future value that's calculated from your entries.

6. If you want to do another calculation, enter new values and click the Calculate button. When you're through, click the Exit button to exit the program. Then, close the IDLE window for the source code.

Run the Guess the Number program of chapter 4

7. Open the guess_the_number.py file that's in this folder:

    murach/python/book_apps/ch04

8. Compile and run the program. Then, guess the number. This demonstrates the type of program that you'll be able to write by the time you complete chapter 4.

9. Close the window for the source code.

Exercise 1-3   Use IDLE to test and debug a program

This exercise guides you through the process of using IDLE to test and debug a program that has one syntax error and one runtime error. This walks you through the procedure that's shown in figure 1-9.

1. Start IDLE and open the future_value_errors.py file that should be in this folder:

   ```
   python/exercises/ch01
   ```

2. Press F5 to compile and run the program. This should display a dialog box for a syntax error.

3. Fix this syntax error by adding a right parenthesis at the end of the statement in the preceding line.

4. Press F5 again, and click OK to save the updated file when the dialog box is displayed. This time, the program should compile cleanly and run in the interactive shell.

5. Enter the values for monthly investment, yearly interest rate, and years. This should cause a NameError exception that says "year" is not defined in this statement:

   ```
   months = year * 12
   ```

6. Fix this runtime error by changing "year" to "years".

7. Compile and run this program again. This time, the program should be able to calculate and display a future value for the three values that you enter.

8. To exit this program, enter "n" at the last prompt. Otherwise, the program will continue running.

2

How to write your first programs

The quickest and best way to *learn* Python programming is to *do* Python programming. That's why this chapter shows you how to write complete Python programs that get input, process it, and display output. When you finish this chapter, you'll have the skills for writing comparable programs of your own.

Basic coding skills

This chapter starts by presenting some basic coding skills. You'll use these skills in every program that you develop.

How to code statements

Figure 2-1 presents the rules for coding Python *statements*. To start, you should know that, unlike many programming languages, the indentation of each line matters in a Python program. With Python, the indentation is typically four spaces, as illustrated in the first example in this figure. As you learn how to code the various types of Python statements, you'll get the specifics for the indentation that's required.

In some cases, you'll want to divide a long statement over two or more lines. Then, you can use *implicit continuation*. To do that, you divide a statement before or after an operator like a plus or minus sign. You can also divide a statement after an opening parenthesis. When you divide the statement, it's a good practice to indent its continuation lines. This is illustrated by the implicit continuation example in this figure.

The other way to continue a statement is to use *explicit continuation*. Then, you code a backslash to show that a line is continued. In general, this is discouraged and isn't usually required, so you shouldn't need to use it often.

In this book, you'll see many examples of statements that require indentation. You'll also see many examples of implicit continuation. For now, you just need to have a general idea of what's required.

The first line in a Python program is often a *shebang line* like the one in this figure. This line is ignored by Windows, but Unix-like systems, including OS X, use this line to determine what interpreter to use to run the program. In this example, the shebang line tells the operating system to use Python 3. In this book, every program has been written for Python 3. As a result, they all use the shebang line shown in this figure.

If you're using IDLE to develop programs, you don't need to include the shebang line at all. However, it's generally considered a good practice to include this line since it clearly indicates what version of Python should be used to run the program. In addition, it can make it easier to run the program on Unix-like operating systems.

shebang line

The Python code for a Test Scores program

```
#!/usr/bin/env python3

counter = 0
score_total = 0
test_score = 0

while test_score != 999:
    test_score = int(input("Enter test score: "))
    if test_score >= 0 and test_score <= 100:
        score_total += test_score
        counter += 1

average_score = round(score_total / counter)

print("Total Score: " + str(score_total))
print("Average Score: " + str(average_score))
```

An indentation error

```
print("Total Score: " + str(score_total))
 print("Average Score: " + str(average_score))
```

Two ways to continue one statement over two or more lines

Implicit continuation

```
print("Total Score: " + str(score_total)   line break before  " + "
    + "\nAverage Score: " + str(average_score))
```

Explicit continuation

```
print("Total Score: " + str(score_total) \
    + "\nAverage Score: " + str(average_score))
```

Coding rules

- Python relies on proper indentation. Incorrect indentation causes an error.
- The standard indentation is four spaces whenever it is required.
- With *implicit continuation*, you can divide statements after parentheses, brackets, and braces, and before or after operators like plus or minus signs.
- With *explicit continuation*, you can use the \ character to divide statements anywhere on a line.

Description

- A *statement* performs a task. Each statement must be indented properly.
- A program typically starts with a *shebang line* that begins with a hash (#) symbol followed by a bang (!) symbol. This line identifies the interpreter to use when running the program.
- If you're using IDLE to run your programs, you don't need a shebang line. However, it's generally considered a good practice to include one.

Figure 2-1   How to code statements

How to code comments

To provide *comments* that describe portions of a program, you use the techniques in figure 2-2. To code a *block comment*, you code a pound sign (#) at the start of each line. To code an *inline comment*, you code the pound sign on the same line but after a Python statement. Since all comments are ignored by the Python interpreter, they have no effect on the operation of the program.

Most of the time, comments are used to document portions of code that are difficult to understand. This can be helpful to the programmer who develops the program as well as to programmers who maintain the program later.

Comments can also be used to disable statements that you don't want to run when you compile and run a program. This is called *commenting out* statements. To do that, you code a pound sign before each statement that you want to comment out. Then, when you're ready to test those statements, you can *uncomment* them by removing the pound signs.

When you're using IDLE, it's easy to comment out or uncomment statements. To do that, you can select the statements. Then, you can use the commands available from the Format menu to comment out or uncomment the selected statements.

○ Block comment:

```
# this is string
str (variable _name)
```

○ inline comment:

```
str (variable _name) # this is string
```

The Test Scores program after comments have been added

```
#!/usr/bin/env python3

# This is a tutorial program that illustrates the use of the while
# and if statements

# initialize variables
counter = 0
score_total = 0
test_score = 0

# get scores
while test_score != 999:
    test_score = int(input("Enter test score: "))
    if test_score >= 0 and test_score <= 100:
        score_total += test_score        # add score to total
        counter += 1                     # add 1 to counter

# calculate average score
#average_score = score_total / counter
#average_score = round(average_score)
average_score = round(           # implicit continuation
    score_total / counter)       # same results as commented out statements

# display the result
print("=====================")
print("Total Score: " + str(score_total)     # implicit continuation
      + "\nAverage Score: " + str(average_score))
```

Block comments

Inline comments

Commented out statements — *disabled statements*

Guidelines for using comments

- Use comments to describe portions of code that are hard to understand, but don't overdo them.
- Use comments to comment out (or disable) statements that you don't want to test.
- If you change the code that's described by comments, change the comments too.

Description

- *Comments* start with the # sign, and they are ignored by the compiler. *Block comments* are coded on their own lines. *Inline comments* are coded after statements to describe what they do.
- Comments are used to document what a program or portion of code does. This can be helpful not only to the programmer who creates the program, but also to those who maintain the program later on.
- Comments can also be used to *comment out* statements so they aren't executed when the program is tested. Later, the statements can be *uncommented* so the statements will be executed when the program is tested. This can be helpful when debugging.
- When you're using IDLE, you can use the Format menu to comment out and to uncomment the statements that you've selected.

Figure 2-2   How to code comments

How to use functions

A *function* is a group of statements that perform a specific task. Python provides many *built-in functions* that you'll use throughout this book. And you'll learn how to create your own functions in chapter 4.

To use one of the built-in functions, you use the syntax shown at the top of figure 2-3. In a syntax summary like this, the italicized words are ones that you have to supply and the brackets indicate portions of the code that are optional.

To *call* a function, then, you code the function name, a set of parentheses, and any *arguments* that are required by the function within the parentheses. If a function requires more than one argument, you separate the arguments with commas.

The print() function shows how this works. This function displays the data that is passed to it as arguments. But note that the arguments are optional. If no argument is passed to this function, it prints a blank line.

This is illustrated by the calls to the print() function in the example. Here, the first print() function prints "Hello out there!" to the console. The second print() function prints a blank line (or skips a line). And the third print() function displays "Goodbye!".

The main point of this figure, though, is to show you how to call any function, not just the print() function. In this chapter, you'll learn more about using the print() function as well as five other functions. And the syntax for using these functions is always the same.

The syntax for calling any function

```
function_name([arguments])
```

The print() function

Function	Description
print([data])	Prints the data argument to the console followed by a new line character.
	If the call doesn't include a data argument, this function prints a blank line to the console.

A script with three statements

```
print("Hello out there!")
print()
print("Goodbye!")
```

blank line *arguments*

The console after the program runs

```
Hello out there!

Goodbye!
```

Description

requires an input!

- A *function* is a reusable unit of code that performs a specific task.

- Python provides many *built-in functions* that do common tasks like getting input data from the user and printing output data to the console.

- When you *call a function*, you code the name of the function followed by a pair of parentheses. Within the parentheses, you code any *arguments* that the function requires, and you separate multiple arguments with commas. *, if you leave it empty — blank line*

- In a syntax summary like the one at the top of this page, brackets [ ] mark the portions of code that are optional. And the italicized portions of the summary are the ones that you have to supply.

- In this chapter, you'll learn to use the print() function plus five other functions.

function_name (argument, argument, argument, ...)

Figure 2-3   How to use functions

How to work with data types and variables

When you develop a Python program, you work with variables that store data. In the topics that follow, you'll learn how to work with three of the most common Python data types.

How to assign values to variables

Figure 2-4 starts by summarizing three of the Python *data types*. The *str* (or *string*) data type holds any characters like "Mike" or "40". The *int* (or *integer*) data type holds whole numbers like 21 or -25. And the *float* (or *floating-point*) data type holds numbers with decimal places like 41.3 or -25.78.

When you work with these data types in a program, you normally assign them to *variables*. To do that, you code *assignment statements* like those in the first group of examples in this figure. These statements consist of a variable name like first_name or quantity1, an equals sign, and the value that should be assigned to the variable. These variables and values are stored in the main memory of the computer.

In this figure, the first group of examples assigns *literal values* to the variables. Here, the *string literal* is coded within quotation marks, but the *numeric literals* aren't. That means that Mike is assigned to the first_name variable, 3 is assigned to the quantity1 variable, 5 is assigned to the quantity2 variable, and 19.99 is assigned to the list_price variable.

The second group of examples shows how to assign a new value to a variable. To start, the first statement sets the first_name variable to Joel. The second statement sets the value of quantity1 to 10. The third statement sets the value of the quantity1 variable to the value of the quantity2 variable, or 5. And the fourth statement sets the value of the quantity1 variable to a string value of "15".

The last example shows that the names of variables are *case-sensitive*. That means an uppercase (or capital) letter is different than a lowercase letter. As a result, Quantity2 is different than quantity2. In this example, then, a NameError exception occurs because you can't set quantity1 equal to a variable that doesn't exist.

As you review this code, note that Python determines the data type for a variable based on the value that's assigned to the variable. For instance, in the second group of examples, the second statement assigns a numeric literal of 10 to the quantity1 variable. As a result, Python uses the int data type for this variable. However, the fourth statement assigns a string literal of "15" to the quantity1 variable. As a result, this variable is now assigned to a value of the str type, not a value of the int type.

Three Python data types

Data type	Name	Examples				
str	String	"Mike"	"40"	'Please enter name: '		
int	Integer	21	450	0	-25	
float	Floating-point	21.9	450.25	0.01	-25.2	3.1416

[handwritten right margin:]
- characters
- whole #s
- # with decimal places

Code that initializes variables and assigns data to them

```
first_name = "Mike"     # sets first_name to a str of "Mike"
quantity1 = 3           # sets quantity1 to an int value of 3
quantity2 = 5           # sets quantity2 to an int value of 5
list_price = 19.99      # sets list_price to a float value of 19.99
```

Code that assigns new data to the variables above

```
first_name = "Joel"        # sets first_name to a str of "Joel"
quantity1 = 10             # sets quantity1 to an int of 10
quantity1 = quantity2      # sets quantity1 to an int of 5
quantity1 = "15"           # sets quantity1 to a str of "15", not an int of 5
```

Code that causes an error because of incorrect case

```
quantity1 = Quantity2  # NameError: 'Quantity2' is not defined
```

[handwritten: does not exist ⟹ case-sensitive]

How to code literal values

[handwritten: print ("string literal")]

- To code a *literal value* for a string, enclose the characters of the string in single or double quotation marks. This is called a *string literal*.

- To code a literal value for a number, code the number without quotation marks. This is called a *numeric literal*.

[handwritten: print (numeric literal)]

Description

- A *variable* can change, or *vary*, as code executes.
- A *data type* defines the type of data for a value. *[handwritten: - int, str, etc.]*
- An *assignment statement* uses the equals sign (=) to assign a value to a variable. The value can be a literal value, another variable, or an expression like the arithmetic expressions in the next figure.
- You can assign a value of any data type to a variable, even if that variable has previously been assigned to a value of a different data type.
- Because variable names are *case-sensitive*, you must be sure to use the correct case when coding the names of variables.

Figure 2-4   How to assign values to variables

How to name variables

Figure 2-5 presents the Python rules for creating variable names. It also lists the Python *keywords* that should *not* be used for variable names. That's because these words are used in other ways by Python.

Besides these rules, though, you should give your variables meaningful names. That means that it should be easy to tell what a variable name refers to and easy to remember how to spell the name. To create names like that, you should avoid abbreviations. If, for example, you abbreviate the name for monthly investment as mon_inv, it's hard to tell what it refers to and hard to remember how you spelled it. But if you spell it out as monthly_investment, both problems are solved.

Similarly, you should avoid abbreviations that are specific to one industry or field of study unless you are sure the abbreviation is widely understood. For example, mpg is a common abbreviation for miles per gallon, but cpm could stand for a number of things and should be spelled out.

To create an identifier that has more than one word in it, most Python programmers use underscores to separate the words in a variable name. For example, the variables named tax_rate and monthly_investment use underscores to separate words. This is known as *underscore notation*.

However, some programmers use a convention called *camel case*. With this convention, the first letter of each word is uppercase except for the first word. For example, the variables named taxRate and monthlyInvestment use camel casing.

In this book, sections 1 and 2 use underscore notation for most variable names. However, since camel case is commonly used with object-oriented programs, sections 3 and 4 use camel casing for all of the object-oriented modules. When you're writing your own programs, you can choose the convention that you prefer. What's most important is to pick one of these conventions and use it consistently within a module.

Handwritten notes:

Rules for naming variables:

① Meaningful, relevant names

② Avoid abbreviations
→ variable names

③ underscore for spaces   : tax_rate

OR

camel case   : TaxRate
↳ object oriented

④ No Python keywords!

Rules for naming variables

- A variable name must begin with a letter or underscore.
- A variable name can't contain spaces, punctuation, or special characters other than the underscore.
- A variable name can't begin with a number, but can use numbers later in the name.
- A variable name can't be the same as a *keyword* that's reserved by Python.

Python keywords

and	except	lambda	while
as	False	None	with
assert	finally	nonlocal	yield
break	for	not	
class	from	or	
continue	global	pass	
def	if	raise	
del	import	return	
elif	in	True	
else	is	try	

can NOT be used for variable names

Two naming styles for variables

```
variable_name        # underscore notation
variableName         # camel case
```

Recommendations for naming variables

- Start all variable names with a lowercase letter.
- Use underscore notation or camel case.   *function_name   functionName*
- Use meaningful names that are easy to remember.
- Don't use the names of built-in functions, such as print().

Description

- When naming variables, you must follow the rules shown above. Otherwise, you'll get errors when you try to run your code.
- It's also a best practice to follow the naming recommendations shown above. This makes your code easier to read, maintain, and debug.
- With *underscore notation*, all letters are lowercase with words separated by underscores.
- With *camel case notation*, the first word is lowercase and subsequent words start with a capital letter.

Figure 2-5   Rules and recommendations for naming variables

How to work with numeric data

The next three figures show you how to work with numeric data. That's something you will do in just about every program that you write.

How to code arithmetic expressions

Figure 2-6 shows how to code *arithmetic expressions*. These expressions consist of two or more *operands* that are operated upon by *arithmetic operators*. The operands in an expression can be either numeric variables or numeric literals.

The first table in this figure summarizes the arithmetic operators. Here, the +, -, and / operators are the same as those used in basic arithmetic, and the * operation is used for multiplication.

Python also has an operator for integer division (//) that truncates the decimal portion of the division. It has a *modulo operator* (%), or *remainder operator*, that returns the remainder of a division. And it has an exponentiation operator (**) that raises a number to the specified power.

The second table in this figure shows some examples of how these operators work. For the most part, this is simple arithmetic. Here, the division operator always returns a floating point number. However, the integer division operator truncates the result and returns an integer, and the modulo operator returns just the remainder of an integer division operation. As a result, 25 divided by 4 is 6.25, but 25 divided by 4 with integer division is 6. And 25 modulo 4 is 1 because that's the remainder.

When an expression includes two or more operators, the *order of precedence* determines which operators are applied first. This order is summarized in the table in this figure. For instance, Python performs all multiplication and division operations from left to right before it performs any addition and subtraction operations.

If you need to override the default order of precedence, you can use parentheses. Then, Python performs the expressions in the innermost sets of parentheses first, followed by the expressions in the next sets of parentheses, and so on. This works the same as it does in algebra, and this is typical of all programming languages. The examples in the last table show how this works.

Python's arithmetic operators

Operator	Name	Description
+	Addition	Adds two operands.
–	Subtraction	Subtracts the right operand from the left operand.
*	Multiplication	Multiplies two operands.
/	Division	Divides the right operand into the left operand. The result is always a floating-point number.
//	Integer division	Divides the right operand into the left operand and drops the decimal portion of the result.
%	Modulo / Remainder	Divides the right operand into the left operand and returns the remainder. The result is always an integer.
**	Exponentiation	Raises the left operand to the power of the right operand.

Examples with two operands

Example	Result
5 + 4	9
25 / 4	6.25
25 // 4	6
25 % 4	1
3 ** 2	9

The order of precedence for arithmetic expressions

Order	Operators	Direction
1	**	Left to right
2	* / // %	Left to right
3	+ –	Left to right

Examples that show the order of precedence and use of parentheses

Example	Result
3 + 4 * 5	23 (the multiplication is done first)
(3 + 4) * 5	35 (the addition is done first)

Description

- An *arithmetic expression* consists of one or more *operands* that are operated upon by *arithmetic operators*.
- You don't have to code spaces before and after the arithmetic operators.
- When an expression mixes integer and floating-point numbers, Python converts the integers to floating-point numbers.
- If you use multiple operators in one expression, you can use parentheses to clarify the sequence of operations. Otherwise, Python applies its *order of precedence*.

Figure 2-6   How to code arithmetic expressions

How to use arithmetic expressions in assignment statements

Now that you know how to code arithmetic expressions, figure 2-7 shows how to use these expressions with variables and assignment statements. Here, the first two examples show how you can use the multiplication and addition operators in Python statements.

This is followed by a table that presents three of the *compound assignment operators*. These operators provide a shorthand way to code common assignment statements. For instance, the += operator modifies the value of the variable on the left of the operator by adding the value of the expression on the right to the value of the variable on the left. When you use this operator, the variable on the left must already exist and have a value assigned to it.

The other two operators in this table work similarly, but the -= operator subtracts the result of the expression on the right from the variable on the left. And the *= operator multiples the result of the expression on the right by the variable on the left.

The first example after this table shows two ways to increment a variable by adding 1 to it, a common coding requirement. Here, the first statement assigns a value of 0 to a variable named counter. Then, the second statement uses an arithmetic expression to add 1 to the value of the counter. This shows how you can code a variable name on both sides of the = operator. In contrast, the third statement adds 1 to the counter by using the += operator. When you use the += operator, you don't need to code the variable name on the right side of the = operator, which makes the code more concise.

The second example after the table shows how the += operator can be used to add variable values to a variable that stores the total of the values. This is a common programming technique that is used in many of the programs in this book. It's followed by an example that shows how all three compound assignment operators work.

The last example illustrates a problem with float values that you should be aware of. Because float values are stored internally as floating-point numbers, the results of arithmetic operations aren't exact. In this example, the tax result is 7.495000000000001, even though it should be 7.495. For now, you just need to be aware of the potential for inaccuracies like this so you won't be surprised by them. Later, you'll learn ways to deal with these inaccuracies. One way to do that is to round the results of calculations as shown later in this chapter.

Code that calculates sales tax

```
subtotal = 200.00
tax_percent = .05
tax_amount = subtotal * tax_percent       # 10.0
grand_total = subtotal + tax_amount       # 210.0
```

Code that calculates the perimeter of a rectangle

```
width = 4.25
length = 8.5
perimeter = (2 * width) + (2 * length)    # (8.5 + 17) = 25.5
```

The most useful compound assignment operators

Operator	Description
+=	Adds the result of the expression to the variable.
-=	Subtracts the result of the expression from the variable.
*=	Multiplies the variable value by the result of the expression.

Two ways to increment the number in a variable

```
counter = 0
counter = counter + 1        # counter = 1
counter += 1                 # counter = 2
```

Code that adds two numbers to a variable

```
score_total = 0              # score_total = 0
score_total += 70            # score_total = 70
score_total += 80            # score_total = 150
```

More statements that use the compound assignment operators

```
total = 1000.0
total += 100.0               # total = 1100.0
counter = 10
counter -= 1                 # counter = 9
price = 100
price *= .8                  # price = 80.0
```

A floating-point result that isn't precise

```
subtotal = 74.95             # subtotal = 74.95
tax = subtotal * .1          # tax = 7.495000000000001
```

Description

- Besides the assignment operator (=), Python provides for *compound assignment operators*. These operators are a shorthand way to code common assignment operations.

- Besides the compound operators in the table, Python offers /=, //=, %=, and **=.

- When working with floating-point numbers, be aware that they are approximations, not exact values. This can cause inaccurate results.

Figure 2-7   How to use arithmetic expressions in assignment statements

How to use the interactive shell for testing numeric operations

Remember the IDLE interactive shell that you learned about in the previous chapter? If you're confused by any of the examples presented in the previous figures, now is a good time to use it! To do that, open the interactive shell as described in the previous chapter. Then, start experimenting with the arithmetic operations as shown in figure 2-8.

In fact, you probably should take a break right now and do some experimenting, especially if you have any doubts about how the arithmetic operations work. For instance, test the use of each arithmetic operator. Test the use of each compound assignment operator. And test the results of floating-point operations. Along the way, you'll probably get some error messages, but that's all part of the learning process. Each one should give you a better understanding of how Python works.

When you get an error, you might want to attempt to fix the entry that caused the error. To do that, you can start by pressing Alt+p (Windows) or Command+p (OS X) to retype the previous entry at the prompt. Then, you can attempt to fix the problem by editing your previous entry and pressing the Enter key to execute it again.

The Python interactive shell as it's used for numeric testing

```
Python 3.5.1 Shell
File  Edit  Shell  Debug  Options  Window  Help
>>> 25 // 4
6
>>> 25 / 4
6.25
>>> 25 / 3
8.333333333333334
>>> counter = 0
>>> counter = counter + 1
>>> counter
1
>>> counter += 1
>>> counter
2
>>> subtotal = 250.00
>>> tax_percent = .04
>>> tax = subtotal * tax_percent
>>> tax
10.0
>>> total = subtotal + tax
>>> total
260.0
>>> total = total - Tax
Traceback (most recent call last):
  File "<pyshell#68>", line 1, in <module>
    total = total - Tax
NameError: name 'Tax' is not defined
>>> |
                                    Ln: 498   Col: 4
```

How to use the shell

- To test a statement, type it at the prompt and press the Enter key. You can also type the name of a variable at the prompt to see what its value is.

- Any variables that you create remain active for the current session. As a result, you can use them in statements that you enter later in the same session.

- To retype your previous entry, press Alt+p (Windows) or Command+p (OS X).

- To cycle through all of the previous entries, continue pressing the Alt+p (Windows) or Command+p (OS X) keystroke until the entry you want is displayed at the prompt.

Description

- The Python interactive shell that you learned about in chapter 1 is an excellent tool for learning more about the way numeric operations work. Just enter a statement or series of statements and see what the results are.

- This type of testing will give you a better idea of what's involved as you work with integer and floating-point numbers. It will also show your errors when you enter a statement incorrectly so you will learn the proper syntax as you experiment.

Figure 2-8   How to use the interactive shell for testing numeric operations

How to work with string data

The next three figures show you how to work with string data. That's another thing that you will do in just about every program you write.

How to assign strings to variables

In figure 2-4, you learned how to assign strings to variables. Now, figure 2-9 expands upon that skill. Here, the first group of examples shows that you can use single or double quotes to create a string literal. You can also create an *empty string* by coding a set of quotation marks with nothing between them. And you can assign a new value to a string variable. This works the same way it does with numeric variables.

How to join strings

This figure also shows how to *concatenate*, or *join*, strings. To do that, you use the + operator as shown in the second example in this figure. Here, the last_name variable is joined with a string literal that contains a comma and a space and then that's joined with the first_name variable. The resulting value is:

`Smith, Bob`

The trouble with this is that you can't join a string and a number. Instead, you need to use the str() function to convert the number to a string before you can join it. This is illustrated by the next set of examples. Here, the name variable is joined with " is ", the age variable, and " years old." However, this code uses the str() function to explicitly convert the age variable to a string before the join takes place. The resulting string is:

`Bob Smith is 40 years old.`

The second part of this example shows what happens if you don't explicitly convert the numeric variable to a string before trying to join it with a string. In this case, a TypeError exception occurs with a message that says Python can't implicitly convert an int object to a string.

If you use joins to create long strings, you will sometimes want to code the statement over two or more lines. To do that, you can use implicit continuation as shown in the last example in this figure. In this case, the statement can be divided before or after the plus signs.

The str() function for converting numbers to strings

Function	Description
str(*data*)	Converts a numeric argument to a string and returns the string.

How to assign strings to variables

```
first_name = "Bob"        # first_name = Bob
last_name = 'Smith'       # last_name = Smith
name = ""                 # name = empty string
name = "Bob Smith"        # name = Bob Smith
```

How to join three strings with the + operator

```
name = last_name + ", " + first_name     # name is "Smith, Bob"
```

How to join a string and a number with the str() function

```
name = "Bob Smith"
age = 40
message = name + " is " + str(age) + " years old."
```

What happens if you don't use the str() function

```
message = name + " is " + age + " years old."
Traceback (most recent call last):
  File "<pyshell#33>", line 1, in <module>
    message = name + " is " + age + " years old."
TypeError: Can't convert 'int' object to str implicitly
```

Implicit continuation of a string over several coding lines

```
print("Total Score: "
      + str(score_total)
      + "\nAverage Score: "
      + str(average_score))
```

Description

- A *string* can consist of one or more characters including letters, numbers, and special characters like *, &, and #.

- To specify the value of a string, you can enclose the text in either double or single quotation marks. This is known as a *string literal*.

- To assign an *empty string* to a variable, you code a set of quotation marks with nothing between them. This means that the string doesn't contain any characters.

- To convert a numeric variable to a string, you can call the str() function with the numeric variable as the argument.

Figure 2-9   How to assign strings to variables and how to join strings

How to include special characters in strings

Figure 2-10 shows how to use *escape sequences* to include special characters in a string. To start, the table shows six of the many escape sequences that you can use with Python. These sequences let you put characters in a string that you can't put in just by pressing the appropriate key on the keyboard. For instance, the \n escape sequence is similar to pressing the Enter key in the middle of a string.

Escape sequences are needed so the Python compiler can interpret the code correctly. For instance, since single and double quotations marks are used to identify strings, coding them within the strings can cause syntax errors. But when the quotation marks are preceded by escape characters, the Python compiler can interpret them correctly.

The first three examples in this figure show how escape characters work in print() functions. In the first two examples, the new line sequence is used to start a new line. In the second example, the tab sequence is also used. And in the third example, the backslash sequence is used.

The last example shows the four ways that you can put quotation marks in a string, even though quotation marks are used to identify a string. The first two statements use escape sequences to insert the marks in a string. The third statement uses single quotes within a string that's marked by double quotes. And the last statement does the reverse.

Common escape sequences

Sequence	Character
\n	New line
\t	Tab
\r	Return
\"	Quotation mark in a double quoted string
\'	Quotation mark in a single quoted string
\\	Backslash

The new line character

```
print("Title: Python Programming\nQuantity: 5")
```

Displayed on the console

```
Title: Python Programming
Quantity: 5
```

The tab and new line characters

```
print("Title:\t\tPython Programming\nQuantity:\t5")
```

Displayed on the console

```
Title:          Python Programming
Quantity:       5
```

The backslash in a Windows path

```
print("C:\\murach\\python")
```

Displayed on the console

```
C:\murach\python
```

Four ways to include quotation marks in a string

```
"Type \"x\" to exit"    # String is: Type "x" to exit.
'Type \'x\' to exit'    # String is: Type 'x' to exit.
"Type 'x' to exit"      # String is: Type 'x' to exit.
'Type "x" to exit'      # String is: Type "x" to exit.
```

Description

- Within a string, you can use *escape sequences* to include certain types of special characters such as new lines and tabs. You can also use escape characters to include special characters such as quotation marks and backslashes.

- Another way to include quotation marks in a string is to code single quotes within a string that's in double quotes, or vice versa.

Figure 2-10   How to include special characters in strings

How to use the interactive shell
for testing string operations

If you have any doubts about how the string operations work, this is a good time to take a break and do some experimenting with them. Figure 2-11 shows how.

As you experiment, you'll probably get a few error messages, but each one should give you a better understanding of how Python works. For instance, can you tell what's wrong with the statement that caused the SyntaxError in this figure? And can you tell what's wrong with the statement that caused the TypeError exception? If there's any doubt, you can retype the statement that caused the error, modify it, and press Enter to execute it again. The more you experiment, the more you'll learn.

The Python interactive shell as it's used for string testing

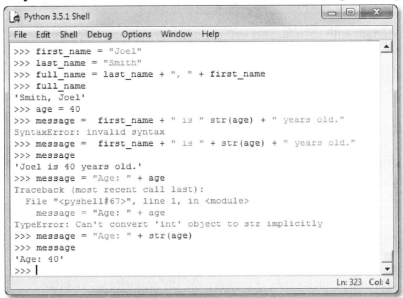

How to use the shell

- To test a statement, type it at the prompt and press the Enter key. You can also type the name of a variable at the prompt to see what its value is.

- Any variables that you create remain active for the current session. As a result, you can use them in statements that you enter later in the same session.

- To retype the previous statement on Windows, press Alt+p. To cycle through all of the previous statements, continue pressing Alt+p. On OS X, use Command+p.

Description

- The Python interactive shell that you learned about in chapter 1 is an excellent tool for learning more about the way string operations work.

- To see how string statements work, just enter a statement or series of statements and see what the results are. This will also show your errors when you enter a statement incorrectly so you will learn the proper syntax as you experiment.

Figure 2-11   How to use the interactive shell for testing string operations

How to use five of the Python functions

When you program with Python, you will use many of its built-in functions. So far, you've been introduced to the print() and str() functions. Now, you'll learn more about the print() function, and you'll learn how to use four other functions.

How to use the print() function

Figure 2-12 starts by showing the syntax for the print() function. In most cases, you'll just code one or more data items as the arguments when you use this function. Although you can also code sep and end arguments, you won't need them in your early programs so don't worry about them right now.

The first group of examples shows print() functions that receive one or more arguments. In this case, the numbers are printed directly to the console. For instance, the first function prints a number. The second function prints a string and a number and automatically puts a space between the two values. And the third function prints four integers with spaces between them.

The next group of examples shows two different ways to get the same results when using print() functions. The first print() function receives four arguments and works like the previous examples. It prints the four values with spaces between them. Note, however, that the escape sequence for a new line is coded at the start of the third argument so that argument is displayed on a new line.

The second example gets the same result by passing a single string argument to the print() function. This string consists of a string, a number, another string, and another number that have been joined together with + operators. In this case, though, the numeric variables need to be converted to strings by using the str() function. Otherwise, this code will cause an exception to occur.

When you start using print() functions, you will probably want to use the first method of coding because it's easier. But as you get more experience, you'll find that the second method isn't much harder, and it lets you get results that you can't get with the first method.

The last group of examples in this figure shows how to use the sep and end arguments. Since you must code the names of these arguments, they're called *named arguments*. Here, the first statement uses the sep argument to separate the integers with a bar character that has a space before and after it. And the second statement uses the end argument to put three exclamation points at the end of the data, instead of ending the data with a new line character. If necessary, you can code both the sep and end arguments in the same function call.

The syntax of the print() function

```
print(data[, sep=' '][, end='\n'])
```

Three print() functions that receive one or more arguments

```
print(19.99)                    # 19.99
print("Price:", 19.99)          # Price: 19.99
print(1, 2, 3, 4)               # 1 2 3 4
```

comma automatically adds a space

Two ways to get the same result

A print() function that receives four arguments

```
print("Total Score:", score_total,
      "\nAverage Score:", average_score)
```

\n: new line
ALWAYS remember backwards slash

A print() function that receives one string as the argument

```
print("Total Score: " + str(score_total) +
      "\nAverage Score: " + str(average_score))
```

The data that's displayed by both functions

```
Total Score: 240
Average Score: 80
```

Examples that use the sep and end arguments

```
print(1,2,3,4,sep=' | ')        # 1 | 2 | 3 | 4
print(1,2,3,4,end='!!!')        # 1 2 3 4!!!
```

Description

- The print() function can accept one or more data arguments.
- If you pass a series of arguments to the print() function, numbers don't have to be converted to strings.
- If you pass just one string as the argument for a print() function, numbers have to be converted to strings within the string argument.   *str (48)*
- In a syntax summary, an argument that begins with a name and an equals sign (=) is a *named argument*. To pass a named argument to a function, you code the name of the argument, an equals sign (=), and the value of the argument.
- The print() function provides a sep argument that can change the character that's used for separating the strings from one space to something else.
- The print() function also provides an end argument that can change the ending character for a print() function from a new line character (\n) to something else.

Figure 2-12   How to use the print() function

How to use the input() function

Most programs get input data from the user and then adjust the processing based on that input. For a program that uses the console, you can use the input() function to get that data. Figure 2-13 shows how.

The input() function can take one string argument that prompts the user to enter data. In the first example, this argument is "Enter your first name:". Then, when Python executes the function, it displays this *prompt* on the console, and the program pauses as it waits for the user to make an entry.

When the user makes that entry and presses the Enter key, the entry is returned by the function so it can be saved in a variable. In this example, it is saved in a variable named first_name.

The second example shows how you can get an entry without using the prompt argument. In this case, you use a print() function to display the prompt. Then, you use an input() function to get the data for that prompt. When you get data this way, the prompt is displayed on one line and the entry on the next.

When you use the input() function, remember that all entries are returned as strings. This is illustrated by the last example. If the user enters 85, and that number is stored in a variable, it is stored with the str data type. Then, if the program tries to add that variable to a variable with a numeric data type, a TypeError exception occurs because you can't add a string to a number.

The input() function for getting data from the console

Function	Description
`input([prompt])`	Pauses the program and waits for the user to enter data at the console. When the user presses Enter, this function returns the data entered by the user as a str value.
	If the call includes a prompt argument, this function prints the prompt to the console before pausing to wait for the user to enter data.

Code that gets string input from the user

```
first_name = input("Enter your first name: ")
print("Hello, " + first_name + "!")
```

The console

```
Enter your first name: Mike
Hello, Mike!
```

Another way to get input from the user

```
print("What is your first name?")
first_name = input()
print("Hello, " + first_name + "!")
```

The console

```
What is your first name?
Mike
Hello, Mike!
```

Code that attempts to get numeric input from the user

```
score_total = 0
score = input("Enter your score: ")
score_total += score      # causes an error because score is a string
```

Description

- You can use the input() function to get user input from the console. Typically, you assign the string that's returned by this function to a variable.
- The input() function always returns string data, even if the user enters a number.

Figure 2-13   How to use the input() function

How to use the int(), float(), and round() functions

Figure 2-14 presents three more functions. The int() and float() functions convert the data argument, which is typically a str value, to int or float values. This is illustrated by the first three groups of examples. In the second and third examples, the input() function returns strings for numeric entries. Then, the strings are converted to int and float values.

In contrast, the round() function rounds a numeric value to the specified number of digits. This is illustrated by the last example. Here, a floating-point number is rounded to two decimal places. By rounding a float value, you can avoid the numeric inaccuracies that can occur when you're working with floating-point data.

How to chain functions

The second part of the second and third examples in this figure shows how you can *chain functions*. To do that, you code one function as the argument of another function. In the chained part of the second example, the input() function is coded as the argument of the int() function. As a result, two functions are chained together in a single statement. In the chained part of the third example, the input() function is coded as the argument of the float() function.

In the fourth example, an arithmetic expression is coded as the first argument of the round() function. Since the second argument of the round() function is 2, the result is rounded to two decimal places. This isn't chaining, but it shows how an arithmetic expression can be coded as the argument of a function.

At first, chaining may seem to make the code more complicated. But chaining is commonly used by professional programmers, so you need to get used to it. A good way to do that is to start by coding your programs without chaining. Then, when you have that working, you can use chaining to combine statements.

Three functions for working with numbers

Function	Description
int(*data*)	Converts the data argument to the int type and returns the int value.
float(*data*)	Converts the data argument to the float type and returns the float value.
round(number [,*digits*])	Rounds the number argument to the number of decimal digits in the digits argument. If no digits are specified, it rounds the number to the nearest integer.

Code that causes an exception

```
x = 15
y = "5"
z = x + y # TypeError: can't add an int to a str
```

How using the int() function fixes the exception

```
x = 15
y = "5"
z = x + int(y)                          # z is 20
```

Code that gets an int value from the user

```
quantity = input("Enter the quantity: ")   # quantity is str type
quantity = int(quantity)                    # quantity is int type
```

How to use chaining to get the int value in one statement

```
quantity = int(input("Enter the quantity: "))
```

Code that gets a float value from the user

```
price = input("Enter the price: ")      # price is str type
price = float(price)                    # price is float type
```

How to use chaining to get the float value in one statement

```
price = float(input("Enter the price: "))
```

Code that uses the round() function

```
miles_driven = 150
gallons_used = 5.875
mpg = miles_driven / gallons_used      # mpg = 25.53191489361702
mpg = round(mpg, 2)                    # mpg = 25.53
```

How to combine the last two statements

```
mpg = round(miles_driven / gallons_used, 2)
```

Description

- If you try to perform an arithmetic operation on a string, an exception occurs. To fix that, you can use the int() and float() functions.

- When you *chain functions*, you code one function as the argument of another function. This is a common coding practice.

Figure 2-14   How to use the int(), float(), and round() functions

Two illustrative programs

This chapter ends by presenting two programs that illustrate the skills that have been presented. This is a good checkpoint for you. If you understand all of the code in these programs, you're on your way.

The Miles Per Gallon program

Figure 2-15 presents a Miles Per Gallon program. In the console, the user enters two values: the number of miles driven and the gallons of gas that were used. Then, the program calculates and displays the miles per gallon. Incidentally, in this console and in all of the console examples in this book, the user entries aren't boldfaced, but the characters displayed by the program are boldfaced.

In the Python code for this program, the first line is a shebang line that's appropriate for programs that are written for Python 3. This is followed by two print() functions that print a title and a blank line to the console.

Next, the program gets two input values from the user and stores them in two variables. In the input() functions, the prompts use escape sequences for tab characters. In addition, each input() function is chained within a float() function. As a result, both of these variables store float values, not str values.

Then, the program calculates the miles per gallon by dividing miles driven by gallons used. This is followed by a statement that rounds the miles per gallon value to two decimal places.

Last, the program uses four print() functions to display the miles per gallon value and a message that indicates that the program is ending. Here, the second print() function uses escape sequences for tab characters. In addition, it uses the str() function to convert the float value for miles per gallon to a string.

When you test a program like this, you should know that you need to enter valid numeric data whenever it is called for. Otherwise, the float() function won't be able to convert the strings to float values. That will cause a ValueError exception, and the program will crash.

For now, you have to accept this weakness of the programs that you write. In chapter 8, though, you'll learn how to handle exceptions and prevent this type of error.

The console

```
The Miles Per Gallon program

Enter miles driven:          150
Enter gallons of gas used:   35.875

Miles Per Gallon:            4.18

Bye
```

The code

```python
#!/usr/bin/env python3

# display a title
print("The Miles Per Gallon program")
print()

# get input from the user
miles_driven= float(input("Enter miles driven:\t\t"))
gallons_used = float(input("Enter gallons of gas used:\t"))

# calculate and round miles per gallon
mpg = miles_driven / gallons_used
mpg = round(mpg, 2)

# display the result
print()
print("Miles Per Gallon:\t\t" + str(mpg))
print()
print("Bye")
```

Description

- This program uses many of the features presented in this chapter.
- The input() function is chained with the float() function to convert the user entries from str values to float values.
- This round() function rounds the result of the calculation to 2 decimal places.
- If the user enters a non-numeric value such as "sixty", this program will crash and display an exception to the console. That's because the input entry can't be converted to a float value. You'll learn how to fix an exception like that in chapter 8.

Figure 2-15   The Miles Per Gallon program

The Test Scores program

Figure 2-16 presents another program that illustrates the skills that are presented in this chapter. This time, the user enters three test scores. Then, the program calculates the average score and displays both the total of the scores and the average score.

You should be able to understand this program without any further explanation. So take some time to study it and see whether there's anything you don't understand. If so, here's a description of what's going on.

The four print statements at the start display the first four lines shown in the console. Then, a total_score variable is set to zero, and three input() functions are used to get three score entries from the user. These entries are converted to integers by the chained int() function, and they are added to the total_score variable by using the += operator.

Next, the average score is calculated by dividing the total score by 3. This arithmetic expression is coded as the argument of a round() function that rounds to zero decimal places. Last, the results are printed, followed by a blank line and "Bye".

This time, the print() function that displays the results receives four arguments, not one long string argument. As a result, the integer variables don't need to be converted to strings before they are displayed. You can see how this print() function formats the data by reviewing the output in the console. You can also see how implicit continuation is used by dividing the statement after a comma.

Like the previous program, this one will crash if the user enters data that can't be converted to integers. So be sure to enter valid integer data when you test this program.

The console

```
The Test Scores program

Enter 3 test scores
=======================
Enter test score: 75
Enter test score: 85
Enter test score: 95
=======================
Total Score:    255
Average Score: 85


Bye
```

The code

```python
#!/usr/bin/env python3

# display a title
print("The Test Scores program")
print()
print("Enter 3 test scores")
print("=======================")

# get scores from the user and accumulate the total
total_score = 0        # initialize the variable for accumulating scores
total_score += int(input("Enter test score: "))
total_score += int(input("Enter test score: "))
total_score += int(input("Enter test score: "))

# calculate average score
average_score = round(total_score / 3)

# format and display the result
print("=======================")
print("Total Score:   ", total_score,
      "\nAverage Score:", average_score)
print()
print("Bye")
```

Description

- This program shows how you can use a variable named total_score to accumulate the total for a series of entries. In this case, the program doesn't store the individual scores in variables. Instead, it just adds them to the total_score variable.

- If the user doesn't enter a valid integer for each test score, this program will crash and display an exception on the console. You'll learn how to fix that in chapter 8.

Figure 2-16   The Test Scores program

Perspective

The goal of this chapter has been to get you started with Python programming and to get you started fast. Now, if you understand the Miles Per Gallon and Test Scores programs, you've come a long way. You should also be able to write comparable programs of your own.

Keep in mind, though, that this chapter is just an introduction to Python programming. So in the next chapter, you'll learn how to code the control statements that drive the logic of your programs. This will take your programs to another level.

Terms

statement	literal
implied continuation	string literal
explicit continuation	numeric literal
shebang line	case-sensitive
comment	keyword
block comment	underscore notation
inline comment	camel case
comment out	arithmetic expression
uncomment	operand
built-in function	arithmetic operator
function	modulo operator
call a function	remainder operator
argument	order of precedence
data type	compound assignment operator
string	empty string
str data type	concatenate
integer	join
int data type	escape sequence
floating-point number	named argument
float data type	prompt
variable	chain functions
assignment statement	

Summary

- A Python *statement* has a simple syntax that relies on indentation. A statement can be continued by using *implicit continuation*.

- Python *comments* can be *block* or *inline*. Comments can also be used to *comment out* portions of code so they won't be executed. Later, the code can be *uncommented* and executed.

- Python provides many *built-in functions* that you can *call* in your programs. When you call a function, you can include any *arguments* that are used by the function.

- Python *variables* are used to store data that changes as a program runs, and you use *assignment statements* to assign values to variables. Variable names are case-sensitive, and they are usually coded with *underscore notation* or *camel case*.

- The str, int, and float *data types* store values for strings, integers, and floating-point numbers.

- When you assign a value to a numeric *variable*, you can use *arithmetic expressions* that include *arithmetic operators*, variable names, and *numeric literals*.

- When you assign a value to a string variable, you can use the + operator to join variables and *string literals*. Within a string literal, you can use *escape sequences* to provide special characters.

- The print() function prints output to the console, and the input() function gets input from the console. The str(), int(), and float() functions convert data from one data type to another. And the round() function rounds a number to the specified number of decimal places.

- To *chain functions*, you code one function as the argument of another function. This is a common coding practice.

Before you do the exercises for this book...

Before you do any of the exercises in this book, you need to install Python. In addition, you need to install the source code for this book from our website (www.murach.com). For details, see the appendix for your operating system.

Exercise 2-1   Modify the Miles Per Gallon program

In this exercise, you'll test and modify the code for the Miles Per Gallon program in figure 2-15. When you're finished, the program will get another user entry and do two more calculations, so the console will look something like this:

```
Enter miles driven:          150
Enter gallons of gas used:   15
Enter cost per gallon:       3

Miles Per Gallon:     10.0
Total Gas Cost:       45.0
Cost Per Mile:        0.3
```

If you have any problems when you test your changes, please refer to figure 1-9 of the last chapter, which shows how to fix syntax and runtime errors.

1. Start IDLE and open the mpg.py file that should be in this folder:
    `python/exercises/ch02`

2. Press F5 to compile and run the program. Then, enter valid values for miles driven and gallons used. This should display the miles per gallon in the interactive shell.

3. Test the program with invalid entries like spaces or letters. This should cause the program to crash and display error messages for the exceptions that occur.

4. Modify this program so the result is rounded to just one decimal place. Then, test this change.

5. Modify this program so the argument of the round() function is the arithmetic expression in the previous statement. Then, test this change.

6. Modify this program so it gets the cost of a gallon of gas as an entry from the user. Then, calculate the total gas cost and the cost per mile, and display the results on the console as shown above.

Exercise 2-2   Modify the Test Scores program

In this exercise, you'll modify the Test Scores program in figure 2-16. When you're finished, the program will display the three scores entered by the user in a single line, as shown in this console:

```
Enter 3 test scores
=====================
Enter test score: 75
Enter test score: 85
Enter test score: 95
=====================
Your Scores:    75 85 95
Total Score:    255
Average Score: 85
```

If you have any problems when you test your changes, please refer to figure 1-9 of the last chapter, which shows how to fix syntax and runtime errors.

1. Start IDLE and open the test_scores.py file that should be in this folder:
   python/exercises/ch02

2. Press F5 to compile and run the program. Then, enter valid values for the three scores. This should display the results in the interactive shell.

3. Modify this program so it saves the three scores that are entered in variables named score1, score2, and score3. Then, add these scores to the total_score variable, instead of adding the entries to the total_score variable without ever saving them.

4. Display the scores that have been entered before the other results, as shown above.

Exercise 2-3   Create a simple program

Copying and modifying an existing program is often a good way to start a new program. So in this exercise, you'll copy and modify the Miles Per Gallon program so it gets the length and width of a rectangle from the user, calculates the area and the perimeter of the rectangle, and displays the results in the console, like this:

```
The Area and Perimeter program

Please enter the length: 25
Please enter the width:  10

Area = 250
Perimeter = 70

Thanks for using this program!
```

1. Start IDLE and open the mpg_model.py file that is in this folder:

   `python/exercises/ch02`

   Then, before you do anything else use the File→Save As command to save the file as rectangle.py.

2. Modify the code for this program so it works for the new program. Remember that the area of a rectangle is just length times width, and the perimeter is 2 times length plus 2 times width.

3

How to code control statements

Like all programming languages, Python provides *control statements* that let you control the execution of a program. These statements include if statements as well as looping statements. Before you can learn how to use these statements, though, you need to learn how to code Boolean expressions.

How to code Boolean expressions

Boolean expressions are expressions that evaluate to either True or False based on a comparison between two or more values. You use these expressions in if statements as well as in looping statements.

How to use the relational operators

Figure 3-1 shows you how to code *Boolean expressions* (or *conditional expressions*) that use the six *relational operators*. To start, the table summarizes the six relational operators. Then, the examples of Boolean expressions show how these operators work.

In the first expression, for instance, if the value of the variable named age is equal to 5, the expression evaluates to True. Otherwise, it evaluates to False. Similarly, in the second expression, if the value of the first_name variable is equal to "John", the expression evaluates to True. Otherwise, it evaluates to False.

The rest of the examples are similar, although they use the other operators. They also show that you can compare a variable with a literal or a variable with another variable. The last example shows that you can compare an arithmetic expression with a literal. Not shown is that you can also compare an arithmetic expression to a variable or another arithmetic expression.

When Python evaluates a Boolean expression, it returns either True or False, and that value can be assigned to a variable. You can also directly assign True or False to a variable as shown by the last group of examples.

When you're coding Boolean expressions, you need to make sure that your expressions compare numbers with numbers and strings with strings. If you compare a number with a string, it doesn't cause an error to occur, but it might not yield the result you expect. On the other hand, if you compare an integer with a floating-point number, the values are compared numerically, so the expression should yield the result you expect.

When you use the equal to operator, you need to remember to use two equal signs, not one. That's because the one equal sign is the assignment operator, not the equal to operator. This is a common mistake when you're learning to program, and it causes a syntax error.

Last, because floating-point values aren't always exact, you shouldn't use the equal to or not equal to operators when comparing them. Instead, you should use the greater than (>) and less than (<) operators.

Relational operators

Operator	Name	Description
==	Equal to	Returns True if both operands are equal.
!=	Not equal to	Returns True if the left and right operands are not equal.
>	Greater than	Returns True if the left operand is greater than the right operand.
<	Less than	Returns True if the left operand is less than the right operand.
>=	Greater than or equal to	Returns True if the left operand is greater than or equal to the right operand.
<=	Less than or equal to	Returns True if the left operand is less than or equal to the right operand.

Boolean expressions

```
age == 5                    # variable equal to numeric literal
first_name == "John"        # variable equal to string literal

quantity != 0               # variable not equal to a numeric literal

distance > 5.6              # variable greater than a numeric literal
fuel_req < fuel_cap         # variable less than a variable

distance >= limit           # variable greater than or equal to a variable
stock <= reorder_point      # variable less than or equal to a variable

rate / 100 >= 0.1           # expression greater than or equal to a literal
```

How to assign a Boolean value to a variable

```
active = True               # variable is set to Boolean True value
active = False              # variable is set to Boolean False value
```

Description

- You can use the *relational operators* to create a *Boolean expression* (or *conditional expression*) that compares two operands and returns a Boolean value..

- A *Boolean value* is either True or False. You can use the True and False keywords to assign a Boolean value to a variable.

- Because the float data type doesn't store floating-point numbers as exact values, you shouldn't use the equal to (==) or not equal to (!=) operators to compare them.

- When coding Boolean expressions, be sure to compare numbers with numbers and strings with strings. Mixed expressions won't work the way you expect them too.

Figure 3-1   How to use the relational operators

How to use the logical operators

To code a *compound conditional expression*, you can use the *logical operators* that are shown in figure 3-2 to combine two or more Boolean expressions. If you use the AND operator, the compound expression only returns True if both expressions are True. If you use the OR operator, the compound expression returns True if either expression is True. If you use the NOT operator, the value returned by the expression is reversed.

Below the table of operators, you can see their *order of precedence*. That is the order in which the operators are evaluated if more than one logical operator is used in a compound expression. This means that NOT operators are evaluated before AND operators, which are evaluated before OR operators. Although this is normally what you want, you can override this order by using parentheses.

The examples in this figure show how these operators work. For instance, the first example uses the AND operator to connect two Boolean expressions. As a result, it evaluates to True if the expression on its left *and* the expression on its right are both True. Similarly, the second example uses the OR operator to connect two Boolean expressions. As a result, it evaluates to True if either the expression on its left *or* the expression on its right is True. Note in these examples that the operators must be coded in lowercase letters, even though we refer to them with uppercase letters in the text.

The third example shows how to use the NOT operator to reverse the value of an expression. As a result, this expression evaluates to True if the age variable is *not* greater than or equal to 65. In this case, using the NOT operator is okay, but often the NOT operator results in code that's difficult to read. That's why it's a good practice to rewrite your code so it doesn't use the NOT operator.

The next four examples show that compound conditions aren't limited to two expressions. For instance, the fourth example uses two AND operators to connect three Boolean expressions, and the fifth example uses two OR operators to connect three expressions.

You can also mix AND and OR expressions as in the sixth and seventh examples. In the sixth example, the parentheses *clarify* the sequence of operations since Python would do the AND operation first anyway. In the seventh example, though, the parentheses *change* the sequence of operations. As a result, Python evaluates the two expressions connected by the OR operator before evaluating the rest of the expression.

When you use the AND and OR operators, Python evaluates them from left to right, and the second expression is only evaluated if necessary. That's why these operators are known as *short-circuit operators*. If, for example, the first expression in an AND operation is False, the second expression isn't evaluated because the entire expression is going to be False. Similarly, if the first expression in an OR operation is True, the second expression isn't evaluated because the entire expression is going to be True.

For most programs, Boolean expressions are relatively simple so they aren't hard to code. In the rest of this chapter and book, you'll see many examples of Boolean expressions.

Logical operators

Operator	Name	Description
and	AND	Returns a True value if both expressions are True. This operator only evaluates the second expression if necessary.
or	OR	Returns a True value if either expression is True. This operator only evaluates the second expression if necessary.
not	NOT	Reverses the value of a Boolean expression.

Order of precedence

1. NOT operator
2. AND operator
3. OR operator

Boolean expressions that use logical operators

```
# The AND operator
age >= 65 and city == "Chicago"

# The OR operator
city == "Greenville" or age >= 65

# The NOT operator
not age >= 65

# Two AND operators
age >= 65 and city == "Greenville" and state == "SC"

# Two OR operators
age >= 65 or age <= 18 or status == "retired"

# AND and OR operators with parens to clarify sequence of operations
(age >= 65 and status == "retired") or age < 18

# AND and OR operators with parens to change sequence of operations
age >= 65 and (status == "retired" or state == "SC")
```

Description

- You can use the *logical operators* to join two or more Boolean expressions. This can be referred to as a *compound conditional expression*.

- The *order of precedence* determines the sequence in which the logical operators are executed. However, you can use parentheses to clarify or change that sequence.

- The AND and OR operators only evaluate the second expression if necessary. As a result, they are known as *short-circuit operators*.

Figure 3-2   How to use the logical operators

How to compare strings

When numbers are compared, they are compared based on their numeric values. In contrast, the comparison of strings is more complicated. They are evaluated on a character by character basis from left to right. Thus, "peach" comes before "pear".

To understand string comparisons, though, you need to know the *sort sequence* of the letters and digits. On most systems, the digits are lower than (come before) all uppercase letters, and uppercase letters are lower than (come before) all lowercase letters. But that means that "Peach" comes before "apple", which isn't usually what you want when you sort or compare two strings.

To help you resolve this problem, Python provides two string *methods* that are summarized in the table in the middle of figure 3-3. The lower() method converts a string to all lowercase letters. The upper() method converts a string to all uppercase letters.

To call a string method, you use the syntax shown after this table. That is, you code the variable name of the string, a dot (period), and the method name including the required pair of parentheses. This is illustrated by the examples that follow.

In the first group of examples, you can see how you could use the IDLE interactive shell to experiment with string comparisons. First, two variables that contain "Mary" and "mary" are compared without using the lower() or upper() method. The result is False.

Then, they are compared after both have been converted to lowercase by the lower() method. Now, the result is True, which is what you want. But note that using the lower() method doesn't change the value of the variable itself.

The last group of examples shows how using the lower() method can simplify a comparison. In the first example, a compound condition is required to test whether a variable named customer_type is equal to either an upper or lowercase "r". In the second example, using the lower() method simplifies this comparison.

Of course, the upper() method could be used instead of the lower() method in these examples. Then, the values would be converted to uppercase before the comparisons.

Some string comparisons

Condition	Boolean result
`"apple" < "Apple"`	False
`"App" < "Apple"`	True
`"1" < "5"`	True
`"10" < "5"`	True

The sort sequence of the digits and letters, from lowest to highest

- Digits from 0-9
- Uppercase letters from A-Z
- Lowercase letters from a-z

Two string methods that you can use in string comparisons

Method	Description
`lower()`	Converts uppercase letters to lowercase without changing the string itself.
`upper()`	Converts lowercase letters to uppercase without changing the string itself.

How to call a string method

```
variableName.methodName()
```

How the lower() method can be used to compare string values

```
string1 = "Mary"
string2 = "mary"
string1 == string2                          # False
string1.lower() == string2.lower()          # True
print(string1)                              # prints 'Mary'
print(string2)                              # prints 'mary'
```

How the lower() method can simplify code

Without the lower() method

```
customer_type == "r" or customer_type == "R"
```

With the lower() method

```
customer_type.lower() == "r"
```

Description

- When strings are compared, the evaluation moves from left to right with numbers coming before letters, and uppercase letters coming before lowercase letters.
- As the syntax summary shows, you call a *method* by coding the variable name of the string, followed by a period (the *dot operator*), and the method name including the required set of parentheses after the method name.

Figure 3-3   How to compare strings

How to code the selection structure

All languages provide statements that implement the *selection structure*. In Python, this structure is implemented by one type of statement: the if statement. And this statement is common to most languages.

How to code if statements

An *if statement* lets you control the execution of statements based on the results of a Boolean expression. This statement is summarized in figure 3-4. To start, the syntax summary shows that each if statement must start with an *if clause*. Then, the brackets [ ] indicate that the if clause can be followed by one or more *elif clauses* (read as *else if clauses*), but they are optional. And any elif clauses can be followed by an *else clause*, but that clause is optional too.

To code an if clause, you code the *if* keyword followed by a Boolean expression, followed by a colon. Then, you code a *block* of one or more indented statements starting on the next line. That block ends when the indentation ends. To code an elif clause, you do the same but with the elif keyword. And to code an else clause, you just code the else keyword, the colon, and the block of indented statements.

For the record, the official Python documentation uses the term *suite*, instead of block. However, since block is a more commonly used term, that's the term we'll use throughout this book.

The three examples in this figure show how this works. Here, the first example shows an if statement without an elif or else clause. Then, if the value of the age variable is greater than or equal to 18, the print() function is executed. Otherwise, this if statement doesn't do anything.

The second example shows an if statement with an else clause. Then, if the Boolean expression evaluates to True, the first print() function is executed. If not, the print() function in the else clause is executed.

The third example shows an if statement with two elif clauses and an else clause. When this statement is executed, if the invoice_total variable is greater than or equal to 500, the discount_percent variable is set to .2. Otherwise, the first elif clause is executed. Then, if the invoice_total variable is greater than or equal to 250, the discount_percent variable is set to .1. Otherwise, the second elif clause is executed. In that clause, if the invoice_total variable is greater than 0, the discount_percent variable is set to zero. Otherwise, the else clause is executed and an error message is displayed.

Note in these examples, that only one block of statements can be executed by each statement. And no statements are executed if none of the conditions in the if or elif clauses are true and the if statement doesn't have an else clause.

Note too that the sequence of the conditions matters when you use elif clauses. For instance, the last example wouldn't work correctly if you reversed the three conditions in the if and elif clauses. That's because the condition in the if clause would test whether the invoice_amount is greater than zero. As a result, the conditions in the elif clauses would never be tested.

The syntax of the if statement

```
if boolean_expression:
    statements...
[elif boolean_expression:
    statements...]...
[else:
    statements...]
```

An if statement with only an if clause

```
if age >= 18:
    print("You may vote.")
```

An if statement with an if clause and an else clause

```
if age >= 18:
    print("You may vote.")
else:
    print("You are too young to vote.")
```

An if statement with two elif clauses and an else clause

```
if invoice_total >= 500:
    discount_percent = .2
elif invoice_total >= 250:
    discount_percent = .1
elif invoice_total > 0:
    discount_percent = 0
else:
    print("Invoice total must be greater than zero.")
```

The operation of an if statement

- An *if statement* always contains an *if clause*. In addition, it may contain one or more *elif clauses* and one *else clause*.
- When an if statement is executed, the if clause is evaluated first. If it is true, the statements in this clause are executed and the if statement ends. Otherwise, the first elif (else if) clause is executed.
- If the statement in the first elif clause is true, the statements in this clause are executed. Otherwise, the next elif clause is evaluated. This continues until the condition in one of the elif clauses is true or the else clause is reached.
- The statements in the else clause are executed if the conditions in all of the preceding clauses are false.
- Only one block of statements can be run for each time an if statement is executed.

Description

- The statements within a clause end when the indentation ends.
- The if statement ends when the indentation for the statements in the last clause ends.

Figure 3-4   How to code if statements

More examples of if statements

To give you a better idea of how if statements can be used, figure 3-5 presents more examples. Here, the first example shows how an if statement can be used to assign letter grades based on numeric scores. It contains three elif clauses and an else clause, and yet its code should be easy to understand.

The second part of this example shows another way to get the same results. In this case, the if and elif clauses use compound conditions. This shows the lower and upper limits for most of the letter grades. One advantage of this approach is that it's easier for other programmers to understand how the code works. Another advantage is that the clauses can be coded in any sequence. The disadvantage of this approach is that it requires more code.

The next example shows how an if statement can be used to check whether data entered by a user is valid. This is known as *data validation*. Here, the user is prompted to enter a test score. Then, the if statement checks to make sure that the entry is between 0 and 100. If it isn't, the entry isn't valid. As a result, the code displays an error message.

The last example shows how an if statement can be used to check whether the user entered an "r" or a "w". Here, the first statement sets a variable named is_valid to True, and the second statement prompts the user to enter a customer type of "r" or "w". Then, an if statement checks whether the user entry is valid. If so, it executes a *pass statement*. This statement does nothing, but it's required since an if clause must contain at least one statement. On the other hand, if the entry is not valid, the else clause displays an error message and sets the is_valid variable to False.

When you code an if statement, you should try to make it as easy to read as possible. That makes it easier to debug and maintain. To do that, you should avoid the use of the NOT operator. This means that you may sometimes need to use a pass statement as shown in the last example, but it's also a good practice to avoid the use of pass statements.

For efficiency, you may also want to start by coding the conditions that are most likely to be true and end with the conditions that are least likely to be true. As you have seen, however, it may be more important to code the conditions in the way that's most readable.

An if statement used for grading

```
score = int(input("Enter test score: "))
if score >= 90:
    grade = "A"
elif score >= 80:
    grade = "B"
elif score >= 70:
    grade = "C"
elif score >= 60:
    grade = "D"
else:
    grade = "F"
```

Another way the if statement could be coded

```
score = int(input("Enter test score: "))
if score >= 90 and <= 100:
    grade = "A"
elif score >= 80 and score < 90:
    grade = "B"
elif score >= 70 and score < 80:
    grade = "C"
elif score >= 60 and score < 70:
    grade = "D"
elif score < 60:
    grade = "F"
```

An if statement that validates the range of a score

```
score = int(input("Enter test score: "))
if score >= 0 and score <= 100:
    total_score += score
else:
    print("Test score must be from 0 - 100.")
```

An if statement that validates the customer type

```
is_valid = True
customer_type = input("Enter customer type (r/w): ")
if customer_type == "r" or customer_type == "w":
    pass            # this statement does nothing
else:
    print("Customer type must be 'r' or 'w'.")
    is_valid = False
```

Description

- If statements are often used to choose one option out of several. They are also used to make sure that user entries are valid (called *data validation*).

- A *pass statement* does nothing. You can use it as a placeholder when a statement is required but you don't want to perform any action.

- If you can code an if statement more than one way and get the same results, you should usually choose the way that's easiest to read and understand.

Figure 3-5   More examples of if statements

How to code nested if statements

In many programs, you will need to code one if statement within a clause of another if statement in order to get the logic right. The result is known as *nested if statements*. This is illustrated by the first example in figure 3-6.

The outer if statement in this example checks for two customer type codes. The if clause tests for the "r" code, and the elif clause tests for the "w" code. If neither test evaluates to True, the else clause sets the discount_percent variable to zero.

Within the outer if clause, a nested if statement sets the discount percent based on the value of the invoice_total variable. Similarly, the outer elif clause uses a nested if statement to set the discount percent variable in a similar way.

When you're coding if statements and the conditions get so complicated that they're hard to follow, it often helps to create a table that summarizes the conditions. This is illustrated by the table in this figure. Once that's done, you can use the table as a guide to the coding of your if statements.

Another option is to consider alternate ways of coding the if statements. For instance, the second example in this figure gets the same results as the first example, but it doesn't use nested if statements. Instead, it uses a series of compound conditions. In addition, it uses comments to describe what the two main portions of the if statement are doing. This makes it fairly easy for other programmers to read and understand this if statement.

The problem with the second if statement is that it duplicates the Boolean expression that checks the customer type in each clause. As a result, it makes your code more difficult to maintain. If, for example, the code for retail customers was changed from "r" to "retail", you'd have to make that change in three places in the second if statement. That's both tedious and error prone. In contrast, you'd only have to change the code in one place in the first example.

Furthermore, it's debatable as to whether the second if statement is any easier to read than the first statement. If the first example included comments similar to the comments for the second if statement, it would probably be easier to read and maintain.

In the first example, both of the nested if statements could use an else clause instead of the last elif clause. For example, the second nested if clause could be coded like this:

```
if invoice_total < 500:
    discount_percent = .4
else:
    discount_percent = .5
```

The advantage of this approach is that it uses less code and is easier to maintain. However, the code in this figure is easier for some people to understand when they're first getting started with programming.

Similarly, in the second example, there's no need to check whether the invoice total is greater than or equal to 250 for retail customers, and there's no need to check whether the invoice total is greater than or equal to 500 for wholesale customers. As a result, you can simplify these statements by cutting the AND operator and the Boolean expression for these conditions.

Nested if statements for applying customer discounts

```
if customer_type.lower() == "r":
    if invoice_total < 100:
        discount_percent = 0
    elif invoice_total >= 100 and invoice_total < 250:
        discount_percent = .1
    elif invoice_total >= 250:
        discount_percent = .2
elif customer_type.lower() == "w":
    if invoice_total < 500:
        discount_percent = .4
    elif invoice_total >= 500:
        discount_percent = .5
else:
    discount_percent = 0
```

A table that summarizes the discount rules

Type code	Invoice total	Discount percent
R (for Retail)	< 100	0
	>= 100 and < 250	.1
	>= 250	.2
W (for Wholesale)	< 500	.4
	>= 500	.5

An if statement that gets the same results

```
# the discounts for Retail customers
if customer_type.lower() == "r" and invoice_total < 100:
    discount_percent = 0
elif customer_type.lower() == "r" and (
    invoice_total >= 100 and invoice_total < 250):
    discount_percent = .1
elif customer_type.lower() == "r" and invoice_total >= 250:
    discount_percent = .2
# the discounts for Wholesale customers
elif customer_type.lower() == "w" and invoice_total < 500:
    discount_percent = .4
elif customer_type.lower() == "w" and invoice_total >= 500:
    discount_percent = .5
# all other customers
else:
    discount_percent = 0
```

Description

- It's possible to code one if statement within a clause of another if statement. The result is known as *nested if statements*.

- In some cases, you can use the logical operators to get the same results that you get with nested if statements.

- To improve the readability of if statements, you can use comments to describe what various clauses do.

Figure 3-6   How to code nested if statements

How to use pseudocode to plan if statements

In most cases, the if statements that you need are relatively simple so you don't need to plan the way you're going to code them. Instead, you can just enter the if statements directly into your programs and test them to make sure that they get the results that you want.

When if statements get complicated, though, you may want to do some planning before you start coding. For that, we recommend the use of *pseudocode*, as shown in figure 3-7. Here, the first example of pseudocode is used to plan the if statements that are used to provide the discount percents for various types of customers and varying invoice totals. This is similar to but simpler than the example in the previous figure.

Pseudocode is just your personal shorthand for what needs to be done. Within the pseudocode, though, you can use the same coding structures that are required by Python. For instance, the first example clearly shows the IF, ELSE IF, and ELSE portions of the nested if statements that are used. Then, the pseudocode is a useful guide to your Python coding.

If you compare the Python code to the pseudocode, you can see how they relate. The benefit of the pseudocode is that you can plan the logic without worrying about coding details like parentheses, quotation marks, and colons. As a result, you can document the logic more quickly and experiment with multiple approaches before you decide on the best one and use it as your guide to the Python coding.

In practice, you often write out your pseudocode by hand. Because you're the only one who is going to use it, it doesn't need to be neat or formal. Then, after you've coded and tested the Python code, you usually throw away the pseudocode.

The second example in this figure shows another use of pseudocode for planning an if statement. Here again, the pseudocode becomes a guide to the Python coding. As you get more experience with if statements, though, you'll find less need for pseudocode. That's because Python itself is so easy to read and understand.

Pseudocode for planning customer discounts

```
Get customer type
IF type = R
    IF invoice total < 250
            discount = 0
    ELSE IF invoice total >= 250
            discount = 20%
ELSE IF type = W
    discount = 40%
ELSE
    print invalid type message
```

The Python code that's based on the pseudocode

```python
customer_type = input("Enter customer type (R or W): ")
if customer_type.lower() == "r":
    if invoice_total < 250:
        discount_percent = 0
    elif invoice_total >= 250:
        discount_percent = .2
elif customer_type.lower() == "w":
    discount_percent = .4
else:
    print("Customer type must be R or W.")
```

Pseudocode for planning the processing of test score entries

```
Get test score
IF score is from 0 to 100
    add score to total score
    add 1 to the number of scores
ELSE IF score = 999
    print end of program message
ELSE
    print error message
```

The Python code that's based on the pseudocode

```python
total_score = 0
score_counter = 0
score = int(input("Enter test score: "))
if score >= 0 and score <= 100:
    total_score += score
    score_counter += 1
elif score == 999:
    print("Ending program...")
else:
    print("Test score must be from 0 through 100. Score discarded.")
```

Description

- *Pseudocode* is just your own shorthand for planning the logic of a program. After you do the planning with pseudocode, you use it as a guide to your Python coding.

Figure 3-7   How to use pseudocode to plan if statements

Two illustrative programs

Now, to illustrate the use of if statements, this chapter presents the code for two programs: an enhanced version of the Miles Per Gallon program and a new Invoice program.

The Miles Per Gallon program

Figure 3-8 presents an enhanced version of the Miles Per Gallon program that was introduced in the previous chapter. This version uses an if statement to do some minimal data validation. It just tests to make sure that both user entries are greater than zero. If they are, the mpg value is calculated and displayed. If either entry isn't valid, an error message is displayed.

Here, the if statement begins by testing whether the miles driven entry is greater than zero. If it isn't, an error message is displayed and the if statement ends. Otherwise, the elif clause is executed. This clause tests whether the gallons used entry is greater than zero. If it isn't, a different error message is displayed and the if statement ends. Otherwise, the else clause calculates and displays the rounded mpg result.

Of course, there are other ways that this if statement could be coded. One of them is shown in this figure. Here, a compound condition is used to test both entries for validity in the if clause. As you code your if statements, then, you should try to code them in the way that's most readable and logical.

The advantage of the second approach is that it uses fewer lines of code. The disadvantage is that it uses the same error message for both entries. As a result, this error message isn't as specific as the error messages in the first approach.

The user interface with invalid data

```
The Miles Per Gallon program

Enter miles driven:          150
Enter gallons of gas used:  0
Gallons used must be greater than zero. Please try again.

Bye
```

The user interface with valid data

```
The Miles Per Gallon program

Enter miles driven:          150
Enter gallons of gas used:  30
Miles Per Gallon:           5.0

Bye
```

The code

```python
# display a welcome message
print("The Miles Per Gallon program")
print()

# get input from the user
miles_driven = float(input("Enter miles driven:          "))
gallons_used = float(input("Enter gallons of gas used:  "))

if miles_driven <= 0:
    print("Miles driven must be greater than zero. Please try again.")
elif gallons_used <= 0:
    print("Gallons used must be greater than zero. Please try again.")
else:
    # calculate and display miles per gallon
    mpg = round((miles_driven / gallons_used), 2)
    print("Miles Per Gallon:          ", mpg)

print()
print("Bye")
```

Another way the if statement could be coded

```python
if miles_driven > 0 and gallons_used > 0:
    mpg = round((miles_driven / gallons_used), 2)
    print("Miles Per Gallon:          ", mpg)
else:
    print("Both entries must be greater than zero. Please try again.")
```

Description

- This Miles Per Gallon program performs some data validation.
- If either user entry is less than zero, a message is displayed. If both are valid, the calculation is done and the results are displayed.

Figure 3-8   The Miles Per Gallon program

The Invoice program

Figure 3-9 presents an Invoice program that uses nested if statements to calculate the discount percent for an invoice. These nested if statements are similar to the nested if statements presented earlier in this chapter. Here again, the discount percent is based on the customer type (R or W) and the invoice total. Both of these values are entered by the user.

To make the nested if statements easier to follow, comments are used before the if, elif, and else clauses of the outer if statement. In the nested if statements, compound conditions are used so each discount bracket is obvious. This also makes the code easier to modify if the brackets change or new brackets are added.

Once the discount percent is established, the program calculates the discount amount and the new invoice total. Then, the old and new invoice totals are displayed along with the discount percent and discount amount.

The user interface

```
The Invoice program

Enter customer type (r/w):  R
Enter invoice total:        250

Invoice total:      250.0
Discount percent:   0.2
Discount amount:    50.0
New invoice total:  200.0
```

The code

```python
#!/usr/bin/env python3

# display a welcome message
print("The Invoice program")
print()

# get user entries
customer_type = input("Enter customer type (r/w):\t")
invoice_total = float(input("Enter invoice total:\t\t"))
print()

# determine discounts for Retail customers
if customer_type.lower() == "r":
    if invoice_total > 0 and invoice_total < 100:
        discount_percent = 0
    elif invoice_total >= 100 and invoice_total < 250:
        discount_percent = .1
    elif invoice_total >= 250 and invoice_total < 500:
        discount_percent = .2
    elif invoice_total >= 500:
        discount_percent = .25
# determine discounts for Wholesale customers
elif customer_type.lower() == "w":
    if invoice_total > 0 and invoice_total < 500:
        discount_percent = .4
    elif invoice_total >= 500:
        discount_percent = .5
# set discount to zero if neither Retail or Wholesale
else:
    discount_percent = 0

# calculate discount amount and new invoice total
discount_amount = round(invoice_total * discount_percent, 2)
new_invoice_total = invoice_total - discount_amount

# display the results
print("Invoice total:\t\t" + str(invoice_total))
print("Discount percent:\t" + str(discount_percent))
print("Discount amount:\t" + str(discount_amount))
print("New invoice total:\t" + str(new_invoice_total))
print()
print("Bye")
```

Figure 3-9   The Invoice program

How to use the iteration structure

Besides the selection structure, most languages provide for an *iteration structure*. Since this structure provides a way to repeatedly execute a block of statements, it's also known as a *repetition structure*. In Python, the iteration structure is implemented by while and for statements.

How to code while statements

Figure 3-10 starts by presenting the syntax of the *while statement* that's used to create *while loops*. This statement starts with the while keyword followed by a Boolean expression and a colon. Then, an indented block of one or more statements starts on the next line. These are the statements in the loop, and they end when the indentation ends.

When Python executes a while statement, it executes the statements in the loop *while* the Boolean expression evaluates to True. Since a while loop uses a condition to determine the number of times it executes, it is known as a *condition-controlled loop*.

The first example in this figure uses a while loop to continue a program while a user enters "y" or "Y". Before the loop, this code creates a variable named choice and sets it to a string of "y". Then, the loop runs while the choice variable equals "y" or "Y".

The first time through the loop, the choice variable equals "y". As a result, the loop always runs at least once. Within the loop, the first statement prints "Hello!" to the console. Then, the second statement asks the user if he or she wants to say hello again and prompts the user to enter "y" for yes or "n" for no.

If the user enters "y" or "Y", the condition at the top of the loop evaluates to True. As a result, the loop runs again. This prints "Hello!" to the console again. Otherwise, the condition at the top of the loop evaluates to False, and the loop ends. This prints "Bye!" to the console.

The second example uses a while loop to display the numbers 0 through 4. Before the while statement starts, this code sets a variable named counter to 0. Within the loop, the first statement prints the value of the counter variable to the console followed by a space, and the second statement increases the value of the counter variable by 1. As a result, each time the loop is executed it displays the new value of the counter variable. When that value reaches 5, the condition (less than 5) at the top of the loop evaluates to False, so the loop ends. Then, the first statement after the loop displays a message that indicates that the loop has ended.

If the condition for a while statement doesn't ever become False, the loop continues indefinitely. This is called an *infinite loop*. When you first start programming, it's common to code an infinite loop by mistake. If you do that, you can use the keystroke combinations shown in this figure to end the loop. However, it's also a common practice to code an infinite loop on purpose to continue to execute statements repeatedly for as long as a program is running. Then, if necessary, you can use a break statement to end the loop as described in figure 3-12.

The syntax of the while statement

```
while boolean_expression:
    statements...
```

A while loop that continues as long as the user enters 'y' or 'Y'

```
choice = "y"
while choice.lower() == "y":
    print("Hello!")
    choice = input("Say hello again? (y/n): ")
print("Bye!")  # runs when loop ends
```

The console after the loop runs

```
Hello!
Say hello again? (y/n): y
Hello!
Say hello again? (y/n): n
Bye!
```

A while loop that prints the numbers 0 through 4 to the console

```
counter = 0
while counter < 5:
    print(counter, end=" ")
    counter += 1
print("\nThe loop has ended.")
```

The console after the loop runs

```
0 1 2 3 4
The loop has ended.
```

Code that causes an infinite loop

```
while True:
    # any statements in this loop run forever
    # unless a break statement is excecuted as in figure 3-12
```

How to end an infinite loop

- Press Ctrl+C (Windows) or Command+C (Max OS X).

Description

- In a *while statement*, Python begins by testing the condition defined by the Boolean expression at the top of the statement. Then, if this condition is True, Python executes the statements in the *while loop* until the condition is False.

- If the condition initially evaluates to False, Python never executes the code in the loop. If the condition never evaluates to False, the loop never ends. This is known as an *infinite loop*.

- Since a while loop uses a Boolean condition to determine the number of times it executes, it is known as a *condition-controlled loop*.

Figure 3-10   How to code while statements

How to code for statements

Figure 3-11 shows how to use *for statements* to define *for loops* that run once for each integer in a collection of integers. The integers in the collection are produced by the range() function that's summarized in the table in this figure. Since Python's for loop executes once for each item in a collection, it's known as a *collection-controlled loop*.

At the top of the figure, the syntax summary shows that the for statement consists of the for keyword, the name of a variable for the integer, the in keyword, a range() function, and the colon. Then, the indented block of statements in the loop start on the next line.

When the for statement is executed, Python stores the first integer returned by the range() function in the int variable that's defined in the for statement. Then, each time through the loop, this variable receives the next integer in the collection that's returned by the range() function. When the loop finishes going through all of the integers in the collection, it ends.

The first example shows how this works by displaying the integers from 0 to 4. Here, the for statement defines an integer variable named i, and it sets the argument for the range() function to 5. Within the loop, a print() function prints the i variable to the console, followed by a space. The first time through the loop the i variable is 0, the second time it's 1, and so on. This continues until the loop goes through all of the numbers in the collection returned by the range() function. Then, the loop ends.

Incidentally, a variable name of i is commonly used for the integer value in a loop. However, you can use any name you want. For instance, this example would work equally well if this variable name was changed from i to counter.

The second example uses a for loop to get the sum of the numbers 1 through 4. Before the loop, this example creates a variable named sum_of_numbers and assigns it a value of 0. Then, this code defines a loop for a range() function that returns the numbers 1 through 4. In other words, this loop executes 4 times. Each time through the loop, the statement within the loop adds the integer in the range() function to the sum_of_numbers variable. When the loop ends, this code prints the sum_of_numbers variable to the console.

The syntax of a for loop that uses the range() function

```
for int_var in range_function:
    statements...
```

The range() function

Function	Description
range(*stop*)	Returns integer values from 0 to the stop value, but not including the stop value.
range(*start*, *stop*[, *step*])	Returns integer values from the start value to the stop value, but not including the stop value. If the optional step value is specified, this function increments or decrements the integers by the step value.

Examples of the range() function

```
range(5)          # 0, 1, 2, 3, 4
range(1, 6)       # 1, 2, 3, 4, 5
range(2, 10, 2)   # 2, 4, 6, 8
range(5, 0, -1)   # 5, 4, 3, 2, 1
```

A for loop that prints the numbers 0 through 4 to the console

```
for i in range(5):
    print(i, end=" ")
print("\nThe loop has ended.")
```

The console after the loop runs

```
0 1 2 3 4
The loop has ended.
```

A for loop that gets the sum of the numbers from 1 through 4

```
sum_of_numbers = 0
for i in range(1,5):
    sum_of_numbers += i
print(sum_of_numbers)    # displays 10 (1+2+3+4)
```

Description

- When you use the *for statement* with the range() function, it executes a *for loop* once for each integer in the collection of integers returned by the range() function.

- Each time through the loop, the integer variable at the top of the loop receives the next integer in the collection that's returned by the range() function. The loop ends after it executes for the last integer in the collection.

- Since Python's for loop executes once for each item in a collection, it's known as a *collection-controlled loop*.

Figure 3-11   How to code for statements

How to code break and continue statements

The break and continue statements give you additional control over loops. The *break statement* breaks out of a loop by causing program execution to jump to the statement that follows the loop. This causes the loop to end. The *continue statement* continues a loop by causing execution to jump to the top of the loop. This causes the loop to execute again by reevaluating its condition.

The first example in figure 3-12 shows how the break statement works. Here, the condition in the while loop is intentionally set to True. This starts an infinite loop. Within the loop, the first statement asks the user to enter an integer to square. If the user enters an integer, this example calculates the square of the integer and displays it. However, if the user enters "exit", this example executes the break statement and the while loop ends. This breaks out of the current loop and executes the statement that follows the loop.

The second example in this figure shows how the continue statement works. This example uses a while loop to calculate the miles per gallon based on two entries made by the user. To start, this loop gets two entries from the user. Then, it checks whether these entries are less than or equal to zero. If so, they aren't valid. As a result, miles per gallon shouldn't be calculated and displayed. In fact, doing that could cause the program to crash because trying to divide by zero causes an exception.

To avoid that, the if statement displays a message that indicates that the entries must be greater than zero. Then, it uses a continue statement to jump to the start of the while loop. This executes the first statement in the loop, which prompts the user for the first entry again.

Although it isn't shown in this figure, you can nest one loop within another. For instance, you can nest a for loop within a while loop. In that case, a break or continue statement applies only to the loop that it's in. If, for example, you code a break statement within an inner loop, it ends the inner loop, not the outer loop.

A break statement that exits an infinite while loop

```
print("Enter 'exit' when you're done.\n")
while True:
    data = input("Enter an integer to square: ")
    if data == "exit":
        break
    i = int(data)
    print(i, "squared is", i * i, "\n")
print("Okay, bye!")
```

The console

```
Enter 'exit' when you're done.

Enter an integer to square: 10
10 squared is 100

Enter an integer to square: 23
23 squared is 529

Enter an integer to square: exit
Okay, bye!
```

A continue statement that jumps to the beginning of a while loop

```
more = "y"
while more.lower() == "y":
    miles_driven = float(input("Enter miles driven:\t\t"))
    gallons_used = float(input("Enter gallons of gas used:\t"))

    # validate input
    if miles_driven <= 0 or gallons_used <= 0:
        print("Both entries must be greater than zero. Try again.\n")
        continue

    mpg = round(miles_driven / gallons_used, 2)
    print("Miles Per Gallon:", mpg, "\n")

    more = input("Continue? (y/n): ")
    print()

print("Okay, bye!")
```

Description

- You can use the *break statement* to break out of the current loop by jumping to the statement that follows the loop.

- You can use the *continue statement* to continue executing the loop by jumping to the top of the loop.

Figure 3-12   How to code break and continue statements

More examples of loops

To give you a better idea of how loops can be used, figure 3-13 presents more examples. To start, the first example answers this question: If you make a one-time investment of $10,000 and you get 5% yearly interest, what will the value be after 20 years?

The answer is derived by using a for loop that is executed 20 times. Before this loop is entered, though, an investment variable is set to 10000. Then, within the loop, the yearly interest is calculated by multiplying the investment variable by .05, and the yearly interest is added to the investment variable. So after one year, the investment variable contains 10500 (10000 plus the first year's interest of 500). After this is repeated 19 times, the loop ends and the investment amount is rounded to two decimal places.

Note in this example that i is used as the counter variable, but that variable isn't used in the loop because it isn't needed. That often happens when using a for loop with the range() function.

The second example shows how to get the same result by using a while loop instead of a for loop. The difference is that this example requires a counter variable named year that varies from 0 to 19 as the loop is executed. This variable is set to zero before the loop starts and is increased by one each time through the loop. The loop ends when this variable is no longer less than 20. Because of the extra coding, while loops are not commonly used for this type of problem.

The third example is similar. The difference is that it calculates the future value of a monthly investment with interest calculated each month. Before the loop, this example assigns starting values to four variables. Then, the for loop executes one time for each month, which in this case is 120. In other words, the loop is executed 120 times.

Within the loop, the first statement adds the monthly investment amount to the future value. The second statement calculates the monthly interest. And the third statement adds the monthly interest to the future value. When the loop ends, the statement after the loop rounds the future value to two decimal places. Here again, the counter variable (month) isn't used in the loop.

The fourth example shows how to work with *nested loops*. Here, the outer for loop executes three times. Then, the inner while loop executes until a user enters a valid test score. As a result, this code continues to run until the user enters three valid test scores.

In this example, the break statement in the if statement jumps out of the inner while loop. That takes control back to the for loop, so the while statement can be executed for the next value in the range. Without the break statement, the inner while loop would never end.

A for loop that calculates the future value of a one-time investment

```
investment = 10000
for i in range(20):
    yearly_interest = investment * .05
    investment = investment + yearly_interest
investment = round(investment, 2)
```

A while loop that gets the same result

```
year = 0
investment = 10000
while year < 20:
    yearly_interest = investment * .05
    investment = investment + yearly_interest
    year += 1
investment = round(investment, 2)
```

A for loop that calculates the future value of a monthly investment

```
monthly_investment = 100
monthly_interest_rate = .08 / 12
months = 120
future_value = 0
for month in range(months):
    future_value += monthly_investment
    monthly_interest_amount = future_value * monthly_interest_rate
    future_value += monthly_interest_amount
future_value = round(future_value, 2)
```

Nested loops that get the total of 3 valid test scores

```
total_score = 0
for i in range(3):
    while True:
        score = int(input("Enter test score: "))
        if score >= 0 and score <= 100:
            total_score += score
            break
        else:
            print("Test score must be from 0 - 100.")
print("Total score:", total_score)
```

The console

```
Enter test score: 110
Test score must be from 0 - 100.
Enter test score: -10
Test score must be from 0 - 100.
Enter test score: 100
Enter test score: 90
Enter test score: 0
Total score: 190
```

Description

- When one loop is coded within another loop, it is known as *nested loops*.

Figure 3-13   More examples of loops

How to use pseudocode to plan a program

You have now seen three types of statements that provide the logic of a program: the if statement, the while statement, and the for statement. This means that you know enough to plan the code for an entire program. To do that, we recommend the use of pseudocode, as shown in figure 3-14.

The first example in this figure shows the pseudocode for a program that gets test scores from a user and then calculates and displays the average of the scores that have been entered. To do that, the pseudocode begins by starting an infinite while loop for the program.

Within the while loop, an if statement tests whether the entry is between 0 and 100. If so, the program adds the score to the score total, and it adds 1 to the number of scores. Then, an else if clause tests to see whether the entry is 999. If so, the loop ends, and the program calculates the average score and displays the results. Otherwise, the entry must be invalid. As a result, the program displays an error message and jumps to the top of the loop.

The second example shows the pseudocode for a program that gets user entries of a monthly investment amount, a yearly interest rate, and a number of years. Then, it calculates the future value of these monthly investments with interest calculated monthly.

In this example, a while loop gets the entries and performs the calculations until the user no longer wants to continue. This while loop starts by getting the three user entries, converting the yearly interest rate to a monthly rate, converting the number of years to months, and setting the future value to zero. Then, a nested for loop calculates the future value one time for each month.

Within the for loop, the code adds the monthly investment amount to the future value, calculates the monthly interest, and adds the monthly interest to the future value. When the for loop ends, the program displays the future value and checks whether the user wants to continue.

The main benefit that you get from using pseudocode is that you can plan what needs to be done...and how to get it done...without worrying about coding details. Then, when you feel good about your plan, you can use the pseudocode as a guide to your Python code.

Pseudocode for a Test Scores program

Display user message
WHILE TRUE
    get score
    IF score is from 0 to 100
        add score to score total
        add 1 to number of scores
    ELSE IF score is 999
        end loop
    ELSE
        print error message
Calculate average score
Display results

Pseudocode for a Future Value program

Display user message
WHILE user wants to continue
    get monthly investment, yearly interest rate, and years
    convert yearly interest rate to monthly interest rate
    convert years to months
    set the future value to zero
    FOR each month
        add monthly investment amount to future value
        calculate interest for month
        add interest to future value
    display future value
    ask if user wants to continue
Display end message

Description

- You can use pseudocode to plan the coding of loops as well as if statements. In fact, you can use pseudocode to plan all the coding for console programs like the ones in the first section of this book.

- When you use pseudocode, you don't need to know how you're actually going to code what you're planning. You can figure that out later. You just need to record what needs to be done.

- Often, you just sketch out your pseudocode with paper and pencil as a guide to your coding. Then, after you've coded and tested the program, you throw the pseudocode away.

Figure 3-14   How to use pseudocode to plan a program

Two illustrative programs

This chapter ends by presenting two more programs. The pseudocode in the previous figure provides the logic for these programs.

The Test Scores program

Figure 3-15 presents the Test Scores program. If you compare this with the pseudocode in the previous figure, you can see how the two match up. The logic is the same, but the Python code has all the implementation details.

The main loop in this program is an infinite while loop that continues until the test_score variable is 999. To make this work, the test_score variable must be initialized outside the loop. In this case, it's set to zero.

Within the while loop, an if statement tests for valid entries and for an entry that's equal to 999. If the entry is a valid score, this code adds the test score to the score total and adds 1 to the counter for test scores. If the entry is 999, a break statement ends the while loop. Otherwise, the entry must be invalid. As a result, this code displays an error message.

In this program, the clauses in the if statement are coded in the sequence in which the conditions are most likely to be true. For instance, a valid entry is most likely. A 999 entry is second most likely. And an invalid entry is least likely. Of course, there are many other ways this if statement could be coded.

The user interface

```
The Test Scores program

Enter 999 to end input
======================
Enter test score: 85
Enter test score: 95
Enter test score: 155
Test score must be from 0 through 100. Score discarded. Try again.
Enter test score: 75
Enter test score: 999
======================
Total Score: 255
Average Score: 85
```

The code

```python
#!/usr/bin/env python3

# display a welcome message
print("The Test Scores program")
print()
print("Enter 999 to end input")
print("======================")

# initialize variables
counter = 0
score_total = 0
test_score = 0

while True:
    test_score = int(input("Enter test score: "))
    if test_score >= 0 and test_score <= 100:
        score_total += test_score
        counter += 1
    elif test_score == 999:
        break
    else:
        print("Test score must be from 0 through 100. "
            + "Score discarded. Try again.")

# calculate average score
average_score = round(score_total / counter)

# format and display the result
print("======================")
print("Total Score:", score_total,
     "\nAverage Score:", average_score)
print()
print("Bye")
```

Figure 3-15   The Test Scores program

The Future Value program

Figure 3-16 presents the Future Value program that matches the pseudocode in figure 3-14. This illustrates the use of nested loops. Here, a while statement loops until the user enters "n" for the last input() function in the loop. Within the while loop, a for statement calculates the future value of the investment entries. When the for loop ends, the future value is displayed.

Before the for loop is started, though, two of the user entries are converted to monthly values. First, the yearly interest rate entry, which is entered as a whole number, is converted to a monthly rate by dividing it first by 12 and then by 100 (so an entry of 12 gets converted to .01). Then, the years entry is converted to months by multiplying it by 12. Within the for loop, these values are used to perform the calculations for each month.

Note that the argument for the range() function is the months variable. So, if the user enters 10 years, the months variable is 120, and the integers returned by the range() function are 0 through 119. As a result, the loop is executed once for each month, or 120 times, which is what you want.

By now, you should be able to understand every line of code in this program. If you can, you're off to a great start with Python. If you can't, you should review the figures that show how to use the statements that you don't understand, even if that means going back to chapter 2.

The user interface

```
Welcome to the Future Value Calculator

Enter monthly investment:       100
Enter yearly interest rate:     12
Enter number of years:          10
Future value:                   23233.91

Continue (y/n)?:
```

The code

```python
#!/usr/bin/env python3

# display a welcome message
print("Welcome to the Future Value Calculator")
print()

choice = "y"
while choice.lower() == "y":

    # get input from the user
    monthly_investment = float(input("Enter monthly investment:\t"))
    yearly_interest_rate = float(input("Enter yearly interest rate:\t"))
    years = int(input("Enter number of years:\t\t"))

    # convert yearly values to monthly values
    monthly_interest_rate = yearly_interest_rate / 12 / 100
    months = years * 12

    # calculate the future value
    future_value = 0
    for i in range(months):
        future_value += monthly_investment
        monthly_interest_amount = future_value * monthly_interest_rate
        future_value += monthly_interest_amount

    # display the result
    print("Future value:\t\t\t" + str(round(future_value, 2)))
    print()

    # see if the user wants to continue
    choice = input("Continue (y/n)?: ")
    print()

print("Bye!")
```

Figure 3-16   The Future Value program

Perspective

In this chapter, you learned how to use the control statements that drive the logic of a program. Now, if you understand the programs in this chapter, you're on your way. Otherwise, you need to study the programs until you understand every line of code in each program.

Terms

control statement	suite of statements
Boolean expression	data validation
conditional expression	pass statement
relational operator	nested if statements
Boolean value	pseudocode
compound conditional expression	iteration structure
logical operator	repetition structure
order of precedence	while statement
short-circuit operator	while loop
sort sequence	condition-controlled loop
method	infinite loop
dot operator	for statement
selection structure	for loop
if statement	collection-controlled loop
if clause	break statement
elif clause	continue statement
else clause	nested loops
block of statements	

Summary

- When you code a *Boolean* (or *conditional*) *expression*, you can use *relational operators* and *logical operators*. You can also use parentheses to override the *order of precedence* for the logical operators.

- To assign a *Boolean value* to a variable, you can use the True and False keywords.

- You can use the lower() and upper() string *methods* to convert the letters in a string to all lowercase or uppercase. This is useful when comparing strings.

- An *if statement* always starts with an *if clause*. It can also have one or more *elif clauses* and a concluding *else clause*, but those clauses are optional.

- The *while* statement loops through a block of statements while a condition evaluates to True. This can be referred to as a *condition-controlled loop*.

- The *for statement* can loop through a block of statements once for each integer in a collection of integers that's specified by the range() function. This can be referred to as a *collection-controlled loop*.

- A *break statement* breaks out of a loop by jumping to the end of it.

- A *continue statement* continues a loop by jumping to the start of it.

- You can use *pseudocode* to plan the logic of a program.

Exercise 3-1   Enhance the Miles Per Gallon program

In this exercise, you'll enhance the Miles Per Gallon program in figure 3-8 so the console display looks something like this:

```
The Miles Per Gallon program

Enter miles driven:          150
Enter gallons of gas used:   15.2
Enter cost per gallon:       4.25

Miles Per Gallon:            9.87
Total Gas Cost:              64.6
Cost Per Mile:               0.4

Get entries for another trip (y/n)? y

Enter miles driven:          225
Enter gallons of gas used:   16
Enter cost per gallon:       4.25

Miles Per Gallon:            14.06
Total Gas Cost:              68.0
Cost Per Mile:               0.3

Get entries for another trip (y/n)?
```

1. Start IDLE and open the mpg.py file that's in this folder:
   murach/python/exercises/ch03

2. Test the program with valid and invalid values.

3. Enhance the program so it lets the user repeat the entries and get the miles per gallon for more than one trip. To do that, use a while loop.

4. Modify this program so it gets the cost of a gallon of gas as another entry from the user, and validate this entry before using it in your calculations. If all three entries are valid, calculate the total gas cost and the cost per mile, and display the results on the console.

Exercise 3-2   Enhance the Test Scores program

In this exercise, you'll enhance the Test Scores program in figure 3-14 so the console display looks something like this:

```
The Test Scores program

Enter test scores
Enter 'end' to end input
======================
Enter test score: 75
Enter test score: 85
Enter test score: 95
Enter test score: end
======================
Total Score: 255
Average Score: 85


Enter another set of test scores (y/n)? y


Enter test scores
Enter 'end' to end input
======================
Enter test score: 95
Enter test score: -85
Test score must be from 0 through 100. Try again.
Enter test score: 85
Enter test score: 60
Enter test score: end
======================
Total Score: 240
Average Score: 80


Enter another set of test scores (y/n)?
```

1. Start IDLE and open the test_scores.py file that's in this folder:
   murach/python/exercises/ch03

2. Test the program with valid and invalid values.

3. Enhance the program so it lets the user enter two or more sets of scores. Use a while loop to do that. That nests one while loop within another.

4. Enhance this program so the user enters "end" to end a set of score entries, but keep the validation of the test scores. To do this, you need to change the if statement within the inner while loop. In fact, you may want to nest one if statement within the else clause of another one to get the results that you want.

Exercise 3-3   Enhance the Future Value program

In this exercise, you'll enhance the Future Value program so the console display looks something like this:

```
Welcome to the Future Value Calculator

Enter monthly investment:       0
Entry must be greater than 0. Please try again.
Enter monthly investment:       100
Enter yearly interest rate:     16
Entry must be greater than 0 and less than or equal to 15.
Please try again.
Enter yearly interest rate:     12
Enter number of years:          100
Entry must be greater than 0 and less than or equal to 50.
Please try again.
Enter number of years:          10

Year =  1  Future Value =   1280.93
Year =  2  Future Value =   2724.32
Year =  3  Future Value =   4350.76
Year =  4  Future Value =   6183.48
Year =  5  Future Value =   8248.64
Year =  6  Future Value =   10575.7
Year =  7  Future Value =   13197.9
Year =  8  Future Value =   16152.66
Year =  9  Future Value =   19482.15
Year =  10 Future Value =   23233.91

Continue (y/n)? n
```

1. In IDLE, open the future_value.py file that's in this folder:

   murach/python/exercises/ch03

2. Test the program, but remember that it doesn't do any validation so enter valid numbers.

3. Add data validation for the monthly investment entry. Use a while loop to check the validity of the entry and keep looping until the entry is valid. To be valid, the investment amount must be greater than zero. If it isn't, an error message like the first one shown above should be displayed.

4. Use the same technique to add data validation for the interest rate and years. The interest rate must be greater than zero and less than or equal to 15. And the years must be greater than zero and less than or equal to 50. For each invalid entry, display an appropriate error message. When you're finished, you'll have three while loops and a for loop nested within an outer while loop.

5. Modify the statements in the for loop that calculates the future value so one line is displayed for each year that shows the year number and future value, as shown above. To do that, you need to work with the integer that's returned by the range() function.

4

How to define and use functions and modules

In chapter 2, you learned how to use some of Python's built-in functions, such as the print() and input() functions. In this chapter, you'll learn how to define and use your own functions. You'll also learn how to store your functions in modules and how to use modules that have been created by others.

How to define and use functions

A *function* is a unit of code that performs a task. Functions are useful because they provide a way to divide the code for a program into manageable chunks. This makes it easier to maintain, test, and debug your code. Besides that, functions can be used by more than one program.

How to define and call a function

Figure 4-1 starts by showing the syntax for *defining* a function. It starts with a def statement that consists of the function name, a set of parentheses, an optional list of *arguments* within the parentheses, and a colon. This is followed by one or more indented statements that are executed when the function is called.

To *call* a function, you use the same syntax that you've been using for calling other functions. That is, you code the function name and a set of parentheses. Then, if the function requires one or more arguments, you code the arguments in the same sequence that they are in the function definition and you use commas to separate the arguments.

This is illustrated by the three examples in this figure. Since the function in the first example doesn't have any arguments, you call it by coding the name of the function followed by a set of parentheses. This just prints a welcome message.

The function in the second example requires one argument, the message that should be printed. As a result, the statement that calls it provides an argument that is a variable for the string that should be printed.

The function in the third example requires two arguments. It multiples the values of the two arguments and then uses a *return statement* to return the result of the calculation to the calling statement. In this case, the calling statement sets a variable named mpg to the result that's returned by the function.

When you code a calling statement, the names that you use for the arguments don't have to be the same as the names that are used in the function definition. In the third example, for instance, the calling statement passes arguments named miles and gallons, but the function defines arguments named miles_driven and gallons_used. However, the arguments in the calling statement must be in the same sequence as the arguments in the function definition. You'll see examples of this in the next few figures.

When you name a function, it's a good practice to start the name with a verb. In addition, the name should do a reasonable job of describing or implying what the purpose of the function is. To do that, you can follow the verb with a noun, with maybe an adjective before the noun. That makes it easier for you to remember what your functions are doing.

Before you continue, you should know that some programmers refer to the arguments as *parameters*. In fact, some programmers use the term *parameter* when referring to a function definition, and the term *argument* when referring to calling statements. In practice, most programmers use these terms interchangeably. In this book, we use the term *argument* for both the function definition and the calling statement.

The syntax for defining a function

```
def function_name([arguments]):
    statements
```

A function that doesn't accept arguments

How to define it

```
def print_welcome():
    print("Welcome to the Future Value Calculator")
    print()
```

How to call it

```
print_welcome()                                  # prints welcome message
```

A function that has one argument

How to define it

```
def print_welcome(message):
    print(message)
    print()
```

How to call it

```
message = "Welcome to the Future Value Calculator"
print_welcome(message)                           # prints welcome message
```

A function that accepts two arguments and returns a value

How to define it

```
def calculate_miles_per_gallon(miles_driven, gallons_used):
    mpg = miles_driven / gallons_used
    mpg = round(mpg, 1)
    return mpg
```

How to call it

```
miles = 500
gallons = 14
mpg = calculate_miles_per_gallon(miles, gallons)    # mpg = 35.7
```

Description

- A *function* is a block of code that can be *called* by other statements.
- To *define* a function, code the def keyword, the name of the function, a set of parentheses that contains zero or more arguments, and a colon. Then, code a block of one or more statements for the function. These statements must be indented.
- To *call* a function, code the name of the function and a set of parentheses. Within the parentheses, code any arguments and separate multiple arguments with commas. But you must pass the values to the function in the same sequence that they're listed.
- Within the body of a function, you can code a *return statement* that returns a value to the calling function.
- When you name a function, it's a good practice to start the name with a verb.

Figure 4-1   How to define and call a function

How to define and call a main() function

When you use one or more functions in a program, it's a good practice to put all of the code for the program in functions. To make that work, you put all of the code that isn't in specific functions in a *main() function*. Then, the code in the main() function starts the operation of the program.

This is illustrated by the main() function in figure 4-2. This is a main() function for a Future Value program like the one in the previous chapter. The difference is that it calls a function named calculate_future_value() to compute the future value. Thus, as you'll see in the next figure, the code for this program is divided into two functions: calculate_future_value() and main().

When all the code of a program is divided into specific functions and a main() function, you need to call the main() function to start the program. This figure shows two ways to do that.

The first way just calls the main() function from outside all of the functions. That works okay as long as no other program imports the program to use its functions. For the programs in this book, that won't happen so this is an acceptable way to call the main() function.

The second way, however, is a more professional way to call the main() function. To understand that, you need to know that a *module* in Python is any file that contains reusable code like a function. That means that the file that contains the Future Value program is a module.

Then, if you run the module without importing it, Python sets its internal __name__ variable to a value of "__main__". As a result, you can use an if statement like the one in this figure to check whether the current module is the main module. If it is, you call the main() function as shown in this program. If it isn't, this means that the current module is not the main module so you should not run its main function.

If that's confusing to you, don't worry. This will be easier to understand after you learn more about importing modules later in this chapter. In the meantime, you can just code the if statement exactly as shown. Or, you can call the main() function using the simple call statement without the if statement.

A main() function that calls another function

```
#!/usr/bin/env python3

def main():
    # display a welcome message
    print("The Future Value Calculator\n")

    # get input
    monthly_investment = float(input("Enter monthly investment:   "))
    yearly_interest = float(input("Enter yearly interest rate: "))
    years = int(input("Enter number of years:      "))

    # get the future value
    future_value = calculate_future_value(
        monthly_investment, yearly_interest, years)

    # display output
    print("Future value:                ", round(future_value, 2))
```

Two ways to call a main() function

Code a simple call statement (not recommended)
```
main()
```

Code a call statement within an if statement
that checks whether the current module is the main module
```
if __name__ == "__main__":    # if this module is the main module
    main()                    # call the main() function
```

Description

- When you code programs that use functions, it's a best practice to put all of the code for the program in functions and to include a function named main(). Then, to start the program, you call the main() function.

- One way to call the main() function is to code a statement that calls the main() function after all functions have been defined. The problem with this approach is that the main() function is also run if you import this module into another program.

- A better way to call the main() function is to code an if statement that checks whether the current module is being run as the main module. If so, it calls the main() function. Otherwise, it doesn't call the main() function. This lets other programs import this module without running the main() function.

Figure 4-2   How to define and call a main() function

The Future Value program with functions

Figure 4-3 should give you a better idea of how to code a program that consists of multiple functions. It shows the complete Future Value program after it has been divided into a function that calculates the future value and a main() function. Here, the program starts by loading the two functions. Then, it executes an if statement like the one in the last figure. This calls the main() function.

The definition of the calculate_future_value() function shows that it requires three arguments. Then, the calling statement passes three arguments to it. In this case, the name of the second argument in the calling statement isn't quite the same as the second argument in the function definition. Remember, though, that these names don't have to be the same. However, they have to be in the same sequence as they are in the function definition.

The last statement in the calculate_future_value() function is a return statement that returns the future value when the for loop ends. This value is then stored in the future_value variable in the main() function. After that, the main() function continues by rounding and displaying this value.

The user interface

```
Enter monthly investment:    100
Enter yearly interest rate: 12
Enter number of years:       10
Future value:                23233.91

Continue? (y/n): y
```

The code

```python
#!/usr/bin/env python3

def calculate_future_value(monthly_investment, yearly_interest, years):
    # convert yearly values to monthly values
    monthly_interest_rate = yearly_interest / 12 / 100
    months = years * 12

    # calculate future value
    future_value = 0.0
    for i in range(0, months):
        future_value += monthly_investment
        monthly_interest = future_value * monthly_interest_rate
        future_value += monthly_interest
    return future_value

def main():
    choice = "y"
    while choice.lower() == "y":
        # get input from the user
        monthly_investment = float(input("Enter monthly investment:\t"))
        yearly_interest_rate = float(input("Enter yearly interest rate:\t"))
        years = int(input("Enter number of years:\t\t"))

        # get and display future value
        future_value = calculate_future_value(
            monthly_investment, yearly_interest_rate, years)

        print("Future value:\t\t\t" + str(round(future_value, 2)))
        print()

        # see if the user wants to continue
        choice = input("Continue? (y/n): ")
        print()

    print("Bye!")

if __name__ == "__main__":
    main()
```

Description

- All of the code in this program is within functions, except the last if statement that calls the main() function if the current module is the main module.

Figure 4-3   The Future Value program with functions

More skills for defining and using functions

The next two figures present three more skills for working with functions. To start, the first figure shows how to work with default values and named arguments. Then, the second figure shows when and how to use local and global variables.

How to use default values for arguments

When you define a function, you can assign default values to one or more of the arguments. To do that, you code the name of the argument, the assignment operator (=), and the default value for the argument. This is illustrated by the third argument in the first example in figure 4-4. When you assign default values, though, you need to code the arguments with default values after any arguments that don't provide default values.

When an argument has a default value, you don't have to code that argument when you call the function. Then, the function uses the default value for the argument. However, if you do code the argument in the calling statement, the argument you pass to the function overrides the default value.

How to use named arguments

The last example in figure 4-4 shows how to use *named arguments* in your call statements to pass arguments to a function. To do that, you code the name of the argument in the function definition, an equals sign (=), and the value or variable name that should be passed to the function.

When you use named arguments in your call statements, the arguments don't have to be in the same sequence that they are in the function definition. As a result, this coding technique can avoid some coding errors, especially when the list of arguments is lengthy.

The calculate_future_value() function with a default value

```
def calculate_future_value(monthly_investment,
                           yearly_interest, years=20):
    # convert yearly values to monthly values
    monthly_interest_rate = yearly_interest / 12 / 100
    months = years * 12

    # calculate future value
    future_value = 0.0
    for i in range(0, months):
        future_value += monthly_investment
        monthly_interest = future_value * monthly_interest_rate
        future_value += monthly_interest

    return future_value
```

How to call the function and use its default value (years = 20)

```
future_value = calculate_future_value(100, 8.5)
```

How to call the function and override its default value

```
future_value = calculate_future_value(100, 8.5, 10)
```

How to call the function with named arguments

```
future_value = calculate_future_value(
    years=10,
    monthly_investment=100,
    yearly_interest=8.5)
```

How to use default values in your function definitions

- You can specify a default value for any argument in a function definition by assigning a value to the argument. However, the arguments with default values must be coded last in the function definition.

- When you call a function, any arguments that have default values are optional. But you can override the default value for an argument by supplying that argument.

How to use named arguments in your calling statements

- To code a *named argument*, code the name of the argument in the function definition, an equals sign, and the value or variable for the argument.

- If you call a function without named arguments, you must code them in the same sequence that they're coded in the function definition.

- If you call a function with named arguments, you don't have to code the arguments in the sequence that they're coded in the function definition.

- It's a good practice to use named arguments for functions that have many arguments. This can improve the readability of the code and reduce errors.

Figure 4-4   How to use default values and named arguments

When and how to use local and global variables

Scope in a programming language refers to the visibility of variables. That is, it tells you where in your program you are allowed to use the variables and functions that you've defined.

When you use Python, *global variables* are variables that are defined outside of all functions. These variables have *global scope* so they can be accessed by any function without passing them to that function. In contrast, *local variables* are variables that are defined within functions. They have *local scope*, which means that they can only be used within the functions that define them. In general, it's considered a good practice to avoid the use of global variables because they often lead to programming problems.

This is illustrated by the examples in figure 4-5. In the first example, tax is a local variable in each of the two functions. As a result, the first function needs to return the tax variable to the main() function that calls it. The main() function can't refer to the tax variable in the calc_tax() function directly. This is the preferred way to work with variables that are used by more than one function.

In the second example, though, tax is defined as a global variable. As a result, the calc_tax() function can access the variable directly. However, if the function is going to change the tax variable, it needs to access the global variable by coding the *global* keyword before the variable, as shown by the first statement in the first function. If the function isn't going to change the global variable, though, this isn't necessary.

In the third example, a local variable *shadows* a global variable. This happens because the local variable has the same name as a global variable. Then, the statements in the calc_tax() function refer to the local tax variable because it's defined there. But the statements in the main() function, refer to the global variable. This of course can lead to debugging problems so shadowing should usually be avoided.

With few exceptions, it's a best practice to use local variables and avoid the use of global variables. This is illustrated by most of the programs in this book. However, the end of this chapter presents a program where global variables help to simplify the code.

The last example shows how to use a *global constant*. This code uses all caps for the name of the global constant, which is a common naming convention in Python and other languages. This clearly indicates that TAX_RATE is a constant. This is considered an acceptable coding practice.

Python doesn't prevent you from changing the value of a global constant. However, within a function, a global constant is read-only by default, which is what you want. To change it, you would have to use the global keyword to access the constant. In most cases, that's a bad practice as it rarely makes sense for a function to change the value of a constant.

Functions that use local variables

```
def calc_tax(amount, tax_rate):
    tax = amount * tax_rate      # tax is a local variable
    return tax                   # return statement is necessary

def main():
    tax = calc_tax(85.0, .05)    # tax is a local variable
    print("Tax:", tax)           # Tax 4.25
```

A function that changes a global variable (not recommended)

```
tax = 0.0                        # tax is global variable

def calc_tax(amount, tax_rate):
    global tax                   # access global variable
    tax = amount * tax_rate      # change global variable

def main():
    calc_tax(85.0, .05)
    print("Tax:", tax)           # Tax 4.25 (the global variable)
```

A local variable that shadows a global variable (not recommended)

```
tax = 0.0                        # tax is a global variable

def calc_tax(amount, tax_rate):
    tax = amount * tax_rate      # tax is a local variable
    print("Tax:", tax)           # Tax 4.25 (the local variable)

def main():
    calc_tax(85.0, .05)
    print("Tax:", tax)           # Tax 0.0 (the global variable)
```

A function that uses a global constant (okay)

```
TAX_RATE = 0.05                  # TAX_RATE is a global constant
def calc_tax(amount):
    tax = amount * TAX_RATE      # the constant is used here
    return tax
```

Description

- A variable defined inside a function is known as a *local variable*. A variable defined outside of all functions is known as a *global variable*.

- A local variable can only be used within the function that defines it. Global variables can be used by all functions.

- Inside a function, a global variable is read-only. To modify its value, you need to precede the variable name with the *global* keyword.

- When a local variable has the same name as a global variable, the local variable *shadows* the global variable. In a function that defines the variable, all operations are done on the local variable. Otherwise, all operations are done on the global variable.

- If you don't use the global keyword to modify a global variable, it becomes a *global constant*. To show that, the variable name is often coded in all uppercase letters.

Figure 4-5   When and how to use local and global variables

How to create and use modules

As mentioned earlier, a Python *module* is just a file that contains reusable code like functions. Now, you'll learn how to create and use modules.

How to create a module

Figure 4-6 shows the code for a module named temperature. It consists of two functions named to_celsius() and to_fahrenheit(), plus a main() function that can be used to test the two functions. To create a temperature module from this code, you just save it in a file named temperature.py.

If you look at the code in this module, you can see that the to_celsius() function receives the value of a Fahrenheit temperature and returns the value as a Celsius temperature. And the to_fahrenheit() function does the reverse.

Then, the code in the main() function uses two for statements to call the two functions multiple times and display the values that are calculated. This can be used for testing the functions before they are made available for use by others. But when the module is used by others, you don't want the main() function to be run.

This illustrates the value of the if statement at the end of this module. If you run the temperature module, Python calls the main() function. This executes the code for testing the other functions in the module. However, if you import this module into another module, Python doesn't run the main() function. Then, you can call the to_celsius() and to_fahrenheit() functions from the other module.

The code in the module that's stored in the temperature.py file

```
def to_celsius(fahrenheit):
    celsius = (fahrenheit - 32) * 5/9
    return celsius

def to_fahrenheit(celsius):
    fahrenheit = celsius * 9/5 + 32
    return fahrenheit

# the main() function is used to test the other functions
# this code isn't run if this module isn't the main module
def main():
    for temp in range(0, 212, 40):
        print(temp, "Fahrenheit =", round(to_celsius(temp)), "Celsius")

    for temp in range(0, 100, 20):
        print(temp, "Celsius =", round(to_fahrenheit(temp)), "Fahrenheit")

# if this module is the main module, call the main() function
# to test the other functions
if __name__ == "__main__":
    main()
```

The console when you run this module

```
0 Fahrenheit = -18 Celsius
40 Fahrenheit = 4 Celsius
80 Fahrenheit = 27 Celsius
120 Fahrenheit = 49 Celsius
160 Fahrenheit = 71 Celsius
200 Fahrenheit = 93 Celsius
0 Celsius = 32 Fahrenheit
20 Celsius = 68 Fahrenheit
...
```

Description

- A file that contains reusable code such as functions is known as a *module*.
- To create a module, you store one or more functions in a Python file.
- The name of the module comes from the name of the file. For example, to create a module named temperature, you store the code in a file named temperature.py.
- The easiest way to make the functions in a module available to other modules is to store the module file in the same directory as the other modules.
- If you want to store the module file in a central location and access it from multiple directories, you need to store the module in a directory that's in the *search path*. How you set this path varies from system to system, but you can search the Internet to find out how.
- This example illustrates why the if statement that calls the main() function is useful. If this module is the main module, its main() function is called to test the other functions. If this module isn't the main module, the main() function isn't called.

Figure 4-6   How to create a module

How to document a module

If a module is going to be used by other programmers, it's good to document the functions of the module. To do that, you can use *docstrings*, as shown in figure 4-7. These strings start and end with three double quotation marks.

Later, to see the documentation for the module, a programmer can first use the Python Shell to import the module (you'll learn more about importing in a moment). Then, the programmer can use the help() function with the name of the module as its argument to see the documentation for the program. This is especially useful for programmers who didn't develop the module and its functions, but who want to use them.

The temperature module with documentation

```
"""
This module contains functions for converting
temperature between degrees Fahrenheit
and degrees Celsius
"""
def to_celsius(fahrenheit):
    """
    Accepts degrees Fahrenheit (fahrenheit argument)
    Returns degrees Celsius
    """
    celsius = (fahrenheit - 32) * 5/9
    return celsius

def to_fahrenheit(celsius):
    """
    Accepts degrees Celsius (celsius argument)
    Returns degrees Fahrenheit
    """
    fahrenheit = celsius * 9/5 + 32
    return fahrenheit
```

How to view the documentation for a module

```
>>> import temperature
>>> help(temperature)
Help on module temperature:

NAME
    temperature

DESCRIPTION
    This module contains functions for converting
    temperature between degrees Fahrenheit
    and degrees Celsius

FUNCTIONS
    to_celsius(fahrenheit)
        Accepts degrees Fahrenheit (fahrenheit argument)
        Returns degrees Celsius

    to_fahrenheit(celsius)
        Accepts degrees Celsius (celsius argument)
        Returns degrees Fahrenheit
```

Description

- A *docstring* begins and ends with three double quotes.
- Docstrings must start at the proper indentation level.
- It's a good practice to use docstrings to document the purpose of the modules and functions that might be used by other programmers.
- To display the documentation for a module, start the interactive shell, import the module, and pass the name of the module to the help() function.

Figure 4-7   How to document a module

How to import a module

If a program is going to use functions that are stored in another module, it needs to first *import* that module. Figure 4-8 shows the several ways that you can do that.

The first way is to use the *import statement*. The syntax summary at the top of this figure shows that you have the option of specifying a namespace when you use this statement. And the two examples that follow show how to import the temperature module into the default namespace and into a specified namespace.

A *namespace* is just an area in main memory that holds a module. By default, the import statement imports a module into a namespace that has the same name as the module. This is illustrated by the first example. Here, the module is imported into the temperature namespace. Then, to call a function in this namespace, you code the name of the namespace, a period (or dot), and the name of the function that you're calling.

If you use the *as* clause with the import statement, the module is imported into the namespace with the name that you specify. This is illustrated by the second example. Here, the namespace is temp. Then, to call the functions in this namespace, you again code the name of the namespace (temp), the dot, and the function name.

The second way to import a module is to use the *from* variation of the import statement. The syntax for this variation and two examples that use it are next in this figure. In this case, though, the module is imported into the *global namespace*.

The trouble with that is that more than one module can be imported into the global namespace. In that case, more than one module may use the same function name. Then, if a program calls a function that's in the global namespace two or more times, a *name collision* occurs, and that's when the debugging problems start. That's why it's a best practice to avoid the use of the global namespace.

The benefit of using the global namespace is that you don't need to use a namespace prefix when you're calling a function in that namespace. To reduce the possibility of name collisions, then, you can import just the functions that you're going to use. This is illustrated by the first example of the from variation of the import statement.

The other alternative is to use the * to import all of the functions in the module. This is illustrated by the last example in this figure. However, since this increases the possibility of name collisions, this practice should be avoided.

The syntax for importing a module into a local namespace

```
import module_name [as namespace]
```

Importing the temperature.py module into the default namespace

```
import temperature
```

Code that calls its functions
```
c = temperature.to_celsius(f)
f = temperature.to_fahrenheit(c)
```

Importing the module into a specified namespace

```
import temperature as temp
```

Code that calls its functions
```
c = temp.to_celsius(f)
f = temp.to_fahrenheit(c)
```

The syntax for importing into the global namespace (not recommended)

```
from module_name import function_name1[, function_name2]...
```

Importing one function into the global namespace

```
from temperature import to_celsius
```

Code that calls its functions
```
c = to_celsius(f)
f = to_fahrenheit(c)        # doesn't work; function hasn't been imported
```

Importing all functions into the global namespace

```
from temperature import *              # use * to get all of the functions
```

Code that calls its functions
```
c = to_celsius(f)
f = to_fahrenheit(c)
```

Description

- Before you can call the functions in a module, you must *import* the module.

- When you use the *import statement*, Python imports the functions into a *namespace*. By default, this namespace has the same name as the module. Then, to call a function in this module, you must prefix it with the name of the namespace.

- To import into a specified namespace, you can use the *as* keyword. Then, you can use the new namespace as the prefix in your function calls.

- To import into the *global namespace*, you use the *from* variation of the import statement. Then, the function names don't need prefixes in your call statements.

- If you import functions from more than one module into the global namespace, two functions could have the same name. This is known as a *name collision*, and this leads to debugging problems.

Figure 4-8   How to import a module

The Convert Temperatures program

To show how the temperature module of figure 4-6 can be used by a program, figure 4-9 shows a Convert Temperatures program. Here, the user enters a 1 or a 2 to indicate what type of conversion should be done followed by the number of degrees to be converted. Then, the program displays the result.

The import statement in the code imports the temperature module into a namespace named temp. Then, that name is used in the statements that call the to_celsius() and to_fahrenheit() functions. Other than that, you shouldn't have much trouble understanding the code in this program. But note that all of the code in this program is in functions except for the import statement and the if statement that calls the main() function.

In a program like this, it's a common practice to arrange the functions in the sequence in which they're called, and to put the main() function last followed by the if statement that calls it. Here, the main() function first calls the display_menu() function and then calls the convert_temp() function, so that's the sequence in which they appear in the code listing. Of course, the to_celsius() and to_fahrenheit() functions don't appear in the code because they're in the temperature module that's imported.

The user interface

```
MENU
1. Fahrenheit to Celsius
2. Celsius to Fahrenhit

Enter a menu option: 1
Enter degrees Fahrenheit: 99
Degrees Celsius: 37.2

Convert another temperature? (y/n): n
```

The code

```python
import temperature as temp

def display_menu():
    print("MENU")
    print("1. Fahrenheit to Celsius")
    print("2. Celsius to Fahrenhit")
    print()

def convert_temp():
    option = int(input("Enter a menu option: "))
    if option == 1:
        f = int(input("Enter degrees Fahrenheit: "))
        c = temp.to_celsius(f)
        c = round(c, 2)
        print("Degrees Celsius:", c)
    elif option == 2:
        c = int(input("Enter degrees Celsius: "))
        f = temp.to_fahrenheit(c)
        f = round(f, 2)
        print("Degrees Fahrenheit:", f)
    else:
        print("You must enter a valid menu number.")

def main():
    display_menu()
    again = "y"
    while again.lower() == "y":
        convert_temp()
        print()
        again = input("Convert another temperature? (y/n): ")
        print()
    print("Bye!")

if __name__ == "__main__":
    main()
```

Figure 4-9   The Convert Temperatures program

How to use standard modules

Python provides many *standard modules* that include functions that you can use in your programs. The table at the top of figure 4-10 lists a few of the standard modules that are presented in this book. To use a standard module, you import it and call its functions, just as if you had created the module yourself.

How to use the random module

The first standard module that you're going to learn how to use in this book is the *random module* that's summarized in figure 4-10. The second table in this figure summarizes just three of its many functions: the random(), randint(), and randrange() functions. The examples that follow show how these functions work.

The first group of examples shows how the random() function works. It returns a float value greater than or equal to 0.0 and less than 1.0. Then, if you want larger values, you can multiply the value that's returned. If, for instance, you multiply the returned value by 100, you get a value from 0.0 to less than 100.0. If you multiply it by 70, you get a value from 0.0 to less than 70.0.

The second group of examples shows how the randint function works. It returns a random integer that's equal to or between the two values that are supplied as arguments.

The third group shows how the randrange() function works. It works similarly to the range() function that you learned about in the previous chapter. However, the randrange() function returns a random integer value within the range of integers that's specified. The default step value is 1, but you can change that by coding the optional third argument.

The last example shows how you can simulate rolling a pair of dice. Here, the first statement gets a random value between 1 and 6, and the second does the same. Then, the third statement prints the values that were rolled.

Some of the standard modules presented in this book

Module	Description
math	Functions for mathematical operations
random	Functions for generating random numbers
decimal	Functions for working with decimal numbers
csv	Functions for working with files that contain comma-separated values
pickle	Functions for persistent data storage
tkinter	Functions for building GUI applications

Three functions of the random module

Function	Description
random()	Returns a random float value that's greater than or equal to 0.0 and less than 1.0.
randint(*min*, *max*)	Returns a random int value that's greater than or equal to the min argument and less than or equal to the max argument.
randrange([*start*,] *stop* [,*step*])	Returns a random value greater than or equal to the start argument, less than the stop argument, and a multiple of the step argument.

A statement that imports the random module

```
import random
```

Examples that use functions of the random module

```
# the use of the random method
number = random.random()         # a float value >= 0.0 and < 1.0
number = random.random() * 100   # a float value >= 0.0 and < 100.0

# the use of the randint method
number = random.randint(1, 100)    # an int from 1 to 100
number = random.randint(101, 200)  # an int from 101 to 200
number = random.randint(0, 7)      # an int from 0 to 7

# the use of the randrange method
number = random.randrange(1, 100)        # an int from 1 to 99
number = random.randrange(100, 200, 2)   # an even int from 100 to 198
number = random.randrange(11, 250, 2)    # an odd int from 11 to 249
```

Code that simulates rolling a pair of dice

```
die1 = random.randint(1, 6)       # assume 6 is returned
die2 = random.randint(1, 6)       # assume 5 is returned
print("Your roll:", die1, die2)   # Your roll: 6 5
```

Description

- The *random module* provides methods for generating random numbers. One of its uses is for game development.

Figure 4-10 How to use the random module

The Guess the Number game

To illustrate the use of the random module, figure 4-11 presents a Guess the Number game. It consists of three functions. The first displays the title. The second plays the game. And the main() function calls those functions as it controls the playing of the game.

In the play_game() function, the randint() function gets the number that the player has to guess. It returns a random number between 1 and 10. Later, a while statement lets the user guess the number until the guess is correct. Then, a return statement returns to the statement in the main() function that's after the call to the play_game() function. This return statement doesn't specify a return value, but it does end the function.

Here again, you should be able to understand the rest of this code without any trouble. And here again, the functions are presented in the sequence in which they are called, followed by the main() function.

Just for fun, this program uses a global constant named LIMIT to set the limit for the guessing game. This isn't necessary, but it does make it easier to change the limit if you want to modify the program. Then, all you have to do is change the global constant, which is easy to find.

The user interface

```
Guess the Number!

I'm thinking of a number from 1 to 10

Your guess: 5
Too low.
Your guess: 8
You guessed it in 2 tries.

Would you like to play again? (y/n): n

Bye!
```

The code

```python
import random

LIMIT = 10

def display_title():
    print("Guess the number!")
    print()

def play_game():
    number = random.randint(1, LIMIT)
    print("I'm thinking of a number from 1 to " + str(LIMIT) + "\n")
    count = 1
    while True:
        guess = int(input("Your guess: "))
        if guess < number:
            print("Too low.")
            count += 1
        elif guess > number:
            print("Too high.")
            count += 1
        elif guess == number:
            print("You guessed it in " + str(count) + " tries.\n")
            return

def main():
    display_title()
    again = "y"
    while again.lower() == "y":
        play_game()
        again = input("Would you like to play again? (y/n): ")
        print()
    print("Bye!")

# if started as the main module, call the main() function
if __name__ == "__main__":
    main()
```

Figure 4-11   The Guess the Number game

How to plan the functions of a program

As a program gets larger and requires more functions, it gets more difficult to decide what the functions should be and how they should relate to each other. To help you make those decisions, you can use a hierarchy chart to plan the modules of the program.

How to use a hierarchy chart

Figure 4-12 show how to plan the functions of a program by using a *hierarchy chart*. For instance, the first hierarchy chart represents the five functions that are used by the Convert Temperatures program in figure 4-9.

This shows that the top-level function (the main() function) calls the display_menu() and convert_temp() functions. The convert_temp() function in turn calls the to_celsius() and to_fahrenheit() functions. Note that these functions are on the chart, even though they're stored in a module that's imported. That makes the hierarchy chart complete.

Similarly, the second chart in this figure shows the functions that are used by the Guess the Number game. Here, the main() function calls the display_title() function and also the play_game() function.

These examples show the chart for an existing program, but you need to learn how to create a chart like this for a new program before the code is written. To do that, you can start with the main() function. That's always the top level. Then, you ask yourself what primary function or functions the main() function needs to call. In the first example, that's the convert_temp() function. In the second example, that's the play_game() function. Once you identify the primary function or functions, you add them to the structure chart.

Next, you ask yourself what functions, if any, need to be called before or after the primary function or functions of the program. In the first example, that's the display_menu() function that's called before the convert_temp() function. After you add those functions to the chart, the first two levels are done: the top-level with the main() function and the next level.

Then, you continue this process for the next levels down, until you've divided all of the functions into their component functions. The example that starts in the next figure shows how this works.

When you add a function to a chart, try to use a name that starts with a verb and ends with a noun, perhaps with one adjective between the verb and noun. That name should provide a good indication of what the function does. Later, when you code the functions of the program, you can create the function names by connecting the words on the flowchart with underscores, so "play game" on your chart becomes play_game in your code.

In practice, programmers often draw hierarchy charts by hand and discard them once the program has been coded and tested. Another alternative is to use a *hierarchy outline* like the one in this figure, instead of a hierarchy chart. An outline like this is a left-to-right view of the structure instead of a top-down view.

A hierarchy chart for the Convert Temperatures program

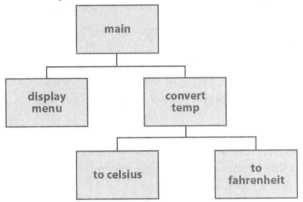

A hierarchy outline for the same program

```
main
    display menu
    convert temp
        to celsius
        to fahrenheit
```

A hierarchy chart for the Guess the Number game

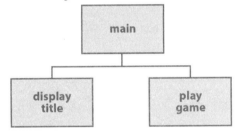

How to build a hierarchy chart

- Start with a box for the main() function.
- At the next level, put boxes for the functions that the main() function needs to call. This usually includes the function that will control the main action of the program, plus any functions that need to be done before or after that function.
- Continue down the levels by dividing the higher-level functions into their component functions until there aren't any more components.

Guidelines for creating hierarchy charts

- The names in a chart should start with a verb and give a good indication of what the function does. Then, the names can easily be converted to Python function names.
- Each function should do everything that is related to the function name and nothing more.

Figure 4-12   How to plan the functions of a program

The hierarchy chart for the Pig Dice game

To show how to develop a hierarchy chart for a new program, figure 4-13 presents the rules for a new game called Pig Dice. In brief, a player rolls a die to try to reach 20 in as few turns as possible. If a player rolls anything but a 1, the points are added to the points for the turn. If the player holds, all the points for the turn are added to the total score. But if the player rolls a 1, all points for that turn are lost.

Now, how would you create the hierarchy chart for this program? Well, the top-level should consist of the main() function, and the next level should consist of the play_game() function that controls the playing of the game and the display_rules() function that displays the rules. But then what?

To play the game, the user has to take a turn. So that's a logical component of the play_game() function. And to take a turn, the player has to either roll the die or hold, so those are the logical components of the take_turn() function. In fact, that may be all that this hierarchy chart needs.

That's the general thought process. If only it were that easy! In practice, you typically have to write some of the code for the top-level functions to get a better idea of how the functions work. In fact, you typically have to go back and forth between the code and the chart before you get it right. However, it's still often helpful to take the time to create a hierarchy chart or outline, especially as your programs become more complicated.

The rules for a Pig Dice game

- For each turn, the player can choose to roll the die or hold.
- A turn ends when the player rolls a 1 or chooses to hold.
- If the player rolls a 1, all points are lost for that turn.
- If the player chooses to hold, all points for that turn are added to the total.
- If the player enters an invalid character, the roll or hold prompt is displayed and the player can make another entry.
- When a player reaches 20 points, the game ends and the number of turns is displayed.

A hierarchy chart for the Pig Dice game

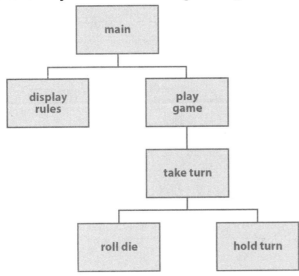

Description

- The Pig Dice game uses the console as the user interface.
- In the hierarchy chart, the main() function calls the play_game() function. If this program lets the user play more than one game, the main() function calls it repeatedly.
- The play_game() function calls the take_turn() function until the game is over.
- The take_turn() function calls the roll_die() function if the user chooses to roll and the hold_turn() function if the user chooses to hold.

Figure 4-13   How to plan the functions of a Pig Dice game

The Pig Dice game with global variables

Figure 4-14 presents the user interface and code for the Pig Dice game introduced in the previous figure. This game has one function for each function in the hierarchy chart presented in the previous figure. It also imports the random module so the game can use the randint() function to simulate the roll of the die.

If you look at the highlighted code in this listing, you can see that the main() function calls the display_rules() and play_game() functions, as indicated by the hierarchy chart. Then, the play_game() function uses a while statement to call the take_turn() function until the game_over variable is set to true. This continues as the take_turn() function calls the roll_die() and hold_turn() functions, just the way it's shown in the hierarchy chart.

The user interface

```
TURN 1
Roll or hold? (r/h): r
Die: 4
Roll or hold? (r/h): h
Score for turn: 4
Total score: 4

TURN 2
Roll or hold? (r/h): r
Die: 1
Turn over. No score.
...
...
You finished in 4 turns!
```

The code   **Page 1**

```python
import random

turn = 1
score = 0
score_this_turn = 0
turn_over = False
game_over = False

def main():
    display_rules()
    play_game()

def display_rules():
    print("Let's Play PIG!")
    print()
    print("* See how many turns it takes you to get to 20.")
    print("* Turn ends when you hold or roll a 1.")
    print("* If you roll a 1, you lose all points for the turn.")
    print("* If you hold, you save all points for the turn.")
    print()

def play_game():
    while not game_over:
        take_turn()
    print()
    print("Game over!")
```

Description

- When coding the functions of a program, be sure that each function does *everything* that its name implies and nothing that isn't implied by its name.

- This program illustrates a possible use for global variables. Otherwise, the five global variables would be local variables that are passed between the functions.

Figure 4-14   The Pig Dice game with global variables (part 1)

When you code a function, you should try to include everything that the name of the function implies...and nothing that the name of the function doesn't imply. For instance, all of the code that's required by the take_turn() function should be included in that function. None of it should be in the play_game() function. And none of the code for the hold_turn() function should be in either the play_game() or take_turn() functions.

If you keep this principle in mind, the code in your calling functions should be relatively simple. In addition, the code in the called modules should contain most of the code for the program. This should make your code easier to maintain, test, and debug.

Another feature that makes this program relatively easy to understand is that it uses five global variables. As a result, none of the functions require that arguments be passed to them. And none of the functions return values. To make that work, the three functions on this page of the code use the global keyword to access the variables that they need to change. That way, those functions can change the global variables. Then, since these variables are global, the other functions can access them without the global keyword as long as they don't need to change them.

But didn't we say that it was a best practice to avoid the use of global variables? Well, here's a case that might be an exception. By using global variables, the code has been simplified considerably. But even then, some programmers would say that it's better to pass local variables between the functions as described in the next figure.

The code

```python
def take_turn():
    global turn_over

    print("TURN", turn)
    turn_over = False
    while not turn_over:
        choice = input("Roll or hold? (r/h): ")
        if choice == "r":
            roll_die()
        elif choice == "h":
            hold_turn()
        else:
            print("Invalid choice. Try again.")

def roll_die():
    global turn, score_this_turn, turn_over

    die = random.randint(1, 6)
    print("Die:", die)
    if die == 1:
        score_this_turn = 0
        turn += 1
        print("Turn over. No score.\n")
        turn_over = True
    else:
        score_this_turn += die

def hold_turn():
    global turn, score_this_turn, score, turn_over, game_over

    print("Score for turn:", score_this_turn)
    score += score_this_turn
    score_this_turn = 0
    print("Total score:", score, "\n")

    turn_over = True
    if score >= 20:
        game_over = True
        print("You finished in", turn, "turns!")
    turn += 1

# if started as the main module, call the main() function
if __name__ == "__main__":
    main()
```

Description

- The global keywords in the functions above identify the global variables that would have to be passed between the functions if only local variables were used.

Figure 4-14   The Pig Dice game with global variables (part 2)

The Pig Dice game with local variables

To show what this program looks like with local variables instead of global variables, figure 14-15 shows the code for the four functions that need to access the variables for the game.

To make this work, this code uses a Python feature known as *multiple assignment*. This feature allows you to use a single statement to assign multiple values to multiple variables. For instance, you can assign three int values to three variables named x, y, and z like this:

```
x, y, z = 1, 2, 3
```

Similarly, in this figure, the play_game() function assigns the three values returned by the take_turn() function to three variables like this:

```
turn, score, game_over = take_turn(turn, score, game_over)
```

This calls the take_turn() function and passes it the turn, score, and game_over variables. Then, it assigns the three variables that are returned by the take_turn() function to the turn, score, and game_over variables.

To make this work, the take_turn() function returns three values by ending with a return statement like this:

```
return turn, score, game_over
```

This shows that a return statement can return multiple values. Similarly, the roll_die() and hold_turn() functions also return multiple values.

Now that you've seen this program with and without global variables, you can make your own decision. Is it worth using global variables in a program like this? This is largely a matter of personal preference. We think that either approach is acceptable.

The code for the four functions that pass variables

```
def play_game():
    turn = 1
    score = 0
    game_over = False
    while not game_over:
        turn, score, game_over = take_turn(turn, score, game_over)
    print()
    print("Game over!")

def take_turn(turn, score, game_over):
    print("TURN", turn)
    score_this_turn = 0
    turn_over = False
    while not turn_over:
        choice = input("Roll or hold? (r/h): ")
        if choice == "r":
            turn, score, score_this_turn, turn_over = \
                roll_die(turn, score, score_this_turn)
        elif choice == "h":
            turn, score, turn_over, game_over =       \
                hold_turn(turn, score, score_this_turn)
        else:
            print("Invalid choice. Try again.")
    return turn, score, game_over

def roll_die(turn, score, score_this_turn):
    die = random.randint(1, 6)
    print("Die:", str(die))
    if die == 1:
        score_this_turn = 0
        turn += 1
        print("Turn over. No score.\n")
        turn_over = True
    else:
        score_this_turn += die
        turn_over = False
    return turn, score, score_this_turn, turn_over

def hold_turn(turn, score, score_this_turn):
    print("Score for turn:", score_this_turn)
    score += score_this_turn
    print("Total score:", score, "\n")
    turn_over = True
    game_over = False
    if score >= 20:
        print("You finished in", turn, "turns!")
        game_over = True
        return turn, score, turn_over, game_over
    turn += 1
    return turn, score, turn_over, game_over
```

Description

- A return statement can return multiple variables.
- An assignment statement can assign multiple values to multiple variables.

Figure 4-15   The Pig Dice game with local variables

Perspective

Now that you've finished this chapter, you should have all the skills that you need for planning, coding, and using the functions and modules that your programs require. These are critical skills that become increasingly valuable as your programs get longer and more complex. By applying these skills, you make your programs easier to understand, test, debug, and maintain.

In section 3 of this book, you'll learn another way to organize the code in your programs. It's called object-oriented programming. Fortunately, many of the skills for working with functions and modules also apply to object-oriented programming. That's why this chapter is so important.

Terms

function	global constant
define a function	module
argument	docstrings
call a function	import a module
return statement	import statement
parameter	namespace
main() function	global namespace
named argument	name collision
scope	standard module
global variable	random module
global scope	hierarchy chart
local variable	hierarchy outline
local scope	multiple assignment statement
shadowing	

Summary

- A *function* is a reusable unit of code that performs a task.

- A function can accept zero or more *arguments* that supply data for the function to operate on. Within the body of a function, a *return statement* can return one or more values to the calling code.

- When you define a function, you can set default values for arguments. When you call a function, you can pass *named arguments*.

- *Global variables* are defined outside of the functions of a program so they have *global scope*. As a result, they can be accessed by any of the functions.

- *Local variables* are defined inside functions so they have *local scope*. As a result, they can only be accessed from within their functions.

- When a local variable has the same name as a global variable, the local variable *shadows* the global variable.

- It's a best practice to avoid the use of global variables and variable shadowing because that often leads to debugging problems.

- A *module* is a file that stores reusable code. When you *import* a module, it is stored in a *namespace*.

- If you import two modules into the *global namespace*, two functions could have the same name. Then, a *name collision* occurs and one function overrides the other, which leads to debugging problems.

- Python provides many *standard modules* that contain functions that you can use in your programs. One of those modules is the *random module*, which provides functions that return random numbers.

- To plan the functions for a program, you can use a *hierarchy chart*. Then, you code one function for each box on the hierarchy chart.

- In Python, a function can return multiple values. Then, an assignment statement can assign those return values to multiple variables. This feature is known as *multiple assignment*.

Exercise 4-1   Enhance the Future Value program

In this exercise, you'll enhance the Future Value program in figure 3-15 so it validates the three user entries with messages that are something like these:

```
Welcome to the Future Value Calculator

Enter monthly investment:      0
Entry must be greater than 0 and less than or equal to 1000
Enter monthly investment:      100
Enter yearly interest rate:    16
Entry must be greater than 0 and less than or equal to 15
Enter yearly interest rate:    12
Enter number of years:         100
Entry must be greater than 0 and less than or equal to 50
Enter number of years:         10

Future Value =                 23233.91

Continue (y/n)? n
```

1. In IDLE, open the future_value.py file that's in this folder:
   python/exercises/ch04

2. Test the program, but remember that it doesn't do any validation, so enter valid numbers.

Add two validation functions to the program

3. In preparation for adding two functions named get_float() and get_int() to the program, create a hierarchy chart or outline that includes those functions. The functions will be used to get valid numbers and integers from the user as described in the next steps.

4. Add a function named get_float() to the program. This function should accept one argument, which is a prompt like "Enter monthly investment: ". Then, this function should use the input function to get an entry from the user using the prompt that's passed to it, and the entry should be converted to a float value. Next, this function should check this entry to make sure it's greater than 0. If it is, the entry is valid and the number should be returned to the calling statement. If it isn't, an appropriate error message should be displayed, and the user should enter another value. To make this work, the function should use a while statement that gets an entry until it is valid.

5. Modify the main() function so it uses this function to get the monthly investment entry. That tests the function.

6. Enhance the get_float() function so it gets three arguments: a prompt, a low validity value, and a high validity value. This function should work as before, except the entry must be greater than the low value and less than or equal to the high value. If the entry is invalid, this function should display error messages like those above using the low and high arguments. Otherwise, it should return the value to the calling statement.

7. Modify the main() function so it uses the get_float() function for the first two entries. The low and high arguments should be 0 and 1000 for the first entry, and 0 and 15 for the second entry.

8. Add a get_int() function that works like the get_float() function, except that it gets an integer entry instead of a float entry. Then, call this function from the main() function so it gets the years entry.

Create a validation module

9. Use the File→Save As command to save a copy of the Future Value program as validation.py. This will be the file for a module that stores the get_float() and get_int() functions. So, delete the calculate_future_value() function, but keep the main() function and the if statement after the main() function.

10. In the main() function, delete everything inside the while loop except the last statement that asks whether the user wants to continue. Within this loop, code two call statements that test the get_float() and get_int() functions.

11. Run the program to test the two functions. When you're through, you can close the file.

Use the validation module in the Future Value program

12. Go back to the future_value.py file. Then, comment out the get_number and get_integer() functions.

13. Add an import statement that imports the validation module.

14. Modify the code in the main() function so it uses the functions in the validation module.

5

How to test and debug a program

If you've been doing the exercises and writing your own programs, you already have some experience with testing and debugging. Now, this chapter reviews some of what you've been experiencing and presents some new skills for testing and debugging. As your programs become more complicated, these testing and debugging skills become more valuable.

An introduction to testing and debugging

When you *test* a program, you run it to make sure that it works correctly. As you test the program, you try every possible combination of input data and user actions to be certain that the program works in every case. In other words, the goal of testing is to *make the program fail*.

When you *debug* a program, you fix the errors (*bugs*) that you discover during testing. Each time you fix a bug, you test again to make sure that the change that you made didn't affect any other aspect of the program.

The three types of errors that can occur

As you test a program, three types of errors can occur. These errors are described in figure 5-1.

Syntax errors prevent your program from compiling and running. Since syntax errors occur when Python attempts to compile a program, they're known as *compile-time errors*. This type of error is the easiest to find and fix. When you use IDLE, it highlights the location of the first syntax error that it finds each time you attempt to run the program. Then, you can correct that error and try again.

Unfortunately, some errors can't be detected until you run a program. These errors are known as *runtime errors*, and they throw *exceptions* that stop the execution of a program.

Even if a program runs without throwing exceptions, it may contain *logic errors* that prevent the program from working correctly. This type of error is often the most difficult to find and fix. For example, the Future Value program in this figure has a logic error that results in an incorrect result. In this case, though, it's hard to tell what the right future value should be. In a moment, though, you'll learn how to make sure that it's correct.

The Future Value program with a logic error

```
Enter monthly investment:   100
Enter yearly interest rate: 12
Enter number of years:      10

Future value:               22903.87

Continue? (y/n):
```

The goal of testing

- To find all errors before the program is put into production.

The goal of debugging

- To fix all errors before the program is put into production.

The three types of errors that can occur

- *Syntax errors* violate the rules for how Python statements must be written. These errors, also called *compile-time errors*, are caught by IDLE and the Python compiler before you run the program.

- *Runtime errors* don't violate the syntax rules, but they throw *exceptions* that stop the execution of the program. Many of these exceptions are due to programming errors that need to be fixed. But some exceptions need to be handled by the program so the program won't crash.

- *Logic errors* are statements that don't cause syntax or runtime errors, but produce the wrong results. In the console for the Future Value program above, the future value isn't correct, which is a logic error.

Description

- To *test* a Python program, you run it to make sure that it works properly no matter what combinations of valid or invalid data you enter.

- When you *debug* a program, you find and fix all of the errors (*bugs*) that occur when you test the program.

Figure 5-1   An introduction to testing and debugging

Common Python errors

Figure 5-2 presents some of the coding errors that are commonly made as you write a Python program. By now, you have certainly encountered many of them. But it's worth taking a quick look at the list to remind yourself to avoid these errors.

The function at the top of this figure illustrates two of these errors. Here, the first line of the for statement doesn't end with a colon. That's an error that's caught by IDLE when you try to run the program.

The second error is in the first statement in the for loop. Here, the first statement in the loop adds a variable named monthly_investment_amount to the future_value variable. However, a variable named monthly_investment_amount has never been defined. Instead, the name should be monthly_investment, the first argument that's defined by the function. This error causes an exception when the program is run.

This figure also describes the problem that Python has with floating-point arithmetic. Near the bottom of this figure, an example shows how floating-point arithmetic can produce strange results even with simple calculations. One way to handle this issue is to round numbers. Another is to use the decimal module so you can work with fixed-point decimal numbers instead of floating-point numbers. You'll learn how to use this module in chapter 9.

By the way, the function in this figure has one logic error that doesn't cause a compile-time error or a runtime exception, but does lead to inaccurate results. You'll learn how to find and fix errors like this in the next two figures.

A Python function that contains errors

```
def calculate_future_value(monthly_investment, yearly_interest, years):
    # convert yearly values to monthly values
    monthly_interest_rate = yearly_interest / 12 / 100
    months = years * 12

    # calculate future value
    future_value = 0.0
    for i in range(1, months)
        future_value += monthly_investment_amount
        monthly_interest = future_value * monthly_interest_rate
        future_value += monthly_interest

    return future_value
```

Common syntax errors

- Misspelling keywords.
- Forgetting the colon at the end of the opening line of a function definition, if clause, else clause, while statement, for statement, try clause, or except clause.
- Forgetting an opening or closing quotation mark or parenthesis.
- Using parentheses when you should be using brackets, or vice versa.
- Improper indentation.

Problems with names and values

- Misspelling or incorrectly capitalizing a variable or function name.
- Using a keyword as a variable or function name.
- Not checking that a value is the right data type before processing it. For example, using a number when it needs to be converted to a string, or vice versa.

Problem with floating-point arithmetic

- The float data type in Python uses floating-point numbers, and that can lead to arithmetic results that are imprecise. For example,
  ```
  sales_amount = 74.95;
  discount = sales_amount * .1;          # result is 7.495000000000001
  ```
- One quick way to fix this problem is to round the result to the right number of decimal places. If necessary, you can also convert it back to a floating-point number:
  ```
  discount = round(discount, 2)          # result is 7.5
  ```
- Another way to fix this problem is to use the standard decimal module, which lets you work with decimal numbers instead of floating-point numbers. You'll learn how to use this module in chapter 9.

Figure 5-2   Common Python errors

Four techniques for testing and debugging

With that as background, this chapter now presents four techniques that you can use to test and debug your programs more efficiently.

How to plan the test runs

When you test a program, you typically do so in at least two phases. In the first phase, you test the program with valid data. In the second phase, you test the program with invalid data. This is illustrated in figure 5-3.

As your programs become more complex, it helps to create a *test plan* for testing a program. This is simply a table or spreadsheet that shows what test data you're going to enter and what the results should be.

In the valid testing phase, you should start with test data that produces results that can be easily verified. This is illustrated by the Miles Per Gallon program in this figure. Here, the first test data entries are 320 miles driven and 10 gallons of gas used, so the result should clearly be 32 miles per gallon, and it is.

But don't stop there. You should also use test data that is more likely to produce an inaccurate result. For example, the next entries are 325 miles driven and 10 miles per gallon. But this time, the result is still 32 miles per gallon when it should be 32.5 miles per gallon. This shows the importance of using a range of valid entries and verifying that the results are accurate, even if they may look okay.

For the invalid testing phase, your test data should include all varieties of invalid entries. This is illustrated by the second example in this figure. This shows the start of a test run for the Future Value program that tests all aspects of the validation that's done by the program. When you create a test plan for invalid data, you try to make the program fail by testing every combination of invalid data and user action that you can think of.

The third example shows the importance of knowing what the results should be so you can verify the results in your test runs. But what should the result in this example be? In this case, calculating the result for just 12 months by hand or with a calculator would be difficult. If you know the formula for calculating the future value, you could use that. But even then, you have to be sure that the formula calculates the future value in the way that produces the correct results for your program. In the next figure, though, you'll learn a simple way to make sure the results are correct.

Yes, there's a lot more to testing than this. In a program that stores its data in a file, for instance, you need to make sure that the data has been written correctly on disk, which creates some new problems. Or, in a GUI program, you need to make sure that all of the controls like check boxes and drop-down lists work correctly. But in all programs, what's critical is (1) to test with all of the possible combinations of data, and (2) to make sure that the results are accurate by comparing them to results that you know are accurate.

The Miles Per Gallon program as it's tested with valid data

```
Enter miles driven:          320
Enter gallons of gas used:   10
Miles Per Gallon:            32.0
Continue? (y/n): y

Enter miles driven:          325
Enter gallons of gas used:   10
Miles Per Gallon:            32.0
```

Starting to test the Future Value program with invalid data

```
Enter monthly investment:    0
Entry must be greater than 0 and less than or equal to 1000.
Enter monthly investment:    1001
Entry must be greater than 0 and less than or equal to 1000.
Enter monthly investment:    100
Enter yearly interest rate: -12
```

The Future Value program as it's tested with valid data

```
Enter monthly investment:    100
Enter yearly interest rate: 12
Enter number of years:       10

Future value:                22903.87
```

The two critical test phases

1. Test the program with valid input data to make sure the results are correct.

2. Test the program with invalid data or unexpected user actions. Try everything you can think of to make the program fail.

How to make a test plan for the critical phases

1. List the valid entries that you're going to make and the correct results for each set of entries. Then, make sure that the results are correct when you test with these entries.

2. List the invalid entries that you're going to make. These should include entries that test the limits of the allowable values.

Two common testing problems

- Not testing a wide enough range of entries.

- Not knowing what the results of each set of entries should be and assuming that the answers are correct because they look correct.

Description

- It's easy to find syntax and runtime errors because the program won't run until you fix them.

- Logic errors can slip through your test runs if you don't check to make sure the results are correct, or if you don't test a wide enough range of entries.

Figure 5-3   How to plan the test runs

A simple way to trace code execution

When you *trace* the execution of a program, you add statements to your code that display messages or variable values at key points in the code. You typically do this to help find the cause of a logic error.

If, for example, you can't figure out why the future value that's calculated by the program is incorrect, you can insert print() functions into the code for the program as shown in figure 5-4. Here, the first print() function prints a message that indicates that program execution is entering the calculate_future_value() function. The second print() function at the end of the for loop prints the values of two important variables used by the loop.

After you run the program, the data that's displayed by these print() functions clearly shows where the calculation is going wrong. Here, the loop is only executed 11 times for one year, but it should be executed 12 times. That means that the arguments for the range() function aren't correct.

In this example, tracing helps you find a bug. However, you can also use tracing to make sure that the results are correct. For instance, you could easily assume that the future value result is correct without checking further. However, tracing the execution of the statements in the loop shows that the result can't possibly be correct.

When you use this tracing technique, you usually start by adding just a few print() functions to the code. Then, if that doesn't help you solve the problem, you can add more. Although this technique is simple, it can help you find the causes of many types of errors. The primary disadvantage of this technique is that it takes time to add the print() functions as you're debugging, and you need to remove these print() functions when you're done debugging.

A function that uses print() functions to trace execution

```
def calculate_future_value(monthly_investment, yearly_interest, years):
    print("Entering calculate_future_value()")
    # convert yearly values to monthly values
    monthly_interest_rate = yearly_interest / 12 / 100
    months = years * 12

    # calculate future value
    future_value = 0.0
    for i in range(1, months):
        future_value += monthly_investment
        monthly_interest = future_value * monthly_interest_rate
        future_value += monthly_interest
        print("i =", i, "future value =", future_value)
    return future_value
```

The data that's printed to the console

```
Enter monthly investment:    100
Enter yearly interest rate: 12
Enter number of years:       1
Entering calculate_future_value()
i = 1 future value = 101.0
i = 2 future value = 203.01
i = 3 future value = 306.0401
i = 4 future value = 410.100501
i = 5 future value = 515.20150601
i = 6 future value = 621.3535210701
i = 7 future value = 728.567056280801
i = 8 future value = 836.852726843609
i = 9 future value = 946.2212541120451
i = 10 future value = 1056.6834666531656
i = 11 future value = 1168.2503013196972

Future value:           1168.25

Continue? (y/n):
```

Description

- A simple way to *trace* the execution of a program is to insert print() functions at key points in the code that display messages or data on the console.

- The messages that are printed to the console can indicate what functions are being executed, or they can display the values of variables.

Figure 5-4   A simple way to trace code execution

How to use top-down coding and testing to simplify debugging

One way to simplify debugging is to code and test just a small portion of a program at a time. This can be referred to as *top-down coding and testing* or just *top-down testing*.

This is illustrated by the example in figure 5-5. This is for the Future Value program that consists of the four functions shown in the hierarchy chart. One of the benefits of dividing a program into functions is that it makes it easy to code and test the program on a top-down basis.

In the first testing phase for a program like this, you code one or two of the functions and the code in the main() function that uses those functions. In this example, you code and test the calculate_future_value() function and the code in the main() function that calls that function and displays its results. When that's fully tested, you go on to phase 2.

In phase 2, you code one of the other functions and adjust the code in the main() function so it uses that function. In this case, you code and test the get_float() function and adjust the main() function accordingly. At this point, you know you that have this program under control and you just need to code and test the rest of the functions.

So, in phase 3, you code and test the get_int() function along with whatever adjustments are needed in the main() function. And in phase 4, you can test all aspects of the program and add whatever finishing touches are needed.

The result is that you're testing a small amount of code at a time. That makes debugging easy because you know that any errors were introduced by functions and code that you've just added. This also makes programming more enjoyable because you're making continuous progress without the frustration of complex debugging problems.

When the hierarchy chart for a program consists of several levels and many functions, you may want to take a few minutes to plan the sequence that you'll use for top-down coding and testing. In most cases, you'll want to code and test the critical functions first so you know that the concept of the program is going to work. But after that, you can usually add the other functions in whatever sequence you prefer.

A hierarchy chart for a Future Value program

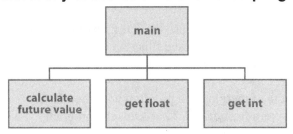

Testing phase 1: The main() function and the calculate function

- Code the calculate_future_value() function.
- Code the main() function or at least the portion that calls the calculate_future_value() function and uses the result that's returned.
- Test what you've coded so far.

Testing phase 2: Add data validation for float entries

- Code the get_float() function.
- Modify the main() function so it uses this function to get the float entries.
- Test what you've coded so far.

Testing phase 3: Add data validation for int entries

- Code the get_int() function.
- Modify the main() function so it uses this function to get the integer entries.
- Test what you've coded so far.

Testing phase 4: Add the finishing touches

- Make any refinements to the code like improving the prompt messages or the display of the results.

Discussion

- When you use *top-down coding and testing*, you start by coding and testing the code for one or two functions plus the code in the main() function that uses these functions. Then, you build on that base by adding the code for one or two functions at a time.
- Top-down testing simplifies debugging because you know that the errors are caused by the code that you've just added. As a result, it's relatively easy to find the errors.

Figure 5-5   How to use top-down coding and testing to simplify debugging

How to use the IDLE shell to test functions

One of the benefits of using IDLE is that you can use the IDLE shell to test any of the functions in your programs. This lets you test a function in variety of ways without running the whole program. Often, that means you can test a function more thoroughly in less time.

Figure 5-6 shows you how to test the functions of a program with the IDLE shell. To do that, you first run the program from IDLE. That loads the program module into the shell. After that, you can use the shell to run any function in the program.

This is illustrated by the first two examples in this figure. In the first example, the Future Value program has been run and thus loaded into the shell. Then, statements are entered into the shell that call the functions in the program. First, the get_float() function is tested with the three arguments it requires. Then, the calculate_future_value() function is executed.

In the second example, the Convert Temperatures program of the last chapter has been run and loaded into the shell. Then, the convert_temp() function of the program is called twice. For each call, this function gets two user entries, and then displays the result.

The third example in this figure shows that you can also use the shell to test the functions of a module that isn't a program. To do that, you first import the module. In this example, the temperature module that's used by the Convert Temperatures program is imported into the shell. Then, its functions are called.

When you test functions this way, you isolate them from the rest of the program or module. That makes it easier to see whether they work the way they're supposed to. As a result, this is an efficient way to test each function of a program with a variety of arguments.

Testing the functions of the Future Value program in the Python shell

```
>>> new_value = get_float("Enter Number: ", 0, 1000)
Enter Number: 0
Entry must be greater than 0 and less than or equal to 1000.
Enter Number: -1
Entry must be greater than 0 and less than or equal to 1000.
Enter Number: 1001
Entry must be greater than 0 and less than or equal to 1000.
Enter Number: 1000
>>> new_value
1000.0
>>> new_value = get_float("Enter Number: ", 0, 10)
Enter Number: 11
Entry must be greater than 0 and less than or equal to 10.
Enter Number: 10
>>> new_value
10.0
>>> calculate_future_value(100, 12, 1)
1168.2503013196972
>>> calculate_future_value(500, 12, 50)
19528669.849965967
>>>
```

Testing the functions of the Convert Temperatures program in the shell

```
>>> convert_temp()
Enter a menu option: 1
Enter degrees Fahrenheit: 212
Degrees Celsius: 100.0
>>> convert_temp()
Enter a menu option: 2
Enter degrees Celsius: 100
Degrees Fahrenheit: 212.0
```

Testing the functions of the temperature module in the shell

```
>>> import temperature as t
>>> t.to_celsius(212)
100.0
>>> t.to_fahrenheit(0)
32.0
>>> t.to_celsius(32)
0.0
>>> t.to_fahrenheit(100)
212.0
```

Description

- To test the functions of a program in the IDLE shell, you first run the program. That loads the program into the IDLE shell. Then, you can call any function in the program from the prompt in the shell.

- To test the functions in a module, you can import the module into the shell. Then, you can call any function in the module.

- This lets you test functions one at a time with arguments that produce verifiable results.

Figure 5-6   How to use the IDLE shell to test functions

How to use the IDLE debugger

So far in this chapter, you've learned the skills that you'll use to solve most of your debugging problems. Occasionally, though, you'll run into bugs that are difficult to isolate. Then, you can use the IDLE debugger to step through the statements of a program, one at a time, and view the changes in the variables at each step.

Most modern IDEs include debuggers. In fact, the debuggers for most modern IDEs are easier to use than the IDLE debugger. So, if you can learn how to use the IDLE debugger, you shouldn't have any problem using other debuggers.

How to set and remove breakpoints

The first step in using the IDLE *debugger* is to set a *breakpoint* at the point in the program that precedes the statements that you think are causing the bug. To set a breakpoint, you right-click on a statement in the IDLE editor and select Set Breakpoint from the context menu. This highlights the statement in the editor, as shown in figure 5-7. Later, when you run the program with the debugger, execution will stop just prior to the statement at the breakpoint.

When debugging, you need to set the breakpoint before the line in the program that's causing the bug. Often, you can figure out where to set a breakpoint by reading the exception information that's displayed when your program crashes. Sometimes, though, you have to experiment before finding a good location to set a breakpoint.

You also need to know that it doesn't usually make sense to set a breakpoint on a comment line or on a line that defines a function. That's because these lines aren't executed, so they don't cause execution to stop. Instead, you typically want to set the breakpoint on an executable statement within a function.

After you set the breakpoint, you need to start the IDLE debugger. To do that, you switch to the shell and select Debug→Debugger. That causes the Debug Control window to appear. In this window, you usually want to check the Source box, which isn't on by default. That way, the text editor highlights the statement that's going to be executed next, and the debugger automatically opens any modules that are used by the program when they are needed.

Then, you switch back to the editor and run the program. This switches you back to the Debug Control window with the first line of the program displayed, as shown in this figure. Next, you click the Go button to run the program until it reaches the first breakpoint. When you do that, you have to go to the shell to enter any data that the program prompts you for. When you reach the breakpoint, you can step through the program as shown in the next figure.

When you're using the debugger, you're actually working with three different IDLE windows. Your program is in the editor. You respond to prompts of the program in the shell. And you step through the program in the debugger. To use the debugger efficiently, it helps to arrange these windows on your monitor so you can see all three at the same time.

The IDLE editor window with a breakpoint

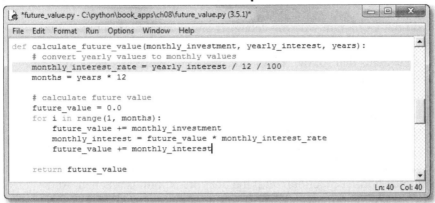

The IDLE Debug Control window when the Future Value program starts

Description

- To set a *breakpoint* for a line, right-click on the line and select Set Breakpoint from the context menu. This highlights the line that contains the breakpoint as shown above.

- To remove a breakpoint from a line, right-click on the line and select Clear Breakpoint from the context menu.

- To turn the debugger on, switch to the shell and select Debug→Debugger. This opens the Debug Control window.

- To start debugging, go back to the editor and run the program. That displays the first line of code for the program in the Debug Control window as shown above.

- To run the program to the breakpoint, click the Go button in the debugger. Along the way, you have to respond to any prompts that the program issues in the interactive shell.

Figure 5-7   How to set and remove breakpoints

How to step through the code

When you run a program with the debugger and it encounters a breakpoint, execution stops just prior to the statement at the breakpoint. Then, you can step through the statements that follow. This is illustrated in figure 5-8. Here, the debugger is shown after the programmer stepped through the statements in the loop one time.

When you *step through a program*, you can click the Step button to execute every statement, one at a time. Or, you can click the Over button if you want to execute a function without stepping into it. You can click the Out button to step out of any function that you don't want to step through. You can click the Go button to continue normal execution until the next breakpoint is reached. And you can click the Quit button to end the execution of the program.

As you step through code, the bottom of the debugger shows the local variables and their values. If you want to view the global variables too, you can check the Globals box. In this figure, the debugger shows all of the local variables. That includes the arguments passed to the function, the variables defined in the function, and the i variable that's used in the for loop. Better yet, the debugger shows how these variables change as each statement is executed.

These are powerful debugging features that can help you find the cause of serious programming problems. Stepping through a program is also a good way to understand how the code in an existing program works. If, for example, you step through an entire program, you'll step through each function within that program. That clearly shows how the program works.

The IDLE Debugger when the Future Value program is running

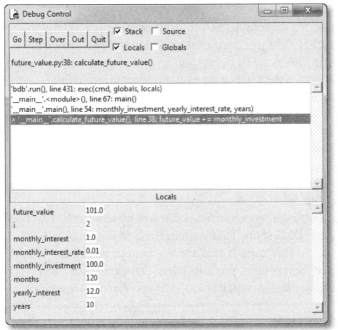

Some of the buttons on the Debug toolbar

Button	Description
Go	Run the program until the next breakpoint.
Step	Step through the code one statement at a time, including statements in called functions.
Over	Step through the code one statement at a time, skipping over called functions, but still executing them.
Out	Finish executing the current function and return to the calling function.
Quit	End the execution of the program.

Description

- When a breakpoint is reached, program execution is stopped before the line is executed.
- When the Source checkbox in the Debug Control window is checked, the current line of code is highlighted in gray in the editor window.
- If the Source checkbox is checked and you step into a function located in a different module, a new editor window opens with the source code for that module.
- If the Locals checkbox is checked, the bottom of the Debug Control window shows the values of the local variables that are currently in scope.
- To show the global variables, check the Globals checkbox.

Figure 5-8   How to step through the code

How to view the stack

When an exception occurs, it's sometimes helpful to view the *stack*. The stack is a list of the functions that have just been executed in reverse sequence in which they were called. This is illustrated in figure 5-9.

The stack in this figure shows a stack when an exception occurred in the calculate_future_value() function of the Future Value program. To start, IDLE's built-in function named runcode() loaded the module for the Future Value program as the __main__ module. That loaded all functions for the module and executed the if statement at the bottom of the module. This if statement called the main() function of the Future Value program. Then, the main() function called the calculate_future_value() function, and the exception occurred when Python attempted to execute line 38.

After an exception occurs, you can open the Stack Viewer by selecting Debug→Stack Viewer from the IDLE shell. That switches you to the Stack Viewer so you can view the stack. However, if you always want to switch to the Stack Viewer when an exception occurs, you can select Debug→Auto-open Stack Viewer. Then, IDLE automatically switches to the Stack Viewer whenever an exception occurs.

In the Stack Viewer, you can click on the plus sign next to a function to expand it. Then, you can view the current values of all local and global variables. In this figure, the plus sign for the calculate_future_value() function has been clicked, and you can see all of the local variables. This is helpful because you can get all this information without running the debugger.

If you want to jump to a function that's listed in the stack, you can double-click on it. This takes you to the code editor window and highlights the relevant line of code.

You probably won't need to view the stack often. Usually, when an exception occurs, you can figure out what caused the problem from the normal exception information that's displayed in the shell. Then, you can fix the problem and continue testing and debugging. In some cases, though, the stack gives you the extra information that you need to find and fix a bug.

A debugging session with the Stack Viewer window displayed

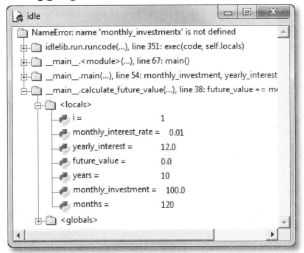

Description

- When an unhandled exception occurs, the Stack Viewer displays a list of the functions that were called, leading up to the exception. This list is called the *stack*.

- To open the Stack Viewer after an exception occurs, select Debug→Stack Viewer from the IDLE shell.

- To automatically open the Stack Viewer whenever an exception occurs, select Debug→Auto-open Stack Viewer.

- To see what the stack looked like when the exception occurred, expand any folder in the Stack Viewer. This includes all the local and global variables that were in scope at the time.

- To jump to a line of code in the editor from the Stack Viewer, double-click on the line. That switches you to the code editor window and highlights the line of code.

Figure 5-9   How to view the stack

Perspective

Before you put a program into production, you should test and debug it thoroughly. If you do a good job of it, your program won't encounter unexpected errors and crash, and it will deliver correct results. Now that you've completed this chapter, you should have all the skills you need for testing and debugging programs like the ones in this book.

Terms

test	test plan
debug	trace execution
bug	top-down coding and testing
syntax error	top-down testing
compile-time error	debugger
runtime error	breakpoint
exception	step through code
logic error	stack

Summary

- To *test* a program, you run it to make sure that it works properly no matter what combinations of valid or invalid data you enter.

- When you *debug* a program, you find and fix all of the errors (*bugs*) that you find when you test the program.

- *Syntax errors* violate the rules for how Python statements must be written. Since they are caught when Python attempts to compile your code, they are a type of *compile-time error*.

- An *exception* is a type of error that causes a program to crash if it isn't handled properly. Since exceptions occur when a program is running, they are a type of *runtime error*.

- *Logic errors* don't cause a program to crash, but they prevent it from working correctly.

- A *test plan* is a table or spreadsheet that shows the data entries that you can use for testing the program as well as the correct results for each set of entries. That way, you can verify that the program's results are correct.

- A simple way to *trace* the execution of a program is to insert print() functions at key points in the code.

- IDLE lets you test one function of a program at a time in the interactive shell.

- IDLE includes a *debugger* that can help you find and fix errors.

- You can set a *breakpoint* on a statement to stop the execution of the program just before that statement. Then, you can *step through the code* and view the values of the variables at each step.

- A *stack* is a list of functions in the reverse order in which they were called.

Exercise 5-1   Test and debug a Test Scores program

In this exercise, you will test and debug a variation of the Test Scores program of chapter 3.

1. In IDLE, open the test_scores.py file that's in this folder:

   `python/exercises/ch05`

   Then, review the code.

2. Create a test plan that thoroughly tests the program with valid data. This can be a handwritten table or a spreadsheet that includes the test data for three or four test runs as well as the expected results.

3. Use your test plan as a guide to testing the program. Then, note any inaccurate results that you discover during testing.

4. Debug any logic errors.

5. Test the program with the same data to be sure it works correctly.

Exercise 5-2   Trace and test the functions of the Future Value program

In this exercise, you will trace the operation of the calculate_future_value() function of a Future Value program. You'll also use the IDLE shell to test the functions in this program.

Use print() functions to trace the execution of a function

1. In IDLE, open the future_value.py file that's in this folder:

   `python/exercises/ch05`

   Then, test the program and note that the future value results are obviously inaccurate. In fact, the calculate_future_value() function has two logic errors.

2. To debug this problem, scroll down to the calculate_future_value() function, and add print() functions that show you how the values of the variables change each time through the for loop.

3. Run the program and review the results.

4. Fix the errors and comment out the print() functions that you added.

Use the IDLE shell to test the functions of this program

5. Run the Future Value program to make sure its functions are loaded into the shell.

6. Test its three functions as shown in figure 5-6. This shows you how easy it is to test a function without running the entire program.

Exercise 5-3   Step through a Future Value program

This exercise guides you through the use of the IDLE debugger as you step through the Future Value program.

Step through the calculate_future_value() function

1. In IDLE, open the future_value.py file that's in this folder:

    `python/exercises/ch05`

    If you did exercise 5-2, this will be a corrected version of this program. Otherwise, it will still contain two logic errors that lead to inaccurate results.

2. In the calculate_future_value() function, set a breakpoint on the first executable statement. Then, go the IDLE shell and start the debugger. That should display the Debug Control window. Now, check the Source checkbox.

3. Try to arrange the editor, shell, and Debug Control windows so you can see all three. That should make it easier for you to switch from one window to another and to see what's happening.

4. Go to the editor, and run the program. That should take you to the Debug Control window. Then, click Go to run the program to the breakpoint, and enter the required values when prompted in the interactive shell.

5. At the breakpoint, click the Step button to step through the function and note how the values of the local variables change. When you see how this works, click the Quit button to end the debugging session.

Step through the entire program

6. In the editor window, remove the breakpoint in the calculate_future_value() function, and set a breakpoint on the first statement of the main module. Then, run the program to the breakpoint as before.

7. Step through the program. This should take you from the main() function to the functions that it calls. This may also take you to Python functions that operate behind the scenes. Since these functions probably won't make much sense to you, you can step out of them right away. In short, experiment with the Step, Over, and Out buttons as you step through the code.

8. When you're through experimenting, click on the Quit button to end the session.

6

How to work with lists and tuples

So far, you have learned how to work with variables that store a single item of data such as a number or a string. However, in programming, you often to need to store a collection of data items. For example, you might need to store a collection of strings or a collection of numbers. This chapter teaches you how to work with two of Python's data structures for collections: lists and tuples.

Basic skills for working with lists

As the name implies, a *list* lets you store a list of *items*. Since a list stores these items in the sequence in which they are added to the list, lists are a type of data structure known as a *sequence*. In some languages, this structure is referred to as an *array* and the items in the array are referred to as *elements*.

How to create a list

Figure 6-1 shows the syntax for creating a list. To do that, you enclose the items you want to include in the list inside brackets ([ ]) and separate the items with commas. Most of the time, a list contains items that have the same data type. This is illustrated by the first two examples after the syntax summary. The first example creates a list of floating-point numbers, and the second example creates a list of strings.

However, you may sometimes need to create a list that contains items of different data types as shown by the third example. This is useful if you want to group all of the data for an entity that consists of both string and numeric data. Finally, you sometimes need to create an *empty list* as shown by the fourth example. Then, you can add items to this list later on.

The next example shows how you can use the *repetition operator* (*) to help create a list. If, for example, you create a list with one item that contains a zero, you can use the repetition operator to repeat that item as many times as you want.

How to get and set items

To refer to an item from a list, you use an *index*, starting at 0. This is illustrated by the next group of examples. Here, the first item in the temps list has an index of 0, the second item has an index of 1, and so on. However, you can also get items starting from the end of the list by using a negative integer as the index. Then, the last item in a list has an index of -1, the second to last item has an index of -2, and so on.

The next group of examples shows how you can get an item in a list and assign its value to a variable. This includes examples for both the temps and inventory lists.

Setting an item in a list works similarly. This is illustrated by the last group of examples. Here, you code the name of the list and the index that accesses the item on the left of the assignment operator (=). Then, you code the data that you want to assign to the item on the right side of the assignment operator.

When you get and set items in a list, keep in mind that you can only access an item if it already exists in the list. If you attempt to access an item that doesn't exist in the list, you'll get an IndexError that indicates that the index is out of range.

The syntax for creating a list

```
mylist = [item1, item2, ...]
```

Code that creates lists

```
temps = [48.0, 30.5, 20.2, 100.0, 42.0]     # 5 float values
inventory = ["staff", "hat", "shoes"]        # 3 str values
movie = ["The Holy Grail", 1975, 9.99]       # str, int, and float values
test_scores = []                             # an empty list
```

How to use the repetition operator (*) to create a list

```
scores = [0] * 5                # test scores = [0, 0, 0, 0, 0]
```

The positive and negative index values for the 5 items in the temps list

```
temps[0]   temps[-5]         # returns 48.0
temps[1]   temps[-4]         # returns 30.5
temps[2]   temps[-3]         # returns 20.2
temps[3]   temps[-2]         # returns 100.0
temps[4]   temps[-1]         # returns 42.0
```

How to get an item in a list

Code that gets items from the temps list

```
temps = [48.0, 30.5, 20.2, 100.0, 42.0]
temp = temps[0]                 # temp = 48.0
temp = temps[4]                 # temp = 42.0
temp = temps[5]                 # IndexError: index out of range
```

Code that gets items from the inventory list

```
inventory = ["staff", "hat", "shoes", "bread", "potion", "scroll"]
item = inventory[5]             # item = "scroll "
item = inventory[3]             # item = "bread"
item = inventory[6]             # IndexError: index out of range
```

How to set an item in a list

```
temps[3] = 98.0                 # replaces 100.0 with 98.0
inventory[4] = "ration"         # replaces "potion" with "ration"
```

Description

- A *list* contains a collection of *items*.

- To refer to the items in a list, you use an *index* where 0 refers to the first item, 1 refers to the second item, and so on.

- You can also use negative values for an index where -1 refers to the last item in the list, -2 refers to the second last item, and so on.

- You can use the repetition operator (*) to repeat the items in a list. This can be a good way to set the items in new list to default values.

Figure 6-1   How to create a list and access its items

How to add and remove items

Figure 6-2 shows how you can add items to a list and remove items from a list. To do that, you can use some of the methods that are available for a list. These are summarized in the table at the start of this figure. For instance, the append() method lets you add an item to the end of a list. The insert() method lets you add an item anywhere in a list. And the remove() method lets you remove an item from the list.

These methods are illustrated by the first group of examples after the table. Here, the first example appends the integer value 99.5 to the end of the list. The second example inserts the string value "robe" at index position 3 in the list and pushes all of the other items up one index position. The third example removes the item that has the value "shoes", and the items at the other index positions are adjusted to fill in that position.

The second group of examples shows how to use the pop() method of a list. If the calling code doesn't pass an argument to the method, this method removes the last item in the list. If the calling code specifies an index argument, this method removes the item at the specified index. When you use this method, it not only removes the item from the list but also returns it to the calling code. In this figure, the code assigns the item returned by the method to a variable named item.

The last group of examples shows how the index() and pop() methods can be used together to remove an item with a specific value. Here, the index() method searches for an item that has a value of "hat". If it finds the item, this method returns the index of the item, and the example assigns that index to the variable named i. Then, the pop() method removes the item at that index.

If the remove() and index() methods don't find the item, they cause a ValueError exception to occur. Since you typically don't want those exceptions to occur, you should make sure the item exists in the list before you call those methods. You'll learn how to do that in the next figure.

List methods for modifying a list

Method	Description
`append(item)`	Appends the specified item to the end of the list. This increases the length of the list by one.
`insert(index, item)`	Inserts the specified item at the specified index. This increases the length of the list by one and shifts all items after the specified index back by one index.
`remove(item)`	Removes the first item in the list that is equal to the specified item. This decreases the length of the list by one and shifts all items after the found item's index forward. If item isn't found, this method raises a ValueError.
`index(item)`	Returns the index of the first occurrence of the specified item in the list. If the item isn't found, this method raises a ValueError.
`pop([index])`	If no index argument is specified, this method gets the last item from the list and removes it. Otherwise, this method gets the item at the specified index and removes it.

How to use the append(), insert(), and remove() methods

```
stats = [48.0, 30.5, 20.2, 100.0]
inventory = ["staff", "hat", "shoes", "bread", "potion"]

stats.append(99.5)              # stats = [48.0, 30.5, 20.2, 100.0, 99.5]

inventory.insert(3, "robe")     # inventory = ["staff", "hat", "shoes",
                                #               "robe", "bread", "potion"]

inventory.remove("shoes")       # inventory = ["staff", "hat", "robe",
                                #               "bread", "potion"]
```

How to use the pop() method

```
inventory = ["staff", "hat", "robe", "bread"]
item = inventory.pop()          # item = "bread"
                                # inventory = ["staff", "hat", "robe"]
item = inventory.pop(1)         # item = "hat"
                                # inventory = ["staff", "robe"]
```

How to remove an item by using the index() and pop() methods

```
inventory = ["staff", "hat", "robe", "bread"]
i = inventory.index("hat")      # i = 1
inventory.pop[i]                # inventory = ["staff", "robe", "bread"]
```

Description

- You can use the list methods to add and remove the items in a list.

Figure 6-2   How to find, add, and remove items

How to process the items in a list

Figure 6-3 shows a variety of ways that you can process the items in a list. To help you do that, you can use the built-in len() function to get the length of the list, which is the number of items in the list. If, for example, there are 10 items in a list, the indexes range from 0 through 9, but the len() function returns 10.

As the first example shows, you can use the *in keyword* to search for an item in a list. This is one way to make sure that an item is in a list before you process it. In this example, the item is removed after the code makes sure it's in the list.

The next example shows that you can use the print() function to print a list to the console. This is often useful when testing a program that works with a list.

The third example shows how you can use a *for statement* to process all of the items in a list. This type of statement creates a *for loop* that's executed once for each item in the list. In this example, the loop just prints each item in the list. However, it's common for a loop to include multiple statements that process each item in the list.

As you review the third example, you should realize that this for loop works the same as the for loop presented in chapter 3. The only difference is that the for loop presented in chapter 3 processed a collection of int values returned by the range() function. Now, in this chapter, the for loop processes a collection of items that are stored in a list.

The last group of examples shows how you can process a list of scores with a for loop or a while loop. Here, both loops add each score in the list to the total. This comparison shows that it's easier to perform this processing by coding a for loop. That's because you don't need to use an index to get each item from the list, you don't need to use a counter variable, and you don't need to know the length of the list.

A built-in function for getting the length of a list

Function	Description
`len(list)`	Returns the length of the list, which is the number of items in the list.

How to use the in keyword to check whether an item is in a list

```
inventory = ["staff", "hat", "bread", "potion"]
item = "bread"
if item in inventory:
    inventory.remove(item)          # inventory = ["staff", "hat", "potion"]
```

How to print a list to the console

```
inventory = ["staff", "hat", "shoes", "bread", "potion"]
print(inventory)
```

The console

```
['staff', 'hat', 'shoes', 'bread', 'potion']
```

The syntax of a for statement that loops through a list

```
for item in list:
    statements
```

Code that prints each item in a list

```
inventory = ["staff", "hat", "shoes"]
for item in inventory:
    print(item)
```

The console

```
staff
hat
shoes
```

How to process the items in a list

With a for loop

```
scores = [70, 80, 90, 100]
total = 0
for score in scores:
    total += score
print(total)                    # total = 340
```

With a while loop

```
scores = [70, 80, 90, 100]
total = 0
i = 0
while i < len(scores):
    total += scores[i]
    i += 1
print(total)                    # total = 340
```

Figure 6-3   How to process the items in a list

How lists are passed to functions

In chapter 4, you learned how to pass number, string, and Boolean arguments to a function. Now, you need to learn more about how this works, and what the difference is when you pass a list to a function. This is summarized in figure 6-4.

To start, you need to know that Python uses *objects* to store data of all data types including strings, integers, floating-point numbers, Boolean values, and lists. When you write code, you often create objects without realizing it. For example, when you code a literal value of "staff", you are using the str type to create a str object for that value. Similarly, when you code a literal value of 1, you are using the int type to create an int object for that value.

When you write code, you often assign an object to a variable so you can use it in your code. In this figure, for instance, the calling code in the first example assigns an int object to the value1 variable. Similarly, the calling code in the second example creates a list object and assigns it to the inventory variable.

Next, you need to know that the str, int, float, and bool data types are *immutable types*. This means that you can't change the data that's stored in these objects. In contrast, a list object is a *mutable type*. This means that you can change the data in the list. If, for example, you append an item to a list, it directly changes the list object.

These concepts come into play when you pass arguments to functions. In that case, the variable name in the calling code and the argument name in the function both refer to the same object. But whether or not you have to return the result of the function depends on whether the argument is immutable or mutable. This is illustrated by the two examples in this figure.

In the first example, the int object for the variable named value1, which has a value of 25, is passed to the double_the_number() function. At this point, the value1 variable and the value argument both refer to the same object. But then, the first statement in the function doubles the value argument. This creates a new int object that's assigned to the value argument. Now, the value1 variable is still assigned to the original object, but the value argument is assigned to a new object with a value of 50. So, to make the new value available to the calling code, this function must return it.

In the second example, you can see the difference when a mutable object is passed to a function. Here, the calling code creates a list object and assigns it to a variable named inventory. Next, it passes the list object to the add_to_list() function along with a second argument for an item to be added to the list. At this point, the variable named inventory and the argument named list both refer to the same list object.

Then, within the add_to_list() function, the code appends the item argument to the list. Because the list is mutable, this changes the list object directly. In other words, there's no need to create a new list object. As a result, this function doesn't need to return the list. That's because the inventory variable in the calling code still refers to the list object that has been changed. So, when the calling code prints the list, it includes the new item that was added by the function.

Four immutable types

```
str
int
float
bool
```

One mutable type

```
list
```

How to work with arguments of the immutable type

The double_the_number() function

```
def double_the_number(value):
    value = value * 2       # a new int object is created
    return value            # the new int object must be returned
```

The calling code in the main() function

```
value1 = 25                        # an int object is created
value2 = double_the_number(value1)
print(value1)                      # 25
print(value2)                      # 50
```

How to work with arguments of the mutable type

The add_to_list() function

```
def add_to_list(list, item):
    list.append(item)                      # the list object is changed
```

The calling code in the main() function

```
inventory = ["staff", "hat", "bread"]  # the list object is created
add_to_list(inventory, "robe")
print(inventory)                       # ["staff", "hat", "bread", "robe"]
```

Description

- Python uses *objects* to store data of all types including integers, strings, floating-point numbers, and lists. When you write code that creates an object, you typically assign it to a variable name, so you can work with it.

- An object that's created from an *immutable type* such as the str or int type can't be changed, but you can create a new object that's based on it.

- An object that's created from a *mutable type* such as a list can be changed.

- When you pass an object to a function, the argument name in the function refers to the same object as the variable name in the calling code.

- When you pass an immutable object to a function, the function can use the argument name to create a new object. But then, it must return that object to make it available to the calling code.

- When you pass a mutable object like a list to a function, the function can change the object. In that case, the function doesn't need to return the object to the calling code because it already has a variable that refers to that object.

Figure 6-4   How lists are passed to functions

The Movie List program

Figure 6-5 presents a Movie List program that illustrates many of the skills that you've just learned. As the console shows, this program maintains a list of movies, and the user can list all the movies, add a movie to the list, or delete a movie from the list.

After the console, this figure shows a hierarchy chart for this program. Here, the main() function calls four other functions to display the command menu, list all the movies, add a movie to the list, or delete a movie from the list.

The user interface

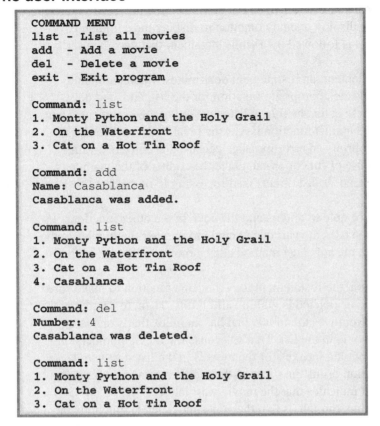

```
COMMAND MENU
list - List all movies
add  - Add a movie
del  - Delete a movie
exit - Exit program

Command: list
1. Monty Python and the Holy Grail
2. On the Waterfront
3. Cat on a Hot Tin Roof

Command: add
Name: Casablanca
Casablanca was added.

Command: list
1. Monty Python and the Holy Grail
2. On the Waterfront
3. Cat on a Hot Tin Roof
4. Casablanca

Command: del
Number: 4
Casablanca was deleted.

Command: list
1. Monty Python and the Holy Grail
2. On the Waterfront
3. Cat on a Hot Tin Roof
```

The hierarchy chart

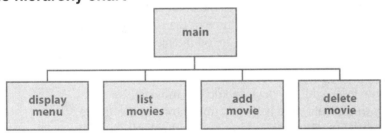

Figure 6-5   The Movie List program (part 1)

Part 2 of this figure shows the Python code for this program. To start, look at the main() function that's last in this listing. It starts by creating a list of three movies. Then, it calls the display_menu() function to display the commands that the user can use. This is followed by a while statement that gets the user's commands.

Within this while statement, an if statement determines which command has been entered and calls the appropriate function for the list, add, and del commands. In each of these calls, the movie list is passed as the argument. Then, for the exit command, the main() function issues the break statement to end the while loop. Otherwise, it prints an error message because the entry is invalid.

This shows how the use of functions can make the coding of the main() function easier to understand. It just directs the processing to one of the other functions.

By now, you should be able to understand the code in the other functions. In the list() function, the loop uses the variable named i to number the movies in the list. In the add() function, the append() method adds a movie to the end of the list.

In the delete() function, the if statement uses the len() function to make sure the index for the movie to be deleted is within valid limits. Then, to delete the movie, the pop() method removes the movie that has an index that's one less than the number of the movie in the list. That's because the movie numbers on the console start with 1, but the indexes for the movies in the list start with 0. Finally, the delete() function prints the name of the movie returned by the pop() method in a message that indicates that the movie was deleted.

What's most interesting, though, is that the add() and delete() functions in this program don't return the movie list after they change it. That's because a list is a mutable type, and the variable in the main() function still refers to it. Then, the main() function can pass that updated list to the other functions.

You might also notice that the names for three of the functions are list(), add(), and delete(), not the longer names that are on the hierarchy chart. That's acceptable in a simple program like this that has only a few functions. However, in a more complex program, you might want to avoid confusion by using longer names such as list_movies(), add_movie(), and delete_movie().

That's especially true because the list() function shown in this figure overrides the built-in list() function that's described in chapter 9. Since the Movie List program presented in this chapter doesn't use the built-in list() function, it doesn't cause any problems for this program. However, it's a bad practice to override built-in functions with your own functions.

You should also know that del() can't be used for the name of the delete() function. That's because Python has a built-in del operator. As a result, del is a keyword, and you can't use a keyword as the name for a variable or function. If do that, you'll get a syntax error when you attempt to compile the program.

The code

```python
def display_menu():
    print("COMMAND MENU")
    print("list - List all movies")
    print("add  - Add a movie")
    print("del  - Delete a movie")
    print("exit - Exit program")
    print()

def list(movie_list):
    i = 1
    for movie in movie_list:
        print(str(i) + ". " + movie)
        i += 1
    print()

def add(movie_list):
    movie = input("Name: ")
    movie_list.append(movie)
    print(movie + " was added.\n")

def delete(movie_list):
    number = int(input("Number: "))
    if number < 1 or number > len(movie_list):
        print("Invalid movie number.\n")
    else:
        movie = movie_list.pop(number-1)
        print(movie + " was deleted.\n")

def main():
    movie_list = ["Monty Python and the Holy Grail",
                  "On the Waterfront",
                  "Cat on a Hot Tin Roof"]

    display_menu()

    while True:
        command = input("Command: ")
        if command.lower() == "list":
            list(movie_list)
        elif command.lower() == "add":
            add(movie_list)
        elif command.lower() == "del":
            delete(movie_list)
        elif command.lower() == "exit":
            break
        else:
            print("Not a valid command. Please try again.\n")

    print("Bye!")

if __name__ == "__main__":
    main()
```

Figure 6-5   The Movie List program (part 2)

How to work with a list of lists

You can create a *list of lists* by storing a list in each item of another list. Since this lets you store data in two dimensions that you can think of as rows and columns, a list of lists is also referred to as a *two-dimensional list*.

How to create a list of lists

Figure 6-6 shows how to create and use a list of lists. This takes what you learned about lists and applies it to a list of lists. For instance, to create a list of lists, you code another list within each item of a first list. This is illustrated by the first two examples in this figure.

The first example consists of a list that contains three items, and each of those items contains a list of four items. As a result, it can be thought of as a list with three rows and four columns. Similarly, the second example can be thought of as a list with three rows and three columns.

The third example shows how you can add to a list of lists through programming. This example starts with a statement that creates a movies list that contains the lists for two movies. Then, to add a movie, the next statement creates an empty list for the movie. This is followed by three statements that append three items to the empty list: the movie name, year, and price. The last statement adds the movie list to the movies list. So at this point, the movies list is the same as the one defined by the first example.

How to process the items in a list of lists

To refer to the items in a list of lists, you use two indexes as illustrated by the fourth example. If necessary, you can also use negative indexes to work from the end of each list, but you usually don't need to do that. In addition, you get an IndexError exception if either index isn't valid.

If you want to display all of the items in a list of list, you can use the print() function as in the fifth example. This is often useful when you're testing a program.

You can also use nested loops to process the items in list of lists. In the last example in this figure, nested for loops are used to display the items in a list of lists, but you can of course use other types of loops with a list of lists. In this example, the end argument is coded with a pipe character (|) as its value so the columns in each row are separated by that character.

In general, then, the skills are the same whether you're working with a list or a list of lists. Applying them, however, is conceptually more difficult because of the second dimension. Also, if you need to, you can extend this syntax so it provides for a third dimension.

How to define a list of lists with 3 rows and 4 columns

```
students = [["Joel", 85, 95, 70],
            ["Anne", 95, 100, 100],
            ["Mike", 77, 70, 80, 85]]
```

How to define a list of lists with 3 rows and 3 columns

```
movies = [["The Holy Grail", 1975, 9.99],
          ["Life of Brian", 1979, 12.30],
          ["The Meaning of Life", 1983, 7.50]]
```

How to add to a list of lists through programming

```
movies = [["The HolyGrail", 1975, 9.99],
          ["Life of Brian", 1979, 12.30]]
movie = []                              # Create empty list for next movie
movie.append("The Meaning of Life")     # Add movie name to movie list
movie.append(1983)                      # Add movie year to movie list
movie.append(7.5)                       # Add movie price to movie list
movies.append(movie)                    # Add movie list to movies list
```

How to access the items in the list of movies

```
movies[0][0]         # "The Holy Grail"
movies[0][2]         # 9.99
movies[0][3]         # IndexError: index out of range
movies[1][0]         # "Life of Brian"
movies[3][0]         # IndexError: index out of range
```

How to print a two-dimensional list

```
print(movies)
```

The console

```
[['The Holy Grail', 1975, 9.99], ['Life of Brian', 1979,
12.3], ['The Meaning of Life', 1983, 7.5]]
```

How to loop through the rows and columns of a 2-dimensional list

```
for movie in movies:
    for item in movie:
        print(item, end=" | ")
    print()
```

The console

```
The Holy Grail | 1975 | 9.99 |
Life of Brian | 1979 | 12.3 |
The Meaning of Life | 1983 | 7.5 |
```

Description

- A Python *list of lists* is a list in which the items are other lists. Then, to access the items in the list of lists, you use two indexes.

- This can also be referred to as a *two-dimensional list*, and you can think of the data as *columns* within *rows*.

Figure 6-6   How to work with a list of lists

The Movie List 2D program

Figure 6-7 presents a Movie List program like the one in figure 6-5. However, this movie list uses a two-dimensional list to store two columns of data for each movie. Otherwise, the programs are similar because they let the user list, add, and delete movies. As a result, this program has the same hierarchy chart and the same functions as the earlier program.

In the list() function, an if statement checks the length of the list to make sure that the list contains at least one item before it displays the movies. That's an enhancement that isn't in the first Movie List program. Then, if there are movies in the list, the for loop displays a numbered list of movies. To do that, this loop uses the i variable to number each row. In addition, it uses the indexes 0 and 1 to get the movie name and year from each column in each row.

In the add() function, the first two statements use input() functions to get the movie and year entries from the user. Then, the next three statements create an empty list for a movie, and append the values of the two user entries to that list. This creates the list that stores the data for the movie. Next, the second to last statement appends the list for the new movie to the list of all movies. In other words, it adds another row to the list of movies. Finally, the last statement displays a message that includes the name of the movie that was added.

The user interface

```
COMMAND MENU
list - List all movies
add -  Add a movie
del -  Delete a movie
exit - Exit program

Command: list
1. Monty Python and the Holy Grail (1975)
2. On the Waterfront(1954)
3. Cat on a Hot Tin Roof (1958)

Command: add
Name: Gone with the Wind
Year: 1939
Gone with the Wind was added.

Command: list
1. Monty Python and the Holy Grail (1975)
2. On the Waterfront (1954)
3. Cat on a Hot Tin Roof (1958)
4. Gone with the Wind (1939)

Command: del
Number: 2
On the Waterfront was deleted.

Command: list
1. Monty Python and the Holy Grail (1975)
2. Cat on a Hot Tin Roof (1958)
3. Gone with the Wind (1939)
```

The code   Page 1

```python
def list(movie_list):
    if len(movie_list) == 0:
        print("There are no movies in the list.\n")
        return
    else:
        i = 1
        for row in movie_list:
            print(str(i) + ". " + row[0] + " (" + str(row[1]) + ")")
            i += 1
        print()

def add(movie_list):
    name = input("Name: ")
    year = input("Year: ")
    movie = []
    movie.append(name)
    movie.append(year)
    movie_list.append(movie)
    print(movie[0] + " was added.\n")
```

Figure 6-7   The Movie List 2D program (part 1)

The delete() function works like the delete() function in the earlier program. Here, the number of the movie to be deleted is one higher than the index of the movie in the list. Then, if that number is between 1 and the length of the movie list, the movie is deleted. To delete the movie, the pop() method uses an index of the movie number minus 1. Then, the print() function uses an index of 0 to get the name of the movie that was just deleted and returned by the pop() method.

The display_menu() and main() functions also work the same as in the earlier program. Here again, the main() function passes the movie list to the list(), add(), and del() functions when it calls those functions. But since a list is mutable, the add() and delete() functions don't need to return the updated list. That's because the movie_list variable in the main() function is assigned to the same list. As a result, it reflects the changes that were made by the add() and delete() functions.

The code   **Page 2**

```python
def delete(movie_list):
    number = int(input("Number: "))
    if number < 1 or number > len(movie_list):
        print("Invalid movie number.\n")
    else:
        movie = movie_list.pop(number-1)
        print(movie[0] + " was deleted.\n")

def display_menu():
    print("COMMAND MENU")
    print("list - List all movies")
    print("add -  Add a movie")
    print("del -  Delete a movie")
    print("exit - Exit program")
    print()

def main():
    movie_list = [["Monty Python and the Holy Grail", 1975],
                  ["On the Waterfront", 1954],
                  ["Cat on a Hot Tin Roof", 1958]]

    display_menu()

    while True:
        command = input("Command: ")
        if command == "list":
            list(movie_list)
        elif command == "add":
            add(movie_list)
        elif command == "del":
            delete(movie_list)
        elif command == "exit":
            break
        else:
            print("Not a valid command. Please try again.\n")
    print("Bye!")

if __name__ == "__main__":
    main()
```

Figure 6-7   The Movie List 2D program (part 2)

More skills for working with lists

The next three figures present more skills for working with lists. Many of these skills are useful for processing the items in a list.

How to count, reverse, and sort the items in a list

The first table in figure 6-8 presents three more methods that you can use with a list. The second table presents a built-in function for sorting the items in the list. Then, the first set of examples shows how the count(), reverse(), and sort() methods can be used with a list of numbers. That's easy enough.

Although the count() and reverse() methods work the same with a list of strings, the sort() method requires a second argument if the list contains strings with mixed cases. That's because uppercase letters come before lowercase letters when strings are compared. Thus, "Pear" comes before "apple" in a simple sort. This is illustrated by the second set of examples.

To fix this, you need to supply a key argument that specifies a function that makes the sort work correctly. In this example, the key argument is set equal to str.lower, which is the string function that converts a string to lowercase letters. Then, the sort works correctly even though the string values in the list haven't been changed.

The same approach is required by the built-in sorted() function. In the third set of examples, this function requires a key argument, just like the sort() method. The difference between the sorted() function and the sort() method is that the sorted() function creates a new list but the sort() method doesn't.

Three more list methods

Method	Description
count(*item*)	Returns the number of occurrences of an item in the list. If the item isn't found in the list, this method returns 0.
reverse(*list*)	Reverses the order of the items in the list.
sort([key=*function*])	Sorts the list items in place. The optional key argument specifies a function to be called on each item before sorting.

A built-in function for sorting the items in a list

Method	Description
sorted(*list*[, key=*function*])	Returns a new list consisting of the sorted items of the original list. The optional key argument specifies a function to be called on each item before sorting.

How to use the count(), reverse(), and sort() methods

```
numlist = [5, 15, 84, 3, 14, 2, 8, 10, 14, 25]
count = numlist.count(14)        # count = 2
numlist.reverse()                # [25, 14, 10, 8, 2, 14, 3, 84, 15, 5]
numlist.sort()                   # [2, 3, 5, 8, 10, 14, 14, 15, 25, 84]
```

How to use the sort() method with mixed-case lists

What happens in a simple sort

```
foodlist = ["orange", "apple", "Pear", "banana"]
foodlist.sort()                  # ["Pear", "apple", "banana", "orange"]
```

How to use the key argument to fix the sort order

```
foodlist.sort(key=str.lower)
# result: ["apple", "banana", "orange", "Pear"]
```

How to use the sorted() function with mixed-case lists

What happens in a simple sort

```
foodlist = ["orange", "apple", "Pear", "banana"]
sorted_foodlist = sorted(foodlist)
print(sorted_foodlist)           # ["Pear", "apple", "banana", "orange"]
```

How to use the key argument to fix the sort order

```
sorted_foodlist = sorted(foodlist, key=str.lower)
print(sorted_foodlist)           # ["apple", "banana", "orange", "Pear"]
```

Description

- Note that the sorted() function creates a new list, but the sort() method doesn't.

Figure 6-8   How to count, reverse, and sort the items in a list

How to use other functions with lists

Figure 6-9 presents two more built-in functions that can be used with lists, and two functions of the random module that you can use to work with lists. The examples in this figure show how these functions work.

The first example uses the min() function to get the lowest value in the list and the max(function) to get the highest value.

The second example uses the choice() function to get a randomly selected item from the list named numlist. Here, choice is used as the variable name even though it is also the name of the function. This is okay because choice isn't one of the Python keywords and the choice() function is in the random module. The last statement in this example uses the shuffle() function to shuffle the numbers in the list named numlist.

Two built-in functions for working with lists

Method	Description
min(*list*)	Returns the minimum value in the list.
max(*list*)	Returns the maximum value in the list.

Two functions of the random module that work with lists

Function	Description
choice(*list*)	Returns a randomly selected item from the list.
shuffle(*list*)	Shuffles the items in the list on a random basis.

How to use the min() and max() functions

```
numlist = [5, 15, 84, 3, 14, 2, 8, 10, 14, 25]
minimum = min(numlist)              # 2
maximum = max(numlist)              # 84
```

How to use the choice() and shuffle() functions

```
import random
numlist = [5, 15, 84, 3, 14, 2, 8, 10, 14]
choice = random.choice(numlist)      # returns random item from numlist
random.shuffle(numlist)              # shuffles numlist items randomly
```

Description

- For working with lists, Python provides some built-in functions, and its random module provides some random functions.

Figure 6-9   How to use other functions with lists

How to copy, slice, and concatenate lists

Figure 6-10 presents three more skills that you may occasionally need when you're working with lists. Here, the first example shows how to make a *shallow copy* of a list. To do that, you assign a variable that contains a list to another variable. Since a list is a mutable type, this causes both variables to refer to the same list. As a result, if you use one variable to change the list, those changes are also available to the other variable.

If that's not what you want, you can use the deepcopy() function to make a *deep copy* of a list. This is illustrated by the second example in this figure. Since this function is in the copy module, you have to import this module in order to use this function. Then, after you use the deepcopy() function, you end up with two variables that refer to two different lists. As a result, you can use one variable to change items in one list, and you can use the other variable to change the items in the other list.

The next set of examples shows the syntax for slicing a list plus a few statements that show how that works. If you only want to supply start and end arguments, you only need to code one colon. If you want to start slicing at the beginning of the list, you can omit the start argument. Or, if you want to continue slicing to the end of the list, you can omit the end argument.

If you include the step argument, it specifies which items in the list should be included. If, for example, you want to get every other item in the list, you can supply a step argument of 2. Or, if you want to reverse the items, you can supply a step argument of -1.

The last set of examples shows how you can concatenate or join two lists by using the + or += operators. This is occasionally useful.

The deepcopy() function of the copy module

Function	Description
`deepcopy(list)`	Returns a deep copy of the list. The deep copy is a separate list with no relation to the original list.

How to make a shallow copy of a list

```
list_one = [1, 2, 3, 4, 5]
list_two = list_one
list_two[1] = 4
print(list_one)         # [1, 4, 3, 4, 5]
print(list_two)         # [1, 4, 3, 4, 5]
```

How to make a deep copy of a list

```
import copy
list_one = [1, 2, 3, 4, 5]
list_two = copy.deepcopy(list_one)
list_two[1] = 4
print(list_one)         # [1, 2, 3, 4, 5]
print(list_two)         # [1, 4, 3, 4, 5]
```

How to slice a list

The syntax for slicing a list

mylist[start:end:step]

Code that slices with the start and end arguments

```
numbers = [52, 54, 56, 58, 60, 62]
numbers[0:2]            # [52, 54]
numbers[:2]             # [52, 54]
numbers[4:]             # [60, 62]
```

Code that slices with the step argument

```
numbers[0:4:2]          # [52, 56]
numbers[::-1]           # [62, 60, 58, 56, 54, 52]
```

How to concatenate two lists with the + and += operators

```
inventory = ["staff", "robe"]
chest = ["scroll", "pestle"]
combined = inventory + chest   # ["staff", "robe", "scroll", "pestle"]
print(inventory)               # ["staff", "robe"]
inventory += chest             # ["staff", "robe", "scroll", "pestle"]
print(inventory)               # ["staff", "robe", "scroll", "pestle"]
```

Description

- The assignment operator makes a *shallow copy* of a list, so both list variables refer to the same list. In contrast, the deepcopy() function of the copy module makes a *deep copy* of the list so the list variables refer to two different lists.

- You can *slice* a list to get a subset of the original list. And you can concatenate lists by using the + operator or the += operator.

Figure 6-10   How to copy, slice, and concatenate lists

How to work with tuples

A *tuple* is a sequence that works much like a list. As a result, you can use many of the same skills that you learned for working with lists when you're working with tuples. The difference is that tuples are *immutable*, so they can't be changed. As a result, you can't use any of the skills for adding, modifying, or removing items. Figure 6-11 shows how to work with tuples.

How to create a tuple

To create a tuple, you use a syntax that's similar to the one for creating a list. The difference is that you use parentheses to enclose the items in a tuple, not brackets.

Most of the time, you'll need to create tuples that contain multiple items like the ones shown in the first example. However, if you need to create a tuple that contains a single item, you must follow that item with a comma like this:

```
scores = (99,)
```

This creates a tuple named scores that contains one int value. Without the comma, this code would not create a tuple. Instead, it would create an int value.

How to get items from a tuple

To access the items in a tuple, you use indexes within brackets, just as you do for the items in a list. However, since a tuple is immutable, you can only use this syntax to get items, not to set them.

The next example shows how you can *unpack* the items in a tuple by using a *multiple assignment statement*. To do that, you code as many variables as there are items in the tuple and then assign the tuple to those items.

The last example shows a function that returns three values. In this case, the function automatically creates a tuple that contains the three values specified by the return statement. Then, the function returns that tuple to the calling code so it can be unpacked.

If you remember, the Pig Dice game presented at the end of chapter 4 used code like this to return multiple values. Note, however, that most languages don't let you return multiple values in this way.

How to create a tuple

```
mytuple = (item1, item2, ...)
```

Code that creates tuples

```
# a tuple of 5 floating-point numbers
stats = (48.0, 30.5, 20.2, 100.0, 48.0)

# a tuple of 6 strings
herbs = ("lavender", "pokeroot", "chamomile",
         "valerian", "nettles", "oatstraw")

# a tuple that stores the data for a movie
movie = ("Monty Python and the Holy Grail", 1975, 9.99)
```

Code that accesses items in a tuple

```
herbs[0]                       # lavender
herbs[-1]                      # oatstraw
herbs[1:4]                     # ('pokeroot', 'chamomile', 'valerian')

herbs[1] = "red clover"
# TypeError: 'tuple' object does not support item assignment
```

Code that unpacks a tuple

```
tuple_values = (1, 2, 3)
a, b, c = tuple_values         # a = 1, b = 2, c = 3
```

A function that returns a tuple

```
def get_location():
    # the code that computes the values for x, y, and z goes here
    return x, y, z
```

Code that calls the get_location() function and unpacks the returned tuple

```
x, y, z = get_location()
```

Description

- Like lists, *tuples* are data structures that can contain multiple items.

- Unlike lists, tuples are *immutable*. In other words, after a tuple has been created, you can't add, remove, or set items.

- You can *unpack* the values of a tuple into multiple variables by using a *multiple assignment statement*.

- Because tuples are immutable, they are more efficient than lists. As a result, you should use a tuple whenever you know the items won't be changed.

Figure 6-11   How to work with tuples

The Number Crunching program

To show how some of skills you've just learned can be applied, figure 6-12 presents a Number Crunching program that works with a tuple and a list. In the main() function, the tuple consists of 11 integers from 0 to 50 counting by fives. In contrast, the list consists of 11 integers where each integer is a random number from 0 to 50. To create this list, the code creates a list that contains 11 items that are initialized to 0. Then, a for loop sets a random number from 0 through 50 in each of the 11 items. Next, the sort method sorts the list so the random numbers are in sequence.

The rest of the main() function prints the items in the tuple and calls the crunch_numbers() function to get and display the statistics for the tuple. Then, it does the same for the list of random numbers. Note that the crunch_numbers() function processes the numbers in both the tuple and the list.

When it's done processing the numbers, the crunch_numbers() function displays the statistics for the tuple and the list: average, median, min, max, and duplicate values (if any). To get those statistics, this function begins by using a for loop to calculate the total of all items in the tuple or list. Then, it calculates the average. Next, it calculates the index for the median value by dividing the number of items by 2 and using the // operator to truncate the result. Then, it uses that index to get the median value, which is the value that half the values are below and half are above. That's followed by two statements that get the minimum and the maximum values.

The get_duplicates() function returns any duplicate values contained by the tuple or list. Of course, the tuple created by this code doesn't contain any duplicate numbers. Although the statements for this function could have been coded in the crunch_numbers() function, there are a couple benefits to breaking this code out into its own function. To start, it breaks a large task down into smaller and more manageable tasks. In addition, the function name clearly identifies what the code does without having to use comments.

In any case, the get_duplicates() function starts by creating an empty list named dups that stores the duplicates, if any, in the list. Then, a for loop cycles through the numbers from 0 to 50, gets the count for each number, and appends the number to the dups list if the count is greater than or equal to 2. When the loop finishes, the return statement returns the dups list to the crunch_numbers() function, which prints the statistics for the tuple or list.

Both of these functions are coded so they work with any odd number of items in the tuple or list. This should give you some idea of how useful lists can be for processing real data. To take this to another level, for example, you can slice the list into four parts and then process the data for each quartile. You can also build a random list with more items. That more items you use, the more the medians and averages should level out.

The user interface

```
TUPLE DATA: (0, 5, 10, 15, 20, 25, 30, 35, 40, 45, 50)
Average = 25 Median = 25 Min = 0 Max = 50 Dups = []

RANDOM DATA: [4, 6, 19, 22, 26, 29, 29, 39, 42, 45, 47]
Average = 28 Median = 29 Min = 4 Max = 47 Dups = [29]
```

The code

```python
import random

def crunch_numbers(data):
    total = 0
    for number in data:
        total += number

    average = round(total / len(data))
    median_index = len(data) // 2
    median = data[median_index]
    minimum = min(data)
    maximum = max(data)
    dups = get_duplicates(data)

    print("Average =", average,
          "Median =", median,
          "Min =", minimum,
          "Max =", maximum,
          "Dups =", dups)

def get_duplicates(data):
    dups = []
    for i in range(51):
        count = data.count(i)
        if count >= 2:
            dups.append(i)
    return dups

def main():
    fixed_tuple = (0,5,10,15,20,25,30,35,40,45,50)
    random_list = [0] * 11
    for i in range(len(random_list)):
        random_list[i] = random.randint(0, 50)
    random_list.sort()

    print("TUPLE DATA:", fixed_tuple)
    crunch_numbers(fixed_tuple)
    print()
    print("RANDOM DATA:", random_list)
    crunch_numbers(random_list)

# if started as the main module, call the main() function
if __name__ == "__main__":
    main()
```

Figure 6-12   The Number Crunching program

Perspective

A *list* is a data structure that is supported by all programming languages. That's why this chapter is important to your development as a programmer. As you progress through this book, you'll see that lists are used in a wide variety of programs.

Terms

sequence	immutable
list	mutable
item	list of lists
array	two-dimensional list
element	shallow copy
index	deep copy
empty list	tuple
in keyword	unpack a tuple
for statement	multiple assignment statement
for loop	

Summary

- A *sequence* is an ordered collection of items such as a list or tuple.

- A *list* contains a collection of items that can be accessed by *index* values.

- To modify a list by adding items or deleting items, you can use the methods of a list including the append(), insert(), remove(), and pop() methods.

- To search for an item in a list, you can use the in keyword or the index() method of a list.

- To process the items in a list, you typically use for loops, but you can also use while loops.

- An object that's created from an *immutable type* such as the str or int type can't be changed, but you can create a new object that's based on it.

- An object that's created from a *mutable type* such as a list can be changed.

- You can use a *list of lists* to store data in a grid of rows and columns. This is also known as a *two-dimensional list*.

- When you make a *shallow copy* of a list, both variables refer to the same list. As a result, any changes to one variable are reflected in the other variable.

- When you make a *deep copy* of a list, both variables refer to their own copy of the list. As a result, changes to one variable aren't reflected in the other variable.

- A *tuple* works much like a list but is immutable instead of mutable. As a result, after you create it, you can't add, set, or remove items.

Exercise 6-1   Use a list for the Test Scores program

In this exercise, you'll modify a Test Scores program that gets the test scores that a user enters and then calculates and displays the average test score. You'll enhance this program by storing the test scores in a list and then getting and displaying other statistics for the test scores, like this:

```
The Test Scores program
Enter 'x' to exit

Enter test score: 75
Enter test score: 85
Enter test score: 95
Enter test score: x

Total:           255
Number of Scores: 3
Average Score:    85
Low Score:        75
High Score:       95
Median Score      85
```

1. In IDLE, open the test_scores.py file that's in this folder:
   python/exercises/ch06

2. Review the code, and test the program.

3. Modify the get_scores() function so the test scores are stored in a list named scores. This list should be returned by the function when all scores have been entered. The function should still make sure that the entries are valid, but the score_total and count variables aren't needed and shouldn't be updated.

4. Modify the process_scores() function so the scores list is its only argument. Then, this function should use a for statement to total the scores in the list. It should use the len() function to get the number of scores in the list. And it should get the average by dividing the total scores by the length.

5. Modify the main() function so the list that's returned by the get_scores() function is stored in a variable. Then, modify the call to the process_scores() function so it passes just the scores list to it.

6. Test this program to make sure everything is working right.

7. Enhance this program by getting and displaying all of the other statistics shown above. For an odd number of scores, the median score is the score that has the same number of scores below it as above it. For an even number of scores, calculate the median by taking the average of the two middle numbers.

Exercise 6-2 Enhance the Movie List 2D program

In this exercise, you'll modify the Movie List 2D program in figure 6-7 so it provides a third column for each movie. Otherwise, this program should work the same way it did before:

```
COMMAND MENU
list - List all movies
add -  Add a movie
del -  Delete a movie
find - Find movies by year
exit - Exit program

Command: add
Name: Gone with the Wind
Year: 1939
Price: 14.95
Gone with the Wind was added.

Command: list
1. Monty Python and the Holy Grail (1975) @ 9.95
2. On the Waterfront (1954) @ 5.59
3. Cat on a Hot Tin Roof (1958) @ 7.95
4. Gone with the Wind (1939) @ 14.95

Command: find
Year: 1954
On the Waterfront was released in 1954

Command:
```

1. In IDLE, open the movie_list_2d.py file that's in this folder:
   python/exercises/ch06

2. Enhance the program so it provides for the price column that's shown above.

3. Enhance the program so it provides a find by year function that lists all of the movies that were released in the year that the user requests, as shown above.

7

How to work with file I/O

So far in this book, you've learned how to work with data in the main memory of your computer. But when the program ends, that data is lost. Now, you'll learn how to save that data in a file and how to read that data from the file. This is known as file input and output, or *file I/O*.

An introduction to file I/O

The first two figures in this chapter show you how file I/O (input and output) works and how to open and close files so you can access their data.

How file I/O works

To start, you should know that Python supports dozens of different file types. These file types can be broken down into the two general types that are summarized at the top of figure 7-1. A *text file* stores all of its data as characters and each line ends with a new line character. Like a text file, a *binary file* can store character data. However, it can also store numeric data types such as the int and float types.

A *CSV (comma-separated values) file* is a type of text file that stores multiple values in each line. Typically, a CSV file uses commas to separate each value.

In this figure, the first example shows what a text file looks like when it's opened by a text editor. More specifically, it shows what a CSV file looks like when it's opened by Notepad. Here, there's one line for each of the three records in the file, and each record contains two values that are separated by commas.

The second example shows what a binary file that contains the same data looks like when it's opened by Notepad. Here, Notepad displays all of the data in a single line since there aren't any new line characters. Also, the values for the years look like gibberish because of the way numbers are stored.

When you use Python to work with one of these file types, you need to follow a sequence of operations. First, you *open* the file. Then, you can *read* the data from the file, or you can *write* data to the file. When you're through processing the file, you need to *close* the file so the resources that are being used are released to the system.

When a program writes data to a file, it saves the data that's in *main memory* (or *RAM*) to disk. Then, when the program ends, it doesn't lose that data. Instead, when it restarts, it can read the data from the disk file into main memory. Since this allows data to *persist* across program restarts, this is known as *persistent data storage*.

When you open, read, write, or close a file, an error called an *exception* can occur. If, for example, you try to open a file that doesn't exist, an exception occurs and the program crashes. In the next chapter, you'll learn how to handle exceptions so you can prevent your program from crashing.

Incidentally, the extension for a plain text file is often txt, and the extension for a CSV file is usually csv. In contrast, the extension for a binary file that contains data is often bin or dat. When you're using Python, though, you can use any extension for any type of file.

Two types of files

Type	Description
Text	Contains one or more lines that contain text characters. In a text file, each line ends with a new line character (\n). On Windows, this character is sometimes preceded by a carriage return character (\r).
	Common types include CSV files, JSON files, XML files, and HTML files.
Binary	Any file that isn't a text file. Many binary file formats contain parts that can be interpreted as text. However, binary files typically contain a sequence of bytes that are intended to be interpreted as something other than text characters.
	Common types include compiled program files, image files, audio files, video files, database files, and compressed files.

A CSV text file that's opened by a text editor

A binary file with the same data that's opened by a text editor

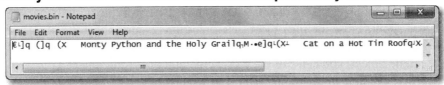

The sequence of file operations

1. *Open* the file.
2. *Write* data to the file or read data from the file.
3. *Close* the file.

Description

- Data that's in *main memory* (*RAM*) is lost when a program ends. But data that's saved in files on disk is available the next time a program needs to access it. Since this data *persists* across program restarts, this is known as *persistent data storage*.

- A *CSV (comma-separated values) file* is a type of text file that stores multiple values per line, typically using commas to separate each value.

- When I/O operations like opening, reading, or writing data to a file fail, an *exception* occurs. In the next chapter, you'll learn how to handle these exceptions.

Figure 7-1   How file I/O works

How to open and close a file

Figure 7-2 shows how to open a file. To do that, you can use the built-in open() function to create a *file object*. This function accepts both a file and a mode argument.

The file argument specifies a path for a file. In this book, the examples only specify the filename. As a result, the open() function looks for the file in the working directory, which is usually the same directory as the program file. If, for example, the program file is in a directory named book_apps/ch07, the open command usually looks in that directory.

The mode argument specifies the mode for the file, and four of these modes are summarized in the second table in this figure. Typically, a program uses read mode to read data from a file, and write mode to write data to a file. However, you can also use append mode to add a line to the end of an existing file. As you will see in figure 7-10, you use binary mode in combination with read or write mode when you're working with binary files.

One of the main differences between the read, write, and append modes is what they do if the open() function can't find the file. In that case, the read mode causes a file not found error to occur. However, the write and append modes create the file and write the appropriate data to the file.

When you open a file object, some of the operating system's resources are used to work with that object. As a result, when you're done working with the file object, you should close the file object. This frees the resources that the file object is using and prevents problems that can occur if you don't close the file.

To close a file object, you can call the close() method of the file object as shown in the first example in this figure. But if an exception occurs between the opening and closing of the file, the close statement is never executed and the resources aren't released.

To avoid this, you should use a *with statement* to automatically close a file when you're done using it, even if an error occurs. In this figure, the syntax summary shows that you code the open() function for a file in the first line of the with statement. Then, you code the block of statements that you want to execute while the file is open. When Python finishes executing that block of statements, it automatically closes the file.

This is illustrated by the last two examples in this figure. The first one opens a file in write mode, and it closes the file after it executes the one statement in the block. The second example opens a file in read mode, and it closes the file after it executes the print() function. In both cases, this code automatically closes the file, even if the statements in the block result in an error that causes the program to crash. For that reason, you should use with statements to open the files in all of your programs.

The built-in open() function

Function	Description
`open(file, mode)`	Returns a file object for the specified file with the specified mode.

A few of the modes of the open() function

Character	Mode	Description
`r`	Read	If the file doesn't exist, this mode causes a file not found error.
`w`	Write	If the file doesn't exist, this mode creates it. If the file already exists, this mode erases all existing data.
`a`	Append	If the file doesn't exist, this mode creates it. If the file already exists, this mode appends the data to the end of the file.
`b`	Binary	Use for binary files along with "r" or "w" mode.

The close() method of a file object

Method	Description
`close()`	Closes the file, which ends all operations and frees all resources.

How to open a file in write mode and close the file manually

```
outfile = open("test.txt", "w")
outfile.write("Test")
outfile.close()
```

How to use with statements to open and close files

The syntax of the with statement for file I/O

```
with open(file, mode) as file_object:
    statements...
```

Code that opens a text file in write mode and automatically closes it

```
with open("test.txt", "w") as outfile:
    outfile.write("Test")
```

Code that opens a text file in read mode and automatically closes it

```
with open("test.txt", "r") as infile:
    print(infile.readline())
```

Description

- When you open a file, you create a *file object*. Then, you can use the methods of the file object to work with the file.

- When you use a *with statement* to open a file, it automatically closes the file after executing its block of statements. That frees all resources used by the file, even if an exception occurs and the program ends prematurely.

- If you don't specify a path for the file, the open() function uses the working directory, which is usually the same directory as the program.

Figure 7-2   How to open and close a file

How to use text files

Now that you know how to open and close files, you're ready to learn how to read and write data to a plain text file. This is the simplest type of text file.

How to write a text file

When you open a file object in write or append mode, you can use its write() method to write or append data to a text file as shown in figure 7-3. With either mode, you pass one string as an argument. However, you can convert other data types such as the int and float types to the str type before you write them to the file. In addition, you can include a new line character to end each line in the text file.

The two examples in this figure show how that works. The first example uses write mode to create a new file and write one line to it. The second example uses append mode to append a line to the file. However, both examples pass a string that ends with a new line character.

The third example shows the contents of a text file that contains the data that was written by the first two examples. This data consists of a name, a new line character, another name, and another new line character. However, if you open this text file in a text editor, the editor doesn't display the new line characters. Instead, it starts a new line after each new line character as shown by the last example in this figure.

The write() method of a file object

Method	Description
write(*str*)	Writes the specified string to the file. If you want to start a new line, you must include the new line character.

How to write one line to a text file

```
with open("members.txt", "w") as file:
    file.write("John Cleese\n")
```

How to append one line to a text file

```
with open("members.txt", "a") as file:
    file.write("Eric Idle\n")
```

The contents of the text file after the two lines have been written

```
John Cleese\nEric Idle\n
```

The contents of the text file when viewed in a text editor

```
John Cleese
Eric Idle
```

Description

- To write data to a text file, you can use the write() method of its file object.
- When you write data to a file, the data is written from main memory (RAM) to a file on a disk drive.

Figure 7-3   How to write a text file

How to read a text file

After you open a file and create a file object, you can use the three methods in the table in figure 7-4 to read data from the file. Or, you can use a for statement to get the data from the lines in the file object.

In this figure, the four examples show how this work. All of these omit the mode argument of the open() method. Then, since read mode is the default, the files are opened in read mode.

In the first example, a for loop gets and prints each line of the file to the console. Since each line already ends with a new line character, this code sets the end argument of the print() method to an empty string. That way, the print() method doesn't add a second new line character to each line. In this example, the code doesn't call any of the read methods in the table. That's because the for loop automatically calls the readline() method to get the next line in the file.

In contrast, the next three examples do call the read methods. For instance, the second example uses the read() method to read the entire file and return its contents as a string. Then, it prints that string to the console.

The third example uses the readlines() method to read the entire file and return its contents as a list. Then, it prints the first two items in the list to the console.

The fourth example uses the readline() method to read the first two lines of the file and print them to the console. This works like the third example, except that it doesn't read the entire file at once. Instead, it reads the first line and prints it to the console. Then, it reads the second line and prints it to the console.

For a small file like the one in this figure, all of the read methods work equally well. However, for a large file, you'll probably want to use the readline() method since it only reads one line into memory at a time. Conversely, the read() and readlines() methods read the entire file into memory at once, which could have a negative impact on performance if the computer doesn't have enough memory to store the entire file.

Three read methods of a file object

Method	Description
`read()`	Reads the entire file and returns its contents as a string.
`readlines()`	Reads the entire file and returns it as a list.
`readline()`	Reads the next line in the file and returns its contents as a string.

How to use a for statement to read each line of the file

```
with open("members.txt") as file:
    for line in file:
        print(line, end="")
    print()
```

How to read the entire file as a string

```
with open("members.txt") as file:
    contents = file.read()
    print(contents)
```

How to read the entire file as a list

```
with open("members.txt") as file:
    members = file.readlines();
    print(members[0], end="")
    print(members[1])
```

How to read each line of the file

```
with open("members.txt") as file:
    member1 = file.readline();
    print(member1, end="")
    member2 = file.readline();
    print(member2)
```

The result that's printed to the console by all four examples

```
John Cleese
Eric Idle
```

Description

- To read data from a text file, you can use a for statement to iterate through the lines in the file object. Or, you can call the read methods of the file object.
- When you read data from a file, the data is read from the file on disk into main memory (RAM).

Figure 7-4   How to read a text file

How to work with a list in a text file

Because it's common for a program to store its data in a list, figure 7-5 shows how to write a list to a text file and how to read a list from a text file. In the first set of examples, two names are stored in a members list. Then, a for loop uses the write() method of the file object to write each member in the list to the file. To make that work, this code adds a new line character to the end of the string for each member.

To read that file, a for loop gets the string for each line in the file. Then, the replace() method of the string replaces the new line character with an empty string. After that, this code appends the string to the members list. When the loop finishes, a print() function prints the members list to the console.

The second set of examples in this figure shows how this works with integer data. The writing example works the same as before, except that the integer for the year must be converted to a string before the string can be written to the file. The reading example works the same as before, except that the year string must be converted to an integer.

In these examples, the replace() method of a string object removes the new line character from each string. You'll learn more about string methods like this in chapter 10.

How to write and read a list of strings

How to write the items in a list to a file

```
members = ["John Cleese", "Eric Idle"]
with open("members.txt", "w") as file:
    for m in members:
        file.write(m + "\n")                    # adds new line character
```

How to read the lines in a file into a list

```
members = []
with open("members.txt") as file:
    for line in file:
        line = line.replace("\n", "")           # removes new line character
        members.append(line)
print(members)
```

The result that's printed to the console

```
['John Cleese', 'Eric Idle']
```

How to write and read a list of numbers

How to write the items in a list to a file

```
years = [1975, 1979, 1983]
with open("years.txt", "w") as years_file:
    for year in years:
        years_file.write(str(year) + "\n")    # converts int to str
```

How to read the items in a list from a file

```
years = []
with open("years.txt") as file:
    for line in file:
        line = line.replace("\n", "")
        years.append(int(line))                 # converts str to int
print(years)
```

The result that's printed to the console

```
[1975, 1979, 1983]
```

Description

- When you read a text file into a list, you typically want to remove the new line character that's at the end of each line. To do that, you can use the replace() method of a string object.

- Before you can write a non-string value to a text file, you must convert it to a string value. Later, when you read that string value, you can convert it back to its original data type.

Figure 7-5   How to work with a list in a text file

The Movie List 1.0 program

Figure 7-6 presents a Movie List program that stores a list of movies in a text file. Like the Movie List program in the previous chapter, this one lets you list the movies, add movies to the list, and delete movies from the list. However, the program in this chapter saves the movie list in a file on disk. As a result, you don't lose your changes to the movie list when you exit the program.

As you review the code for this program, keep in mind that it only works if the file already exists. In practice, you can create a file like this by writing a separate program that writes the starting set of lines to the file. Or, you can use a text editor to do that. Once that's done, a program like this can read the file without causing an exception.

With that in mind, the Python code begins by defining a global constant named FILENAME that stores the name of the text file. Then, the code defines two functions that use this global constant to write and read this file. Since this constant only specifies the name of the file, not the path, the file must be in the working directory, which is usually the same directory as the program file.

The write_movies() function gets the list that contains movies as its argument. Then, it writes each movie in the list to the file by using the write() method of the file object. But first, it adds a new line character to the end of each movie name.

The read_movies() function reads each line in the file and appends it to the movies list. But first, it replaces the new line character with an empty string. When all of the movies have been read into the list, the function returns the list.

You should be able to follow the rest of this code since it's so similar to the code in the previous chapter. The main difference is that the program calls the write_movies() function whenever the user updates the movies list. As a result, the add_movie() and delete_movie() functions call the write_movies() function after they've updated the movies list.

The user interface

```
The Movie List program

COMMAND MENU
list - List all movies
add -  Add a movie
del -  Delete a movie
exit - Exit program

Command: list
1. Monty Python and the Holy Grail
2. Cat on a Hot Tin Roof
3. On the Waterfront

Command: add
Movie: Casablanca
Casablanca was added.

Command: list
1. Monty Python and the Holy Grail
2. Cat on a Hot Tin Roof
3. On the Waterfront
4. Casablanca

Command: del
Number: 4
Casablanca was deleted.
```

The code   Page 1

```python
FILENAME = "movies.txt"

def write_movies(movies):
    with open(FILENAME, "w") as file:
        for movie in movies:
            file.write(movie + "\n")

def read_movies():
    movies = []
    with open(FILENAME) as file:
        for line in file:
            line = line.replace("\n", "")
            movies.append(line)
    return movies

def list_movies(movies):
    for i in range(len(movies)):
        movie = movies[i]
        print(str(i+1) + ". " + movie)
    print()
```

Figure 7-6   The Movie List 1.0 program (part 1)

In the second part of this figure, you should note that the main() function calls the read_movies() function to read the movies list before it calls any of the other functions. If the file doesn't exist, an exception occurs and the program crashes.

However, if the file exists, the main() function reads the data into a movies list, and it passes the list to the list_movies(), add_movie(), and delete_movie() functions whenever it calls those functions. This works because the movies list is mutable. As a result, the add_movie() and delete_movie() functions can add and remove items in the list, and these changes are available to the main() function because it has a variable that's assigned to the same list.

The code

```python
def add_movie(movies):
    movie = input("Movie: ")
    movies.append(movie)
    write_movies(movies)
    print(movie + " was added.\n")

def delete_movie(movies):
    index = int(input("Number: "))
    movie = movies.pop(index - 1)
    write_movies(movies)
    print(movie + " was deleted.\n")

def display_menu():
    print("The Movie List program")
    print()
    print("COMMAND MENU")
    print("list - List all movies")
    print("add -  Add a movie")
    print("del -  Delete a movie")
    print("exit - Exit program")
    print()

def main():
    display_menu()
    movies = read_movies()
    while True:
        command = input("Command: ")
        if command == "list":
            list_movies(movies)
        elif command == "add":
            add_movie(movies)
        elif command == "del":
            delete_movie(movies)
        elif command == "exit":
            print("Bye!")
            break
        else:
            print("Not a valid command. Please try again.")

if __name__ == "__main__":
    main()
```

Figure 7-6   The Movie List 1.0 program (part 2)

How to use CSV files

When you use a plain text file to store data, the only separators are the new line characters. So, if you want to store several items of data on a single line, you can use CSV files for your data. Then, each line is a *row* (or *record*) that ends with a new line character, and each row consists of one or more *columns* (or *fields*) that are typically separated by commas. To make it relatively easy to work with this type of file, Python provides a csv module.

How to write a CSV file

Figure 7-7 shows how to write a movies list with three rows and two columns to a CSV file. Before you can write the list to disk, though, you need to import the csv module. Then, you can use the functions and objects available from the csv module.

The third example shows how to write the data in the list to the CSV file. Here the with statement begins by using the open() function to open the CSV file. This works much like opening a text file, but the open() function specifies a third argument named newline with a value of an empty string This enables *universal newlines mode*, which allows the csv module to read and write new lines correctly for all operating systems.

Inside the with statement, the first statement calls the writer() function of the csv module to get a CSV *writer object*. Then, the second statement calls the writerows() method of that object to write the movies list to the CSV file. This creates a CSV file with the format shown in this figure.

The writer() function of the CSV module

Function	Description
writer(*file*)	Returns a CSV writer object for the file. This writer object converts the data into comma-separated values.

The writerows() method of the CSV writer object

Method	Description
writerows(*rows*)	Writes all specified rows to the file specified by the writer object using the CSV format specified by the writer object.

A 2-dimensional list with 3 rows and 2 columns

```
movies = [["Monty Python and the Holy Grail", 1975],
          ["Cat on a Hot Tin Roof", 1958],
          ["On the Waterfront", 1954]]
```

How to import the csv module

```
import csv
```

How to write the list to a CSV file

```
with open("movies.csv", "w", newline="") as file:
    writer = csv.writer(file)
    writer.writerows(movies)
```

The contents of the CSV file

```
Monty Python and the Holy Grail,1975
Cat on a Hot Tin Roof,1958
On the Waterfront,1954
```

Description

- A *comma-separated values (CSV) file* stores tabular data in a text file. Within this file, each line is a *row* that ends with a new line character, and each row contains one or more *columns* that are typically separated by commas.

- Rows and columns can also be referred to as *records* and *fields*.

- To write data to a CSV file, you use the writer() function of the csv module to get a *writer object*. Then, you use the methods of the writer object to write data.

- When you open a CSV file for reading or writing, you typically specify an argument named newline with a value of an empty string. This enables *universal newlines mode*, so the reading and writing operations work correctly for all operating systems.

Figure 7-7   How to write a CSV file

How to read a CSV file

The first example in figure 7-8 shows how to read the CSV file that was created by the code in the previous figure. To start, it opens the CSV file. Here again, since this code doesn't specify the mode for opening the file, Python uses the default mode, which is read mode.

Inside the with statement, the first statement calls the reader() function of the csv module to get a CSV *reader object* for the file. Then, a for loop gets each row in the reader object. Within this loop, a print() function displays the name of the movie followed by its year in parentheses. Since the year value in the movies list was stored as an integer, that integer has to be converted to a string before it can be displayed by the print() function.

How to modify the CSV format

Historically, one of the problems with the CSV format has been that it doesn't work correctly if the data itself contains commas, quotation marks, or new line characters. If, for example, an address field contains a comma, the comma is interpreted as the end of the field and the start of another field.

With Python, though, the csv module automatically handles this by adding double quotes around any columns that contain special characters such as commas and new line characters. It does that before writing the data to disk, and it doesn't enclose any other fields with double quotes. Then, when the csv module reads this data, it interprets the data correctly.

Occasionally, though, you may have to read a file that has been created in a slightly different format. For example, all of the fields might be enclosed in double quotation marks. Or, single quotation marks might be used to enclose the fields. Or, tab characters might be used as the field separators instead of commas.

To handle these variations, the csv module lets you customize the file formatting by using optional arguments when you read and write files. To illustrate, the table in this figure summaries a few of the formatting arguments. As the examples after the table show, you code these arguments when you create a reader or writer object. Both of these examples change the field separator from commas to tabs.

The reader() function of the csv module

Function	Description
`reader(file)`	Returns a CSV reader object for the file. This reader object gets the data from the CSV file.

How to read data from a CSV file

```
with open("movies.csv", newline="") as file:
    reader = csv.reader(file)
    for row in reader:
        print(row[0] + " (" + str(row[1]) + ")")
```

The console

```
Monty Python and the Holy Grail (1975)
Cat on a Hot Tin Roof (1958)
On the Waterfront (1954)
```

Some optional arguments that can be used to change the CSV format

Argument	Description
`quoting=csv.QUOTE_MINIMAL`	Specifies when quotes are written and read. It can be set to any of the QUOTE constants in the csv module. It defaults to QUOTE_MINIMAL, which only adds quotes to columns that contain special characters such as the delimiter, quote, or end of line characters.
`quotechar='"'`	Specifies the character that's used to quote columns. It defaults to a double quote (").
`delimiter=","`	Specifies a one-character string used to separate fields. It defaults to a comma.

Code that changes the delimiter for the writer object

```
writer = csv.writer(file, delimiter="\t")
```

Code that changes the delimiter for the reader object

```
reader = csv.reader(file, delimiter="\t")
```

Description

- To read data from a CSV file, you use the reader() function of the csv module to create a *reader object*. Then, you can use a for statement with the reader object to read the data in the file.

- By default, reader and writer objects use commas to delimit the columns of a row and only add quotes to columns when necessary. However, when you create reader and writer objects, you can specify arguments that change that behavior.

Figure 7-8   How to read a CSV file and how to modify the CSV format

The Movie List 2.0 program

Figure 7-9 presents a Movie List 2.0 program that stores a two-dimensional list of movies in a text file. Here, the data for each movie consists of the movie name and the year that it was released. Like the Movie List 2D program in the previous chapter, this one lets you list the movies, add movies to the movies list, and delete movies from the movies list. However, the program in this chapter stores this data in a file. As a result, any changes the user makes to the list are available even if the user exits and restarts the program.

Like the Movie List 1.0 program presented earlier in this chapter, the Movie List 2.0 program only works if the file already exists. In practice, you can create a file like this by writing a separate program that writes the starting set of rows to the file. Or, you can use a spreadsheet program like Excel to create the starting file and save it in CSV format. Once that's done, a program should be able to read the file without causing an exception.

With that in mind, the Python code for this program begins by defining a global constant named FILENAME that stores the name of the CSV file. Then, the code defines two functions that use this global constant to write and read this file. Since this constant only specifies the name of the file, not the path, the file must be in the working directory, which is usually the same directory as the program file.

The write_movies() function gets the list that contains the movies as its argument. Then, it writes each movie in the list to the file by using the writerows () method of the writer object. This automatically handles the formatting of the CSV records that are written to the disk.

The read_movies() function starts by creating an empty movies list. Then, it uses a for statement to read each row in the reader object and append it to the movies list. When it finishes appending all of the movies to the movies list, this function returns the list.

The user interface

```
The Movie List program

COMMAND MENU
list - List all movies
add -  Add a movie
del -  Delete a movie
exit - Exit program

Command: list
1. Monty Python and the Holy Grail (1975)
2. Cat on a Hot Tin Roof (1958)
3. On the Waterfront (1954)

Command: add
Name: Gone with the Wind
Year: 1939
Gone with the Wind was added.

Command: list
1. Monty Python and the Holy Grail (1975)
2. Cat on a Hot Tin Roof (1958)
3. On the Waterfront (1954)
4. Gone with the Wind (1939)

Command: del
Number: 4
Gone with the Wind was deleted.
```

The code   Page 1

```python
import csv

# a file in the current directory
FILENAME = "movies.csv"

def write_movies(movies):
    with open(FILENAME, "w", newline="") as file:
        writer = csv.writer(file)
        writer.writerows(movies)

def read_movies():
    movies = []
    with open(FILENAME, newline="") as file:
        reader = csv.reader(file)
        for row in reader:
            movies.append(row)
    return movies
```

Figure 7-9   The Movie List 2.0 program (part 1)

You should be able to follow the rest of the code in this program since it's so similar to the code in the previous chapter. The main difference is that this program calls the write_movies() function whenever the user updates the movies list. To do that, the add_movie() and delete_movie() functions call the write_movies() function after they update the movies list. That way, the program always saves changes to the file and never loses data even if the program crashes later.

You should also note that the main() function calls the read_movies() function to get the movies list before any of the other functions are called. Then, it passes that list to the list(), add(), and delete() functions whenever it calls them. This works because the movies list is mutable. As a result, the main() function, the add_movie() function, and the delete_movie() function all work with the same movie list.

The code   **Page 2**

```python
def list_movies(movies):
    for i in range(len(movies)):
        movie = movies[i]
        print(str(i+1) + ". " + movie[0] + " (" + movie[1] + ")")
    print()

def add_movie(movies):
    name = input("Name: ")
    year = input("Year: ")
    movie = []
    movie.append(name)
    movie.append(year)
    movies.append(movie)
    write_movies(movies)
    print(name + " was added.\n")

def delete_movie(movies):
    index = int(input("Number: "))
    movie = movies.pop(index - 1)
    write_movies(movies)
    print(movie[0] + " was deleted.\n")

def display_menu():
    print("The Movie List program")
    print()
    print("COMMAND MENU")
    print("list - List all movies")
    print("add -  Add a movie")
    print("del -  Delete a movie")
    print("exit - Exit program")
    print()

def main():
    display_menu()
    movies = read_movies()
    while True:
        command = input("Command: ")
        if command.lower() == "list":
            list_movies(movies)
        elif command.lower() == "add":
            add_movie(movies)
        elif command.lower() == "del":
            delete_movie(movies)
        elif command.lower() == "exit":
            break
        else:
            print("Not a valid command. Please try again.\n")
    print("Bye!")

if __name__ == "__main__":
    main()
```

Figure 7-9   The Movie List 2.0 program (part 2)

How to use binary files

To make it easier to work with binary files, Python provides a standard *pickle module*. This module automates the process of storing an object in a binary file. Although this module works with most Python objects, it's commonly used with lists.

How to work with a binary file

Figure 7-10 shows how to work with a binary file. As the table in this figure shows, the pickle module provides a dump() method that saves an object such as a list in a binary file. It also provides a load() method that reads an object such as a list from a binary file.

Before you can use the pickle module to write an object to a file, you must import it as shown in the second example in this figure. Then, the third example shows how to write the movies list in this figure to a binary file. To do that, you need to add b to the mode argument of the open() function to indicate that you want to open a binary file. In this case, the code sets the mode to "wb" or "write binary" mode.

Once this code opens the binary file in write binary mode, the dump() method of the pickle module writes the movies list to a binary file. In Python, this is known as *pickling* an object, but it's more generally known as *serializing* an object.

The fourth example shows how to read the movies list from a binary file. To start, it opens the binary file named movies.bin in "rb" or "read binary" mode. Then, it calls the load() method of the pickle module and passes it the file object. This causes the pickle module to read the list that's stored in the specified file. In Python, this is known as *un-pickling* an object, but it's more generally known as *de-serializing* an object.

The fourth example also prints the list to the console. Note that the console doesn't include quotes around the movie's year. This shows that the binary file stores the year as an int value, not as a str value as it would be in a text file.

Two methods of the pickle module

Method	Description
dump(*object*, *bfile*)	Writes the specified object to the binary file.
load(*bfile*)	Reads an object from the specified binary file.

A 2-dimensional list with 3 rows and 2 columns

```
movies = [["Monty Python and the Holy Grail", 1975],
          ["Cat on a Hot Tin Roof", 1958],
          ["On the Waterfront", 1954]]
```

How to import the pickle module

```
import pickle
```

How to write an object to a binary file

```
with open("movies.bin", "wb") as file:    # use wb mode for write binary
    pickle.dump(movies, file)
```

How to read an object from a binary file

```
with open("movies.bin", "rb") as file:    # use rb mode for read binary
    movie_list = pickle.load(file)
    print(movie_list)
```

The console

```
[['Monty Python and the Holy Grail', 1975], ['Cat on a Hot
Tin Roof', 1958], ['On the Waterfront', 1954]]
```

Description

- You can use methods of the *pickle module* to work with binary files. It can be used to *dump* (write) an object like a list to a file and to *load* (read) an object like a list from a binary file.

- Storing an object in a binary file is known as object *serialization*, and reading an object from a binary file is known as *de-serialization*.

Figure 7-10   How to work with a binary file

The Movie List 3.0 program

Figure 7-11 presents the Movie List 3.0 program. This program works like the Movie List 2.0 program, but it stores the list of movies in a binary file instead of a CSV file. Since the user interface is the same for both programs, the difference in file type is transparent to the user of the program. Also, because most of the code for the Movie List 3.0 program is the same as the code for the Movie List 2.0 program, this figure only shows the code that's different.

Here again, this program only works if the file already exists. If necessary, you can create a file like this by writing a separate program that writes the starting list to the file. Once that's done, a program can read the file without causing an exception because the file doesn't exist.

In the Python code, the write_movies() and read_movies() functions use the pickle module to write and read the list of movies in a binary file. To make that possible, the code for this program begins by importing the pickle module. Then, it defines a FILENAME constant for a binary file named movies.bin.

The write_movies() function accepts the list of movies that's created by the program as an argument. Then, it uses the dump() method of the pickle module to write this list to the binary file. But since this program uses a binary file, this code doesn't need to convert the year for each movie from an int value to a str value. Instead, the binary file just stores the int value.

Similarly, the read_movies() function uses the pickle module to read the list object from the binary file. Since this program writes the list to a binary file, it reads the year for each movie as an int value, not as a str value. As a result, the list_movies() function must convert this int value to a str value before it can display it on the console. To do that, the list_movies() function uses the str() function.

The user interface

```
The Movie List program

COMMAND MENU
list - List all movies
add -  Add a movie
del -  Delete a movie
exit - Exit program

Command: list
1. Monty Python and the Holy Grail (1975)
2. Cat on a Hot Tin Roof (1958)
3. On the Waterfront (1954)

Command: add
Name: Gone with the Wind
Year: 1939
Gone with the Wind was added.
```

The code for the two file I/O functions

```python
import pickle

FILENAME = "movies.bin"

def write_movies(movies):
    with open(FILENAME, "wb") as file:
        pickle.dump(movies, file)

def read_movies():
    movies = []
    with open(FILENAME, "rb") as file:
        movies = pickle.load(file)
    return movies
```

The code for the list_movies() function

```python
def list_movies(movies):
    for i in range(len(movies)):
        movie = movies[i]
        print(str(i+1) + ". " + movie[0] + " (" + str(movie[1]) + ")")
    print()
```

Description

- The user interface for the Movie List 3.0 program is the same as the interface for the Movie List 2.0 program, and most of the code for these programs is the same. That's why this figure presents only the functions that have been changed.

- The write_movies() and read_movies() functions use the pickle module to write the list of movies to a binary file and to read the list from the binary file.

- The list_movies() function must convert the movie's year from an int value to a string in order to display it because the binary file stores the year as an int value.

Figure 7-11   The Movie List 3.0 program

Perspective

In this chapter, you learned how to store data in plain text, CSV, and binary files. To do that, you learned how to use file objects, as well as the csv and pickle modules.

But you should also know that Python provides modules for working with other types of files such as JSON and XML files. In addition, third-party modules exist for working with other types of files such as spreadsheet files.

Beyond that, you should know that most serious applications store their data in databases. That's why chapter 17 shows how to use Python to work with a database.

Terms

file I/O	field
text file	universal newlines mode
binary file	writer object
CSV (comma-separated values) file	reader object
main memory (RAM)	pickle module
persistent data storage	dump a binary file
exception	load a binary file
file object	pickling
with statement	un-pickling
row	serializing
column	de-serializing
record	

Summary

- Data that's stored in *main memory (RAM)* is lost when the program ends. But if you save that data to a file, you provide *persistent data storage*. Then, that data is available the next time the program runs.

- Python supports several different types of *text files*, including *CSV (comma-separated values) files*. Python also supports several different types of *binary files*.

- You can use a *with statement* to open a *file object* that's only available for its block of statements. After Python executes the block of statements, it automatically closes the file object, even if an error occurs.

- In a CSV file, each line in the file is a *row*, and each row consists of one or more *columns* that are typically separated by commas. Rows and columns can also be referred to as *records* and *fields*.

- You can use the pickle module to write a Python object to a binary file or to read a Python object from a binary file. In Python, this is known as *pickling* and *un-pickling* an object. It's more generally known as *serializing* and *de-serializing* an object.

Exercise 7-1   Create a CSV file for trip data

In this exercise, you'll modify the Miles Per Gallon program so it stores the data for each calculation in a CSV file. Then, the program that you develop for exercise 7-2 should be able to display the data like this:

```
Distance     Gallons     MPG
225          17          13.24
1374         64          21.47
2514         79          31.82
```

1. In IDLE, open the mpg_write.py file that's in this folder:
   `python/exercises/ch07`

2. Review the code, and run the program so you remember how it works.

3. Enhance the program so it stores the data for each calculation, or trip, in a two-dimensional list. For each calculation, these values should be put in the list: miles driven, gallons of gas used, and the calculated MPG value.

4. Enhance the program so it saves the data in the list to a file named trips.csv when the user wants to exit from the program.

5. Test the program to make sure it works. To do that, you can open the CSV file with a spreadsheet program like Excel.

Exercise 7-2   Keep trip data in a CSV file

In this exercise, you'll modify the Miles Per Gallon program so it adds to the data in the file that you created in exercise 7-1. This program should display the data for each trip that's entered in a CSV file as shown here:

```
The Miles Per Gallon program

Distance     Gallons     MPG
225          17          13.24
1374         64          21.47
2514         79          31.82

Enter miles driven:      274
Enter gallons of gas:    18.5
Miles Per Gallon:        14.81

Distance     Gallons     MPG
225          17          13.24
1374         64          21.47
2514         79          31.82
274.0        18.5        14.81

More entries? (y or n):
```

1. In IDLE, open the mpg.py file that's in this folder:
   `python/exercises/ch07`

2. Add a write_trips() function that writes the data from a two-dimensional list named trips that's passed to it as an argument. This list contains the data for each trip that's entered, and it should be written to a CSV file named trips.csv. As the console above shows, the data for each trip consists of miles driven, gallons of gas used, and the calculated MPG value.

3. Add a read_trips() function that reads the data from the trips.csv file and returns the data for the trips in a two-dimensional list named trips.

4. Add a list_trips() function that displays the data in the trips list on the console, as shown above.

5. Enhance the main() function so it starts by getting the data from the CSV file and listing it as shown above.

6. Enhance the main() function so it adds the last trip that's entered to the trips list after it calculates the MPG. Then, display the data for the updated trips list.

7. Test all aspects of the program until you're sure that it works correctly.

Exercise 7-3   Keep trip data in a binary file

In this exercise, you'll modify the programs that you created for exercises 7-1 and 7-2 so they create and use a binary file instead of a CSV file. Otherwise, everything should work the same.

Modify the CSV version of the write program
1. Open the mpg_write.py file that you created in exercise 7-1. Then, save it as mpg_write_binary.py in the same directory.

2. Modify this program so it saves the list as a binary file instead of a CSV file. The file should be named trips.bin.

3. Test the program to make sure it works. To do that, add statements that read the file at the end of the program and display the list that has been read.

Modify the CSV version of the trip program
4. Open the mpg.py file that you created in exercise 7-2. Then, save it as mpg_binary.py.

5. Modify this program so it works the same as it did with the CSV file.

6. Test this program to make sure it works.

8

How to handle exceptions

In chapter 1, you were introduced to exceptions. By now, you have most likely experienced many of them as you developed and tested your programs. In this chapter, you will learn how to handle exceptions so your programs don't crash when an exception occurs.

How to handle a single exception

For some statements, only one kind of error can occur. In that case, you only need to handle that kind of error. The next three figures show how.

How exceptions work

Figure 8-1 shows how an *exception* can occur. In this example, the first statement uses the int() function to convert a user entry, which is always a string, to an integer value. But if the user enters a value that the int() function can't convert to an integer, an *exception is thrown* (occurs) and an error message like the one in the second console is displayed.

The information that's displayed typically includes the line of code that caused the exception, the name of the exception, and a brief message about the exception. In this figure, for example, the second console shows the name of the file that stores the code, the number of the line that caused the exception, and the line of code itself. Then, this information displays the type of the exception (ValueError) and a brief description of the exception.

In some cases, an exception is thrown because of a programming error like using a variable name that doesn't exist. You need to fix this type of error before your program is ready for use. In other cases, like the entry error in this example, the exception should be handled by the program so it doesn't cause the program to crash. That's called *exception handling*, and that's what this chapter is about.

Code that can cause a ValueError exception

```
number = int(input("Enter an integer: "))
print("You entered a valid integer of " + str(number) + ".")
print("Thanks!")
```

The console for a valid integer

```
Enter an integer: 5
You entered a valid integer of 5.
Thanks!
```

The console for an invalid integer

```
Enter an integer: five
Traceback (most recent call last):
  File "C:\murach\python\book_figs\ch07\fig1.py", line 1, in <module>
    number = int(input("Enter a valid integer: "))
ValueError: invalid literal for int() with base 10: 'five'
```

Two functions that can cause a ValueError exception

Function	Reason for exception
int(*data*)	Can't convert the data argument to an int value.
float(*data*)	Can't convert the data argument to a float value.

Description

- When an error occurs at runtime, it can be referred to as *throwing an exception*.

- When an exception is thrown, Python ends the program and prints information about the exception to the console. The last line of this information includes the type of the exception and a brief description of the exception.

- Some exceptions occur due to programming errors. You need to fix those errors before the program is ready for use.

- Some exceptions occur due to causes outside of the program. These exceptions need to be *handled* by your Python code so the program doesn't crash when they occur.

Figure 8-1   How exceptions work

How to use a try statement to handle one type of exception

To handle exceptions, you use a *try statement*, as shown in figure 8-2. As the syntax summary shows, you start by coding a *try clause* that contains a block of one or more statements that may cause an exception. Then, you code an *except clause* that contains a block of one or more statements that should be executed if an exception is thrown in the try block.

The first example in this figure shows how this works for a user entry that can't be converted to a valid integer. Here, the int() function is coded within a try clause, and an except clause is coded for the exception named ValueError. Then, if the user enters a valid int value, the int() function converts the input to the int value, the first print statement prints a message to the console, and the program continues with the print() function after the try statement.

However, if the user enters an invalid integer so a ValueError is thrown, program execution skips the print() function in the try clause and continues with the statements in the except clause. In this case, the except clause just displays an error message. Then, execution continues with the print statement after the try statement.

In this example, the except clause specifies the ValueError so it is only executed if that type of exception occurs. In contrast, the second example doesn't specify the name of the exception. As a result, Python not only executes the except clause if a ValueError occurs, but also if any other type of exception occurs.

In general, it's a good practice to code the name of the exception in the except clause. That way, your code can handle the exception in the way that's best for that type of exception. You'll learn more about this in a moment.

The syntax for a try statement that catches an exception

```
try:
    statements
except [ExceptionName]:
    statements
```

How to handle a ValueError exception

```
try:
    number = int(input("Enter an integer: "))
    print("You entered a valid integer of " + str(number) + ".")
except ValueError:
    print("You entered an invalid integer. Please try again.")
print("Thanks!")
```

The console for a valid integer

```
Enter an integer: 5
You entered a valid integer of 5.
Thanks!
```

The console for an invalid integer

```
Enter an integer: five
You entered an invalid integer. Please try again.
Thanks!
```

How to handle all exceptions

```
try:
    number = int(input("Enter an integer: "))
    print("You entered a valid integer of " + str(number) + ".")
except:
    print("You entered an invalid integer. Please try again.")
print("Thanks!")
```

Description

- In a *try statement*, you code any statements that may throw an exception in the *try clause*. Then, you can code an *except clause* that handles any exceptions that occur.

- If you don't code the name of an exception type in the except clause, the except clause handles all types of exceptions that can occur.

- When an exception occurs, Python skips any remaining statements in the try clause and executes the statements in the except clause.

- This is known as an *exception handling*.

Figure 8-2   How to use a try statement to handle one type of exception

The Total Calculator program

To show how you can use a try statement in a program, figure 8-3 presents the Total Calculator program. This program handles the ValueError exceptions that can occur when the program tries to convert the strings that the user enters for price and quantity to float and int values.

In the get_price() function for this program, a while loop gets an entry from the user until it successfully converts the entry to a float value. When that happens, the function returns the price to the calling statement and the while loop ends. Otherwise, the except clause displays an error message, and the while loop continues. This prompts the user for another entry.

The get_quantity() function works the same way, except that it prompts the user for a quantity instead of a price. In addition, the entry must be a valid int value, not a valid float value.

The main() function uses the get_price() and get_quantity() functions to get the price and quantity from the user. Then, it uses the values that are returned in a calculation knowing that both values are valid. Last, it displays the results.

In this program, the get_price() and get_quantity() function do a type of *data validation*. However, this validation could be enhanced by checking to make sure that both values are greater than zero. These functions could also check to make sure these entries don't exceed maximum values. You'll see enhanced data validation like this later in this chapter.

The user interface

```
The Total Calculator program

Enter price: ten
Invalid decimal number. Please try again.
Enter price: 9.99
Enter quantity: 2.5
Invalid integer. Please try again.
Enter quantity: 3


PRICE:     9.99
QUANTITY: 3
TOTAL:     29.97
```

The code

```python
def get_price():
    while True:
        try:
            price = float(input("Enter price: "))
            return price
        except ValueError:
            print("Invalid decimal number. Please try again.")

def get_quantity():
    while True:
        try:
            quantity = int(input("Enter quantity: "))
            return quantity
        except ValueError:
            print("Invalid integer. Please try again.")

def main():
    print("The Total Calculator program\n")

    # get the price and quantity
    price = get_price()
    quantity = get_quantity()

    # calculate the total
    total = price * quantity

    # display the results
    print()
    print("PRICE:     ", price)
    print("QUANTITY: ", quantity)
    print("TOTAL:     ", total)

if __name__ == "__main__":
    main()
```

Figure 8-3   The Total Calculator program

How to handle multiple exceptions

For some programs, such as the file I/O programs in the previous chapter, a block of code could cause several different types of exceptions to occur. In that case, it often makes sense to provide different exception handling code for each of type of exception.

How to use a try statement to handle multiple exceptions

Figure 8-4 starts by showing the Python hierarchy for five of the common exceptions. Each of these exceptions is defined by a *class*, and you'll learn more about classes in section 3 of this book. For now, you just need to know that a class defines a type of *exception object*.

The Exception class is the most general type of exception and the *parent class* of the *child* OSError and ValueError classes, which define more specific exceptions. The OSError class in turn is the parent class of two even more specific child classes: FileExistsError and FileNotFoundError.

In this figure, the example shows a try statement that uses three except clauses to handle three different types of exceptions. When you code a statement like this, the except clauses must be coded in sequence from the most specific exception to the most general exception. Here, the try block contains some file I/O code that could cause a FileNotFoundError or an OSError to occur. As a result, except clauses are coded for both types of exceptions. The third exception clause is for any other type of exception.

The benefit of using multiple except clauses is that you can handle each type of exception in an appropriate way. Here, the code just displays a different message for each type of exception, but the code could do more than that. In some cases, for example, you might want to save as much data as possible and shut down the program as gracefully as possible.

Keep in mind that some exceptions are caused by programming errors like attempting to use an invalid index to access an item in a list. Although these errors cause exceptions, you typically don't want to handle these exceptions with try statements. Instead, you should fix your code to prevent these exceptions from occurring in the first place.

The hierarchy for five common exceptions

```
Exception
    OSError
        FileExistsError
        FileNotFoundError
    ValueError
```

The syntax for a try statement with multiple except blocks

```
try:
    statements
except ExceptionName:
    statements
[except ExceptionName:
    statements] ...
```

Code that handles multiple exceptions

```
filename = input("Enter filename: ")
movies = []
try:
    with open(filename) as file:
        for line in file:
            line = line.replace("\n", "")
            movies.append(line)
except FileNotFoundError:
    print("Could not find the file named " + filename)
except OSError:
    print("File found - error reading file")
except Exception:
    print("An unexpected error occurred")
```

The console when a FileNotFoundError occurs

```
Could not find the file named films.txt
```

The console when an OSError occurs

```
File found - error reading file
```

The console when any Exception occurs

```
An unexpected error occurred.
```

Description

- In the hierarchy of the five common exceptions, Exception is the *parent class* of the OSError and ValueError classes. These classes in turn can be referred to as *child classes* of the Exception class.

- Similarly, the OSError class is the parent class of two child classes, the FileExistsError and FileNotFoundError classes.

- The except clauses must be coded in sequence starting with the most specific exception and ending with the least specific.

Figure 8-4   How to handle multiple exceptions

How to get the information
from an exception object

The exception object for each type of exception contains some information about the exception like the name of the exception class and its error message. In figure 8-5, the code gets this information from the exception object. In addition, it uses the exit() function of the sys module to terminate a program.

To get the information from the exception object, you start by coding the as keyword in the except clause followed by a name that you can use for the exception object. Then, you can use that name in a print() function to display the error message for the exception. In this figure, the code does that for the FileNotFoundError and OSError exceptions.

You can also use the built-in type() function to get the class of the exception object. In this figure, the code does that for the Exception class in the last except clause. Here, the print() function displays the class name, followed by the error message for the exception object. This isn't illustrated by a console in this figure, because it's hard to predict what type of exception will be caught by this clause.

Remember that an except clause for the Exception class is executed for any exception that isn't handled by the preceding except clauses. In this case, the type() function of the exception object is useful because it provides a way to display the exception class. In contrast, the other except clauses know the classes of the exceptions that they are going to handle so they don't need to use the type() function.

In all three clauses, the exit() function of the sys module stops the execution of a program. This is something you'll frequently want to do for file I/O errors when the program can't continue due to the type of exception that has occurred. This is illustrated by the OSError that's handled by the second except clause. Here, the message is "permission denied". So before the program can continue, the permissions problem has to be resolved.

When you're coding the exception handling routines in your programs, you could handle all exceptions with one except clause for the Exception class. Then, you could use the same code to handle each type of exception. For example, the write_movies() function in the Movie List program that's presented later in this chapter uses one except clause to handle all exceptions that might occur.

In general, though, it's a better practice to code one except clause for each type of exception that is likely to occur because you will often want to do more than just display an error message and end the program. Then, you can finish with an except clause for the Exception class that handles any unexpected exceptions.

The built-in type() function

Function	Description
type(*object*)	Returns the class for the specified object.

The exit() function of the sys module

Function	Description
exit()	Exits the Python program.

The complete syntax for the except clause

```
except [ExceptionName] [as name]:
    statements
```

Code that handles multiple exceptions

```python
import sys

filename = input("Enter filename: ")
movies = []
try:
    with open(filename) as file:
        for line in file:
            line = line.replace("\n", "")
            movies.append(line)
except FileNotFoundError as e:
    print("FileNotFoundError:", e)
    sys.exit()
except OSError as e:
    print("OSError:", e)
    sys.exit()
except Exception as e:
    print(type(e), e)
    sys.exit()
```

The console when a FileNotFoundError occurs

```
FileNotFoundError: [Errno 2] No such file or directory: 'films'
```

The console when an OSError occurs

```
OSError: [Errno 13] Permission denied: 'movies.csv'
```

Description

- When an exception occurs, an *exception object* is created. Then, you can use the *as* keyword in an except clause to provide a name for accessing that object.
- To cancel a program as part of your exception handling routine, you can use the exit() function of the sys module.

Figure 8-5   How to get the information from an exception object

The Movie List 2.0 program

Figure 8-6 presents another version of the Movie List 2.0 program in the previous chapter. But this version handles the exceptions that may occur when the user enters data, and it handles the exceptions that may occur if the program isn't able to read or write the file that stores the data.

The first console in this figure shows how the program handles invalid user input. If the user attempts to delete a movie, but enters an invalid integer such as "x", the program displays an appropriate error message and lets the user try again. Or, if the user attempts to delete a movie, but enters a number that doesn't correspond with a movie, the program displays an appropriate error message and lets the user try again.

The second console in this figure shows how the program handles the file I/O exceptions that might occur. Since the program can't function properly if it can't read and write the file that stores its data, it displays a message and exits the program.

Because the code for this program is mostly the same as the Movie List 2.0 program in the previous chapter, this figure only presents the code that has been added or changed. To make it easy to see the differences, this figure highlights the changes.

The read_movies() function includes a try statement that handles the exceptions that might occur when the code in the try block attempts to read the movies.csv file. If a FileNotFoundError is thrown, its except clause prints an error message to the console. Then, it calls the exit_program() function.

If any other type of exception is thrown, the except clause for the Exception class prints the type of the exception and its error message to the console. Then, it calls the exit_program() function to exit the program. This prints a relatively user-friendly error message to the console. However, it hides a lot of the useful debugging information that's in the stack trace that's printed to the console if you don't handle the exception.

A console that handles user input exceptions

```
COMMAND MENU
list - List all movies
add -  Add a movie
del -  Delete a movie
exit - Exit program

Command: list
1. Monty Python and the Holy Grail (1975)
2. Cat on a Hot Tin Roof (1958)
3. On the Waterfront (1954)
4. Gone with the Wind (1939)
5. Wizard of Oz (1939)

Command: del
Number: x
Invalid integer. Please try again.
Number: 6
There is no movie with that number. Please try again.
Number: 4
Gone with the Wind was deleted.
```

A console that handles a file I/O exception

```
COMMAND MENU
list - List all movies
add -  Add a movie
del -  Delete a movie
exit - Exit program

Could not find movies.csv file.
Terminating program.
```

The code   Page 1

```python
import csv
import sys

FILENAME = "movies.csv"

def read_movies():
    try:
        movies = []
        with open(FILENAME, newline="") as file:
            reader = csv.reader(file)
            for row in reader:
                movies.append(row)
        return movies
    except FileNotFoundError:
        print("Could not find " + FILENAME + " file.")
        exit_program()
    except Exception as e:
        print(type(e), e)
        exit_program()
```

Figure 8-6   The Movie List 2.0 program with exception handling (part 1)

The write_movies() function gets the movies list as an argument, and it uses a try statement to handle the exceptions that might occur when the code in the try block attempts to write the movies.csv file from the list. Since an exception isn't raised if the movies.csv file can't be found, this function doesn't need to include an except clause for a FileNotFoundError. Instead, it just includes an except clause for the Exception class, which displays a message and calls the exit_program() function.

The exit_program() function prints a message and uses the exit() function of the sys module to exit the program. As a result, the sys module has to be imported at the start of the program.

The delete_movie() function gets the movies list as an argument, and it uses a try clause to get an integer entry from the user. If the entry can't be converted to an integer, the except clause for a ValueError is executed. That displays an error message and executes the continue statement, which causes the loop to be repeated. If the user enters a valid integer, the function continues with the if statement that's after the try statement.

This if statement checks whether the integer that the user entered is within a range that corresponds to one of the movie numbers. If not, it prints an appropriate error message, and the loop continues by executing the try statement again. This is complete data validation.

When the entry is valid, a break statement ends the loop and the rest of the statements in the function are executed. Those statements remove the movie from the list, call the write_movies() function to update the file on disk, and display a message that shows the movie was deleted.

This figure shows the main() function too. However, it's the same as the main() function in the Movie List 2.0 program in the previous chapter.

The code   **Page 2**

```python
def write_movies(movies):
    try:
        with open(FILENAME, "w", newline="") as file:
            writer = csv.writer(file)
            writer.writerows(movies)
    except Exception as e:
        print(type(e), e)
        exit_program()

def exit_program():
    print("Terminating program.")
    sys.exit()

def delete_movie(movies):
    while True:
        try:
            number = int(input("Number: "))
        except ValueError:
            print("Invalid integer. Please try again.")
            continue
        if number < 1 or number > len(movies):
            print("There is no movie with that number. " +
                    "Please try again.")
        else:
            break
    movie = movies.pop(number - 1)
    write_movies(movies)
    print(movie[0] + " was deleted.\n")

def main():
    display_menu()
    movies = read_movies()
    while True:
        command = input("Command: ")
        if command == "list":
            list_movies(movies)
        elif command == "add":
            add_movie(movies)
        elif command == "del":
            delete_movie(movies)
        elif command == "exit":
            break
        else:
            print("Not a valid command. Please try again.\n")
    print("Bye!")
```

Figure 8-6   The Movie List 2.0 program with exception handling (part 2)

Two more skills

The skills you've learned so far are the only ones you'll need for most of the programs that you develop. But this chapter finishes with two more skills that you may need if you continue with programming.

How to use a finally clause

After its except clause or clauses, a try statement can include a *finally clause*, as shown in figure 8-7. A finally clause is executed even if the code in the try clause executes a return statement or causes an exception to occur. Typically, a finally clause is used to clean up the system resources that an object in the try block is using, but it can be used for other purposes too.

When you use Python 3 or later, you typically don't need to code a finally clause because you can use a with statement to automatically clean up the resources that an object is using. This works because some objects, such as a file object, define standard clean-up actions. As a result, the with statement automatically executes those clean-up actions when it finishes executing its block of statements, even if the block of statements causes an exception to occur.

In this figure, the first example shows a function that uses a with statement to automatically clean up the resources used by the file object. In this function, there is one try clause that contains all of the file I/O code, and one except clause that displays a message if an exception is thrown. But whether or not an exception occurs, the with statement automatically calls the close() function of the file object to clean up its resources.

The second example performs the same task as the first example. However, this example doesn't use a with statement. Instead, it uses a finally clause to close the file and clean up the system resources. As a result, it's significantly more complicated. In fact, it requires nested try statements.

The outer try statement handles the FileNotFoundError that occurs if the file can't be found. In this case, the file can't be opened so there's no need for a finally clause to close the file object. However, if the code finds the file and opens it, an exception could occur when the code tries to read the file. That's why the inner try statement contains an except clause and a finally clause. Then, if an exception is thrown, the except clause prints a message to the console. But whether or not an exception occurs, the finally clause is executed, and it calls the close() function of the file object to clean up its resources.

The complete syntax for a try statement

```
try:
    statements
 except [ExceptionName] [as name]:
    statements
[except [ExceptionName] [as name]:
    statements] ...
[finally:
    statements]
```

A function that uses a with statement to clean up resources

```
def read_movies(filename):
    try:
        with open(filename, newline="") as file:
            movies = []
            reader = csv.reader(file)
            for row in reader:
                movies.append(row)
        return movies
    except Exception as e:
        print(e)
```

A function that uses a finally clause to clean up resources

```
def read_movies(filename):
    try:
        file = open(filename, newline="")
        try:
            movies = []
            reader = csv.reader(file)
            for row in reader:
                movies.append(row)
            return movies
        except Exception as e:
            print(type(e), e)
        finally:
            file.close()
    except FileNotFoundError as e:
        print(e)
```

Description

- Some objects such as a file object define standard clean-up actions. For them, you can use a with statement to automatically clean up the resources that they're using, even if an exception occurs during the execution of the with statement.

- For objects that don't define standard clean-up actions, you can use a *finally clause* to manually clean up the resources that the object is using.

- A finally clause is always executed, even if an exception occurs or a return statement is executed in the try block.

Figure 8-7   How to use a finally clause

How to raise an exception

When you define a function, you sometimes need to *raise an exception* (force an exception to occur). For example, you may want to raise exceptions for testing your exception handling routines. Or, you may want to raise an exception if your function isn't passed the correct arguments. Or, you may want to handle an exception, perform some processing, and then raise the exception again so it can be handled by the calling function.

Figure 8-8 shows how to use a *raise statement* to raise an exception. After the raise keyword, you code the name of the exception class that you want to use and an error message in parentheses. This is illustrated by the first example, which raises a ValueError exception with a message that says: "Invalid value".

The second example shows how you can raise an exception to test an exception handler. This technique is especially useful for exceptions that are difficult to produce otherwise. For example, you can test a handler for the FileNotFoundError by providing a file name that doesn't exist. However, testing a handler for an OSError can be difficult. Sometimes, the easiest way to test exceptions like that is to use raise statements. Of course, when you use a raise statement for testing, you must remember to remove it when you finish your testing.

The third example shows a function that accepts one argument and raises a ValueError exception if this argument contains an empty string. This is a good coding practice for a function that's going to be used by other programmers. The exception tells the other programmers that they're passing arguments that are unacceptable so they need to fix their calling statements.

The fourth example shows a function that handles an exception by writing its error message to a log file. A log file is a file that keeps a record of the events that occur during the execution of a program. In this case, the function calls a function named log_exception() to record the error message. Then, it raises that exception again so it can be handled by the calling function.

The syntax for the raise statement

```
raise ExceptionName("Error message")
```

Raising a ValueError exception

```
raise ValueError("Invalid value")
```

Raising an exception for testing an exception handler

```
def get_movies(filename):
    try:
        with open(filename, newline="") as file:
            raise OSError("OSError")       # for testing
            movies = []
            reader = csv.reader(file)
            for row in reader:
                movies.append(row)
        return movies
    except Exception as e:
        print(type(e), e)
```

Raising an exception that should be handled by the calling function

```
def get_movies(filename):
    if len(filename) == 0:
        raise ValueError("The filename argument is required.")
    with open(filename, newline="") as file:
        movies = []
        reader = csv.reader(file)
        for row in reader:
            movies.append(row)
    return movies
```

Logging an exception and raising it for the calling function

```
def get_movies(filename):
    try:
        with open(filename, newline="") as file:
            movies = []
            reader = csv.reader(file)
            for row in reader:
                movies.append(row)
        return movies
    except Exception as e:
        log_exception(e)
        raise e
```

Description

- To *raise an exception*, you can use a *raise statement* that creates an exception object.
- You can raise an exception for the Exception class or any class that's a child class of the Exception class.

Figure 8-8   How to raise an exception

Perspective

In this chapter, you have learned some of the best practices for handling exceptions in Python. As a result, you should now be able to write programs that handle exceptions so your programs don't crash. And that's what you need to do in a professional program.

Now that you've finished this chapter, you're done with the first section of this book. That means you have developed a complete subset of skills that you will use for most of the programs you write.

At this point, you can go on to section 2 to learn more concepts and skills for developing procedural programs like the ones presented in this section. Or, you can skip to section 3 to learn how to develop object-oriented programs. Of course, you should eventually study both sections, but if you're eager to get into object-oriented programming, you have all the skills you need to do that now.

Terms

exception	exception class
throw an exception	exception object
exception handling	parent class
try statement	child class
try clause	finally clause
except clause	raise an exception
data validation	raise statement

Summary

- When an error occurs at runtime, an *exception* is *thrown*.

- In a *try statement*, you code any statements that may throw an exception in the *try clause*. Then, you can code an *except clause* for each type of error that is likely to occur. This is known as *exception handling*.

- When you code multiple except clauses in a try statement, they must be coded from the most specific to the least specific. This is determined by the Python hierarchy of *parent* and *child* exception *classes*.

- When an exception occurs, Python creates an *exception object*. To get information from the object, you can access the object in an except clause.

- If necessary, you can code a *finally clause* at the end of a try statement. The code in a finally block is always executed, even if the code in the try block executes a return statement or causes an exception to occur.

- You can use a *raise statement* to *raise an exception* that can be handled by the calling code.

Exercise 8-1 Add exception handling to the Future Value program

In this exercise, you'll modify the Future Value program so the user can't cause the program to crash by entering an invalid int or float value.

1. In IDLE, open the future_value.py file that's in this folder:
   python/exercises/ch08

2. Review the code and study the get_valid_number() and get_valid_integer() functions. Note that they receive three arguments: the prompt for a user entry, the low value that the entry must be greater than, and the high value that the entry must be less than or equal to. Then, review the calling statements in the main() function and note how these functions are used.

3. Test the program. Note that you can cause the program to crash by entering values that can't be converted to float and int values.

4. Add exception handling to the get_valid_number() and get_valid_integer() functions so the user has to enter valid float and int values. Then, test these changes to make sure the exception handling and the data validation work correctly.

Exercise 8-2 Enhance the Movie List 2.0 program

In this exercise, you'll modify the Movies List 2.0 program so it does more exception handling. You'll also use a raise statement to test for exceptions.

1. In IDLE, open the movies2.py file that's in this folder:
   python/exercises/ch08

2. Add data validation to the add_movie() function so the year entry is a valid integer that's greater than zero. Then, test this change, and note that this creates a problem in the list_movies() function because the year needs to be converted to a string before it can be displayed. So, fix this and test again.

3. Modify the write_movies() function so it also handles any OSError exceptions by displaying the class name and error message of the exception object and exiting the program.

4. Test this by using a raise statement in the try block that raises a BlockingIOError. This is one of the child classes of the OSError. Then, comment out the raise statement.

5. In the read_movies() function, comment out the two statements in the except clause for the FileNotFoundError. Instead, use this except clause to return the empty movies list that's initialized in the try block. This should cause the program to continue if the file can't be found by allowing the program to create a new file for the movies that the user adds.

6. Test this by first running the program with the same CSV file. That should work as before. Then, change the file name in the global constant to movies_test.csv, run the program again, and add a movie. That should create a new file. If that works, run the program again to check whether it works with the new file.

Section 2

Other concepts and skills

This section is designed to add to the skillset that you developed in section 1 of this book. The chapters in this section are designed so you can read them in the sequence that you prefer. In other words, you don't have to read them in sequence.

If, for example, you want to learn more about working with strings, you can skip to chapter 10. Or if you want to learn how to work with dates and times, you can skip to chapter 11. Eventually, though, you'll want to read all of the chapters. This includes chapters on working with numbers, dictionaries, and recursion.

9

How to work with numbers

In previous chapters, you learned the basics of working with numbers, including how to initialize numeric variables, how to use arithmetic expressions, and how to compare numeric values. In this chapter, you'll learn more about working with numbers, including how to format them and how to avoid floating-point errors by using decimal numbers.

Basic skills for working with numbers

To start, this chapter gives you more information about floating-point numbers and how they can lead to programming errors. Then, you'll learn how to use the standard math module.

How floating-point numbers work

Figure 9-1 begins by reviewing two data types for storing numbers. The int type uses 4 bytes to store an integer. And the float type uses 8 bytes to store *floating-point numbers* that can include a decimal point. These floating-point numbers can be much larger or smaller than the integers stored by the int type. However, the float type can only use 16 *significant digits* to store the number.

To express the value of a floating-point number, you can use *scientific notation*, as shown by the second group of examples in this figure. This notation consists of an optional plus sign or a required minus sign, a decimal value for the significant digits, the letter *e* or *E*, and a positive or negative exponent. For example:

```
2.302e+5
```

In this example, the number contains four significant digits (2.302), and the exponent specifies how many places the decimal point should be moved to the right or to the left. Here, the exponent is positive so the point is moved to the right and the value is:

```
230,200
```

But if the exponent was negative (e-5), the point would be moved to the left and the value would be:

```
.00002302
```

As its name implies, scientific notation is typically used for scientific programs that work with very large and small numbers. So, if you're not developing these types of programs, you might never need to use it.

More importantly, the third example shows that floating-point numbers are *approximate values*, not exact values. As a result, they sometimes cause floating-point errors that yield unexpected results as shown in this example. Here, the result of the first three statements should be 300.3. Instead, it is 300.2999999999999995. By contrast, integers are *exact values*. As a result, you don't have to worry about unexpected results when you're working with integers.

You can easily fix the floating-point error shown in the third example by rounding to 2 decimal places as shown in the fourth example. Still, if you aren't aware of this issue, these approximate values can lead to errors in your programs. Later in this chapter, you'll learn another way to fix this issue that's appropriate for programs such as financial programs that typically need to use exact values, not approximate values.

Two numeric data types

Type	Bytes	Use
int	4	Integers from -2,147,483,648 to 2,147,483,647.
float	8	Floating-point numbers from -1.7E308 to +1.7E308 with up to 16 significant digits.

Examples of float values

```
21.5        # a positive float value
-124.82     # a negative float value
-3.7e-9     # floating-point notation for -0.0000000037
```

Variables that are set with scientific notation

```
value1 = 2.382E+5    # 2.382 * 10^5 (or 238,200)
value2 = 3.25E-8     # 3.25 * 10^-8 (or .0000000325)
```

An example of a floating-point error

```
balance = 100.10
balance += 100.10
balance += 100.10
print("Balance =", balance)
```

The result

```
Balance = 300.29999999999995
```

Code that fixes the floating-point error

```
balance = round(balance, 2)
print("Balance =", balance)
```

The result

```
Balance = 300.3
```

Description

- A *floating-point number* consists of a positive or negative sign, a decimal value for the significant digits, and an optional exponent.
- Floating-point numbers provide for very large and very small numbers, but with a limited number of *significant digits*.
- To express the value of a floating-point number, you can use *scientific notation*.
- An integer is an *exact value* that yields expected results.
- A floating-point number is an *approximate value* that can yield unexpected results known as *floating-point errors*.

Figure 9-1   How floating-point numbers work

How to use the math module

The standard math module for Python provides many functions for mathematical, trigonometric, and logarithmic operations. Figure 9-2 begins by presenting four of the functions that you're most likely to use. In addition, it presents the pi constant that's available from this module.

To use these functions, you begin by importing the math module as shown in the first example. Then, you can call functions from this module and use the pi constant. This is illustrated by the examples that follow.

The second group of examples shows how to use the pow() and sqrt() functions. Remember, though, that you can also use the exponentiation operator (**) to raise a number to a power like this:

```
2**3
```

This returns 8 just as the first statement in this group of examples does.

The third statement in this group shows how you can use the pow() function to get the cube root of 125. To do that, you pass 1/3 to the pow() function. This should return a value of 5, but instead it returns a value of 4.999999999999999 on most systems. This is another example of a floating-point error.

The third example shows how to use the pi constant to calculate the circumference and area of a circle. To calculate the circumference, the second statement multiplies the pi constant by the radius multiplied by two. To calculate the area, the third statement multiples the pi constant by the radius squared. The fourth statement performs the same calculation, but it uses the exponentiation operator (**) instead of the pow() function. This shows that the exponentiation operator is more concise and easier to read.

The fourth example shows how to use the floor and ceil operators. This shows that you can use the ceil() function if you always want to round up (towards the ceiling). And you can use the floor() function if you always want to round down (towards the floor).

However, these functions return int values, no matter how many decimal places the argument has. As a result, if you want to round to a specified number of decimal places, you can use the trick shown in the last two examples. Here, you multiply the argument by 10 for each decimal place that you want, pass the result of that calculation to the function, and divide the return value by 10 for each decimal place that you want.

Some common functions of the math module

Function	Description
pow(*num, pow*)	Raises the number to the specified power.
sqrt(*num*)	Returns the square root of the specified number.
ceil(*num*)	Rounds the floating-point number up to the nearest integer.
floor(*num*)	Rounds the floating-point number down to the nearest integer.

A constant of the math module

Constant	Description
pi	The value of pi to 15 decimal positions.

How to import the math module

```
import math as m
```

How to use the pow() and sqrt() functions

```
result = m.pow(2, 3)              # 8.0 (the cube of 2)
result = m.sqrt(16)               # 4.0
result = m.pow(125, 1/3)          # 4.999999999999999 (cube root of 125)
```

How to use the pi constant

```
radius = 12
circumference = m.pi * radius * 2    # 75.39822368615503
area = m.pi * m.pow(radius, 2)       # 452.3893421169302
area = m.pi * radius**2              # 452.3893421169302
```

How to use the floor() and ceil() functions

```
result = m.floor(12.545)          # 12
result = m.ceil(12.545)           # 13
result = m.floor(-3.432)          # -4
result = m.ceil(-3.432)           # -3
```

How to use the ceil() function to work with decimal places

```
m.ceil(2.0083)                    # 3
m.ceil(2.0083 * 10) / 10          # 2.1
m.ceil(2.0083 * 100) / 100        # 2.01
```

How to use floor() function to work with decimal places

```
m.floor(2.0083)                   # 2
m.floor(2.0083 * 10) / 10         # 2.0
m.floor(2.0083 * 1000) / 1000     # 2.008
```

Description

- The math module contains functions for commonly used mathematical operations.
- The ceil() and floor() functions return integers. But if you want to use them with decimal numbers, you can multiply and then divide by multiples of 10.

Figure 9-2   How to use the math module

How to format numbers

So far, you've learned how to use the built-in round() function to round numbers to the correct number of decimal places. Now, you'll learn other ways to format numbers.

How to use the format() method of a string

Figure 9-3 shows how to use the format() method of a string to format numbers with commas and decimal places. To start, this figure presents the syntax for working with the format() method. The best way to understand this syntax is to study the examples in this figure. Once you do that, the syntax should make sense.

In the first group of examples, the statements format and print the floating-point value that's stored in a variable named fp_number. Here, the argument of each print() function starts with a string that contains the format specification for the value to be formatted. For instance, the string that contains the format specification in the first print statement is:

```
"{:.2f}"
```

In this case, the format specification is .2f, which means to format the floating point number with two decimal places. Note that the specification starts with {: and ends with }, which are enclosed in quotes. That's true for all format specifications.

The format specification, which is a string, is then followed by a period and the format() method of the string. The argument for this method is the value to be formatted. So the first format() method formats the value stored in the variable named fp_number and returns a result of 12345.68, which shows that the value has been rounded to two decimal places.

If you understand how the first format() method works, you should be able to understand the other examples in this group. For instance, the second format() method specifies four decimal positions. The third one specifies two decimal positions and uses a comma to separate thousands. And the fourth one specifies a field width of 15. This adds 6 spaces to the left of the 9-character result for a total of 15 characters.

The examples that follow show how format specifications can be used for integers, percentages, and scientific notation. For these specifications, you need to know that percent values are multiplied by 100 and followed by a percent sign, so a value of .125 becomes 12.5%.

The last group of examples shows how you can use a single format() method to format multiple values. In this case, each format string includes three format specifications. Then, the code passes one value for each specification to the format() method.

In addition, this shows how you can use field widths to align values in columns. When you do that, numbers are right aligned and strings are left aligned by default. However, you can use the < and > operators to change this as in the second and third string values in the first statement.

The syntax for the string format() method

```
"{:format_specification}...".format(data_item...)
```

The syntax for the format specification

```
[field_width][comma][.decimal_places][type_code]
```

Common type codes

Code	Meaning	Description
d	Integer	Decimal positions can't be specified.
f	Floating-point number	Decimal positions can be specified.
%	Percent	Multiplies the value by 100 and puts a percent sign after it.
e	Scientific notation	Converts the number to scientific notation.

Examples

```
fp_number = 12345.6789
print("{:.2f}".format(fp_number))          # 12345.68
print("{:.4f}".format(fp_number))          # 12345.6789
print("{:,.2f}".format(fp_number))         # 12,345.68
print("{:15,.2f}".format(fp_number))       # 12,345.68


int_number = 12345
print("{:d}".format(int_number))           # 12345
print("{:,d}".format(int_number))          # 12,345


fp_number = .12345
print("{:.0%}".format(fp_number))          # 12%
print("{:.1%}".format(fp_number))          # 12.3%


fp_number = 12345.6789
print("{:.2e}".format(fp_number))          # 1.23e+04
print("{:.4e}".format(fp_number))          # 1.2346e+04
```

How to use field widths to align results

```
print("{:15} {:>10} {:>5}".format("Description", "Price", "Qty"))
print("{:15} {:10.2f} {:5d}".format("Hammer", 9.99, 3))
print("{:15} {:10.2f} {:5d}".format("Nails", 14.5, 10))
```

The console

```
Description          Price  Qty
Hammer                9.99    3
Nails                14.50   10
```

Description

- You can use the format() method of a string to format a single value or a series of values by converting them into strings. But that doesn't change the values of the variables that are being formatted.

- When you use a field-width specification, numbers are right aligned and strings are left aligned by default. However, you can use the < and > symbols to override that.

Figure 9-3   How to use the format() method of a string

How to use the locale module

As you probably know, the formatting for currency varies from one country to another. In the United States, for example, you format a currency value of 1002.5 as $1,002.50. But in some parts of Europe, you format that same value as +1.002,50. To provide for these variations, Python provides the locale module.

Figure 9-4 shows how to use the locale module. To start, of course, you need to import the module as shown in the examples. Then, you can use the three functions in the table at the top of this figure.

Before you can call the currency() or format() function, you need to set the locale using the setlocale() function. Here, the category argument determines the type of values that the setting applies to. In the examples, all of the setlocale() functions use the LC_ALL constant to apply this locale to all categories. As a result, it applies to both the currency() and format() functions. However, you can also use the LC_NUMERIC constant to apply this locale only to numbers, or you can use the LC_MONETARY constant to apply this locale only to monetary values.

The second argument for the setlocale() function is a code that specifies the locale that should be used for formatting. On most Windows systems, you can set this explicitly by specifying its ISO two-letter country code, like "us" for the United States, "uk" for United Kingdom, or "de" for Germany. However, on most Mac OS X systems, you need to use a longer code that specifies the language and the country, like "en_US" for English/United States.

If you set the second argument to an empty string, Python attempts to use the default locale for the user's computer. However, this fails on most Mac OS X systems, and the setlocale() function returns a code of "C". To prevent your program from crashing, you can check whether the setlocale() function has returned a code of "C". If so, you can set the locale to the most likely locale for your program. In this figure, for instance, the third example sets the locale to English/United States.

Once the locale is set, you can use the currency() function to format specific values. For this function, the first argument specifies the monetary value and is the only required argument. However, it's common to set the optional grouping argument to True to separate the thousands in large numbers as shown by the fourth example.

The format() function works similarly to the currency() function. However, the first argument specifies a string that you can use to specify the format for the number. This works much like the format specification shown in the previous figure. However, the format specification begins with a percent sign (%).

The fifth example shows how this works. Here, the first format() function uses a format specification of "%d" to format an integer, and the second format() function uses a format specification of "%.2f" to format a floating-point value with two decimal places.

Commonly used functions of the locale module

Function	Description
`setlocale(category, locale)`	Sets the locale for the specified category to the locale for the specified country code and returns a string for the locale. If category is set to LC_ALL, the locale is applied to all categories.
	If locale is an empty string, it attempts to set the locale to the user's default locale. If this isn't possible, it returns a code of "C".
`currency(num[, grouping])`	Returns the specified number formatted as currency. If grouping is set to True, the number includes thousands separators.
`format(format, num[, grouping])`	Returns the specified number formatted for the current locale. If grouping is set to True, the number includes thousands separators.

Codes for working with locales

Locale	Short code	Long code	Currency Format
English/United States	us	en_US	$12,345.15
English/United Kingdom	uk	en_UK	£12,345.15
German/Germany	de	de_DE	+12.345,15

How to import the locale module into the lc namespace

```
import locale as lc
```

How to set the locale to English/United States

```
lc.setlocale(lc.LC_ALL, "us")        # works on most Windows systems
lc.setlocale(lc.LC_ALL, "en_US")     # works on most Mac OS X systems
```

How to set the locale on most systems

```
result = lc.setlocale(lc.LC_ALL, "")   # works on most Windows systems
if result == "C":                       # if 'C' code is returned,
    lc.setlocale(lc.LC_ALL, "en_US")    # set default for Mac OS X systems
```

How to use the currency() function

```
print(lc.currency(12345.15, grouping=True))        # $12,345.15 (for US)
```

How to use the format() function

```
print(lc.format("%d", 12345, grouping=True))        # 12,345 (for US)
print(lc.format("%.2f", 12345.15, grouping=True))   # 12,345.15 (for US)
```

Description

- The convention for formatting numbers varies depending on the user's locale.
- Python's locale module allows you to format numbers properly for a user's locale.

Figure 9-4   How to use the locale module

How to fix rounding errors

Figure 9-5 begins by showing the user interface for a program that has *rounding errors*. Here, the discount is 10.01 and that's subtracted from 100.05, so the subtotal should be 90.04. But instead, it's 90.05!

The code in the first example allows this error to occur because it doesn't round the results after each calculation. Instead, it allows the code that displays the results to round each value. But by then, it's too late.

To start, the user enters an order total of 100.05. Next, the program calculates a discount of 10%. This yields a discount of 10.005. Then, it subtracts that amount from the order total. This yields a subtotal of 90.045. Then, when the program displays the results, the format method rounds the discount up to 10.01, and it rounds the subtotal up to 90.05.

So, to fix this bug, you need to round any results that can have more than two decimal places immediately after they are calculated as shown in the second example. Here, the discount and the sales tax can have more than two decimal positions. As a result, this code rounds those values to two decimal places. That way, the code rounds the discount to 10.01 before it subtracts it from the order total of 100.05, yielding a subtotal of 90.04, which is correct.

The trouble with this solution is that it isn't always easy to figure out which values to round and when they need to be rounded. That's partly because floating-point numbers sometimes yield unexpected results. For example, figure 9-1 showed that adding together three floating-point numbers that have two decimal places can yield a number that has more than two decimal places.

For most programs, you can fix these errors easily enough by using the round() function as shown in this figure. However, for some programs, including some financial programs, it's better to eliminate unexpected results by using the decimal module as shown in the next few figures.

The user interface with incorrect results

```
Enter order total: 100.05

Order total:         100.05
Discount amount:      10.01
Subtotal:             90.05
Sales tax:             4.50
Invoice total:        94.55
```

The code that yields incorrect results

```python
# get user entry
order_total = float(input("Enter order total: "))
print()

# determine discount percent
if order_total > 0 and order_total < 100:
    discount_percent = 0
elif order_total >= 100 and order_total < 250:
    discount_percent = .1
elif order_total >= 250:
    discount_percent = .2

# calculate the results
discount = order_total * discount_percent
subtotal = order_total - discount
sales_tax = subtotal * .05
invoice_total = subtotal + sales_tax

# display the results
print("Order total:     {:10,.2f}".format(order_total))
print("Discount amount: {:10,.2f}".format(discount))
print("Subtotal:        {:10,.2f}".format(subtotal))
print("Sales tax:       {:10,.2f}".format(sales_tax))
print("Invoice total:   {:10,.2f}".format(invoice_total))
print()
```

The code that fixes this problem

```python
# calculate results with rounding
discount = round(order_total * discount_percent, 2)
subtotal = order_total - discount
sales_tax = round(subtotal * .05, 2)
invoice_total = subtotal + sales_tax
```

Description

- When you use decimal numbers for financial calculations, you can get *rounding errors* if you don't round the results to two decimal places after any calculation that can result in more than two decimal places.

Figure 9-5   How to fix rounding errors

How to work with decimal numbers

As you have learned, floating-point numbers are approximate values, not exact values. As a result, working with floating-point numbers sometimes yields unexpected results. One way to cope with that is to use rounding, but a more reliable way is to use the decimal module to work with *decimal numbers*. Decimal numbers work like a floating-point numbers, except that they are exact values, not approximate values.

How to use the decimal module

Figure 9-6 shows how to use the decimal module. When you use this module, you don't have to worry about the unexpected results that can be introduced by floating-point numbers.

The first example shows how you can use this module to create decimal numbers. To start, you import the *Decimal class* from the decimal module. Then, you use the *constructor* of the Decimal class to construct *Decimal objects* from string values. To do that, you code a set of parentheses after the Decimal class, and you supply the string for the decimal number within those parentheses.

Once you create Decimal objects, you can use most of the standard arithmetic operators on them. You can even code expressions that mix decimal numbers with integers. That's because both data types represent exact values. However, you can't code expressions that mix decimal numbers with floating-point numbers. Because floating point numbers don't represent exact values, that would introduce the type of unexpected results that the decimal module is intended to fix.

Whenever necessary, you can use the quantize() method to round decimal values to the specified number of decimal places. To do that, the first argument specifies a Decimal object that has the correct number of decimal places. For example, you can specify two decimal places like this:

```
Decimal("1.00")
```

Here, 1.00 specifies two decimal positions, 1.000 specifies three decimal places, and so on. This is a good way to code this argument, but you should know that you can get the same results with any values that have the right number of decimal places, like 9.99 and 9.999.

By default, the quantize() method uses the ROUND_HALF_EVEN rounding constant as shown in the second example. Here, the value of 10.005 is rounded down to 10.00 because the 5 is preceded by a 0, which is an even number. However, a value of 10.015 would be rounded up to 10.01.

For business math, you often want to use the ROUND_HALF_UP constant to round a value like 10.005 up to 10.01 regardless of whether the 5 is preceded by an even or odd number. To do that, you can import this constant and use it to specify the rounding mode as shown in the third example.

How to create Decimal objects and use them in calculations

```
from decimal import Decimal

order_total = Decimal("100.05")
discount_percent = Decimal(".1")
discount = order_total * discount_percent    # 10.005

subtotal = order_total - discount            # 90.045
tax_percent = Decimal(".05")
sales_tax = subtotal * tax_percent           # 4.50225
invoice_total = subtotal + sales_tax         # 94.54725

test1 = subtotal * 2     # Legal. You can mix Decimal and int
test2 = subtotal * 3.5   # Error! You can't mix Decimal and float
```

The syntax of the quantize() method of a Decimal object

```
object.quantize(Decimal("positions_code")[, rounding_constant])
```

Three of the rounding constants for the quantize() method

Constant	Description
ROUND_HALF_UP	Round up if the neighbors are equidistant. This is the constant that's used for most business math.
ROUND_HALF_DOWN	Round down if the nearest neighbors are equidistant.
ROUND_HALF_EVEN	When the nearest neighbors are equidistant, round up for odd numbers, round down for even numbers. This is the default.

How to specify the number of decimal places

```
discount = Decimal("10.005")
discount = discount.quantize(Decimal("1.00"))            # 10.00
```

How to override the default rounding mode

```
from decimal import ROUND_HALF_UP

discount = Decimal("10.005")
discount = discount.quantize(Decimal("1.00"), ROUND_HALF_UP)   # 10.01
```

Description

- You can use the decimal module to create *decimal numbers* that are exact values and don't yield unexpected results.

- When you work with decimal numbers, you usually import the Decimal class and any rounding constants you need from the decimal module.

- To create a *Decimal object* that stores a decimal number, pass a string for the decimal number to the *constructor* of the *Decimal class*.

- You can use most arithmetic operators with Decimal objects. In addition, it's legal to code expressions that mix Decimal objects with int values. However, it's illegal to code expressions that mix Decimal objects with float values.

Figure 9-6   How to use the decimal module

At this point, you might be asking, "If decimal numbers are more accurate than floating-point numbers, why don't we use them all the time?" First, floating-point calculations are faster than decimal calculations. Second, the code for working with floating-point numbers is simpler. Third, floating-point calculations are accurate enough for most programs. As a result, decimal numbers are typically used for financial calculations.

The Invoice program with decimal numbers

Figure 9-7 shows a version of the Invoice program that uses the decimal module so it works with decimal numbers instead of floating-point numbers. To start, the Decimal class and the ROUND_HALF_UP constant are imported from the decimal module.

The body of this program begins by using the constructor of the Decimal class to convert the user's entry into a decimal number. Then, it uses the quantize() method to make sure the user entry contains two decimal places. As a result, if the user enters 100, this stores a value of 100.00. Conversely, if the user enters 100.005, this stores a value of 100.01.

After getting the user entry, this code uses an if statement to create a decimal number for the discount percentage. Since the constructor of the Decimal class can't convert floating-point numbers to decimal numbers, this code uses strings to specify the discount percentage as a decimal number.

The next group of statements calculates the results. To do that, this code uses normal arithmetic operators for multiplication (*), subtraction (-), and addition (+). In addition, this code uses the quantize() method to round the results to two decimal positions whenever a multiplication operation might yield a result that has more than two decimal places. That means that all values used in the addition and subtraction calculations have two decimal places. So, all of the results of these calculations also have two decimal places.

To finish, this program uses print() functions and the string format() method to display the results. Here, the format specifies that each field should have a width of 10 characters, and that commas should be used to separate thousands. As a result, the decimal values are aligned on the right. However, the format string doesn't specify the number of decimal places. This shows that all of the results calculated by this program have two decimal places.

The user interface with correct results

```
Enter order total: 100.05

Order total:            100.05
Discount amount:         10.01
Subtotal:                90.04
Sales tax:                4.50
Invoice total:           94.54

Continue? (y/n):
```

The code

```python
from decimal import Decimal
from decimal import ROUND_HALF_UP

choice = "y"
while choice == "y":

    # get the user entry
    order_total = Decimal(input("Enter order total:    "))
    order_total = order_total.quantize(Decimal("1.00"), ROUND_HALF_UP)
    print()

    # determine the discount percent
    if order_total > 0 and order_total < 100:
        discount_percent = Decimal("0")
    elif order_total >= 100 and order_total < 250:
        discount_percent = Decimal(".1")
    elif order_total >= 250:
        discount_percent = Decimal(".2")

    # calculate the results
    discount = order_total * discount_percent
    discount = discount.quantize(Decimal("1.00"), ROUND_HALF_UP)
    subtotal = order_total - discount
    tax_percent = Decimal(".05")
    sales_tax = subtotal * tax_percent
    sales_tax = sales_tax.quantize(Decimal("1.00"), ROUND_HALF_UP)
    invoice_total = subtotal + sales_tax

    # display the results
    print("Order total:      {:10,}".format(order_total))
    print("Discount amount: {:10,}".format(discount))
    print("Subtotal:         {:10,}".format(subtotal))
    print("Sales tax:        {:10,}".format(sales_tax))
    print("Invoice total:    {:10,}".format(invoice_total))
    print()

    choice = input("Continue? (y/n): ")
    print()

print("Bye")
```

Figure 9-7   The Invoice program with decimal numbers

The Future Value program with decimal numbers

Figure 9-8 presents another program that uses decimal numbers. This time, it's a version of the Future Value program that also uses the locale module to format the currency values. This program begins by importing the locale module and the Decimal class from the decimal module.

The main() function of this program prompts the user to enter a monthly investment, a yearly interest rate, and the number of years. Then, this code creates Decimal objects for both the monthly investment and the yearly interest. However, because the number of years is an integer, which is an exact type, this code doesn't need to convert it to a Decimal object.

After getting the user input, the main() function calls the get_future_value() function and passes it the values entered by the user. This function begins by converting the yearly values entered by the user to monthly values. Then, it initializes the future_value variable to a decimal value of 0.00. Next, the code enters a loop that's executed once for each month.

Within this loop, the second statement calculates the interest for the month. This results in a number that has more than two decimal places. Then, the third statement adds the monthly interest to the future value, which uses as many decimal places as needed to store the result.

When the loop finishes, the function returns the future value to the main() function. But first, it uses the quantize() method to round the future value to two decimal places. Note here that the rounding isn't done in the loop because that might impact the accuracy of the final result.

Back in the main() function, the code continues by setting all categories of the locale to the user's default locale if that's possible. Otherwise, it sets the locale to English/United States. Then, a series of print() functions display the monthly investment, interest rate, years, and future value. Within those print() functions, the currency() function applies currency formatting to the monthly investment amount and future value.

In addition, the format() method right aligns the numeric values. To do that, this code calls the format() method from a variable named line that's initialized before the print() functions. This variable contains the format specifications that left align the first column and right align the second column. Since this stores the format specification in one location, it reduces code duplication, which makes the code easier to maintain. If, for example, you want to make the right column wider, you only need to change the number of characters in one place, not four.

The user interface

```
Enter monthly investment:   100
Enter yearly interest rate: 12.5
Enter number of years:      10

Monthy investment:        $100.00
Interest rate:              12.5
Years:                        10
Future value:         $23,938.13

Continue? (y/n):
```

The code

```python
from decimal import Decimal
import locale as lc

def get_future_value(monthly_investment, yearly_interest, years):
    monthly_interest_rate = yearly_interest / 12 / 100
    months = years * 12
    future_value = Decimal("0.00")
    for i in range(months):
        future_value += monthly_investment
        monthly_interest = future_value * monthly_interest_rate
        future_value += monthly_interest
    future_value = future_value.quantize(Decimal("1.00"))
    return future_value

def main():
    choice = "y"
    while choice.lower() == "y":
        # convert user input to Decimal and int values
        monthly_investment = Decimal(input("Enter monthly investment:   "))
        yearly_interest = Decimal(input("Enter yearly interest rate: "))
        years = int(input("Enter number of years:      "))
        future_value = get_future_value(
            monthly_investment, yearly_interest, years)
        print()

        # format and display the results
        result = lc.setlocale(lc.LC_ALL, "")
        if result == "C":
            lc.setlocale(lc.LC_ALL, "en_US")
        line = "{:20} {:>10}"
        print(line.format("Monthy investment:",
            lc.currency(monthly_investment, grouping=True)))
        print(line.format("Interest rate:", yearly_interest))
        print(line.format("Years: ", years))
        print(line.format("Future value:",
            lc.currency(future_value, grouping=True)), "\n")

        choice = input("Continue? (y/n): ")
        print()

if __name__ == "__main__":
    main()
```

Figure 9-8   The Future Value program with decimal numbers

Perspective

Now that you've completed this chapter, you should be able to use the functions of the math module. You should be able to format and align numbers and currency values. And you should be able to use the decimal module and decimal numbers to avoid the errors that can occur when you use floating-point numbers. These are skills that you won't use in every program, but they come in handy when you do need them.

Terms

floating-point number	rounding error
significant digits	decimal number
scientific notation	Decimal class
approximate value	constructor
exact value	Decimal object

Summary

- A *floating-point number* provides for very large and very small decimal numbers, but with a limited number of *significant digits*. To express the value of a floating-point number, you can use *scientific notation*.

- A floating-point number is an *approximate value* that can yield unexpected results known as *floating-point errors*. An integer is an *exact value* that yields expected results.

- The math module contains functions and constants for common mathematical, trigonometric, and logarithmic operations.

- The format() method of a string lets you format and align numbers.

- The locale module provides functions for formatting numbers and monetary values so they're appropriate for locales throughout the world.

- When you use Python for financial calculations, you can get *rounding errors* if you don't round the results to two decimal places after any calculation that can result in more than two decimal places.

- You can use the decimal module to create *decimal numbers* that are exact values and don't yield unexpected results. To do that, you use the *constructor* of the *Decimal class* to create a *Decimal object* that stores a decimal number.

Exercise 9-1   Enhance the Invoice program

In this exercise, you'll enhance a version of the Invoice program so two of the currency values are formatted correctly. You'll also add a shipping cost to the invoice:

```
Enter order total:      10554.23

Order total:        $10,554.23
Discount amount:      2110.85
Subtotal:             8443.38
Shipping cost:         717.69
Sales tax:             422.17
Invoice total:       $9,583.24

Continue? (y/n):
```

Use the locale module for the currency values

1. In IDLE, open the invoice_decimal.py file that's in this folder:

   python/exercises/ch09

2. Modify this program so it displays the order total and invoice total as currency values in the United States.

Add a shipping cost

3. Add a shipping cost as shown in the console data above. This charge should be .085 of the subtotal. As a result, it could cause a rounding error. To prevent this error from occurring, use the decimal module to make sure each monetary value has the correct number of decimal places.

4. Test and debug this program and make sure that it works with all input values.

10

How to work with strings

In chapter 2, you learned some basic skills for working with strings, including how to create a string, how to concatenate strings, and how to work with escape characters. Now, in this chapter, you'll expand that set of skills.

Basic skills for working with strings

The figures that follow present some basic skills for working with strings. Many of these are similar to the basic skills for working with lists.

Unicode, indexes, slicing, duplicating, and multiline strings

Figure 10-1 presents some of the basic skills for working with strings. To start, you should know that a string consists of *Unicode* characters. Unicode maps each character to an integer, or *ordinal*, value. For instance, the first example uses the built-in ord() function to show that the character "5" maps to the ordinal value of 53, "A" maps to 65, and "a" maps to 97.

The ordinal value determines the sort order for the characters. As a result, digits come before uppercase letters and uppercase letters come before lowercase letters.

To refer to a character in a string, you can use an index, as shown by the second example. This shows that positive indexes start from the left side of a string and begin with 0, and negative indexes start from the right side of a string and begin with -1. These indexes work the same as the indexes for the items in a list. However, unlike a list, a string is *immutable*. As a result, if you attempt to assign a new character to a string index, a TypeError occurs, as shown by the last statement in this example.

Just as you can slice a list, you can slice a string. This is illustrated by the third example. You can also use the repetition operator with a string, as shown in the fourth group.

The last example shows that you can use three single quotes to create a multiline string. This technique is commonly used to create string constants that are used within the program, not for display in a console or GUI interface. When you use this technique, the string includes any new line characters or other whitespace that's included between the triple quotes. In this example, this technique is used for coding a SQL statement like the ones you'll learn about in chapter 17.

Two built-in functions

Function	Description
ord(*char*)	Returns the integer (ordinal) value for the Unicode character.
len(*str*)	Returns an integer for the length of the specified string.

How to get the ordinal value of a Unicode character

```
print("5 =", ord("5"))          # 5 = 53
print("A =", ord("A"))          # A = 65
print("a =", ord("a"))          # a = 97
```

How to use an index to access a character in a string

```
message = "Hello out there!"
message[0]                      # "H"
message[1]                      # "e"
message[-1]                     # "!"
message[16]                     # IndexError: string index out of range
message[0] = "J"                # TypeError: string is immutable
```

How to slice a string

```
string[start:end:step]
```

Examples

```
message = "Hello out there!"
message[:5]                     # "Hello"
message[6:9]                    # "out"
message[10:]                    # "there!"
message[:-1]                    # "Hello out there"
```

How to use the repetition operator (*)

```
print("=" * 20)                 # ====================
print("A horse! " * 2)          # "A horse! A horse!"
```

How to use triple quotes to create a multiline string

```
query = '''SELECT categoryID, name AS categoryName
           FROM Category WHERE categoryID = ?'''
```

Description

- With version 3.0 and later, Python uses *Unicode* to store the characters in strings. Unicode maps each character to an integer (*ordinal*) value and provides for most characters in most of the world's languages.

- A string is *immutable*, which means that you can't change its characters. If you attempt to do that, Python raises a TypeError.

- If you use an index that doesn't exist in the string, Python raises an IndexError that indicates that the index is out of range.

- Slicing and duplicating a string works the same as slicing or duplicating a list.

- Triple quotes are used for strings that are used within programs, not for display.

Figure 10-1   Unicode, indexes, slicing, duplicating, and multiline strings

How to search a string

Figure 10-2 shows how you can use the in keyword to search for a substring within a string. To start, you can use this keyword in an if statement to test whether a string contains a specific substring. Then, you can execute a block of code depending on whether the condition is True or False.

How to loop through the characters in a string

This figure also shows how to loop through the characters in a string. This is similar to looping through the items in a list. Here, the second to last example loops over the three characters in a string of "Hi!" and prints each one on its own line. Then, the last example uses a loop with the ord() function to print the Unicode ordinal value for each character in the string.

The syntax for using the in keyword to search a string

```
term in string
```

Some examples that use the in keyword to search a string

```
spam = "Congratulations. You've won a million dollars."
"million" in spam              # True
"Million" in spam              # False - search is case-sensitive
"on" in spam                   # True - doesn't need to be whole word
" million " in spam            # True - uses spaces to find a whole word
" dollars " in spam            # False - ends with a period, not a space
```

Code that uses an if statement to check a search

```
search_term = input("Enter search term: ")
if search_term in spam:
    print("Term found!")
```

The console

```
Enter search term: dollar
Term found!
```

The syntax for looping over each character in a string

```
for character in string:
    statements
```

Code that loops over each character in a string

```
message = "Hi!"
for char in message:
    print(char)
```

The console

```
H
i
!
```

Code that prints the ordinal value for each character in a string

```
message = "0123 ABCD abcd"
for char in message:
    print(ord(char), end=" ")
```

The console

```
48 49 50 51 32 65 66 67 68 32 97 98 99 100
```

Figure 10-2   How to search a string and loop through its characters

How to use basic string methods

To make it easier to work with strings, Python provides many methods that you can call from strings. Figure 10-3 summarizes some of the ones that are both useful and easy.

The first example shows how you can use the isdigit() method to determine whether all of the characters in a string are digits. The isalpha(), ispper(), and islower() methods work similarly.

The second example shows how you can use the startswith() method to determine whether a string starts with a specific substring. The endswith() method works similarly.

The third example shows how you can use the title() method to convert a string to title case. As you can see, this method converts the first letter of each word to uppercase and the other characters in each word to lowercase. The upper() and lower() methods work similarly, but they convert all letters to uppercase or lowercase.

The fourth example shows how you can use the strip() method to remove whitespace from the start and end of a string. Whitespace consists of characters that aren't visible such as spaces, tabs, new line characters, and other characters. The strip() method is commonly used to remove whitespace at the start and end of a user entry. However, whenever necessary, you can use the lstrip() and rstrip() methods to remove whitespace from just the left or right side of a string.

The last example shows how you can use the ljust() and rjust() methods to align the data in print statements. Here, the code left justifies the string in the left column by adding spaces to the right side of the string until the column is 14 characters wide, and it right justifies the string in the right column by adding spaces to the left side of the string until it is 10 characters wide. In some cases, these methods work better for aligning data than using the format() method presented in chapter 9.

Basic string methods

Method	Description
isalpha(*str*)	Returns True if all characters are alphabetic letters; otherwise False.
islower(*str*)	Returns True if all characters are lowercase letters; otherwise False.
isupper(*str*)	Returns True if all characters are uppercase letters; otherwise False.
isdigit(*str*)	Returns True if all characters are digits (0 through 9); otherwise False.
startswith(*str*)	Returns True if the string starts with the specified string; otherwise False.
endswith(*str*)	Returns True if the string ends with the specified string; otherwise False.
lower()	Converts the string to lowercase and returns it.
upper()	Converts the string to uppercase and returns it.
title()	Converts the string to title case and returns it.
lstrip()	Strips whitespace from the left and returns the string.
rstrip()	Strips whitespace from the right and returns the string.
strip()	Strips whitespace from both sides and returns the string.
ljust(*width*)	Returns a left-justified string with spaces added to fill out the width.
rjust(*width*)	Returns a right-justified string with spaces added to fill out the width.
center(*width*)	Returns a centered string with spaces added to fill out the width.

How to check if a string contains all digits

```
entry = "12345"
is_integer = entry.isdigit()                    # True
```

How to check the if a string starts with a substring

```
title = "The Meaning of Life"
starts_with_the = title.startswith("The")    # True
```

How to change a string to title case

```
movie = "the meaning of life"
movie = movie.title()                       # "The Meaning Of Life"
```

How to strip whitespace from the start and end of a string

```
ssn = "   392 55 7722   "
ssn = ssn.strip()                           # "392 55 7722"
```

How to align strings by using left and right justification

```
print("Hammer".ljust(14), "$9.99".rjust(10))
print("Nails".ljust(14), "$14.50".rjust(10))
```

The console

```
Hammer              $9.99
Nails              $14.50
```

Figure 10-3   How to use basic string methods

How to find and replace parts of a string

In many programs, you need to find or replace parts of a string. Figure 10-4 shows how to use string methods to do that.

The first two examples show how to use the find() method. The first example shows how you can use this method to do some simple validation of an email address entry. Here, the first find() method gets the index of the @ sign. Then, the second find() method starts from that index and looks for a period. That's because a period must come after the @ sign in an email address. Otherwise, the address is invalid.

After these find() methods, this example uses an if statement to check whether either find() method returns -1. If so, the email address is invalid. In this example, the @ sign in the email address is after the period, so the second find() method doesn't find a period and returns -1. As a result, this code displays a message that says the address is invalid.

Of course, this example doesn't identify all invalid email addresses. For instance, joel@.com is an invalid email address, but this example wouldn't catch that. Still, this should give you a good idea of how you can use the find() method for data validation.

The second example of the find() method shows how to get the first word in a string. Here, the find() method gets the index of the first space in a title. Then, if a space is found, the code uses slicing to get the characters from the beginning of the string to the index of the space.

The next three examples show how to use the replace() method. The first example replaces dashes with spaces in a credit card number. The second example removes dashes from a phone number by replacing them with empty strings. And the third example replaces just the first dash with an empty string and keeps the second dash. Then, it uses slicing and concatenations to add parentheses around the first three digits, which is a common way to format phone numbers in North America.

The find() and replace() methods of a string

Method	Description
find(str[, *start*][, *end*])	Searches for the specified substring and returns the index of the first occurrence or -1 if the string isn't found. The optional start and end parameters let you set the starting and ending indexes for the search.
replace(*old*, *new*[, *num*])	Returns a new string with occurrences of the old substring replaced by the new substring. The optional third parameter allows you to specify the number of occurrences to replace.

Find examples

How to search for specific characters

```
email = "joel.murach@com"

at_index = email.find("@")                   # at_index = 11
dot_index = email.find(".", at_index)        # dot_index = -1

if at_index == -1 or dot_index == -1:        # True
    print("Invalid email address:", email)
```

How to get the first word in a string

```
title = "The Meaning of Life"
i = title.find(" ")                          # i = 3
if i == -1:
    first_word = "This title doesn't contain a space."
else:
    first_word = title[0:i]                  # "The"
```

Replace examples

How to replace dashes with spaces in a credit card number

```
cc_number = "4012-881022-88810"
cc_number = cc_number.replace("-", " ")      # 4012 881022 88810
```

How to remove dashes from a phone number

```
phone_number = "555-555-1234"
phone_number = phone_number.replace("-", "") # 5555551234
```

How to replace the first dash in a phone number and then add parentheses

```
phone_number = "555-555-1234"

# replace the first dash
phone_number = phone_number.replace("-", "", 1) # 555555-1234

# add parentheses to the area code
phone_number = "(" + phone_number[:3] + ") " + phone_number[3:]
print(phone_number)                          # (555) 555-1234
```

Figure 10-4 How to use the find() and replace() methods of a string

The Create Account program

To show you how the skills presented in the previous figures can be used in a larger program, figure 10-5 presents the Create Account program. This program asks the user to enter a full name and a password until both are valid. In the real world, of course, a user would need to enter more data to create an account, but this shows how string-handling skills can be used to validate user entries.

The main() function in this program calls the get_full_name() and get_password() functions to get valid user entries. Then, the main() function calls the get_first_name() function to get the first name from the full name, and it displays a thank you message.

The get_full_name() function begins by defining a while loop that runs until the entry is valid. Within this loop, the first statement prompts the user to enter a full name, and it uses the strip() method to strip any accidental whitespace from the front or back of the entry. Then, the code checks whether the entry contains a space. If so, the code returns the name, which exits the loop and the function. Otherwise, the code displays a message that indicates that the entry isn't valid and execution continues at the top of the loop.

The get_password() function gets a password entry and checks it for validity. For this program, a valid password must have at least 8 characters, including at least one uppercase letter and one digit. When the entry is valid, this function returns the entry.

This function begins by defining a while loop that runs until the entry is valid. Here again, the first statement prompts the user for the entry and strips any whitespace from the front or back of the entry. Then, it uses a for statement to loop through the characters in the entry and to check each character for a digit and an uppercase letter. If it finds a digit, it changes the digit variable from False to True. Similarly, if it finds an uppercase letter, it changes the cap_letter variable from False to True.

After the for loop, this code checks whether the digit variable is False, the cap_letter variable is False, or the entry contains less than 8 characters. If so, it displays an error message and execution continues at the top of the while loop. Otherwise, the code returns the password.

The get_first_name() function accepts the full name as an argument. Within the function, the first statement gets the index of the first space in full name. Then, the second statement uses slicing to get the first name, and the third statement returns the first name.

The user interface

```
Enter full name:        Eric
You must enter your full name.
Enter full name:        Eric Idle

Enter password:         sesame
Password must be 8 characters or more
with at least one digit and one uppercase letter.
Enter password:         sesaMe123

Hi Eric, thanks for creating an account.
```

The code

```python
def main():
    full_name = get_full_name()
    print()

    password = get_password()
    print()

    first_name = get_first_name(full_name)
    print("Hi " + first_name + ", thanks for creating an account.")

def get_full_name():
    while True:
        name = input("Enter full name:       ").strip()
        if " " in name:
            return name
        else:
            print("You must enter your full name.")

def get_password():
    while True:
        password = input("Enter password:        ").strip()
        digit = False
        cap_letter = False
        for char in password:
            if char.isdigit():
                digit = True
            elif char.isupper():
                cap_letter = True
        if digit == False or cap_letter == False or len(password) < 8:
            print("Password must be 8 characters or more \n" +
                    "with at least one digit and one uppercase letter.")
        else:
            return password

def get_first_name(full_name):
    index1 = full_name.find(" ")
    first_name = full_name[:index1]
    return first_name

if __name__ == "__main__":
    main()
```

Figure 10-5   The Create Account program

How to split and join strings

The next two figures show how to split a string into a list of strings. In addition, it shows how to join strings. This includes how to join a list of strings into a single string.

How to split a string into a list of strings

Figure 10-6 shows how you can use the split() method to split a string into a list of strings. By default, the *delimiter* for this method is a space or other whitespace character. Then, the method uses this delimiter to split the string into the items of a list.

The first example shows how this works. Here, the second statement splits a sentence into a list that contains eight strings. Then, the next five statements show how you can access these strings with an index. For instance, you can use an index of 0 to access the first item in the list, the word "These". You can use an index of 3 to access the fourth item in the list, the word "times". And you can use an index of 7 or -1 to access the last item. Note, however, that the last item in the list is "souls." with a period at the end. Note too that an IndexError occurs if the index is out of range.

The second example shows how you can specify the delimiter. In this case, the first statement specifies a date in the MM/DD/YYYY format that's commonly used in the United States. Then, the second statement splits this date using a front slash (/) as the delimiter. This returns a list that contains strings for the month, day, and year of the date. When working with dates, you often need to convert strings like these into integers as shown in this example. In chapter 11, you'll learn more about how to work with dates like this one.

The third example shows how you can split a row of data that's separated by a delimiter into a list that stores each column as an item. Here, the first statement defines a row of data that stores a person's name and address using the vertical bar (|) as the delimiter. Then, the second statement splits this row into columns, and the next three statements display the person's name and address on the console.

The split() method of a string

Method	Description
split([*delimiter*][, *num*])	Uses a delimiter to split a string into substrings and returns a list of those substrings. By default, the delimiter is any whitespace.
	The second parameter lets you specify the number of occurrences to replace.

How to split a string on whitespace

```
quotation = "These are the times that try men's souls."
words = quotation.split()
print(words[0])          # 'These'
print(words[3])          # 'times'
print(words[7])          # 'souls.'
print(words[-1])         # 'souls.'
print(words[8])          # IndexError: list index out of range
```

How to split a date on a delimiter

```
date = "11/9/1972"
date = date.split("/")
month = int(date[0])     # 11
day =   int(date[1])     # 9
year =  int(date[2])     # 1972
year =  int(date[3])     # IndexError: list index out of range
```

How to split a row of data on a delimiter

```
address = "John Doe|1500 Any Street|New York|NY|10001"
address = address.split("|")
print(address[0])
print(address[1])
print(address[2] + ", " + address[3] + " " + address[4])
```

The console

```
John Doe
1500 Any Street
New York, NY 10001
```

Description

- A *delimiter* is a character that's used to divide a string into multiple parts.

Figure 10-6   How to split a string into a list of strings

How to join strings

The first two examples in figure 10-7 show how to join strings with the **+** and **+=** operators. Although chapter 2 showed how to use the **+** operator with strings, this book has only shown how to use the **+=** operator used with numbers, not strings. That's because the **+=** operator usually isn't as efficient as the other techniques for joining strings, especially the join() method.

The third example shows how to use the join() method to join a list of strings into a single string. Here, the second statement specifies the vertical bar (|) as the delimiter for the strings in the list. As a result, the joined string consists of each item in the list separated by the vertical bar.

The fourth example shows how you can use the join() method to join the characters in a string. This method works on both lists and strings because both lists and strings are a type of collection known as a *sequence*. A list is a sequence of items, and a string is a sequence of characters. In this example, the second statement specifies a single space as the delimiter. As a result, the characters in the joined string are separated by spaces.

The fifth example shows an error that Python programmers sometimes make because it seems like the join() method would join one string to another. However, if you attempt to use the join() method to join two strings, it doesn't join the two strings together. Instead, it uses the first string as the delimiter between each character in the second string. Obviously, that's not what you typically want. The solution, of course, is to use the **+** operator instead as shown in the first example.

How to join strings with the + and += operators

With the + operator
```
first_name = "Eric"
last_name = "Idle"
full_name = last_name + ", " + first_name    # Idle, Eric
```

With the += operator
```
first_name = "Eric"
last_name = "Idle"
full_name = last_name
full_name += ", "
full_name += first_name                          # Idle, Eric
```

The join() method of a string

Method	Description
join(*sequence*)	Joins the elements of a sequence into a string that uses the current string as the delimiter.

How to join the items of a list
```
address = ["John Doe","1500 Any Street","New York","NY","10001"]
address = "|".join(address)
print(address)
```

The console
```
John Doe|1500 Any Street|New York|NY|10001
```

How to join the characters in a string
```
letters = "HORSE"
letters_spaced = " ".join(letters)
print(letters_spaced)
```

The console
```
H O R S E
```

A common error when using the join() method
```
name = "John"
address = "15 E St"
full_address = name.join(address)
print(full_address)                    # 1John5John JohnEJohn JohnSJohnt
```

Description

- Both lists and strings are type of collection known as a *sequence*. A list is a sequence of items, and a string is a sequence of characters.

- You can use the join() method to join the elements in a sequence into a string. This is more efficient than using the **+** or **+=** operator to concatenate strings.

Figure 10-7   How to join strings

The Movie List 2D program

To show how to use the split() and join() methods in a larger program, figure 10-8 shows how to use them in the Movie List program that was presented in chapter 7. But this time, instead of storing its data in a CSV file, the Movie List program stores its data in a plain text file and uses a vertical bar to separate each column.

Most of the code for this program is the same as the Movie List program from chapter 7. In fact, the write_movies() and read_movies() functions are the only functions affected by this change. As a result, this figure only shows the code for these functions.

The write_movies() function uses the join() method to join the columns for each movie into a line using the vertical bar as the delimiter. Then, it writes this line to the text file.

The read_movies() function begins by reading each line in the file. For each line, this function replaces the new line character with an empty string, and uses the split() method to split the line into a list of strings. To do that, it uses the vertical bar as the delimiter. Then, it appends the list for the movie to the list of all movies.

The console

```
COMMAND MENU
list - List all movies
add -  Add a movie
del -  Delete a movie
exit - Exit program

Command: list
1. Monty Python and the Holy Grail (1975)
2. On the Waterfront (1954)
3. Cat on a Hot Tin Roof (1958)

Command: add
Name: Gone with the Wind
Year: 1939
Gone with the Wind was added.
```

The data in the text file after one record has been added to it

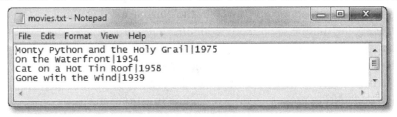

The code

```python
# a file in the current directory
FILENAME = "movies.txt"

def write_movies(movies):
    with open(FILENAME, "w") as file:
        for movie in movies:
            line = "|".join(movie)
            file.write(line + "\n")

def read_movies():
    movies = []
    with open(FILENAME) as file:
        for line in file:
            line = line.replace("\n", "")
            movie = line.split("|")
            movies.append(movie)
        return movies
```

Figure 10-8   The Movie List 2D program with a plain text file for I/O

The Word Counter program

Just for fun, figure 10-9 presents another program that uses some of the skills that you've just learned to count the words in some text that's read from a text file. First, it displays the number of words in the file and the number of unique words. Then, it displays each unique word and the number of times it is used in the text.

In the get_words_from_file() function, the first statement reads the text from the file. Then, the next three statements remove the new line characters, commas, and periods from the text. This is followed by a statement that converts all of the letters to lowercase. The last three statements split the text into a list of words, sort the words alphabetically, and return the list.

The get_unique_words() function starts by creating a new list named unique_words to store the unique words. Then, it sets the first item in the unique words list to the first item in the words list. After that, it defines a for loop that executes once for each word in the words list. However, this loop starts with the second word in the list, the word that's at the index of 1.

Within the loop, an if statement checks whether the current word is equal to the previous word. If so, the unique list already contains that word. That's true because the words list has been sorted alphabetically. As a result, if the current word is equal to the previous word, the code continues at the top of the loop, which processes the next word in the list. Otherwise, the code appends the word to the unique list. Once the loop processes all words, this function returns the unique words list.

The main() function begins by calling the get_words_from_file() and get_unique_words() functions to get the lists for the words and unique words. Then, it displays the number of words and unique words. To do that, this code uses the len() function to get the number of items in each list.

The main() function continues by using a for statement to display each word in the unique list and the number of times it is used. However, to get the number of times each unique word is used, the statement in the loop uses the count() method of the *words* list, not the *unique words* list. This method returns the number of times an item is in the list.

Although this program shows how to work with lists as much as it shows how to work with strings, it should give you some ideas about how you can apply both skillsets to solve a programming problem. In chapter 12, you'll learn how using a dictionary instead of a list makes this type of problem easier to solve.

The console

```
The Word Counter program

Number of words = 260
Number of unique words =  142
Word occurrences:
    a = 7
    above = 1
    add = 1
    ...
```

The code

```python
def get_words_from_file(filename):
    with open(filename) as file:
        text = file.read()                  # read str from file

    text = text.replace("\n", "")
    text = text.replace(",", "")
    text = text.replace(".", "")
    text = text.lower()

    words = text.split(" ")                 # convert str to list
    words.sort()
    return words

def get_unique_words(words):
    unique_words = []
    unique_words.append(words[0])

    for i in range(1, len(words)):
        if words[i] == words[i - 1]:
            continue
        else:
            unique_words.append(words[i])
    return unique_words

def main():
    filename = "gettysburg_address.txt"
    print("The Word Counter program\n")

    # get words and unique words
    words = get_words_from_file(filename)     # get list of words
    unique_words = get_unique_words(words)

    # display number of words and unique words
    print("Number of words =", len(words))
    print("Number of unique words = ", len(unique_words))

    # display unique words and their word counts
    print("Unique word occurrences:")
    for word in unique_words:
        print("    ", word, "=", words.count(word))

if __name__ == "__main__":
    main()
```

Figure 10-9   The Word Counter program

The Hangman game

To conclude this chapter, the next two figures present a program that lets you play a console version of the Hangman game. This program uses many of the string-handling skills that you've learned in this chapter. Beyond that, it should give you some insights into game programming.

The user interface

Figure 10-10 presents the console for the Hangman game. Although it doesn't draw the hangman like you might have done as a child, it works the same otherwise. First, the program picks a word that the player needs to guess. Then, the player guesses the letters that might be in the word. If a guess is correct, the program displays all occurrences of the letter in the word. Otherwise, the program increments the wrong count. If the player makes 10 wrong guesses before getting the word, the player loses. Otherwise, the player wins.

The hierarchy chart

This figure also presents the hierarchy chart for this program. Here, the main() function calls the play_game() function each time the player starts a new game. Then, the play_game() function calls the get_word() function to get the word that the player has to guess. It calls the draw_screen() function to draw the screen that shows the number of letters in the word with the correct letters (if any) filled in, the number of guesses, the number of wrong guesses, and the letters that have already been tried. And it calls the get_letter() function to get each guess from the player.

At the next level, the get_random_word() function gets the word for the game. Here, the function name is italicized to show that it is in a separate module. You can use a convention like this to distinguish the functions that aren't in the main module from those that are.

At the same level, the add_spaces() function adds spaces after the letters in the word as shown in the console. This function is called by the draw_screen() function.

The user interface for the Hangman game

```
Play the H A N G M A N game
-----------------------------------------------------------------------
Word: _ _ _ _ _ _ _       Guesses: 0    Wrong: 0    Tried:
Enter a letter: a
-----------------------------------------------------------------------
Word: _ _ _ _ A _ _       Guesses: 1    Wrong: 0    Tried: A
Enter a letter: e
-----------------------------------------------------------------------
Word: _ _ _ _ A _ _       Guesses: 2    Wrong: 1    Tried: A E
Enter a letter: i
-----------------------------------------------------------------------
Word: _ _ _ _ A _ _       Guesses: 3    Wrong: 2    Tried: A E I
Enter a letter: o
-----------------------------------------------------------------------
     (The game continues)
-----------------------------------------------------------------------
Word: B O U N _ A R Y     Guesses: 13   Wrong: 6    Tried: A E I O U S N C
L M R Y B
Enter a letter: d
-----------------------------------------------------------------------
Word: B O U N D A R Y     Guesses: 14   Wrong: 6    Tried: A E I O U S N C
L M R Y B D
-----------------------------------------------------------------------
Congratulations! You got it in  14 guesses.

Do you want to play again (y/n)?:
```

The hierarchy chart for the Hangman game

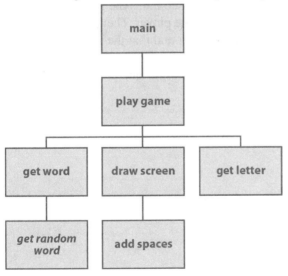

Description

- To show that a function is in another module, you can italicize the function name. In this example, this convention is used for the get_random_word() function.

Figure 10-10   The user interface and hierarchy chart for the Hangman game

The wordlist module

Figure 10-11 presents the wordlist module that contains the get_random_word() function. This module starts by defining a list of words that were downloaded from the website shown in the comment. Then, the get_random_word() function uses the choice() function of the random module to get a random word from the list. After that, it returns the word to the calling module.

The hangman module

In the hangman module, the get_word() function calls the get_random_word() function of the wordlist module to get the word for the game. Then, it returns this word after it converts it to uppercase letters.

The add_spaces function accepts a word as an argument. Then, it uses the join() method to add spaces after each letter in that word, and it returns the word with spaces.

The draw_screen() function begins by printing a line of 79 dashes. That's what separates each drawing of the screen. Then, it draws the screen by displaying the four arguments that are passed to it. To display the fourth argument, which represents the current status of the word to be guessed including the correct letters, this code calls the add_spaces() function. It also calls the add_spaces() function to display the third argument, which contains the letters that the player has guessed.

The get_letter() function accepts an argument that contains the guessed letters. This function begins by getting a letter from the player. Then, it checks to make sure that the player has only entered one letter and that the player hasn't already guessed that letter. If so, this function converts the letter to uppercase and returns it. Otherwise, it displays an appropriate message and gives the player another chance to enter a letter.

The wordlist module

```
import random

# List of words from http://www.free-teacher-worksheets.com/
words = [
    "aardvark",
    "air",
    ...
    ...
    "zipper",
    "zoo"
    ]

def get_random_word():
    word = random.choice(words)
    return word
```

The hangman module

```
import wordlist

# Get a random word from the word list
def get_word():
    word = wordlist.get_random_word()
    return word.upper()

# Add spaces between letters
def add_spaces(word):
    word_with_spaces = " ".join(word)
    return word_with_spaces

# Draw the display
def draw_screen(num_wrong, num_guesses, guessed_letters, displayed_word):
    print("-" * 79)
    print("Word:", add_spaces(displayed_word),
        "  Guesses:", num_guesses,
        "  Wrong:", num_wrong,
        "  Tried:", add_spaces(guessed_letters))

# Get next letter from user
def get_letter(guessed_letters):
    while True:
        guess = input("Enter a letter: ").strip().upper()

        # Make sure the user enters a letter and only one letter
        if guess == "" or len(guess) > 1:
            print("Invalid entry. " +
                    "Please enter one and only one letter.")
            continue
        # Don't let the user try the same letter more than once
        elif guess in guessed_letters:
            print("You already tried that letter.")
            continue
        else:
            return guess
```

Figure 10-11   The code for the Hangman game (part 1)

As the hierarchy chart shows, the play_game() function drives the logic of the Hangman game. After it gets the random word for the game, it sets up the variables for the game. That includes the displayed_word variable, which starts as one underscore character for each letter in the word. Then, this function calls the draw_screen() function to draw the screen for the game. For a word that has eight letters, the first screen should look like this:

```
Word: _ _ _ _ _ _ _ _         Guesses: 0   Wrong: 0   Tried:
```

At this point, the player hasn't guessed any letters so the word is all underscores and the guessed letters string is empty.

After drawing the first screen, the play_game() function enters a while loop that continues as long as the player has less than 10 wrong guesses and there are some remaining letters that the player hasn't guessed. Within that loop, the first two statements get a letter from the player and concatenate it to the guessed_letters variable.

The next statement uses the find() method to check whether the guessed letter is in the word. If so, it sets the displayed_word variable to an empty string and sets the remaining_letters variable to the length of the word. Then, it loops through each character in the word and adjusts the values of these variables.

Within this loop, if the letter is in the guessed_letters variable, the code concatenates that letter to the displayed_word variable and subtracts 1 from the remaining_letters variable. Otherwise, the code concatenates an underscore to the displayed_word variable. When the loop finishes, the displayed_word variable contains the correct letters interspersed with the underscores for the remaining letters, and the remaining_letters variable contains the number of letters that haven't been guessed yet.

If the guessed letter isn't in the word, the code adds 1 to the variable that stores the number of wrong guesses. That ends the if statement in the loop. Then, whether or not the letter is in the word, the code adds 1 to the variable that stores the total number of guesses. Next, this code calls the draw_screen() function to draw the screen with the new variables.

When the player makes 10 wrong guesses or guesses all of the letters in the word, the while loop ends. Then, the code prints a line of 79 dashes and uses an if statement to check whether the remaining_letters variable equals zero. Then, it either prints a "Congratulations!" message or a "Sorry, you lost" message.

This module ends with the main() function and the statement that calls it. Here, the main() function enters a while loop that lets the players play one or more games.

The hangman module (continued)

```python
# The input/process/draw technique is common in game programming
def play_game():
    word = get_word()

    word_length = len(word)
    remaining_letters = word_length
    displayed_word = "_" * word_length

    num_wrong = 0
    num_guesses = 0
    guessed_letters = ""

    draw_screen(num_wrong, num_guesses, guessed_letters, displayed_word)

    while num_wrong < 10 and remaining_letters > 0:
        guess = get_letter(guessed_letters)
        guessed_letters += guess

        pos = word.find(guess, 0)
        if pos != -1:
            displayed_word = ""
            remaining_letters = word_length
            for char in word:
                if char in guessed_letters:
                    displayed_word += char
                    remaining_letters -= 1
                else:
                    displayed_word += "_"
        else:
            num_wrong += 1

        num_guesses += 1

        draw_screen(num_wrong, num_guesses, guessed_letters, displayed_word)

    print("-" * 79)
    if remaining_letters == 0:
        print("Congratulations! You got it in",
              num_guesses, "guesses.")
    else:
        print("Sorry, you lost.")
        print("The word was:", word)

def main():
    print("Play the H A N G M A N game")
    while True:
        play_game()
        print()
        again = input("Do you want to play again (y/n)?: ").lower()
        if again != "y":
            break

if __name__ == "__main__":
    main()
```

Figure 10-11   The code for the Hangman game (part 2)

Perspective

In this chapter, you've learned the string-handling skills that are often used for validating user entries. You've learned how to split a string into a list of strings and how to join the items in a list into a string, which can be useful when you're working with text files. You've also seen how these skills can be used for getting statistics from strings and for writing game programs.

Terms

Unicode	delimiter
ordinal	sequence
immutable	

Summary

- In Python 3 and later, *Unicode* maps each character to an integer (*ordinal*) value that also determines the sort order of the characters. To get the ordinal value for a character, you can use the built-in ord() function.

- To access the characters in a string, you can use positive and negative indexes starting with index 0 for the first character and -1 for the last character. You can also use the len() function to get the length of a string.

- You can use the in operator to search for a substring within a string, and you can use a for loop to loop through the characters in a string.

- Python provides many methods for working with strings, including the find() and replace() methods.

- You can use the split() method to split a string into a list of strings based on a specified *delimiter*. You can use the join() method to join a list of strings into a single string that separates the list items with the specified delimiter.

- Strings are *immutable*, which means they can't be changed. So if you want to keep the changes made by a string method, you need to assign the string that's returned to a new variable.

Exercise 10-1   Enhance the Create Account program

In this exercise, you'll enhance the Create Account program in figure 10-5 so it gets a valid email address and a valid phone number, as shown here:

```
Enter full name:        Joel Murach
Enter password:         Extra54321
Enter email address:    joelmurach.com
Please enter a valid email address.
Enter email address:    joel.murach@com
Please enter a valid email address.
Enter email address:    joel@murach.com
Enter phone number:     (555) 555-555
Please enter a 10-digit phone number.
Enter phone number:     (555) 555-SPAM
Please enter a 10-digit phone number.
Enter phone number:     (555) 555-5555

Hi Joel, thanks for creating an account.
We'll text your confirmation code to this number: 555.555.5555
```

1. In IDLE, open the create_account.py file that's in this folder:
    python/exercises/ch10

2. Create and use a function to get a valid email address. To be valid, the address has to contain an @ sign and end with ".com".

3. Create and use a function to get a valid phone number. To do that, remove all spaces, dashes, parens, and periods from the number. Then, check to make sure it the phone number consists of 10 characters that are digits.

4. When all of the entries are valid, display the message shown above, including the phone number format that uses dots to group the digits.

Exercise 10-2   Enhance the Word Counter program

In this exercise, you'll enhance the Word Counter program in figure 10-9 so it also displays the number of sentences in the text string, as shown here:

```
The Word Counter program

Number of sentences = 11
Number of words = 260
Number of unique words =   142
Unique word occurrences:
    a = 7
    ...
```

1. In IDLE, open the word_counter.py file that's in this folder:
    python/exercises/ch10

2. Create and use a function to get the number of sentences. To keep this simple, this function can read the text file just as the function for getting the number of words does. Then, the main() function should display the number of sentences as shown above.

Exercise 10-3   Enhance the Hangman game

In this exercise, you'll enhance the Hangman game in figure 10-11 so it displays
a graphic hangman as shown here:

```
Play the H A N G M A N game
_____
      |
      O
     \|/
      |
     / \


-----------------------------------------------------------------
_____
      |

Word: _ _ _ _     Guesses: 0    Wrong: 0    Tried:
Enter a letter: b
-----------------------------------------------------------------
_____
      |
      O

Word: _ _ _ _     Guesses: 1    Wrong: 1    Tried: B
Enter a letter: f
-----------------------------------------------------------------
     (The game continues)
-----------------------------------------------------------------
_____
      |
      O
     \|/
      |
     / \

Word: _ A _ E     Guesses: 9    Wrong: 7    Tried: B F A E I C D G H
-----------------------------------------------------------------
Sorry, you lost.
The word was: RAKE
```

1. In IDLE, open the hangman.py file that's in this folder:
    `python/exercises/ch10`

2. Enhance this program so it displays a hangman graphic when the program
    starts as shown above. This hangman consists of the letter O, bars, slashes,
    and backslashes. To display it, create a draw_hangman() function that is called
    from the main() function.

3. Enhance this program so it adds one character to the hangman each time the
    player guesses wrong, starting with O for the head. To do this, enhance the
    draw_hangman() function so it gets the number of wrong guesses as its only
    argument. Then, it should display that many hangman characters. This function
    should be called by the draw_screen() function as well as the main() function.
    In this version of the game, the player only gets 7 wrong guesses. So, make
    sure to modify the program accordingly.

11

How to work with dates and times

In the last two chapters, you learned how to work with two of the essential data types: numbers and strings. Now, you'll learn how to work with a third essential type: dates and times. These skills are important because you use dates and times in most applications, from business applications to games.

Although Python provides several modules for working with dates and times, this chapter shows you how to use the datetime module. That's because it's the most useful module. Note, however, that this module is somewhat different than most of the other modules you have been using because it is an *object-oriented module*. As a result, you will work with classes, constructors, methods, and attributes.

The good news is that the syntax is similar to what you're familiar with so you shouldn't have any trouble using this module. That will be especially true if you've already read chapter 14 on object-oriented programming.

How to get started with dates and times

This topic shows you how to get started with dates and times. As you might expect, the first step is to create an object that stores a date, a time, or a date and a time.

How to create date, time, and datetime objects

Figure 11-1 begins by showing two methods and three constructors that you can use to create a date object, a time object, or a datetime object. As you will learn in chapter 14, a *constructor* is a special type of method that is used to create *objects*.

Collectively, the objects created by the constructors in this figure can be referred to as *date/time objects*. You can use the date() constructor to create a *date object* that contains a date, but not a time. You can use the time() constructor to create a *time object* that contains a time, but not a date. And you can use the datetime() constructor to create a *datetime* object that contains a date and a time.

Before you create a date/time object, you import one or more classes from the datetime module. As you will also learn in chapter 14, a *class* contains the constructors and methods that can be used to create and work with objects.

In the first group of examples in this figure, the statements import the date, time, and datetime classes. Then, the second example shows another way to import all three of these classes. Of course, you only need to import the classes that you're going to use.

The third example uses the today() and now() methods to create date/time objects. Here, the first statement calls the today() method directly from the date class to get a date object for the current date. Then, the second statement calls the now() method directly from the datetime class to get a datetime object for the current date and time.

The fourth example uses the constructors of the date, time, and datetime classes to create date/time objects. Here, the first statement creates a date object for October 31, 1988. The second statement creates a time object for 2:30 PM by using the 24-hour notation to supply the hour (2 PM is 14 hours into the 24-hour day). And the third statement creates a datetime object. Since this code doesn't set the seconds, they default to 0. Finally, the fourth statement creates a datetime object that sets seconds.

Note that none of the examples set the milliseconds or microseconds. Since a *millisecond* is one thousandth of a second and a *microsecond* is one millionth of a second, few applications need to track time that precisely.

You should also know that all of the objects in this chapter are *naïve*. This means that they are not *aware* of time zones or daylight savings time. If you want to create datetime and time objects that are aware, you can set the optional tzinfo parameter of the datetime() and time() constructors, but you won't need to do that for most applications.

Two common methods of the date and datetime classes

Method	Description
`date.today()`	Returns a date object for the current date.
`datetime.now()`	Returns a datetime object for the current date and time.

The constructors for creating date, time, and datetime objects

Constructor	Description
`date(year, month, day)`	Returns a date object set to the specified date.
`time([hour][, min][, sec][, microsec])`	Returns a time object set to the specified time. All time arguments are optional and default to 0.
`datetime(year, month, day` `[,hour][, min][, sec][, microsec])`	Returns a datetime object for the specified date and time. All time arguments are optional and default to 0.

Code that imports the date, time, and datetime classes

```
from datetime import date
from datetime import time
from datetime import datetime
```

Another way to import the date, time, and datetime classes

```
from datetime import date, time, datetime
```

Code that uses methods to create date and datetime objects

```
invoice_date = date.today()                        # Current date
invoice_date = datetime.now()                       # Current date and time
```

Code that uses constructors to create naïve date/time objects

```
halloween = date(1988, 10, 31)                      # 10/31/1988
meeting = time(14, 30)                              # 2:30 PM
appointment = datetime(2016, 10, 28, 14, 30)        # 10/28/2016 2:30 PM
entry_time = datetime(2017, 10, 28, 14, 32, 48)     # 10/28/2017 2:32:48 PM
```

Description

- The datetime module contains *constructors* for constructing dates and times. To use constructors, you pass arguments to them in the same way that you pass arguments to methods.

- Both datetime objects and time objects can be either *aware* or *naïve*. Aware objects account for time zones and daylight savings time. Naïve objects do not.

- By default, datetime objects and time objects are naïve. However, you can make them aware by providing an optional tzinfo argument that you can learn about in the documentation for the datetime module.

- You can't make date objects aware because they don't store time info.

- A *millisecond* is one thousandth of a second. A *microsecond* is one millionth of a second, or one thousand milliseconds.

Figure 11-1   How to create date, time, and datetime objects

How to create datetime objects by parsing strings

When creating date/time objects, it's common to need to create a datetime object from a string. For example, in a console application, you may want to prompt the user to enter a string for a date or time. Then, you may want to convert the string entered by the user to a datetime object. To do that, you can use the strptime() method of the datetime class as shown in figure 11-2. Here, the p stands for *parse*. In other words, you can use this method to create a datetime object by parsing a string.

The strptime() method accepts two arguments: (1) the string representation of the date and time and (2) a format string that specifies what each part of the input string represents. The table in this figure shows the most commonly used formatting codes for the format string, although the datetime module provides many more.

The first example shows how this works. Here, the first statement sets a date using the common U.S. format of MM/DD/YYYY. In other words, the month goes first, followed by a slash, followed by the day, followed by another slash, followed by the year. Since this doesn't specify a time, all of the time values default to 0.

The second and third statements work similarly. However, the second statement sets a date using the common European format of DD-MM-YYYY, and the third statement sets a date using the ISO format of YYYY-MM-DD.

The fourth statement sets both a date and a time. In this case the format string specifies the date in the common U.S. format of MM/DD/YYYY, and it specifies the time in the normal format of hours and minutes, where the hours and minutes are separated by a colon, and the hours are in 24-hour format.

The second example shows how to get a date from a user. Here, the first statement prompts the user to enter a date in the MM/DD/YYYY format. Then, the second statement parses the string entered by the user into a datetime object. Next, the third statement prints the datetime object to the console. This displays the date using the default format of YYYY-MM-DD HH:MM:SS. Since this code didn't prompt the user to enter a time, it probably doesn't make a lot of sense to display the hours, minutes, and seconds here. Fortunately, you can format date/time objects as described in the next figure so they only display the parts that you want to display.

The strptime() method of the datetime class

Method	Description
`datetime.strptime(datetime_str, format_str)`	Uses the specified format string to convert the date/time string to a datetime object.

Common format string codes

Code	Description
`%d`	Day of month as a number
`%m`	Month as a number
`%y`	2-digit year
`%Y`	4-digit year
`%H`	Hour of day in 24 hour format
`%M`	Minute as number
`%S`	Second as number

Code that creates datetime objects using format strings

```python
halloween = datetime.strptime("10/31/1988", "%m/%d/%Y")
halloween = datetime.strptime("31-10-1988", "%d-%m-%Y")
halloween = datetime.strptime("1988-10-31", "%Y-%m-%d")
halloween = datetime.strptime("10/31/1988 22:30", "%m/%d/%Y %H:%M")
```

Code that gets a date from the user and prints it to the console

```python
date_str = input("Enter date of birth (MM/DD/YYYY): ")
birth_date = datetime.strptime(date_str, "%m/%d/%Y")
print("Date of birth:", birth_date)
```

The console

```
Enter date of birth (MM/DD/YYYY): 2/4/1968
Date of birth: 1968-02-04 00:00:00
```

Description

- The p in the strptime() method stands for *parse*. You can use this method to create a datetime object by parsing a string. To specify the format of the string, you can use format string codes.

Figure 11-2   How to create datetime objects by parsing strings

How to format dates and times

Figure 11-3 shows how to use the strftime() method of a date/time object to *format* a date/time object. This method accepts a single argument that specifies a format string. This string works similarly to the format string for the strptime() method described in the previous figure.

The table in the figure shows some of the most common formatting codes that you can use in formatting strings. Many are the same as in the previous figure. Most are self-explanatory, except for the last three.

The %c specifier prints the current date and time according to what is common in the locale for the current computer. For example, in the United States, this would print the abbreviated day of the week, followed the abbreviated month, followed by the day, and then the time. In other locales, the output might look different.

The %x format character gets the shorthand notation for the current date according to the current locale. For example, in the U.S, it gets 10/31/88. In most European countries, where it's conventional to list the day before the month, it would print 31-10-16. Finally, the %X format character prints the current time according to local formatting conventions.

The first example creates a datetime object for a date of October 31, 1988 and a time of 22:48. Then, the next two examples format this date.

The second example shows six statements that format a datetime object. Here, the statements show that you don't have to include the time in the format, even though the datetime object stores hours and minutes. They show how to use names for the month and the day. And they show how to work with the 24-hour and 12-hour formats.

The third example shows two statements that print the date and time according to conventions used in a locale. Here, the first statement prints the date and time according to the local conventions, and the second statement prints the date only.

Although the table in this figure contains the most common formatting codes, many other format codes are available. For more information, you can view the documentation for the strftime() method.

The strftime() method of all date/time objects

Method	Description
`strftime(format_str)`	Uses the specified format string to convert a date/time object to a formatted string.

Some commonly used formatting codes

Code	Description	Example
`%a`	Abbreviated weekday name	`Sat`
`%A`	Full weekday name	`Saturday`
`%b`	Abbreviated month name	`Oct`
`%B`	Full month name	`October`
`%d`	Zero-padded day of month as a number	`01`
`%m`	Zero-padded month as a number	`01`
`%Y`	4-digit year	`1977`
`%y`	2-digit year	`77`
`%H`	Hour of day in 24-hour format	`13`
`%I`	Hour of day in 12-hour format	`01`
`%M`	Minute as number	`59`
`%S`	Second as number	`59`
`%p`	AM/PM specifier	`AM`
`%f`	Microsecond	`0153219`
`%c`	Date and time formatted for locale	`Mon Oct 31 01:15:15 2016`
`%x`	Date formatted for locale	`10/31/16`
`%X`	Time formatted for locale	`01:15:15`

Code that creates a datetime object that has a date and time

```
halloween = datetime(1988, 10, 31, 22, 48)
```

Code that uses format codes to specify format

```
halloween.strftime("%Y-%m-%d")              # 1988-10-31
halloween.strftime("%m/%d/%Y")              # 10/31/1988
halloween.strftime("%m/%d/%y")              # 10/31/88
halloween.strftime("%B %d, %Y (%A)")        # October 31, 1988 (Monday)
halloween.strftime("%B %d, %H:%M")          # October 31, 22:48
halloween.strftime("%B %d, %I:%M %p")       # October 31, 10:48 PM
```

Code that formats for locale

```
halloween.strftime("%c")                    # Mon Oct 31 22:48:00 1988
halloween.strftime("%x")                    # 10/31/88
```

Description

- The f in the strftime() method stands for *format*. You can use this method to get a string for the datetime object with the specified format.

Figure 11-3   How to format dates and times

How to work with spans of time

Figure 11-4 shows how you can use a *timedelta object* to work with a *span of time*. This allows you to add a span of time to a date/time object or to subtract a span of time from date/time object. In addition, it allows you to store the span of time that's returned when you subtract one date/time object from another.

The constructor of the timedelta class accepts seven possible arguments. Typically, since you only need to specify one or two of these arguments, you use named arguments. That's also a good coding practice since it makes your code easier to read and understand.

The first example shows how to import the timedelta class from the datetime module. Then, the second example shows how to create three time spans. This shows how you can use one or more arguments to specify time spans of different lengths.

The third example shows how to add and subtract a time span from a date/time object. Here, the first statement adds a time span to create a new date object that's exactly 3 weeks from the current date. The second statement subtracts a time span to create a new date object that's exactly 3 weeks before the current date. And the third statement creates a new datetime object that's exactly 3 hours from now. Depending on the current time, this may or may not cause the date to change. For example, if the current date and time is December 31, 2017 22:00, this causes the new datetime object to be January 1, 2018 01:00.

The fourth example shows how to get the time span between two different date/time objects. To do that, you can subtract one date from the other. This returns a timedelta object that stores the time span. In this example, the first statement creates a datetime object for Halloween 2017. Then, the second subtracts the current date and time from the first datetime object to get a timedelta object. Note, however, that you will get a negative time span if the current date is after Halloween 2017.

After that, the next four statements use three of the *attributes* and one method of the timedelta object to get the days, seconds, microseconds, and total seconds including microseconds. Here, the seconds and microseconds are added to the days value. In other words, the seconds attribute doesn't store the total number of seconds. If you want to get the total number of seconds, including microseconds, you can call the total_seconds() method of the timedelta object.

The last two statements print representations of the time span. To start, the first statement prints the number of days, seconds, and microseconds between the two datetime objects. Then, the second statement prints the total number of seconds. You can see the results in the console below these statements.

The last example shows another way to get the time span between two dates. It works like the fifth example, but it doesn't create a variable name for the result of the calculation. Instead, it encloses the calculation in parentheses and gets the days attribute of the timedelta object directly from the result of the calculation.

The constructor for a timedelta object

```
timedelta([days][, seconds][, microseconds][, milliseconds]
          [, minutes][, hours][, weeks])
```

Code that imports the timedelta class

```
from datetime import timedelta
```

Code that creates time spans

```
three_weeks = timedelta(weeks=3)
two_hours_thirty_minues = timedelta(hours=2, minutes=30)
time_span = timedelta(weeks=2, days=3, hours=8, minutes=14)
```

Code that adds and subtracts a span of time

```
three_weeks_from_today = date.today() + timedelta(weeks=3)
three_weeks_ago = date.today() - timedelta(weeks=3)
three_hours_from_now = datetime.now() + timedelta(hours=3)
```

Three attributes and a method of a timedelta object

Attribute/method	Description
`days`	Number of days.
`seconds`	Number of seconds in addition to days.
`microseconds`	Number of microseconds in addition to days and seconds.
`total_seconds()`	Total number of seconds and microseconds.

Code that gets the time span between two date objects

```
halloween = datetime(2017, 10, 31)
time_span = halloween - datetime.now()         # Time span between dates

days = time_span.days                          # Number of days
seconds = time_span.seconds                    # Number of seconds
microseconds = time_span.microseconds          # Number of microseconds
total_seconds = time_span.total_seconds()      # Total seconds / microseconds

print(days, "days", seconds, "seconds, and", microseconds, "microseconds.")
print(total_seconds, "seconds and microseconds.")
```

The console

```
405 days, 34951 seconds, and 289282 microseconds.
35026951.289282 seconds and microseconds.
```

Another way to get the time span between two dates

```
days = (halloween - datetime.now()).days    # Number of days
```

Description

- A timedelta object stores a *span of time*.

- You can adjust a date or datetime object by adding or subtracting a timedelta object.

- You can get the span of time between two date/time objects by subtracting one from the other. This returns a timedelta object that contains days, seconds, and microseconds.

Figure 11-4   How to work with spans of time

The Invoice Due Date program

Figure 11-5 presents a program that uses some of the skills presented so far in this chapter. The user interface for this program prompts the user to enter an invoice date in the MM/DD/YY format. Then, it displays the invoice date, the due date, and the current date. In this case, the program calculates the due date as 30 days after the invoice date. If the invoice is overdue, the program displays a message that indicates the number of days overdue. Otherwise, the program displays a message that indicates the number of days until due.

The code for this program begins by importing the datetime and timedelta classes from the datetime module. These are the only two classes needed by this program.

This is followed by the get_invoice_date() function. The first statement in this function prompts the user to enter an invoice date in MM/DD/YY format and stores the user entry as a string. The second statement uses the strptime() method to parse the string into a datetime object. This object is then returned to the main() function.

The main() function contains a while loop that executes until the user exits the program. The first statement in this loop calls the get_invoice_date() function to get the datetime object for the invoice date.

After getting the invoice date object, the main() function calculates the due date by adding 30 days to the object. Next, the code gets the current date. Then, it calculates the number of days between the two dates by subtracting the due date from the current date and storing the result in a variable named days_overdue.

After calculating the days overdue, this code prints the dates to the console. To do that, it uses the strftime() method to return a string for each datetime object that's in a user-friendly format. Then, the code checks whether the days_overdue variable stores a value that's greater than 0. If so, the code prints a message that indicates the number of days overdue. Otherwise, the days_overdue variable stores a negative value or a value of 0. In that case, the code multiplies the days_overdue variable by -1 to convert it to a positive number that represents the number of days until the invoice is due. Then, it prints a message that indicates the number of days until due.

As you review this code, note that it stores all of the dates as datetime objects. In other words, even though the user interface only displays the date part of the object, the program stores the time part too. For the invoice date, the user doesn't enter a time part, so it's set to 00:00:00.0000000. Similarly, since the due date is calculated by adding 30 days, its time part is also 00:00:00.0000000.

The user interface

```
The Invoice Due Date program

Enter the invoice date (MM/DD/YY): 7/14/17

Invoice Date: July 14, 2017
Due Date:     August 13, 2017
Current Date: September 12, 2017

This invoice is 30 day(s) overdue.

Continue? (y/n):
```

The code

```python
from datetime import datetime, timedelta

def get_invoice_date():
    invoice_date_str = input("Enter the invoice date (MM/DD/YY): ")
    invoice_date = datetime.strptime(invoice_date_str, "%m/%d/%y")
    return invoice_date

def main():
    print("The Invoice Due Date program")
    print()

    while True:
        invoice_date = get_invoice_date()
        print()

        # calculate due date and days overdue
        due_date = invoice_date + timedelta(days=30)
        current_date = datetime.now()
        days_overdue = (current_date - due_date).days

        # display results
        print("Invoice Date: " + invoice_date.strftime("%B %d, %Y"))
        print("Due Date:     " + due_date.strftime("%B %d, %Y"))
        print("Current Date: " + current_date.strftime("%B %d, %Y"))
        if days_overdue > 0:
            print("This invoice is", days_overdue, "day(s) overdue.")
        else:
            days_due = days_overdue * -1
            print("This invoice is due in", days_due, "day(s).")
        print()

        # ask if user wants to continue
        result = input("Continue? (y/n): ")
        print()
        if result.lower() != "y":
            print("Bye!")
            break

if __name__ == "__main__":
    main()
```

Figure 11-5   The Invoice Due Date program

The Timer program

Now that you've seen a program that works with dates, you're ready to see a program that works with times like the Timer program presented in figure 11-6. The user interface for this program begins by prompting the user to press Enter to start the timer. When the user presses Enter, the program displays the date and time for the start time. Then, it prompts the user to press Enter to stop the timer. When the user presses Enter the second time, the program displays the date and time for the stop time. In addition, it displays the amount of time that has elapsed between the start and stop times.

The code begins by importing the datetime and time classes from the datetime module. These are the only classes used by this program.

Then, this code gets the start time. To do that, it uses an input statement to prompt the user to press Enter. This pauses the program until the user presses Enter. When the user presses that key, the code gets the current date and time, stores it in the start_time variable, and prints it to the console. Incidentally, an empty string is returned when the user presses the Enter key, but there's no need to store it in a variable.

The code that gets the stop time works similarly. Then, after getting the start and stop times, the program calculates the elapsed time. To do that, it subtracts the start time from the stop time. This returns a timedelta object that stores the days, seconds, and microseconds for the elapsed time. Then, to convert the seconds to minutes, this code uses integer division ($//$) to divide the seconds by 60. To get the leftover seconds, it uses the remainder operator. And to get the microseconds, it uses the microsecond attribute,

The next two statements use a similar technique to break down the minutes into hours and leftover minutes. Then, the code creates a time object from the hours, minutes, seconds, and microseconds. Last, it displays the elapsed time by printing the time object to the console. But first, it checks whether the number of days is greater than 1. If so, it prints the number of elapsed days to the console before it prints the elapsed time to the console. Of course, it would be unusual for a user to wait more than a day to press Enter the second time, but this provides for that possibility.

As you review this code, note that it uses the default display format for the datetime objects for the start time and end time, and it uses the default display format for the time object for the elapsed time. For this program, these formats are adequate. If necessary, though, you could use the strftime() method to change the formatting for these objects.

The user interface

```
The Timer program

Press Enter to start...
Start time: 2016-09-16 15:24:08.633025

Press Enter to stop...
Stop time:  2016-09-16 15:24:25.320605

ELAPSED TIME
Time: 00:00:16.687580
```

The code

```python
from datetime import datetime, time

def main():
    print("The Timer program")
    print()

    # start timer
    input("Press Enter to start...")
    start_time = datetime.now()
    print("Start time:", start_time)
    print()

    # stop timer
    input("Press Enter to stop...")
    stop_time = datetime.now()
    print("Stop time: ", stop_time)
    print()

    # calculate elapsed time
    elapsed_time = stop_time - start_time
    days = elapsed_time.days
    minutes = elapsed_time.seconds // 60
    seconds = elapsed_time.seconds % 60
    microseconds = elapsed_time.microseconds

    # calculate hours and minutes
    hours = minutes // 60
    minutes = minutes % 60

    # create time object
    time_object = time(hours, minutes, seconds, microseconds)

    # display results
    print("ELAPSED TIME")
    if days > 0:
        print("Days:", days)
    print("Time:", time_object)

if __name__ == "__main__":
    main()
```

Figure 11-6   The Timer program

More skills for working with dates and times

If you understand the Invoice Due Date program and the Timer programs, you have already learned the most useful skills for working with dates and times. However, there's always more to learn. That's why this chapter continues by presenting two more skills that you commonly need when you work with dates and times.

How to get date and time parts

Earlier in this chapter, you learned how to use the constructors of the date/time classes to create date/time objects by specifying int values for the year, month, day, hour, minute, second, and microsecond. Now, figure 11-7 shows how to get those values from a date/time object. To do that, you can call the attributes summarized at the top of this figure. However, date objects only provide the year, month, and day attributes. Similarly, time objects only provide the hour, minute, second, and microsecond attributes.

The first example shows how to access each attribute. To start, the first statement creates a datetime object for October 31, 1988 14:32:30. Since this statement doesn't set the microsecond attribute, it defaults to 0.

When you work with dates and times, you sometimes need to use an if statement to check part of the object as shown in the second example. Here, the first statement gets a date object for the current day. Then, the second statement checks whether the month is 10 and the day is 31. If so, it prints a message that says, "Happy Halloween!". Otherwise, it prints a message that indicates that it's not Halloween.

Other times, you may need to create a new date/time object that's based on the parts of an existing date/time object as shown in the third example. Here, the first statement gets a date object for the current date. Then, the second statement gets the previous year by subtracting 1 from the current year. Finally, the third statement creates a new date object that uses the same month and day as the current date, but uses the previous year as the year. In other words, it creates a date object for one year ago today.

The fourth example works like the third example. However, it adjusts the datetime object by adding 1 to the year. In addition, it creates a datetime object that includes non-default values for the hour and minute.

Attributes that return the parts of a date/time object

Attribute	Description
year	Returns the year as a four-digit number
month	Returns the month as a number from 1 to 12
day	Returns the day as a number from 1 to 31
hour	Returns the hour as a number from 0 to 23
minute	Returns the minute as a number from 0 to 59
second	Returns the second as a number from 0 to 59
microsecond	Returns the microsecond as a number from 0 to 9999999

Code that gets the parts of a datetime object

```
halloween = datetime(1988, 10, 31, 14, 32, 30)
year = halloween.year                    # 1988
month = halloween.month                  # 10
day = halloween.day                      # 31
hour = halloween.hour                    # 14
minute = halloween.minute                # 32
second = halloween.second                # 30
microsecond = halloween.microsecond      # 0
```

Code that checks parts of a date object

```
today = date.today()
if (today.month == 10 and today.day == 31):
    print("Happy Halloween!")
else:
    print("Dang, it's not Halloween today.")
```

Code that creates a new date based on the current date

```
today = date.today()
last_year = today.year - 1
one_year_ago_today = date(last_year, today.month, today.day)
```

Code that creates a new date and time based on the current date and time

```
now = datetime.now()
this_time_next_year = datetime(now.year + 1, now.month, now.day,
                               now.hour, now.minute)
```

Description

- You can get the various parts of a date/time object by accessing its attributes.
  However, these attributes are read-only, so you can't set them.

Figure 11-7   How to get date and time parts

How to compare date/time objects

Figure 11-8 shows how you can compare date/time objects. In Python, this is easy to do because you can use the same comparison operators that you use to compare numbers.

The first example begins by getting a date object for the current day. Then, it creates a date object for Halloween 2017. Next, an if statement checks whether the current date is greater than, less than, or equal to Halloween 2017. Each clause within the statement prints an appropriate message.

In the first example, checking for equality works because both objects are date objects. As a result, this example checks whether the year, month, and day are equal. However, if you were using datetime objects, the equality checking would only work if the time parts were also equal.

The second example prints the number of days until Halloween. Here, the first statement gets a date object for the current date. Then, the second statement creates a date object for the Halloween that's in the same year as the current date. Next, an if statement checks whether Halloween is after the current date, which is true for all dates in November and December. In that case, this code adjusts the date object for Halloween by creating a new date object that's one year later. Then, it gets and displays the number of days until Halloween.

The third example works much like the first example. However, it checks whether the current date and time are within the specified start and end times for the meeting, which is an hour long. In addition, it checks whether the current time is less than the start time or greater than the end time.

The fourth example uses the comparison operators to automatically adjust a two-digit year so it's correct for the program. Here, the first statement prompts the user to enter a birth date in this format MM/DD/YY. This makes it easy for the user to enter a year. Then, the second statement parses the string and converts it to a datetime object. Unfortunately, if the user enters a year in the 1900s, this converts the year into the 2000s. For example, if the user enters 2/4/68, this returns a year of 2068, not 1968, which would be correct for a birth date.

To fix this issue, this code checks whether the birth date year is greater than the current year. If so, it subtracts 100 from the birth date year. For example, it would subtract 100 from 2068 to return a value of 1968. Then, it creates a new datetime object for the correct birth date. Finally, this example prints the birth date to the console with a 4-digit year format, so you can make sure that the code has corrected the date.

Of course, this code doesn't work correctly for people who are over 100 years old. For example, if you were born in 1915, this program would not adjust the two-digit year correctly.

Code that compares two date objects

```
today = date.today()
halloween = date(2017, 10, 31)
if today > halloween:
    print("Halloween 2017 has come and gone.")
elif today < halloween:
    print("Halloween 2017 is coming soon.")
elif today == halloween:
    print("Happy Halloween 2017!")
```

Code that prints the number of days until Halloween

```
today = date.today()
halloween = date(today.year, 10, 31)
if today > halloween:
    next_year = today.year + 1
    halloween = date(next_year, 10, 31)
days_until = (halloween - today).days
print(days_until, "day(s) until Halloween.")
```

Code that compares two datetime objects

```
meeting_start = datetime(2017, 12, 2, 9, 30)
meeting_end = meeting_start + timedelta(hours=1)
now = datetime.now()
if now > meeting_start and now < meeting_end:
    print("This meeting is happening now.")
elif now < meeting_start:
    print("This meeting is coming up.")
elif now > meeting_end:
    print("This meeting already took place.")
```

Code that automatically adjusts a two-digit year to be correct

```
# get input and convert to a datetime object
birth_date = input("Enter birth date (MM/DD/YY): ")
birth_date = datetime.strptime(birth_date, "%m/%d/%y")

# if necessary, subtract 100 to fix birth year
if birth_date > datetime.now():
    fixed_birth_year = birth_date.year-100
    birth_date = datetime(fixed_birth_year, birth_date.month,
                          birth_date.day)

print("Birth date: " + birth_date.strftime("%m/%d/%Y"))
```

The console

```
Enter date of birth (MM/DD/YY): 2/4/68
Date of birth: 02/04/1968
```

Description

- You can use the comparison operators to compare date/time objects just like you can use them to compare numbers.

Figure 11-8   How to compare date/time objects

The Hotel Reservation program

To illustrate the use of many of the skills presented so far, this chapter ends with a Hotel Reservation program. As the user interface shows, it begins by prompting the user for an arrival date and a departure date in the YYYY-MM-DD format. Once the user enters those dates, the user interface prints the arrival date, the departure date, and the price per night in user-friendly formats. In addition, it prints the total number of nights and the total price, also in user-friendly formats.

If the arrival date is in August, the price per night is $105 and the user interface displays a message that indicates that August is high season. Otherwise, the price per night is $85 and the user interface doesn't display any message about the price per night.

The code for this program begins by importing the datetime class from the datetime module. This is the only class needed to work with the dates and times in the program. In addition, the code imports the locale module that is presented in chapter 9. This is the module that's used to format the currency values. This is followed by the code for the two functions that are called by the main() function.

The get_arrival_date() function gets a valid arrival date. It begins by entering a loop that continues as long as the arrival date isn't valid. Within this loop, the first statement prompts the user to enter the arrival date in the YYYY-MM-DD format. However, if the strptime() method isn't able to parse the string entered by the user into a datetime object, a ValueError occurs. As a result, a try statement is used to catch this error, print an error message, and let the execution continue at the top of the loop. If the user enters a date in the valid format, though, the code creates a datetime object for the arrival date.

At this point, the code checks whether the arrival date is today or later. To do that, this code creates a datetime object named today that stores the current year, month, and day. However, since this code doesn't set the time values, they all default to 0. As a result, all of the dates used by this program are actually datetime objects with the time values set to 0. This allows the comparisons and calculations of this program to work correctly.

If the arrival date is less than today, this code displays an error message and code execution continues at the top of the loop, which prompts the user for another arrival date. Otherwise, this code returns the arrival date, which ends the loop.

The user interface

```
The Hotel Reservation program

Enter arrival date (YYYY-MM-DD): 2017-8-15
Enter departure date (YYYY-MM-DD): 2017-8-19

Arrival Date:    August 15, 2017
Departure Date: August 19, 2017
Nightly rate:    $105.00 (High season)
Total nights:    4
Total price:     $420.00

Continue? (y/n): y

Enter arrival date (YYYY-MM-DD): 2017-9-15
Enter departure date (YYYY-MM-DD): 2017-9-19

Arrival Date:    September 15, 2017
Departure Date: September 19, 2017
Nightly rate:    $85.00
Total nights:    4
Total price:     $340.00

Continue? (y/n): n

Bye!
```

The code   **Page 1**

```python
from datetime import datetime
import locale

def get_arrival_date():
    while True:
        date_str = input("Enter arrival date (YYYY-MM-DD): ")
        try:
            arrival_date = datetime.strptime(date_str, "%Y-%m-%d")
        except ValueError:
            print("Invalid date format. Try again.")
            continue

        # strip non-zero time values from datetime object
        now = datetime.now()
        today = datetime(now.year, now.month, now.day)
        if arrival_date < today:
            print("Arrival date must be today or later. Try again.")
            continue
        else:
            return arrival_date
```

Figure 11-9   The Hotel Reservation program (part 1)

The get_departure_date() function works like the get_arrival_date() function, but with a few minor differences. To start, it accepts a parameter for the arrival date. This is necessary because this function checks to make sure the departure date is after the arrival date.

In the main() function, a while statement starts the main program loop. Within this loop, the first two statements use the get_arrival_date() and get_departure_date() functions to get valid arrival and departure dates. For the get_departure_date() function, the argument specifies the arrival_date because a valid departure date must be after the arrival date.

After getting the dates from the user, the program gets the nightly rate and its corresponding message. To do that, it sets a default rate to 85.0 and it sets a default message of an empty string. However, if the month of the arrival date is August, this code sets the nightly rate to 105.0 and it sets a message of "(High Season)".

After getting the nightly rate and its message, the program calculates the total nights by subtracting the departure date from the arrival date and accessing the days attribute. Then, it calculates the total cost by multiplying the rate by the total nights.

Now that the program has calculated the results, it can format them. To do that, this code defines a date format string that specifies the full name of the month, the day of the month, a comma, and then the year. Then, it uses the setlocale() function of the locale module to set the locale so the currency values will be formatted the way the user would expect them for his or her locale. Next, it uses a series of print() functions to print the date to the console. These print() functions use the strftime() method of the datetime objects to format the dates, and they use the currency() function of the locale module to format the currency values.

Note that the print() function for the nightly rate also prints the message that's associated with the nightly rate. Of course, for most months, this message is an empty string. As a result, printing it to the console doesn't do anything.

As you review this program, you might wonder why it uses datetime objects instead of date objects. The main reason is that the strptime() method returns datetime objects, not date objects. As a result, there's no built-in way to parse a string into date objects. However, if you wanted to, you could build your own function to parse the user entry into a date object. Then, you could refactor this program to use date objects instead of datetime objects with the time values set to zero.

The code   **Page 2**

```
def get_departure_date(arrival_date):
    while True:
        date_str = input("Enter departure date (YYYY-MM-DD): ")
        try:
            departure_date = datetime.strptime(date_str, "%Y-%m-%d")
        except ValueError:
            print("Invalid date format. Try again.")
            continue

        if departure_date <= arrival_date:
            print("Departure date must be after arrival date. Try again.")
            continue
        else:
            return departure_date

def main():
    print("The Hotel Reservation program\n")
    while True:
        # get datetime objects from user
        arrival_date = get_arrival_date()
        departure_date = get_departure_date(arrival_date)
        print()

        # calculate nights and cost
        rate = 85.0
        rate_message = ""
        if arrival_date.month == 8:      # August is high season
            rate = 105.0
            rate_message = "(High season)"
        total_nights = (departure_date - arrival_date).days
        total_cost = rate * total_nights

        # format results
        date_format = "%B %d, %Y"
        locale.setlocale(locale.LC_ALL, '')
        print("Arrival Date:  ", arrival_date.strftime(date_format))
        print("Departure Date:", departure_date.strftime(date_format))
        print("Nightly rate:  ", locale.currency(rate), rate_message)
        print("Total nights:  ", total_nights)
        print("Total price:   ", locale.currency(total_cost))
        print()

        # check whether the user wants to continue
        result = input("Continue? (y/n): ")
        print()
        if result.lower() != "y":
            print("Bye!")
            break

if __name__ == "__main__":
    main()
```

Figure 11-9   The Hotel Reservation program (part 2)

Perspective

Now that you've completed this chapter, you should be able to use the datetime module to work with dates and times. For most applications, this module provides all of the functionality that you need.

You should know, however, that Python provides several other modules for working with dates and times. For instance, the calendar module provides functionality for displaying and working with calendars. And the time module provides much of the same functionality as the datetime module, but it is procedural, not object-oriented.

Terms

constructor	millisecond
class	microsecond
object	naïve object
date object	aware object
time object	timedelta object
datetime object	span of time
date/time object	attribute

Summary

- A *date object* stores the year, month, and day for a date. A *time object* stores the hours, minutes, seconds, and microseconds for a time. A *datetime object* stores both a date and a time.

- A *date/time object* is a generic term for a date object, a time object, or a datetime object.

- When you use the datetime module to work with dates and times, you import the *classes* that you need like the date, time, or datetime classes. Then, you can use the *constructors* in those classes to create date, time, and datetime objects.

- *Aware* date/time objects account for time zones and daylight savings time. *Naïve* date/time objects do not.

- The p in the strptime() method stands for *parse*. You can use this method to parse a string to create a datetime object.

- The f in the strftime() method stands for *format*. You can use this method to format a datetime object.

- A *timedelta object* stores a *span of time* that's measured in days, seconds, and microseconds. Once created, you can use the *attributes* of the object to get the values of the days, seconds, and microseconds.

Exercise 11-1   Modify the Invoice Due Date program

In this exercise, you'll modify the Invoice Due Date program so it uses date objects, not datetime objects. In addition, you'll add some code that makes sure the user enters a valid date.

```
The Invoice Due Date program

Enter the invoice date (MM/DD/YYYY): 7-14-2017
Invalid date format! Try again.
Enter the invoice date (MM/DD/YYYY): 7/14/2099
Date must be today or earlier. Try again.
Enter the invoice date (MM/DD/YYYY): 7/14/2017

Invoice Date: July 14, 2017
Due Date:     August 13, 2017
Current Date: September 12, 2017

This invoice is 30 day(s) overdue.

Continue? (y/n):
```

Review the code and make sure it works correctly

1. In IDLE, open the invoice.py file that's in this folder:

   python/exercises/ch11

2. Review the code and run the program to see how it works.

Use date objects to store the three dates

3. Modify the get_invoice_date() function so it uses a four-digit year.

4. Modify the program so it uses date objects, not datetime objects, to store the three dates. To do that, you can create a date object from the parts of the datetime object that's created in the get_invoice_date() function.

Add validation

5. Run the program, and enter an invalid date. This should cause the program to crash. Then, add code to the get_invoice_date() function that prevents the program from crashing and makes sure the user enters a valid date.

6. Add code to the get_invoice_date() function that makes sure the user enters a date that's either today or in the past.

Exercise 11-2   Modify the Timer program

In this exercise, you'll modify the Timer program so it displays the time like this:

```
The Timer program

Press Enter to start...
Start time: 15:09:53.206009

Press Enter to stop...
Stop time:  15:12:24.982324

ELAPSED TIME
Hours/minutes: 00:02
Seconds: 31.776315
```

This makes it easier to read the timer for elapsed times that are less than one day.

Review the code and test it

1. In IDLE, open the timer.py file that's in this folder:

    `python/exercises/ch11`

2. Review the code and run the program to see how it works.

Modify the way the elapsed time is displayed

3. Modify the code that displays the start and stop times so it only displays the time part, not the date part.

4. Modify the code that displays the elapsed time so it only shows hours/minutes and seconds. Also, the program should only display the hours/minutes data if it contains a non-zero value.

12

How to work with dictionaries

In chapter 6, you learned how to work with a type of data structure called a list. In this chapter, you'll learn how to work with another type of data structure called a dictionary. In other languages, dictionaries are often called associative arrays.

How to get started with dictionaries

Like a list, a *dictionary* stores a collection of items. However, a list stores a collection of *ordered* items, and a dictionary stores a collection of *unordered* items. In other words, when you work with a list, the items always stay in the sequence in which you insert them. That's why a list is known as a *sequence*. However, when you work with a dictionary, the items typically don't stay in the sequence in which you insert them.

How to create a dictionary

Figure 12-1 shows how to create a dictionary. To do this, you enclose the dictionary inside braces (`{}`). Within these braces, each dictionary entry consists of a *key*, followed by a colon, and a *value* that corresponds with the key. This is known as a *key/value pair*. In other words, unlike lists, which are accessed by an integer index, dictionaries are accessed by a key that's typically a string but can be any immutable data type.

The examples in this figure show how this works. The first example uses a string as the key. This string contains a two-letter code for a country. Each key corresponds with the name of the country, which is also stored as a string.

The second example uses numbers as keys. But even when you use numbers as keys, Python doesn't guarantee that it will maintain the sequence of the numbers. In fact, for efficiency, Python may reorder the key/value pairs in a dictionary at any time. As a result, you can't loop through the items in a dictionary and expect them to be in the same order in which you inserted them into the dictionary.

The third example creates a dictionary that stores the data for a movie. This dictionary uses a string as the key, but it uses different data types to store the values for each key. Here, the value for the name key is a string, the value for the year key is an integer, and the value for the price key is a floating-point number.

The fourth example shows how to create an empty dictionary. To do that, you just code a set of braces with nothing in between. Then, you can add items to the dictionary later as shown in the next figure.

When you create dictionaries, Python ignores the whitespace between items. As a result, you can format your code to make the structure of the dictionary obvious as shown in these examples.

The last example prints the dictionary created by the first example to the console. This is often useful when debugging code that uses dictionaries. In the console, note that the whitespace has been removed from the dictionary. Note also that the items are in a different order than they are in the statement that created the dictionary. This shows that Python doesn't maintain the sequence of the items in a dictionary.

The syntax for creating a dictionary

```
dictionary_name = {key1:value1, key2:value2 ...}
```

Code that creates dictionaries

```
# strings as keys and values
countries = {"CA": "Canada",
             "US": "United States",
             "MX": "Mexico"}

# numbers as keys, strings as values
numbers = {1: "One", 2: "Two", 3: "Three", 4: "Four", 5: "Five"}

# strings as keys, values of mixed types
movie = {"name": "The Holy Grail",
         "year": 1975,
         "price": 9.99}

# an empty dictionary
book_catalog = {}
```

Code that prints a dictionary to the console

```
print(countries)
```

The console

```
{'MX': 'Mexico', 'CA': 'Canada', 'US': 'United States'}
```

Description

- Unlike a list, which is an ordered collection of items, a *dictionary* is an *unordered* collection of items. As a result, there's no guarantee that the items in a dictionary remain in the same order.

- In a dictionary, each item consists of a *key/value pair* where each *value* in the dictionary is indexed by a unique *key*.

- The key can be any immutable data type, but it's usually a string.

- The value for a key can be a simple data type such as number or a string. Or, it can be a complex data type such as a list or another dictionary.

- Whitespace is ignored between dictionary items. As a result, you can use whitespace to format a dictionary so the code is easier to read.

- In some languages, dictionaries are called *associative arrays*.

Figure 12-1   How to create a dictionary

How to get, set, and add items

Figure 12-2 shows how to get, set, and add dictionary items. After the code for creating a dictionary named countries, this figure shows three ways to access items.

The first way is to use a key as shown by the syntax summary for accessing a value. In other words, you just code the key within brackets after the name of the dictionary. This is similar to coding an index to access an item in a list. Then, if the key exists in the dictionary, its value is returned. If the key doesn't exist, a KeyError occurs. This is illustrated by the first example after the syntax summary.

Then, the second example shows how to set a value for a key. To do that, you again use brackets to specify the key. Then, you can assign a new value to that key. If the key exists in the dictionary, it sets the key to the new value.

The third example shows how you can use this syntax to add a key/value pair to a dictionary. Here, if the key doesn't exist in the dictionary, the key and value are added to the dictionary.

The second way to access an item is to use the *in* keyword, as shown by the second syntax summary in this figure. This lets you check whether the key already exists in the dictionary, which can help you prevent a KeyError. It also lets you know whether you're updating or adding an item when setting values. In the example after the syntax summary, the if statement checks whether a key of "IE" is in the dictionary named countries. If so, it prints the name of the country to the console. Otherwise, it prints a message that there is no country for that key.

The third way to access an item is to use the get() method of a dictionary. This method takes a key as an argument and returns the value for that key. The advantage of the get() method is that it doesn't raise a KeyError if the key doesn't exist. Instead, by default, the get() method returns a value of None if the key doesn't exist. However, you can use the optional second argument if you want a different value returned if the key doesn't exist.

This is illustrated by the fourth example in this figure. Here, the second statement returns a value of None, which is not a string, but the third statement returns a value of "Unknown", which is a string.

The countries dictionary

```
countries = {"CA": "Canada",
             "US": "United States",
             "GB": "Great Britain",
             "MX": "Mexico"}
```

The syntax for accessing a value

```
dictionary_name[key]
```

Code that gets a value from a dictionary

```
country = countries["MX"]                 # "Mexico"
country = countries["IE"]                 # KeyError: Key doesn't exist
```

Code that sets a value if the key is in the dictionary

```
countries["GB"] = "United Kingdom"
```

Code that adds a key/value pair if the key isn't in the dictionary

```
countries["FR"] = "France"
```

The syntax for checking whether a key is in a dictionary

```
key in dictionary
```

Code that checks if a key is in a dictionary before getting its value

```
code = "IE"
if code in countries:
    country = countries[code]
    print(country)
else:
    print("There is no country for this code: " + code)
```

The get() method of a dictionary object

Method	Description
get(*key*[, *default_value*])	If the specified key exists, this method returns its value. Otherwise, this method returns None or the default value if it is supplied.

Code that uses the get() method

```
country = countries.get("MX")             # "Mexico"
country = countries.get("IE")             # None
country = countries.get("IE", "Unknown")  # "Unknown"
```

Description

- Attempting to get a value for a key that isn't in the dictionary causes a KeyError.
- If you set a value for an existing key, Python updates the old value with the new value.
- If you set a value for a key that doesn't exist, Python adds a new key/value pair to the dictionary.
- To prevent a KeyError from occurring, you can use the get() method of a dictionary.

Figure 12-2   How to get, set, and add dictionary items

How to delete items

Figure 12-3 begins by showing how to delete an item from a dictionary. To do that, you can code the del keyword, followed by the variable that contains the dictionary, and the key you want to delete within brackets. In the first example, the first statement deletes the country with a code of "MX". If the key doesn't exist in the dictionary, the del keyword causes a KeyError to occur as shown in the second statement.

To prevent the KeyError from occurring, you can check if the key exists before attempting to delete its corresponding item as shown in the second example. This works much like the if statement in the previous figure that prevents the KeyError when getting an item. However, this if statement deletes the item if its key exists.

Alternately, you can delete an item by using the pop() method of a dictionary. This method returns the value for the specified key, and it deletes the key/value pair from the dictionary. If the key doesn't exist, this method causes a KeyError to occur. However, you can prevent this error from occurring by supplying the optional second argument of the pop() method. In that case, the pop() method returns the value specified by the second argument instead of causing a KeyError to occur.

So which approach should you use to remove items from a dictionary? If you don't need to store the deleted value in a variable, they both work equally well. If you need to store the deleted value in a variable, you should use the pop() method. That's especially true if you want to prevent a KeyError from occurring. For instance, the fourth example in this figure gets the same results as the second example but with fewer lines of code.

If you want to delete all items from a dictionary, you can use the clear() method. This method deletes all key/value pairs from the dictionary, leaving an empty dictionary.

You might wonder if you can accomplish the same thing by assigning an empty dictionary to the variable like this:

```
countries = {}
```

Although this may appear to have the same effect, assigning an empty dictionary to the countries variable just causes the variable to refer to a new dictionary. It doesn't actually delete any items from the old dictionary. Since this causes problems if you have more than one variable referencing the same dictionary, you should use the clear() method to delete all items from the dictionary.

The syntax for deleting an item

```
del dictionary_name[key]
```

Code that uses the del keyword to delete an item

```
del countries["MX"]
del countries["IE"]                          # KeyError: Key doesn't exist
```

Code that checks if a key is in a dictionary before deleting the item

```
code = "IE"
if code in countries:
    country = countries[code]
    del countries[code]
    print(country + " was deleted.")
else:
    print("There is no country for this code: " + code)
```

Two dictionary methods for deleting items

Method	Description
pop(*key*[, *default_value*])	Returns the value of the specified key and deletes the key/value pair from the dictionary. The optional second argument is a value to return if the key doesn't exist.
clear()	Deletes all items.

Code that uses the pop() method to delete an item

```
country = countries.pop("US")               # "United States"
country = countries.pop("IE")               # KeyError: Key doesn't exist
country = countries.pop("IE", "Unknown")    # "Unknown"
```

Code that uses the pop() method to prevent a KeyError from occuring

```
code = "IE"
country = countries.pop(code, "Unknown country")
print(country + " was deleted.")
```

Code that uses the clear() method to delete all items

```
countries.clear()
```

Description

- You can use the del keyword or the pop() and clear() methods to delete items from a dictionary.

Figure 12-3   How to delete items from a dictionary

How to loop through keys and values

Figure 12-4 begins by showing three dictionary methods for getting keys and values. All of these methods return a *view object* that contains the keys or values of the dictionary. Since a view object is an *iterator*, you can use a loop to iterate over the values contained in the object.

A view object is also linked to the dictionary. As a result, if you modify the items in the dictionary, Python automatically updates the view object to reflect the changes.

The first example shows how you can use the keys() method to loop through all keys in a dictionary. Within the loop, the statement uses the key to get the value for each item. However, since the default iterator for a dictionary contains its keys, you can get the same result with the code in the example that follows. In other words, you don't need to explicitly call the keys() method.

The second example shows how the items() method can make it easier to loop through all keys and values. This method returns a view object that contains a tuple for each item, and the for statement unpacks this tuple into two variables. Within the for loop, the statements can use these variables to access the key and value for each item.

The third example shows how to use the values() method to loop through all of the values in a dictionary. This is useful if you want to work with the values for a dictionary but don't need to work with the corresponding keys.

The consoles for these examples show once again that dictionaries are unordered. For instance, all of the consoles display Mexico first even though Canada was added first when the dictionary was created.

If you want to sort the items for a list or keep them in some other order, you can convert a view object to a list as shown in the next figure. However, if you do this, you should realize that the list object isn't linked to the dictionary like a view object is. As a result, if the dictionary changes, the list isn't updated and vice versa.

Three dictionary methods for getting all keys and values

Method	Description
keys()	Returns a view object that contains all of the keys in the dictionary. This is the default iterator for a dictionary.
items()	Returns a view object that contains a tuple for each key/value pair in the dictionary.
values()	Returns a view object that contains all of the values in the dictionary.

Code that loops through all keys and values

```
for code in countries.keys():
    print(code + "      " + countries[code])
```

Another way to get the same result since the default iterator contains keys

```
for code in countries:
    print(code + "      " + countries[code])
```

The console

```
MX      Mexico
US      United States
CA      Canada
```

Code that unpacks a tuple as it loops through all keys and values

```
for code, name in countries.items():
    print(code + "      " + name)
```

The console

```
MX      Mexico
US      United States
CA      Canada
```

Code that loops through all values

```
for name in countries.values():
    print(name)
```

The console

```
Mexico
United States
Canada
```

Description

- These methods return a *view object*. Since a view object is an *iterator*, you can iterate over its contents with a for loop.

- You can use tuple unpacking to loop over each key/value pair in the view object.

- If a dictionary is updated, the corresponding keys or values in the view object are also updated. If you don't want these automatic updates, you can use the built-in list() constructor to convert the view object to a list as shown in the next figure.

Figure 12-4   How to loop through keys and values

How to convert between dictionaries and lists

If you need to convert a view object to a list, you can use the list() constructor as shown in the first example of figure 12-5. Here, the first statement uses the list() constructor to create a list object from the view object that's returned by the keys() method. Then, the second statement calls the sort() method of the list object to sort the keys alphabetically. Finally, the for statement loops through all of the keys in the list and displays the key from the list and the value for that key in the dictionary.

When you write code like this, remember that the list object is not linked to the dictionary as a view object would be. As a result, Python won't automatically update the list if the dictionary changes. In this example, this shouldn't cause any problems since the list is only used for a short time. However, if a long list stays in scope for a long time and is used by other parts of the program, this could cause problems if you expect it to always contain updated keys.

If you need to convert a list of lists to a dictionary, you can use the dict() constructor as shown in the second example. However, the lists within the list can only contain two items: one for the key and one for the value. In this example, the list contains three more lists, and each one contains two values. If any of the lists contain fewer or more than two values, the dict() constructor causes a ValueError that says the length of the sequence isn't correct. As you would expect, this is also true for a list of tuples or a tuple of tuples.

Built-in constructors for creating dictionaries and lists

Constructor	Description
list(*view*)	Converts the specified view object to a list.
dict(*list*)	Converts the specified two-dimensional list or tuple to a dictionary. In the two-dimensional list or tuple, each row must contain exactly two values.

Code that converts the keys of a dictionary to a list and sorts them

```
countries = {"CA": "Canada",
             "US": "United States",
             "MX": "Mexico"}
codes = list(countries.keys())
codes.sort()
for code in codes:
    print(code + "       " + countries[code])
```

The console

```
CA      Canada
MX      Mexico
US      United States
```

Code that converts a two-dimensional list to a dictionary

```
countries = [["GB", "United Kingdom"],
             ["NL", "Netherlands"],
             ["DE", "Germany"]]
countries = dict(countries)
print(countries)
```

The console

```
{'NL': 'Netherlands', 'GB': 'United Kingdom', 'DE': 'Germany'}
```

Description

- You can use two built-in constructors to convert between dictionaries and lists.

Figure 12-5   How to convert between dictionaries and lists

The Country Code program

Now that you have the basic skills for working with a dictionary, you're ready to see those skills used within the context of a program. That's why figure 12-6 presents the Country Code program.

The console for this program shows that the user can enter four commands to work with the program. If, for example, the user enters the view command, the program displays an alphabetical list of two-letter country codes. Then, it prompts the user to enter a country code. After the user enters a country code, the program displays the country name that corresponds with the code.

The add and del commands work similarly. However, they prompt the user for the required data. Then, they display a message that indicates whether the command was successful.

The code begins by defining two of the functions of the program. The display_menu() function displays the command menu for the program. The display_codes() function displays an alphabetical list of the country codes in single line, separating each code with a space.

The user interface

```
COMMAND MENU
view - View country name
add  - Add a country
del  - Delete a country
exit - Exit program

Command: view
Country codes: CA MX US
Enter country code: mx
Country name: Mexico.

Command: add
Enter country code: nl
Enter country name: netherlands
Netherlands was added.

Command: view
Country codes: CA MX NL US
Enter country code: nl
Country name: Netherlands.

Command: del
Enter country code: us
United States was deleted.

Command: exit
Bye!
```

The code   Page 1

```python
def display_menu():
    print("COMMAND MENU")
    print("view - View country name")
    print("add  - Add a country")
    print("del  - Delete a country")
    print("exit - Exit program")
    print()

def display_codes(countries):
    codes = list(countries.keys())
    codes.sort()
    line = "Country codes: "
    for code in codes:
        line += code + " "
    print(line)
```

Figure 12-6   The Country Code program (part 1)

The view() function begins by calling the display_codes() function to display the country codes on a single line. Then, it prompts the user to enter one of these codes. Next, it uses the upper() method of the string to convert the code to uppercase. That way, even if the user enters "mx", the program uses "MX" as the key for the dictionary. This is necessary because a search done with the in keyword is case-sensitive.

After making sure that the country code is uppercase, the view() function uses an if statement to check if the specified code is in the countries dictionary. If so, it gets the name from the dictionary and displays it. Otherwise, it displays a message that indicates that there's no country for that code.

The add() function begins by getting a country code from the user and by converting that code to uppercase. Then, it checks whether the code is in the countries dictionary. If so, it prints a message that indicates that another country is already using that code. Otherwise, it gets a country name from the user, uses the title() method described in chapter 10 to convert that name to title case, adds the name to the dictionary, and displays an appropriate message.

The delete() function also begins by getting a country code from the user, converting that code to uppercase, and checking whether that code exists in the countries dictionary. If so, this code deletes the country from the dictionary and displays an appropriate message. Otherwise, this code displays a message that indicates that there's no country with that code.

The main() function begins by creating a dictionary named countries that contains the codes and names for three countries. Then, it displays the command menu and enters the main loop for the program.

The only other thing to note is that this code passes the countries dictionary to the add() and delete() functions. But since a dictionary is a mutable type, these functions can make changes to the countries dictionary directly. As a result, these changes are also available to the main() function.

The code

```python
def view(countries):
    display_codes(countries)
    code = input("Enter country code: ")
    code = code.upper()
    if code in countries:
        name = countries[code]
        print("Country name: " + name + ".\n")
    else:
        print("There is no country with that code.\n")

def add(countries):
    code = input("Enter country code: ")
    code = code.upper()
    if code in countries:
        name = countries[code]
        print(name + " is already using this code.\n")
    else:
        name = input("Enter country name: ")
        name = name.title()
        countries[code] = name
        print(name + " was added.\n")

def delete(countries):
    code = input("Enter country code: ")
    code = code.upper()
    if code in countries:
        name = countries.pop(code)
        print(name + " was deleted.\n")
    else:
        print("There is no country with that code.\n")

def main():
    countries = {"CA": "Canada",
                 "US": "United States",
                 "MX": "Mexico"}

    display_menu()
    while True:
        command = input("Command: ")
        command = command.lower()
        if command == "view":
            view(countries)
        elif command == "add":
            add(countries)
        elif command == "del":
            delete(countries)
        elif command == "exit":
            print("Bye!")
            break
        else:
            print("Not a valid command. Please try again.\n")

if __name__ == "__main__":
    main()
```

Figure 12-6   The Country Code program (part 2)

The Word Counter program

To show another use of a dictionary, figure 12-7 presents a Word Counter program that counts the number of times a word occurs in a text file. This is a variation of the Word Counter program in chapter 10 that shows how using a dictionary can make this easier. This program begins by converting a text file into a list of words and then creating a dictionary with a key for each word and a value that stores the number of times the word occurs in the text file.

The code for this program starts with the get_words_from_file() function that opens the text file and reads its contents into a string named text. Then, this function uses some of the string-handling skills of chapter 10 to work with the text string. To start, it uses the replace() method to replace new line characters with a space and to replace commas and periods with empty strings. Next, it uses the lower() method to convert all of the letters to lowercase. Then, it uses the split() method to split the text string into a list of words. Last, this function returns the list of words.

The count_words() function accepts the list of words as an argument. Then, it uses the techniques in this chapter to create a dictionary that has a key for each word in the list and a value that stores the number of times that the word occurs in the list.

Within this function, the first statement defines an empty dictionary named word_count. Then, the second statement defines a loop that loops through each word in the list of words. Within the loop, the code checks whether the word (the key) is in the dictionary. If so, this code increments the count (the value) of the word by 1. Otherwise, it adds the word to the dictionary and sets its count to 1. Finally, this function returns the word count dictionary.

The display_word_count() function accepts the word count dictionary as an argument. Within this method, the first statement gets a view object for the keys of the word count dictionary and converts it to a list of words. Then, the second statement sorts the list of words alphabetically. Next, the code loops through each word in the sorted list and prints the word (the key) and its count (the value).

The main() function just sets the filename for the file that stores the text. Then, it calls the functions to get the words from the file, to count them, and to display the word counts.

The user interface

```
The Word Counter program

a = 7
above = 1
add = 1
...
```

The code

```python
def get_words_from_file(filename):
    with open(filename) as file:
        text = file.read()                  # read str from file

    text = text.replace("\n", "")
    text = text.replace(",", "")
    text = text.replace(".", "")
    text = text.lower()

    words = text.split(" ")                 # convert str to list
    print(words)
    return words

def count_words(words):
    # define a dict to store the word count
    word_count = {}
    for word in words:
        if word in word_count:
            word_count[word] += 1           # increment count for word
        else:
            word_count[word] = 1            # add word with count of 1
    return word_count

def display_word_count(word_count):
    words = list(word_count.keys())
    words.sort(key=str.lower)
    for word in words:
        count = word_count[word]
        print(word, "=", count)

def main():
    print("The Word Counter program")
    print()

    # change filename to switch text file
    filename = "gettysburg_address.txt"

    # get words, count, and display
    words = get_words_from_file(filename)   # get list of words
    word_count = count_words(words)         # create dict from list
    display_word_count(word_count)

if __name__ == "__main__":
    main()
```

Figure 12-7   The Word Counter program

More skills for working with dictionaries

So far, you've learned the basic skills for working with dictionaries. However, you may also need to work with dictionaries that store lists, tuples, or other dictionaries as their values.

How to use dictionaries with complex objects as values

So far, all of the examples in this chapter use dictionaries to store values of simple data types such as the str, int, and float types. However, dictionaries can also store values of complex data types such as lists, tuples, and other dictionaries. This works similarly to working with lists of lists as described in chapter 6.

In figure 12-8, the first example creates a dictionary named contacts that contains three more dictionaries. Here, each embedded dictionary contains the street address, city, state, postal code, and phone number for a contact.

When you store complex objects in a dictionary, you can use multiple keys to access the values in the embedded dictionary. In the second example, the first statement gets the phone number for Anne. Then, the second statement attempts to get the email address for Anne. However, since the "email" key doesn't exist, this statement causes a KeyError to occur.

If you want to check whether a key exists within an embedded dictionary, you can use bracket notation as shown in the third example. This example checks whether the "email" key exists within the dictionary for Anne.

If you want to use the get() method to get a value from an embedded dictionary, you can use method chaining as shown in the fourth example. The advantage of this technique is that it doesn't cause a KeyError to occur if the key doesn't exist.

However, if the first key doesn't exist in the dictionary, it causes an AttributeError to occur because the first get() method returns a value of None, and None doesn't have a get() method. To work around this problem, you can use the optional second argument of the get() method to specify an empty dictionary as shown in the fourth statement. That way, if the first key doesn't exist, the first get() method returns an empty dictionary, and the second get() method returns a value of None.

The last set of examples shows a dictionary that stores a list of scores for three students. Here, the key is the student's name, and the value is a list of scores. As a result, you can use the dictionary key to get a list of scores for each student, and you can use the list index to get each score from the list. This is illustrated by the last example.

A dictionary that contains other dictionaries as values

```
contacts = {
    "Joel":
        {"address": "1500 Anystreet", "city": "San Francisco",
         "state": "California", "postalCode": "94110",
         "phone": "555-555-1111"},
    "Anne":
        {"address": "1000 Somestreet", "city": "Fresno",
         "state": "California", "postalCode": "93704",
         "phone": "125-555-2222"},
    "Ben"
        {"address": "1400 Another Street", "city": "Fresno",
         "state": "California", "postalCode": "93704",
         "phone": "125-555-4444"}
}
```

Code that gets values from embedded dictionaries

```
phone = contacts["Anne"]["phone"]           # "125-555-2222"
email = contacts["Anne"]["email"]           # KeyError
```

Code that checks whether a key exists within another key

```
key = "email"
if key in contacts["Anne"]:
    email = contacts["Anne"][key]
    print(email)
else:
    print("Sorry, there is no email address for this contact.")
```

Code that uses the get() method with embedded dictionaries

```
phone = contacts.get("Anne").get("phone")       # "555-555-1111"
phone = contacts.get("Anne").get("email")       # None
phone = contacts.get("Mike").get("phone")       # AttributeError
phone = contacts.get("Mike", {}).get("phone")   # None
```

A dictionary that contains lists as values

```
students = {"Joel":[85, 95, 70],
            "Anne":[95, 100, 100],
            "Mike":[77, 70, 80, 85]}
```

Code that gets a value from an embedded list

```
scores = students["Joel"]            # [85, 95, 70]
joel_score1 = students["Joel"][0]    # 85
```

Description

- The value for a key can be a complex data type such as another dictionary, a tuple, or a list.

- You can use two sets of brackets to access an item in an embedded dictionary or list.

- You can also use get() method chaining to access an item in an embedded dictionary.

Figure 12-8   How to use dictionaries with complex objects as values

The Book Catalog program

To show how you can use a dictionary of dictionaries, figure 12-9 presents a Book Catalog program. This program lets you look up a book by title, add books, edit books, and delete books from the catalog.

As the code in the main() function in the next figure shows, this dictionary of dictionaries has this structure:

```
book_catalog = {
    "Moby Dick": {"author":"Herman Melville", "pubyear":"1851"},
    "The Hobbit": {"author":"J. R. R. Tolkien", "pubyear":"1937"}
}
```

Here, the main dictionary has book titles as the keys and embedded dictionaries as the values. Then, each embedded dictionary has key/value pairs for the author and publication year.

The code for this program starts with the show_book() function. This function accepts the book_catalog dictionary as its only argument. Within this function, the code prompts the user to enter a book title. Then, it checks whether the title exists in the catalog. If so, the code gets the embedded dictionary for the book, and stores it in the book variable. Then, it displays the title, author, and publication year. However, if the title doesn't exist in the catalog, the program displays a message that indicates that the book doesn't exist in the catalog.

The add_edit_book() function provides the code for adding or editing a book. This code is all stored in a single function because most of the code for adding and editing a book is identical. To make this possible, this function accepts a second argument named mode that indicates whether the function is adding or editing a book. When the main() function calls the add_edit_book() function, this argument is set to "add" if the program is adding a book, and it is set to "edit" if the program is editing a book.

To start, the add_edit_book() function prompts the user for a book title. Then, an if clause checks whether the program is in "add" mode and whether the title is already in the catalog. If both conditions are true, the user is attempting to add a book that already exists in the catalog. In that case, the program informs the user that the title already exists and asks the user if he or she wants to edit it instead. If the user enters "y" to answer yes, the function continues and allows the user to edit the book instead of adding it. Otherwise, this code executes a return statement.

The elif clause works similarly to the if clause. However, the elif clause checks whether the program is in "edit" mode and the title is not in the catalog. If this is true, the user can enter "y" for yes to add the title instead of editing it. Or, the user can enter "n" for no to return to the main() function.

After the elif clause, the program prompts the user for an author and publication year. Then, it creates a new dictionary and sets the "author" and "pubyear" keys to the values entered by the user. Next, the code accesses the book catalog dictionary using the title as the key and sets its value to the book dictionary. Since adding a new key to the dictionary and editing an existing key are done the same way, this code works for both adding and editing book.

The user interface

```
COMMAND MENU
show - Show book info
add -  Add book
edit - Edit book
del -  Delete book
exit - Exit program

Command: show
Title: Heart of Darkness
Sorry, Heart of Darkness doesn't exist in the catalog.

Command: add
Title: Heart of Darkness
Author name: Joseph Conrad
Publication year: 1890

Command: edit
Title: Heart of Darkness
Author name: Joseph Conrad
Publication year: 1899

Command:
```

The code   Page 1

```python
def show_book(book_catalog):
    title = input("Enter the title for the book: ")
    if title in book_catalog:
        book = book_catalog[title]
        print("Title:    " + title)
        print("Author:   " + book["author"])
        print("Pub year: " + book["pubyear"])
    else:
        print("Sorry, " + title + " doesn't exist in the catalog.")

def add_edit_book(book_catalog, mode):
    title = input("Enter title of the book: ")
    if mode == "add" and title in book_catalog:
        print(title + " already exists in the catalog.")
        response = input ("Would you like to edit it? (y/n): ").lower()
        if(response != "y"):
            return
    elif mode == "edit" and title not in book_catalog:
        print(title + " doesn't exist in the catalog.")
        response = input("Would you like to add it? (y/n): ").lower()
        if (response != "y"):
            return

    # Get book data and create a dictionary for the data
    author = input("Enter author name: ")
    pubyear = input("Enter publication year: ")
    book = {"author": author, "pubyear": pubyear}

    # Add the book data to the catalog using title as key
    book_catalog[title] = book
```

Figure 12-9   The Book Catalog program (part 1)

Like the previous two functions, the delete_book() function accepts the book catalog dictionary as an argument. Then, it prompts the user for the title of the book he or she wants to remove. Next, this code checks whether the title is in the book catalog. If so, it deletes the book from the catalog and displays an appropriate message. Otherwise, it displays a message that indicates that the title doesn't exist in the catalog.

Skip now to the main() function. It starts with the code for a dictionary within dictionaries that consists of three books.

Next, the main() function calls the function that displays the menu commands. That is followed by a while loop that gets the commands from the user until the user enters "exit". However, to make sure the user can enter commands in either upper or lowercase, the user entry is converted to lowercase before it is tested by the if statement.

As you review this code, note that the main() function passes the book catalog dictionary to the add_edit_book() and delete_book() functions. However, these functions don't return the modified dictionary to the main() function. Here again, this isn't necessary because a dictionary is a mutable type. As a result, any changes that the add_edit_book() and delete_book() functions make to the book catalog dictionary are also available to the main() function.

The code   **Page 2**

```python
def delete_book(book_catalog):
    title = input("Title: ")
    if title in book_catalog:
        del book_catalog[title]
        print(title + " removed from catalog.")
    else:
        print(title + " doesn't exist in the catalog.")

def display_menu():
    print("The Book Catalog program")
    print()
    print("COMMAND MENU")
    print("show - Show book info")
    print("add -  Add book")
    print("edit - Edit book")
    print("del -  Delete book")
    print("exit - Exit program")

def main():
    book_catalog = {
        "Moby Dick":
            {"author" : "Herman Melville",
             "pubyear" : "1851"},
        "The Hobbit":
            {"author" : "J. R. R. Tolkien",
             "pubyear" : "1937"},
        "Slaughterhouse Five":
            {"author" : "Kurt Vonnegut",
             "pubyear" : "1969"}
        }

    display_menu()

    while True:
        print()
        command = input("Command: ").lower()
        if command == "show":
            show_book(book_catalog)
        elif command == "add":
            add_edit_book(book_catalog, mode="add")
        elif command == "edit":
            add_edit_book(book_catalog, mode="edit")
        elif command == "del":
            delete_book(book_catalog)
        elif command == "exit":
            print("Bye!")
            break
        else:
            print("Unknown command. Please try again.")

if __name__ == "__main__":
    main()
```

Figure 12-9   The Book Catalog program (part 2)

Perspective

In this chapter, you learned how to work with simple dictionaries as well as dictionaries of dictionaries, lists, or tuples. But you should also know that you can store a dictionary in a list. In fact, a list of dictionaries is a common data structure when working with databases.

Terms

dictionary
associative array
key/value pair
key

value
view object
iterator

Summary

- A *dictionary* is an *unordered* collection of items. In other languages, dictionaries are often called *associative arrays*.
- In a dictionary, each item consists of a *key/value pair* in which each *value* in the dictionary is indexed by a unique *key*.
- You can use brackets that contain keys to access the items in a dictionary. But if you attempt to access an item with a key that doesn't exist, a KeyError occurs.
- You can use the in keyword to check if an item exists in a dictionary, and you can use the get() method of a dictionary object to both check whether an item exists and get the item if it does.
- You can use the del keyword as well as the pop() and clear()methods of a dictionary to remove items from a dictionary.
- *View objects* are *iterators* that allow you to loop over the keys and values of a dictionary. View objects are automatically updated if the dictionary changes.
- You can use the built-in list() and dict() constructors to convert a list to a dictionary and vice versa. When you convert a list to a dictionary, though, the list must be two-dimensional with exactly two items in each row.
- The value for a dictionary can be a simple data type such as a string or a complex data type such as a dictionary, list, or tuple.

Exercise 12-1   Add a list method to the Book Catalog program

In this exercise, you'll enhance the Book Catalog program so it offers a list command that will list all of the books in the catalog, as shown here:

```
COMMAND MENU
list - List all books
show - Show book info
add -  Add book
edit - Edit book
del -  Delete book
exit - Exit program

Command: list

Title:     Slaughterhouse Five
Author:    Kurt Vonnegut
Pub year:  1969

Title:     The Hobbit
Author:    J. R. R. Tolkien
Pub year:  1937

Title:     Moby Dick
Author:    Herman Melville
Pub year:  1851

Command:
```

1. In IDLE, open the book_catalog.py file that's in this folder:
   python/exercises/ch12

2. Review the code and run it.

3. Add the list command.

Exercise 12-2   Enhance the Movie List 2D program

In this exercise, you'll enhance the Movie List program of chapter 6 so it uses a list of dictionaries instead of a list of lists to store the data for the movies. This is similar to how the movie data would be stored if you were retrieving it from a database as shown in chapter 17.

Open and test the program

1. In IDLE, open the movie_list_2d.py file that's in this folder:
   python/exercises/ch12

2. Review the code and run it to refresh your memory about how it works.

Modify the code so it uses a dictionary

3. In the main() function, modify the code so it stores a list of dictionaries where each dictionary stores the data for a movie. Use "name" as the key for the movie's name and "year" as the key for the movie's year

4. In the list() function, modify the code in the loop that displays each movie so it uses the correct key to get the name and year of the movie. Note that this makes the code easier to read and understand.

5. In the add() function, modify the code that stores the data for the movie so that it uses a dictionary instead of a list. Note that you should still use a list to store the list of movies, but you should use a dictionary to store the data for each movie.

6. In the delete() function, modify the code so it works correctly now that the data for the movie is stored in a dictionary.

7. Run the program. It should work as it did before. However, it's now using a dictionary to store the data for each movie.

13

How to work with recursion and algorithms

In chapter 3, you learned how to use loops, or iteration, to execute a block of statements multiple times. Now, this chapter shows how to use recursion to execute a block of statements multiple times. This will give you some insight into how recursion can be used to solve complex problems that are difficult to solve in other ways. Keep in mind, though, that an iterative solution will almost always perform more efficiently than a recursive solution.

An introduction to recursion

In simple terms, *recursion* occurs when a function calls itself. As a result, recursion can be used to execute the same action repeatedly until a certain condition is reached. As you will see, however, there are some important differences between recursive functions and functions that use while and for loops.

How recursion works in Python

Figure 13-1 begins with an *iterative function* that contains an infinite while loop. This loop prints the message "Press Ctrl+C to stop!" repeatedly until the user interrupts the program by pressing Ctrl+C (or Command+C on a Mac).

In the second example, though, a *recursive function* gets the same result by calling itself. Here, the first statement prints the message, and the second statement calls the function again. Then, this process continues infinitely until the user interrupts the program. In other words, from the perspective of a user, this function behaves the same as the first one.

Under the surface, however, these two programs behave differently. To start, these functions differ in the ways that they use the *stack*. In chapter 5, you learned that the stack stores all function calls that are in scope in the reverse order in which they were called. So each time a function is called, Python pushes it onto the stack. Then, when the function ends, Python pops the function call off the stack.

In these examples, when the iterative function is called, Python only pushes one function call onto the stack. In contrast, Python pushes a call to the recursive function onto the stack each time the function is called. Also, since the recursive function never ends, Python doesn't ever pop any function calls off the stack.

Since each function on the stack requires memory, the recursive function will eventually use up all available memory in the system, at which point, it will stop. In contrast, the iterative function will theoretically run forever (as long as nothing interrupts it).

If you interrupt either of these functions, you can see how this works. For the iterative function, you'll see just one function call. For the recursive function, you'll see numerous calls. This shows that Python pushes a new copy of the function onto the stack each time it is called.

An iterative function that loops infinitely

```
def display_message():
    while True:
        print("Press Ctrl+C to stop!")
```

The console

```
Press Ctrl+C to stop!
Press Ctrl+C to stop!
Press Ctrl+C to stop!
...
```

The stack after you interrupt the iterative function

```
display_message()
```

A recursive function that loops until memory runs out or the user interrupts the program

```
def display_message():
    print("Press Ctrl+C to stop!")
    display_message()
```

The console

```
Press Ctrl+C to stop!
Press Ctrl+C to stop!
Press Ctrl+C to stop!
...
```

The stack after you interrupt the recursive function

```
display_message()
display_message()
display_message()
...
```

Description

- *Recursion* occurs when a function calls itself.
- Each time a *recursive function* calls itself, Python adds the function call to the *stack*, which is the list of the function calls that are waiting to be called in the reverse order in which they were called.
- Each time an *iterative function* is called, Python puts one function call on the stack.
- In IDLE, you can stop an infinite loop by pressing Ctrl+C on a Windows system or Command+C on a Mac. Then, IDLE displays an exception message on the console that includes the current stack.

Figure 13-1   How recursion works in Python

How to use recursion to add a range of numbers

In the previous figure, you learned that a recursive function uses the stack differently than an iterative function. Now, figure 13-2 shows some other ways that recursion differs from iteration. To do that, it presents an iterative function and a recursive function that get the sum of a range of numbers.

To start, the first example shows a function that uses a loop to sum all numbers from 0 to the upper limit. By now, you shouldn't have any trouble understanding how this function works. In short, it uses a loop to add all of the numbers in the range to the total before it returns the total. So, for an upper limit of 5, the function adds 0, 1, 2, 3, 4, and 5 and gets a total of 15.

The second example uses a recursive function to do the same thing. This function breaks the problem down into smaller problems until it reaches the simplest possible form of the problem. This simplest form of the problem is known as the *base case*. In this example, the simplest form of the problem is if the upper limit is 0. In that case, there's no need to do any addition. Instead, the function can just return the upper limit. Otherwise, the upper limit is greater than 0, and the function needs to call itself to perform the addition.

To understand how this works, it's helpful to walk through an example. Suppose the call to the function supplies an upper limit of 5. The function begins by checking whether the upper argument is equal to 0. At this point, it isn't. In other words, the base case hasn't been reached. As a result, the code breaks down the problem by returning the result of adding the upper limit to the result of calling the function with an argument of the upper limit minus 1.

The key here is that the addition operation can't be performed yet because it depends on the result of a function call, and the result of that function call isn't known yet. That means the first addition operation has to be performed later. This known as a *deferred action*. You can think of a deferred action as being like a note telling the program that it must come back and perform this action later. And this note is stored on the stack.

The second call to the function supplies an upper argument of 4. Because this argument still isn't equal to 0, the function makes another call to itself, once again adding the upper argument to the result of the function call with an argument of upper minus 1. But once again, the first addition operation in the return statement can't be performed because the result of the function call isn't known yet. And so another deferred action is created and stored on the stack.

This process continues until the upper variable equals 0. At that point, the function returns the upper variable, which ends the recursion. This pops all of the previous recursive function calls off the stack, one at a time, in the reverse order from which they were pushed onto it. This causes Python to add the return value of each recursive function call to the upper variable. When it's done performing all of those deferred actions, it returns the final result of the upper variable.

In this case, Python pushes the recursive function call onto the stack 6 times before it begins executing those calls. This can be referred to as *recursion depth*. If you exceed Python's maximum recursion depth, a RecursionError occurs. This limits the types of calculations you can perform with recursion.

An iterative function that sums all numbers from zero to an upper limit

```python
def add_numbers(upper):
    total = 0
    for number in range(upper + 1):
        total += number
    return number
```

A recursive function that does the same thing

```python
def add_numbers(upper):
    if upper == 0:
        return upper
    else:
        return upper + add_numbers(upper - 1)
```

Code that calls the above functions

```python
def main():
    total = add_numbers(5)      # total = 15
```

The stack for the recursive function

```
main()
add_numbers()   # puts add_numbers(4) on stack
    upper = 5
add_numbers()   # puts add_numbers(3) on stack
    upper = 4
add_numbers()   # puts add_numbers(2) on stack
    upper = 3
add_numbers()   # puts add_numbers(1) on stack
    upper = 2
add_numbers()   # puts add_numbers(0) on stack
    upper = 1
add_numbers()   # sums all return values and returns the result
    upper = 0
```

Description

- A recursive function breaks down a complex problem that it can't solve yet into smaller problems that it can solve when it reaches the simplest form of the problem. The simplest form of the problem is known as the *base case*.

- Each call to a recursive function that can't be performed yet is known as a *deferred action*. In other words, Python puts the function call on the stack, which allows it to "remember" that it has to go back and complete that call later.

- When a function call is added to the stack, it includes the arguments that were passed to the function as local variables.

- Each call to the recursive function moves closer to the base case. When execution reaches the base case, the recursion ends. Then, Python combines the return values from each function call to solve the larger problem.

- The number of recursive function calls that are on the stack at the same time can be referred to as *recursion depth*. If you exceed the maximum recursion depth that's allowed by Python, a RecursionError occurs. Typically, Python's maximum recursion depth is set to less than 1000.

Figure 13-2   How to use recursion to add a range of numbers

Some common recursive algorithms

An *algorithm* is a step-by-step series of operations that perform calculations, process data, or automate reasoning tasks. There are often multiple algorithms for performing a task, and it's up to the programmer to use the algorithm that works best for the task at hand.

In the rest of this chapter, you'll see two mathematical problems and a puzzle that are commonly solved with recursive algorithms. For these tasks, using recursion allows you to write code that's clean and concise. However, you can almost always improve the performance by using iteration instead of recursion.

How to compute the factorial of a number

The factorial of a number is defined as the product of all numbers that are equal to or less than that number, with the special case that the factorial of 0 is 1. As a result, the factorial of 5 is 120. This is shown by the first set of examples in figure 13-3. These examples use the traditional mathematical notation of an exclamation point (!) to indicate the factorial of a number.

Given the definition of a factorial, you can create an algorithm for computing the factorial of a number as shown in the second example. Here, the factorial of 5 can be recursively defined as 5 times the factorial of 4. The factorial of 4 can be defined as 4 times the factorial of 3. And so on until the factorial of 0, which is defined as 1. In other words, this algorithm breaks down the problem of computing the factorial of 5 into smaller problems until it reaches the simplest possible case, the base case.

Using this algorithm, you can write a recursive function for computing factorials as shown in the third example. Since the factorial of 0 is 1, that's the base case. As a result, if the number equals 0, the function returns 1. Otherwise, it returns the number multiplied by the factorial of the number minus one. Here, the multiplication step is a deferred action because it needs the result of a function call, and the result of that function call isn't known until later.

The last example shows an iterative function that calculates the factorial of a number by looping over the range of numbers. If the specified number is 0, the loop isn't executed, and the function returns the fact variable, which is set to a starting value of 1. However, if the specified number is greater than 0, the function loops over the range of numbers. Within the loop, the code updates the fact variable by multiplying it by the next number in the sequence. Then, when the loop finishes, it returns the final value of the fact variable.

How to calculate the factorial of a number

```
0! = 1
1! = 1 * 1 = 1
2! = 2 * 1 = 2
3! = 3 * 2 * 1 = 6
4! = 4 * 3 * 2 * 1 = 24
5! = 5 * 4 * 3 * 2 * 1 * 1 = 120
```

An algorithm for calculating the factorial of a number

```
if n = 0, return 1
if n > 0, return n * (n-1)!
```

A recursive function that calculates the factorial of a number

```python
def factorial(num):
    if num == 0:
        return 1
    else:
        return num * factorial(num - 1)
```

The stack for the recursive function

```
factorial()   # puts factorial(4) on stack
    num = 5
factorial()   # puts factorial(3) on stack
    num = 4
factorial()   # puts factorial(2) on stack
    num = 3
factorial()   # puts factorial(1) on stack
    num = 2
factorial()   # puts factorial(0) on stack
    num = 1
factorial()   # performs multiplication and returns the result
    num = 0
```

An iterative function that calculates the factorial of a number

```python
def factorial(num):
    fact = 1
    for number in range(1, num+1):
        fact = number * fact
    return fact
```

Description

- An *algorithm* is a step-by-step series of operations that performs calculations, processes data, or automates reasoning tasks. Algorithms are commonly used in mathematics and computer science.

- Usually, more than one algorithm can provide a solution to a problem. Then, the programmer should try to pick the algorithm that works best for the problem.

- All problems that can be solved recursively can also be solved iteratively. In Python, an iterative solution almost always runs faster and uses less memory. However, for some problems, a recursive solution may be more apparent and easier to code.

- To get the factorial of a number, you multiply all the numbers that are less than or equal to that number. By definition, the factorial of 0 is 1.

Figure 13-3   How to compute the factorial of a number

How to compute a Fibonacci series

A *Fibonacci series* is a series of numbers named after the Italian mathematician Leonardo Fibonacci. Calculating the numbers in this series lends itself to a recursive algorithm that is used as an example of recursion in many mathematics and computer science textbooks.

Figure 13-4 begins by showing the first 16 numbers of the Fibonacci series. In this series, the first number is 0, the second number is 1, and every other number in the sequence is the sum of the previous two numbers. So, this series has two base cases.

The recursive function named fib() presented in the second example uses those two base cases. If the number equals 0, it returns a value of 0. If the number equals 1, it returns a value of 1. However, for any numbers larger than 1, the function uses recursion to add the previous two Fibonacci numbers.

From a readability point of view, this is an elegant way to solve the problem. It requires seven lines of code, and it's easy to understand. However, from a performance point of view, this code has a serious problem.

To illustrate the source of the problem, this figure shows a diagram of the recursive calls. To start, the top-level function calls the fib() function with an argument of 5. Since 5 is greater than 1, the fib() function makes two recursive calls. This causes the function calls to branch into a tree. The left side of the tree (n-1) is called with 4, and the right side (n-2) is called with 3. On both sides of the tree, the number is still greater than 1, and the function makes two more recursive calls. As a result, the tree splits again. This continues until the base cases are reached. If this seems confusing, remember that each function call has its own local variables and that changes to local variables in one function call do not change the values of local variables in any the other calls.

So, the problem is that the fib() function gets called with the same values and duplicates an enormous amount of work. For example, the diagram in this figure calls the fib() function with value of 2 three times. Furthermore, the number of recursive calls increases exponentially. As it turns out, this way of computing a Fibonacci series is so inefficient, that it becomes virtually unusable with values much larger than 32.

The last example shows an iterative function that solves the same problem. This code isn't as elegant as the code for the recursive function, but it works much more efficiently.

If you call these two functions with an argument of 5, you probably won't notice much difference in the efficiency. However, if you use a number such as 32, the iterative version executes much more quickly than the recursive version. If you call both versions with a number like 100, the iterative version finishes almost instantly, but the recursive version takes an unreasonably long time to execute. The takeaway lesson here is that some recursive algorithms rapidly grow to the point of being unusable.

So, if you had to code a function to calculate a Fibonacci number, which algorithm would you use? Well, if you want to allow your users to calculate more than the first 30 or so numbers of this series, and you probably do, you should almost certainly use the iterative algorithm.

The Fibonacci series

```
0, 1, 1, 2, 3, 5, 8, 13, 21, 34, 55, 89, 144, 233, 377, 610, ...
```

A recursive function that calculates a Fibonacci series

```python
def fib(n):
    if n == 0:
        return 0
    elif n == 1:
        return 1
    else:
        return fib(n - 1) + fib(n - 2)
```

A statement that prints the first 10 numbers of the Fibonacci series

```python
for i in range(10):
    print(fib(i), end=", ")
```

The tree of function calls that calculate the 5ᵗʰ number in the series

The tree of function calls that calculate the 5th number in the series

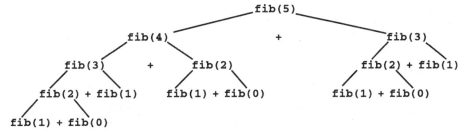

An iterative function that computes a Fibonacci sequence

```python
def fib(n):
    if n == 0:
        return 0
    elif n == 1:
        return 1
    n1 = 0
    n2 = 1
    fib = 0
    for i in range(2, n+1):
        fib = n1 + n2
        n1 = n2
        n2 = fib
    return fib
```

Description

- A recursive Fibonacci algorithm uses two recursive calls that split off in two directions. This is known as *tree recursion* because each recursive call is like the branch of a tree.

- With tree recursion, the number of recursive calls grows exponentially.

- Tree recursion can be extremely inefficient because it needlessly computes some branches multiple times.

- Two functions can work identically from a user's standpoint, but have very different performance depending on the algorithm used to obtain the results.

Figure 13-4   How to compute a Fibonacci series

An algorithm for solving the Towers of Hanoi puzzle

This chapter ends by showing a common example of recursion known as the Towers of Hanoi puzzle. This puzzle consists of three pegs (A, B, and C) and a number of different sized disks that fit onto each peg as shown in figure 13-5. To start, all of the disks are stacked on peg A with the largest one at the bottom and the smallest one at the top.

To solve the puzzle, you must move all of the disks to peg C so that they are in the same order as they were on peg A. However, when you're moving the disks, you can only move one disk at a time, you must move the disk to one of the pegs, and you can't place a larger disk on top of a smaller disk.

This figure starts by showing the seven moves necessary to solve the Towers of Hanoi puzzle with 3 disks. If you follow the steps in order, a recursive pattern begins to emerge that you can apply to any number of disks. Solving this puzzle for 10 disks might seem daunting. But it's not so bad once you notice the pattern.

This puzzle can be solved for more disks by using the recursive algorithm that's described next. This algorithm moves n-1 disks from peg A to peg B, uses peg C as a temporary peg, moves the remaining disk from peg A to peg C, and then moves n-1 disks from peg B to peg C using peg A as a temporary peg.

The function that follows shows how this algorithm can be implemented in Python. It accepts the number of disks as its first argument and the names of the three pegs as its next three arguments. It begins by checking to see if the number of disks is equal to 0. In other words, the base case is reached when there are no disks left to move. In that case, the function uses a return statement to end the function.

If there are disks left to move, the function calls itself to move the disks. Here, the first statement is a recursive call that says "Move all disks except the largest one (disk n) from peg A to peg B, using peg C as a temporary holder." This places one branch of recursive functions on the stack. Then, the second statement prints the message for moving the largest disk (disk n).

The third statement is a recursive call that says "move all disks except for the largest one from peg B to peg C, using peg A as a temporary holder." This places the second branch of recursive functions on the stack. When the number of disks reaches 0, Python begins popping the branches off the recursive tree. This results in a symmetric pattern on each side of the number n.

This puzzle is based on a legend. Although there are many versions of this legend, most versions state that a group of monks has been following rules of this puzzle since ancient times to move a stack of 64 gold disks from one tower to another. According to the legend, when the monks complete this task, the world will end in a clap of thunder. Fortunately, even if the monks could move one disk per second, it would still take them over 500 billion years to complete this task!

How to solve the Towers of Hanoi puzzle with 3 disks

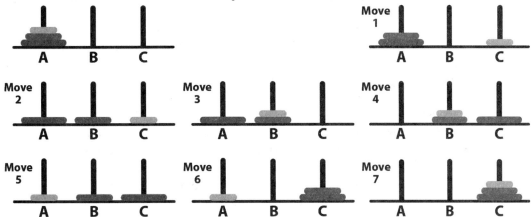

The rules

- The goal is to move all disks from peg A to peg C so they end up in the same order as on the original peg.
- You can only move one disk at a time.
- You must move the disk to one of the three pegs.
- You can't place a larger disk on top of a smaller disk.

A recursive algorithm for solving the puzzle

1. Move n-1 disks from peg A to peg B using peg C as a temporary holder.
2. Move disk n from peg A to peg C.
3. Move n-1 disks from peg B to peg C using peg A as a temporary holder.

A function that implements the recursive algorithm

```python
def move_disk(n, src, dest, temp):
    if n == 0:
        return
    else:
        move_disk(n-1, src, temp, dest)
        print("Move disk", n, "from", src, "to", dest)
        move_disk(n-1, temp, dest, src)
```

Description

- You can use a recursive algorithm to solve the Towers of Hanoi puzzle.
- To code a function that implements this algorithm, you can use tree recursion to create one branch that implements step 1 and another branch that implements step 3.

Figure 13-5   An algorithm for solving the Towers of Hanoi puzzle

The code for solving the Towers of Hanoi puzzle

Figure 13-6 presents the Python code for solving the Towers of Hanoi puzzle. In the user interface, you can see that the program starts by prompting the user to enter the number of disks. Then, it displays the instructions necessary to move all disks from peg A to peg C. When it finishes printing these instructions, the program prints a message before exiting.

The Python code begins with a move_disk() function that's the same as the function described in figure 13-5. Then, the main() function prompts the user to enter the number of disks. Next, it begins the recursion by calling the move_disk() function and passing it the number of disks and the names for the pegs. There's nothing special about the names of the pegs. They're just used to display a user-friendly message to the console.

When Python finishes making all of the recursive calls to the move_disk() function, execution returns to the main() function. Then, it prints a message and exits.

To test this program, run it with different numbers of disks. Start with a small number of disks and gradually increase to larger values. Also, try odd and even numbers of disks. Note that the series of moves is different depending on whether there are an odd or even number of disks. Also, note how fast the number of recursive calls grows. For example, solving the puzzle for 4 disks takes 15 moves, 5 disks takes 31 moves, 6 disks takes 63 moves, and so on. From this, you can determine that each additional disk doubles the required number of moves, plus 1. So, solving the puzzle for 32 disks takes 4,294,967,295 moves.

Because the number of recursive calls grows so rapidly, using larger numbers of disks can quickly make it so the program won't finish in a reasonable amount of time. That's true even if you remove the print statement from the move_disk() function, which slows the function considerably.

The user interface

```
**** TOWERS OF HANOI ****

Enter number of disks: 4

Move disk 1 from A to B
Move disk 2 from A to C
Move disk 1 from B to C
Move disk 3 from A to B
Move disk 1 from C to A
Move disk 2 from C to B
Move disk 1 from A to B
Move disk 4 from A to C
Move disk 1 from B to C
Move disk 2 from B to A
Move disk 1 from C to A
Move disk 3 from B to C
Move disk 1 from A to B
Move disk 2 from A to C
Move disk 1 from B to C

All disks have been moved.
```

The code

```python
def move_disk(n, src, dest, temp):
    if n == 0:
        return
    else:
        move_disk(n-1, src, temp, dest)
        print("Move disk", n, "from", src, "to", dest)
        move_disk(n-1, temp, dest, src)

def main():
    print("**** TOWERS OF HANOI ****")
    print()
    num_disks = int(input("Enter number of disks: "))
    print()

    move_disk(num_disks, "A", "C", "B")

    print()
    print("All disks have been moved.")

if __name__ == "__main__":
    main()
```

The pattern for 4 disks (15 moves)

```
1 2 1 3 1 2 1 4 1 2 1 3 1 2 1
```

The pattern for 5 disks (31 moves)

```
1 2 1 3 1 2 1 4 1 2 1 3 1 2 1 5 1 2 1 3 1 2 1 4 1 2 1 3 1 2 1
```

Figure 13-6   The code for solving the Towers of Hanoi puzzle

Perspective

In this chapter, you learned how to work with recursion. You also learned that you can use different algorithms to solve the same problem. In particular, you learned that any problem that can be solved with recursion can also be solved with a loop.

So, when should you use loops and when you should you use recursion? In short, you should almost always use loops. The only time you might want to use recursion is when a recursive algorithm is more obvious and easier to code and when performance isn't a primary concern. With the Towers of Hanoi puzzle, for example, it's easy to code a recursive algorithm, and it works adequately for a small number of disks. Although an iterative algorithm would perform better, it would be more difficult to code.

Terms

recursion	deferred action
interative function	algorithm
recursive function	Fibonacci series
stack	recursion depth
base case	tree recursion

Summary

- *Recursion* occurs when a function calls itself.

- Each time a *recursive function* calls itself, Python adds the function call to the *stack*, which is the current list of the called functions in the reverse order from which they were called. This function call includes the arguments that were passed to it so it can be executed properly later on.

- A recursive function breaks down a complex problem that it can't solve yet into smaller problems that it can solve when it reaches the simplest form of the problem. This simplest form is known as the *base case*.

- Each call to a recursive function that can't is known as a *deferred action*. Then, when the base case is reached and the recursion ends, all the deferred actions are completed.

- The number recursive function calls that are on the stack at the same time can be referred to as *recursion depth*.

- An *algorithm* is a step-by-step series of operations that performs calculations, processes data, or automates reasoning tasks. Algorithms are commonly used in mathematics and computer science.

- A recursive algorithm that uses two recursive calls splits off in two directions. This is known as *tree recursion* because each recursive call is like the branch of a tree. With tree recursion, the number of recursive calls increases exponentially.

Exercise 13-1   Test the Fibonacci program

In this exercise, you'll test the recursive function that prints part of the Fibonacci series. Then, you'll test an iterative function that does the same thing, but more efficiently.

Open and test the recursive Fibonacci program

1. In IDLE, open the fibonacci_recursion.py file that's in this folder:

   `python/exercises/ch13`

2. Review the code and run it to make sure it works correctly. It should print the first 16 numbers of the Fibonacci series.

3. Modify the code so it calculates a Fibonacci series for 32 numbers, and run it again. Note how slowly it runs.

View the stack for the program

4. Modify the code so it calculates a Fibonacci series for 100 numbers, and run it again. While it's running press Ctrl+C on a Windows system or Command+C on a Mac to interrupt the calculation and view the stack trace. Note that the fib() function has been placed on the stack numerous times.

5. From the IDLE shell, select Debug→Stack Viewer. In the Stack Viewer, expand a few of the fib() functions and note that they include the values for the local variable named n.

Open and test the iterative Fibonacci program

6. Open the fibonacci_loop.py file that's in the same folder.

7. Review the code and run it to make sure it works correctly.

8. Modify the code so it calculates a Fibonacci series for 100 numbers, and run it. Note how quickly it runs compared to the recursive program.

Exercise 13-2 Test the Towers of Hanoi puzzle

In this exercise, you'll test the Towers of Hanoi puzzle.

Open and test the program

1. In IDLE, open the towers_of_hanoi.py file that's in this folder:

   `python/exercises/ch13`

2. Review the code and run it for 3, 4, and 5 disks. Note that the pattern is slightly different depending on whether the number is even or odd.

3. Continue testing with larger numbers until the program begins running too slowly to be acceptable.

Add a print statement that traces the calls on the stack

4. Add a statement to the start of the move_disk() function that prints the name of the function and the values of the arguments that are being passed to it. When you're done, the console should look like this for 4 disks:

```
**** TOWERS OF HANOI ****

Enter number of disks: 4

    move_disk(n=4, src=A, dest=C, temp=B)
    move_disk(n=3, src=A, dest=B, temp=C)
    move_disk(n=2, src=A, dest=C, temp=B)
    move_disk(n=1, src=A, dest=B, temp=C)
    move_disk(n=0, src=A, dest=C, temp=B)
Move disk 1 from A to B
    move_disk(n=0, src=C, dest=B, temp=A)
Move disk 2 from A to C
    move_disk(n=1, src=B, dest=C, temp=A)
    move_disk(n=0, src=B, dest=A, temp=C)
Move disk 1 from B to C
    move_disk(n=0, src=A, dest=C, temp=B)
Move disk 3 from A to B
    move_disk(n=2, src=C, dest=B, temp=A)
    move_disk(n=1, src=C, dest=A, temp=B)
    move_disk(n=0, src=C, dest=B, temp=A)
...
```

5. Study the console and note how the move_disk() functions are pushed onto the stack and popped off the stack.

Section 3

Object-oriented programming

So far in this book, you have learned how to create objects from the built-in classes that are provided by Python. This includes the int, float, str, and list classes. In addition, you have learned how to organize your programs into a series of functions that process the data of your program. This is known as *procedural programming*.

In the next three chapters, you'll learn how to define your own classes. In addition, you'll learn how to create and use objects from your own classes. This allows you to group the data for your programs and the procedures for operating on that data into an object. This is known as *object-oriented programming*, and it can speed the development of large programs and make your code more reusable.

Because each chapter in this section builds on the previous chapter, we recommend that you read these chapters in sequence. We also recommend that you read at least chapters 14 and 15 in this section before going on to section 4. That's because the chapters in section 4 expect you to have a basic understanding of how object-oriented programming works.

14

How to define and use your own classes

So far in this book, you have learned how to create and use objects from the built-in classes that are provided by Python. Now, you'll learn how to define your own classes. In addition, you'll learn how to create objects from those classes and use them in your programs. Fortunately, this works the same as creating and using objects from the built-in classes provided by Python.

An introduction to classes and objects

This chapter starts by introducing classes and objects. This introduction includes two diagrams for a Product class, the complete code for a Product class, and code that creates objects from this class and uses them. As you read this topic, remember that it's only an overview and that the details for defining a class are presented in the next topic. However, if you have experience with other object-oriented programming languages, you might understand many of the details of this code.

Two UML diagrams for the Product class

Figure 14-1 begins by showing a *class diagram* for a *class* named Product. This diagram uses a simplified version of *Unified Modeling Language* (*UML*), a modeling language that is the industry standard for working with all object-oriented programming languages including Python.

In this diagram, the class contains three *attributes* named name, price, and discountPercent. In addition, it contains three *methods* named __init__, getDiscountAmount, and getDiscountPrice.

Of these methods, the __init__() method is a special method that creates an object from the class and initializes its attributes. This method accepts three parameters that are used to set the values of the three attributes. On the other hand, the getDiscountAmount() method doesn't accept any parameters. Instead, it calculates the discount amount from the data that's stored in the object and returns the resulting value.

This shows how objects allow you to group related variables (attributes) and functions (methods) into *data structures* called *objects*. This is the foundation of *object-oriented programming* (*OOP*), and it's fundamentally different than procedural programming, which passes data between a series of functions.

The second diagram shows that a *class* can be thought of as a template or blueprint from which one or more objects can be created. Here, the diagram shows only the attributes, not the methods, of the class and its objects. In this case, two objects named product1 and product2 are created from the Product class. Within these objects, each attribute contains some data. In other words, an object is an *instance* of a class. As a result, the process of creating an object from a class is sometimes called *instantiation*.

Once you create an object from a class, the object has an *identity* (a unique address), a *state* (the data that it stores), and *behavior* (the methods that it contains). As a program runs, an object's state may change.

A diagram of the Product class

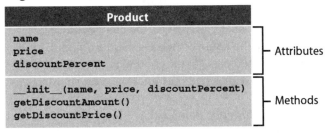

The relationship between a class and its objects

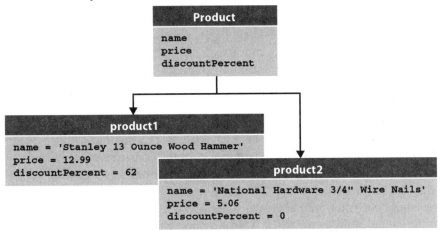

Description

- *Object-oriented programming* (*OOP*) groups related variables and functions into *data structures* called *objects*.

- A *class* can be thought of as a template or blueprint from which *objects* are made.

- The *attributes* of a class define the type of data that an object can store.

- The *methods* of a class define the tasks that an object can perform. Often, these methods provide a way to modify the attributes of the object.

- Once you create an object from a class, the object has an *identity* (a unique address), a *state* (the data that it stores), and *behavior* (the methods that it contains). As a program runs, an object's state may change.

- An object is an *instance* of a class. In other words, you can create more than one object from a single class. The process of creating an object from a class is sometimes called *instantiation*.

UML diagramming notes

- *UML* (*Unified Modeling Language*) is the industry standard used to describe the classes and objects of an object-oriented application.

- A UML *class diagram* describes the attributes and methods of one or more classes.

Figure 14-1   Two UML diagrams for the Product class

Code that defines a Product class

Figure 14-2 shows the code for the Product class. Here, the class definition starts with the class keyword followed by the name of the class and a colon. By convention, it's common to start user-defined class names with an uppercase letter. However, many of the built-in class names (such as int, float, and str) start with a lowercase letter.

After defining the name of the class, this code defines the __init__() method for the Product class. This is a special method that's known as the class *constructor*, and it's automatically called whenever a Product object is created from the Product class.

In this example, the constructor takes four parameters. Of these parameters, the first parameter is a reference to the object itself. This is required for all methods, including the constructor. By convention, this reference is named *self*. We recommend that you follow that convention, although you can use another name if you want.

Within the body of the constructor, the first statement creates the name *attribute* and initializes it to the value that's stored in the name parameter. The second statement creates and initializes the price attribute in a similar fashion. And so on. In other words, the last three parameters of the constructor initialize the three attributes of the object. You can think of these attributes as variables that store the data for an object.

For now, these attributes are *public*. As a result, code outside the class can get and set the values of these attributes. This is a good way to get started with attributes. Later in this chapter, you'll learn how to make them private and control access to them.

After the constructor method, the class defines two *public methods*. Both of these methods perform calculations on the data that's stored in the attributes and return the result. For example, the getDiscountAmount() method calculates the discount amount from the price and discountPercent attributes and returns the result.

Code that uses a Product class

The code that uses the Product class begins by importing the Product class from the objects module. As a result, this code doesn't need to prefix the name of the class with the name of the module. This is often a good way to import classes.

After importing the Product class, this code creates two product objects. Here, the constructor sets the values for all three attributes of each object. Then, this code prints the data for the first product object to the console. To do that, the first three statements use the attributes of the object to get the values for the three attributes. Then, the last two statements use methods to get the data that's calculated from the attributes.

The Product class in the module named objects

```
class Product:
    # a constructor that initializes 3 attributes
    def __init__(self, name, price, discountPercent):
        self.name = name                               # attribute 1
        self.price = price                             # attribute 2
        self.discountPercent = discountPercent         # attribute 3

    # a method that uses two attributes to perform a calculation
    def getDiscountAmount(self):
        return self.price * self.discountPercent / 100

    # a method that calls another method to perform a calculation
    def getDiscountPrice(self):
        return self.price - self.getDiscountAmount()
```

A script that creates two Product objects and uses one of them

```
from objects import Product

# create two product objects
product1 = Product("Stanley 13 Ounce Wood Hammer", 12.99, 62)
product2 = Product('National Hardware 3/4" Wire Nails', 5.06, 0)

# print data for product1 to console
print("PRODUCT DATA")
print("Name:             {:s}".format(product1.name))
print("Price:            {:.2f}".format(product1.price))
print("Discount percent: {:d}%".format(product1.discountPercent))
print("Discount amount:  {:.2f}".format(product1.getDiscountAmount()))
print("Discount price:   {:.2f}".format(product1.getDiscountPrice()))
```

The console

```
PRODUCT DATA
Name:             Stanley 13 Ounce Wood Hammer
Price:            12.99
Discount percent: 62%
Discount amount:  8.05
Discount price:   4.94
```

Description

- Coding and calling methods works similarly to coding and calling a function.
- A *constructor* is a special method named __init__() that defines the attributes for an object and initializes the values of those attributes.
- All methods, including the constructor, must take a reference to the object itself as their first parameters. By convention, this reference is named *self*.
- When writing object-oriented code, it's common to use camel case notation for names such as method names. However, underscore notation works too.

Figure 14-2   Code that defines and uses the Product class

How to create and use objects

Figure 14-3 presents the coding details for creating objects from a user-defined class. In particular, it shows how to create objects from the Product class defined in the previous figure. Then, it shows how to use the attributes and methods of these objects. These skills are the same as the skills for working with built-in objects, so this should mostly be review.

To start, if the class is in a different module, you must import the module. When working with classes, it often makes sense to import the class from the module as shown in the first example.

Then, you can create an object from the class by coding the name of the class followed by a set of parentheses as shown in the second example. These parentheses call the constructor for the object, so you must code any parameters required by the constructor within these parentheses.

For this to work correctly, you must specify the correct number of parameters, in the correct sequence, and with compatible data types. In this example, for instance, the first statement creates a Product object with a name of "Stanley 13 Ounce Wood Hammer", a price of 12.99, and a discount of 62 percent. This works since the constructor for the Product class accepts three parameters: a string for the name, a number for the price, and a number for the discount percent.

Once you create an object, you can get or set its attributes as shown in the third example. To do that, you code the object name, followed by the dot operator, followed by the attribute name. In this example, both statements work with the Product object named product1. The first statement sets the discountPercent attribute to a value of 40. The second statement gets the value stored in the discountPercent attribute and assigns it to a variable named percent.

Similarly, you can call the methods of an object as shown in the fourth example. Calling a method is similar to accessing an attribute. However, you must code a set of parentheses after the name of the method. Then, if the method requires parameters, you code the parameters within the parentheses, separating multiple parameters with commas. In this example, the first statement calls the getDiscountAmount() method to get the discount amount and assign it to a variable named discount. The second statement calls the getDiscountPrice() method to get the discount price and assign it to a variable named salePrice.

Neither of the methods shown in this figure accept parameters. As a result, you just code an empty set of parentheses after the name of the method. However, if the method accepted parameters, you would code the parameters within the parentheses, just as you do for functions. In fact, calling a function is similar to calling a method. The main difference is that you must preface the method with the name of the object and the dot operator. That way, the method can work with the attributes of the object.

How to import a class

The syntax
```
from module_name import ClassName1[, ClassName2]...
```

Import the Product class from the objects module
```
from objects import Product
```

How to create an object

The syntax
```
objectName = ClassName([parameters])
```

Create two Product objects
```
product1 = Product('Stanley 13 Ounce Wood Hammer', 12.99, 62)
product2 = Product('National Hardware 3/4" Wire Nails', 5.06, 0)
```

How to access the attributes of an object

The syntax
```
objectName.attributeName
```

Set an attribute
```
product1.discountPercent = 40          # sets discountPercent to 40
```

Get an attribute
```
percent = product1.discountPercent     # percent = 40
```

How to call the methods of an object

The syntax
```
objectName.methodName([parameters])
```

Call the getDiscountAmount() method
```
discount = product1.getDiscountAmount()
```

Call the getDiscountPrice() method
```
salePrice = product1.getDiscountPrice()
```

Description
- To create an object, you code the name of the class and a set of parentheses. Inside the parentheses, you code the parameters for the constructor separated by commas.
- To access the attributes of an object, you code the name of the object followed by the dot operator (**.**) and the name of the attribute.
- To call a method from an object, you code the name of the object followed by the dot operator (**.**), the name of the method, and a set of parentheses. Inside the parentheses, you code the parameters for the method separated by commas.

Figure 14-3   How to create and use objects

How to define a class

The next few figures show the coding details for defining a class. This includes how to code a constructor that initializes data attributes. In addition, it includes how to code methods that process the data that's stored in those attributes.

How to code a constructor and attributes

Figure 14-4 shows how to code a *constructor*, which is the special method that's automatically executed when a new object is created from a class. The syntax for coding a constructor is similar to the syntax for coding a function. However, there are two significant differences. First, the constructor must be named __init__ (with two underscores before and after). Second, within the parentheses, the first parameter must be a reference to the object itself.

By convention, the reference to the object itself is named *self*. This parameter provides a way for the programmer to access the attributes and methods of an object from within the class. To do that, you code the self parameter, followed by a dot operator, followed by the name of the attribute or method. However, the self parameter isn't visible to other programmers who use the class. As a result, code that calls a constructor shouldn't supply a parameter that corresponds with the self parameter.

In Python, a class can only contain one constructor. However, there are many different ways to code that constructor. To give you a clearer idea of how constructors work, this figure shows three possible ways to code the constructor for the Product class.

The first example shows a constructor that doesn't accept any parameters from the calling code. However, it does specify the parameter that's a reference to the object itself. As mentioned earlier, this is required for all methods of a class, including the constructor. Then, the body of this constructor defines three attributes and sets them to default values. As a result, when you use this constructor to create an object, you typically need to set the attributes of the object.

When you code a constructor, it's a common practice to code parameters that supply the initial values for the attributes of the object as shown in the second example. Here, the constructor accepts three parameters from the calling code. Then, the body of this constructor uses these three parameters to set the initial values for the three attributes. As a result, when you use this constructor to create an object, you typically don't need to set the attributes of the object.

If you need more flexibility in the number of parameters that the calling code can supply to a constructor, you can use named parameters as shown in the third example. Here, the constructor provides default values for all three parameters. As a result, the code that creates an object can supply all three parameters. Or, it can supply zero, one, two, or three parameters. To do that, this code can use named parameters whenever that's necessary or whenever it makes the code easier to read. Then, the constructor uses the default value for any parameter that isn't supplied.

The syntax

```
def __init__(self[, parameters]):      # the constructor
    self.attrName1 = attrValue1        # first attribute
    self.attrName2 = attrValue2        # second attribute
    ...
```

A constructor with no parameters

```
def __init__(self):
    self.name = ""
    self.price = 0.0
    self.discountPercent = 0
```

Code that uses this constructor to create an object

```
product = Product()
```

Code that sets the attributes of the object

```
product.name = "Stanley 13 Ounce Wood Hammer"
product.price = 12.99
product.discountPercent = 62
```

A constructor with three parameters

```
def __init__(self, name, price, discountPercent):
    self.name = name
    self.price = price
    self.discountPercent = discountPercent
```

Code that uses this constructor to create an object and set its attributes

```
product = Product("Stanley 13 Ounce Wood Hammer", 12.99, 62)
```

A constructor with default values for its parameters

```
def __init__(self, name="", price=0.0, discountPercent=0):
    self.name = name
    self.price = price
    self.discountPercent = discountPercent
```

Code that supplies all three parameters

```
product = Product("Stanley 13 Ounce Wood Hammer", 12.99, 62)
```

Code that supplies just two parameters
so the default value is used for discountPercent

```
product = Product(name="Stanley 13 Ounce Wood Hammer", price=12.99)
```

Description

- The constructor for a class is executed when an object is created from the class. It typically defines and initializes the attributes of the object, but it can run other initialization code too.

- The constructor must take a reference to the object itself as its first parameter. By convention, this reference is named self.

- You can only code one constructor per class.

Figure 14-4   How to code a constructor and attributes

How to code methods

Figure 14-5 shows how to code the methods of a class. The syntax for coding a method is almost identical to the syntax for coding a function. The only difference is that the first parameter for the method must be a reference to the object itself. This lets a method access the attributes of the class, and this works just as it does for the constructor of a class. As a result, if you understand how to code functions, and you understand the previous figure, you shouldn't have any trouble coding methods.

The first example shows how to code and call a method named getDiscountAmount(). Since this method doesn't accept any parameters from the calling code, it just supplies the self parameter that's a reference to the object itself. Within the body of this method, the first statement uses the self parameter to access the object's price and discountPrice attributes; it uses those attributes to calculate the discount amount; and it stores the discount amount in a local variable named discountAmount. Then, the second statement returns this value to the calling code.

The second example shows a more concise way to code the getDiscountAmount() method. Here, the body of the method skips the intermediate step of storing the discount amount in a variable. If you compare the calling code in these first two examples, you'll notice that it's exactly the same. This shows that you can change the code in the body of a method without having to change the code that calls the method.

The third example shows how to code and call a method named getDiscountPrice. Like the getDiscountAmount() method, this method doesn't accept any parameters from the calling code and returns a calculated value. To do that, the getDiscountPrice() method uses the self parameter to call the getDiscountAmount() method of the object. This shows that you can use the self parameter to access the attributes or call the methods of the current object.

The fourth example shows how to code a method named getPriceStr. This method accepts one parameter, which is a 2-letter country code that identifies a country. Within the body of this method, the first statement converts the price attribute to a string named priceStr that displays two decimal places. Then, this code checks the country code and appends an appropriate three-letter currency code to the priceStr.

When coding methods, many programmers who are new to Python forget to include the self argument. If you do that, you'll get an error message like the one shown in this figure when you call the method. At first, this error message might be confusing because it says that the getPriceStr() method "only takes one positional argument, but two were given". It says this even though the calling code only supplies one parameter. The explanation is that Python automatically passes a reference to the object itself as the first parameter. As a result, even though the calling code only supplies one parameter, Python is actually passing two parameters to the method.

Another common mistake made by new Python programmers is to forget to prefix attribute names with the self parameter. If you do this, you create a local

The syntax

```
def methodName(self[, parameters]):
    statements
```

A method that returns a value

```
def getDiscountAmount(self):
    discountAmount = self.price * self.discountPercent / 100
    return discountAmount
```

Code that calls this method

```
discountAmount = product.getDiscountAmount()
```

A more concise way to code this method

```
def getDiscountAmount(self):
    return self.price * self.discountPercent / 100
```

Code that calls this method

```
discountAmount = product.getDiscountAmount()
```

A method that calls another method of the class

```
def getDiscountPrice(self):
    return self.price - self.getDiscountAmount()
```

Code that calls this method

```
discountPrice = product.getDiscountPrice()
```

A method of the Product class that accepts a parameter

```
def getPriceStr(self, country):
    priceStr = "{:.2f}".format(self.price)
    if country == "US":
        priceStr += " USD"
    elif country == "DE":
        priceStr = priceStr + " EUR"
    return priceStr
```

Code that calls this method

```
print("Price: " + product.getPriceStr("US"))
```

The error that's displayed if you forget to code the self parameter

```
TypeError: getPriceStr() takes 1 positional argument but 2 were given
```

Description

- To code a method in a class, you code the def keyword followed by the name of the method, an optional parameter list in a set of parentheses, a colon, and then a block of statements to execute.
- A method must take a reference to the object itself as its first parameter. By convention, this reference is named self.

Figure 14-5   How to code methods

variable instead of accessing the attribute. This local variable behaves like any other local variable. In other words, it's only available inside the current method and loses its value when the method returns. It's perfectly legal and common to use local variables inside methods. However, if you want to work with an attribute of the object instead of a local variable, you need to remember to prefix the attribute name with the self parameter.

The Product Viewer 1.0 program

Figure 14-6 shows a simple but complete program named Product Viewer 1.0 that uses objects created from a Product class. This program begins by displaying a numbered list of three products. Then, the user can view the data for a product by entering its number.

The code for the Product class is stored in a module named objects. In other words, it's stored in a file named objects.py. This code defines a constructor that initializes the attributes that store the name, price, and discount percent for the object. Then, it defines two methods that get the discount amount and price for the object. To do that, these methods access the object's attributes and methods.

The product_viewer module contains the code for the program. To start, this code imports the Product class from the objects module. Then, this code defines the functions that make up the program.

The show_products() function displays a numbered list of products. It accepts a parameter that's a list or tuple that contains one or more Product objects. To display these Product objects, a for loop iterates through each Product object. Within the loop, the first statement uses the index to get a Product object from the list. Then, the second statement displays a number that's one greater than the index followed by the name of the Product object.

The show_product() function displays the data that's available from a product. To do that, it accepts a parameter that's a Product object. Then, it uses the three attributes of the product to display the name, price, and discount percent. Finally, it uses the two methods of the product to display the discount amount and discount price.

The console

```
The Product Viewer program

PRODUCTS
1. Stanley 13 Ounce Wood Hammer
2. National Hardware 3/4" Wire Nails
3. Economy Duct Tape, 60 yds, Silver

Enter product number: 1

PRODUCT DATA
Name:              Stanley 13 Ounce Wood Hammer
Price:             12.99
Discount percent: 62%
Discount amount:  8.05
Discount price:   4.94

View another product? (y/n):
```

The objects module

```python
class Product:
    def __init__(self, name, price, discountPercent):
        self.name = name
        self.price = price
        self.discountPercent = discountPercent

    def getDiscountAmount(self):
        return self.price * self.discountPercent / 100

    def getDiscountPrice(self):
        return self.price - self.getDiscountAmount()
```

The product_viewer module

```python
from objects import Product

def show_products(products):
    print("PRODUCTS")
    for i in range(len(products)):
        product = products[i]
        print(str(i+1) + ". " + product.name)
    print()

def show_product(product):
    print("PRODUCT DATA")
    print("Name:              {:s}".format(product.name))
    print("Price:             {:.2f}".format(product.price))
    print("Discount percent: {:d}%".format(product.discountPercent))
    print("Discount amount:  {:.2f}".format(product.getDiscountAmount()))
    print("Discount price:   {:.2f}".format(product.getDiscountPrice()))
    print()
```

Figure 14-6   The Product Viewer 1.0 program (part 1)

The main() function begins by displaying the title of the program. Then, it creates a tuple of Product objects. Note that this code doesn't provide a variable that refers to these Product objects. Instead, it calls the constructor of the Product class to create each object, and it stores each object in the tuple without going through the intermediate step of creating a variable name that refers to the object.

After creating the tuple of product objects, this code passes that tuple to the show_products() function defined earlier in the module. This displays the numbered list of products. Then, this code prompts the user to enter a number that corresponds with a product. Next, this code gets the corresponding Product object from the tuple of Product objects, and passes that Product object to the show_product() function. This displays the data for the product object.

The product_viewer module (continued)

```python
def main():
    print("The Product Viewer program")
    print()

    # a tuple of Product objects
    products = (Product("Stanley 13 Ounce Wood Hammer", 12.99, 62),
                Product('National Hardware 3/4" Wire Nails', 5.06, 0),
                Product("Economy Duct Tape, 60 yds, Silver", 7.24, 0))
    show_products(products)

    while True:
        number = int(input("Enter product number: "))
        print()

        product = products[number-1]
        show_product(product)

        choice = input("View another product? (y/n): ")
        print()
        if choice != "y":
            print("Bye!")
            break


if __name__ == "__main__":
    main()
```

Figure 14-6   The Product Viewer 1.0 program (part 2)

How work with object composition

Object composition is a way to combine simple objects into more complex data structures. In the last few figures, you learned how to define a class that has attributes that store built-in objects such as str, float, and int objects. Now, you'll see how to define a class that stores one or more user-defined objects.

How object composition works

Figure 14-7 presents a diagram that shows how object composition works. More specifically, this diagram shows that the Dice object uses one or more Die objects. To show this relationship, this diagram uses an arrow with a closed (shaded) arrowhead to point from the Dice class to the Die class. However, a Die object doesn't use the Dice object. As a result, there's no arrow pointing from the Die class to the Dice class. It may not seem like much, but being able to define an object that can contain other user-defined objects is a powerful feature that allows you to create complex data structures that you can customize for each program that you develop.

The Die and Dice classes

This figure also shows the dice module that contains the code for the Die and Dice classes. This module begins by importing the random module that's used by the Die class.

The Die class has a single attribute, the value attribute. When you create a Die object, the constructor sets the value attribute to 1. However, since the value attribute is *public*, the calling code can set it to another value if necessary. In addition, the calling code can call the roll() method to set the value attribute to a random value from 1 to 6.

The Dice class also has a single attribute, the list attribute. When you create a Dice object, it initializes this attribute to an empty list. Then, you can use the addDie() method to add a Die object to this list. To do that, this method calls the append() method of the list object to add the die parameter to the end of the list.

After you have added one or more Die objects to the list attribute, you can use the rollAll() method to roll all of the Die objects. To do that, this code loops through each Die object in the list attribute and calls the roll() method on each one.

A UML diagram for two classes that use composition

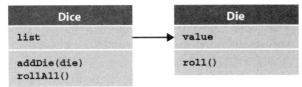

The dice module

```python
import random

class Die:
    def __init__(self):
        self.value = 1

    def roll(self):
        self.value = random.randrange(1, 7)


class Dice:
    def __init__(self):
        self.list = []

    def addDie(self, die):
        self.list.append(die)

    def rollAll(self):
        for die in self.list:
            die.roll()
```

Description

- *Object composition* is a way to combine simple objects into more complex ones. For example, one Dice object can store multiple Die objects.

Figure 14-7   How object composition works

The Dice Roller 1.0 program

Figure 14-8 shows a program named Dice Roller 1.0 that's stored in a module named dice_roller. To start, this module imports the Die and Dice classes from the dice module.

The main() function of this module starts by printing the title of the program. Then, it prompts the user to enter the number of dice to roll. Next, it creates a Dice object and uses a loop to create the correct number of Die objects and add them to the Dice object.

After creating the Dice object, the code enters an infinite loop that's the main loop for the program. This loop begins by calling the rollAll() method of the Dice object to roll all of the dice. Then, it loops through each of the Die objects and prints the value of each Die object to the console.

After displaying the roll, this code asks the user if he or she wants to roll again. If the user enters "y" for yes, program execution jumps back to the top of the loop, which rolls the dice and displays the result again. Otherwise, this code prints a goodbye message and uses a break statement to cause execution to jump out of the loop, which ends the program.

At this point, you may realize that you could accomplish the same results with less code by accessing the random module directly and not using the Die and Dice objects. So, why bother creating these objects?

One advantage of using these objects is that it shields the programmer who uses these classes from the technical details of how the class works. In this case, the Die class shields the programmer who uses that class from how the random value is generated. In other words, the programmer doesn't need to know how to use the random module to be able to create a Die object that can be rolled to get a random value from 1 to 6. That might not be a big selling point for a simple class like the Die class, but it is for more complex classes where the underlying technical details are more complex.

Another advantage is that these objects promote code reusability. In other words, the Dice Roller program isn't the only program that can use Die and Dice objects. Other programs that need to roll six-sided dice can also use this module, especially if you continue to add functionality to this module and to make the other improvements that are described later in this chapter.

The console

```
The Dice Roller program

Enter the number of dice to roll: 5
YOUR ROLL: 1 5 1 2 6

Roll again? (y/n): y
YOUR ROLL: 1 1 4 3 4

Roll again? (y/n): y
YOUR ROLL: 5 4 6 2 2

Roll again? (y/n): n
Bye!
```

The dice_roller module

```python
from dice import Dice, Die

def main():
    print("The Dice Roller program")
    print()

    # get number of dice from user
    count = int(input("Enter the number of dice to roll: "))

    # Dice object and add Die objects to it
    dice = Dice()
    for i in range(count):
        die = Die()
        dice.addDie(die)

    while True:
        # roll the dice
        dice.rollAll()
        print("YOUR ROLL: ", end="")
        for die in dice.list:
            print(die.value, end=" ")
        print("\n")

        choice = input("Roll again? (y/n): ")
        if choice != "y":
            print("Bye!")
            break

if __name__ == "__main__":
    main()
```

Description

- The Dice Roller program uses one Dice object to store multiple Die objects.

Figure 14-8   The Dice Roller 1.0 program

How to work with encapsulation

So far, all of the user-defined objects in this chapter have used *public attributes* to store their data. As a result, the code that uses these objects can directly access their attributes. This is a good way to get started with object-oriented programming, and it's an approach that's adequate for many programs.

Unfortunately, this approach can allow other programmers to use your user-defined objects in ways that may cause them to not work properly. In addition, it can make it more difficult for other programmers to figure out how to use your objects, which makes your objects less user-friendly and reusable. If you encounter these types of problems, you can use object encapsulation to control access to your data attributes.

How object encapsulation works

Encapsulation is a fundamental concept of object-oriented programming. It allows you to prevent direct access to the data attributes of an object. In other words, it allows you to hide the object's data from the calling code. As a result, encapsulation is also known as *data hiding*.

To hide data, you code *private attributes* that other code can't access directly. After you code private attributes, you must provide an indirect way to access them. To do that, you can code *public methods* or *properties*, which are a special type of method.

So far in this chapter, the Die class has used a public attribute named value to store its value. The first step in encapsulating the Die object is to change this public attribute to a private attribute. In Python, you can do that by beginning the attribute name with two underscores as shown in the diagrams in figure 14-9.

In other words, both of these diagrams use a private attribute named __value. Then, in the first diagram, the getValue() and setValue() methods provide an indirect way to get the private __value attribute or to set it to a specified value. In the second diagram, on the other hand, the value property provides an indirect way to get the private __value attribute or to set it to a specified value. In both diagrams, the roll() method provides an indirect way to set the private __value attribute to a random value.

An *interface* allows a programmer to use an object without understanding its internal code. If the interface of an object remains the same, a programmer can change the internal code for the object without needing to change any of the code that uses the object. For example, since the second diagram uses a property named value to get and set the value attribute, it has the same interface as the Die object presented earlier in this chapter that directly accesses a public attribute named value.

When you're using Python to code classes, you can often start by coding public attributes. Later, if you determine that you need to encapsulate these attributes, you can convert them to properties.. Since the interface of the object doesn't change, there is little or no impact on any calling code.

A Die class that uses methods to provide encapsulation

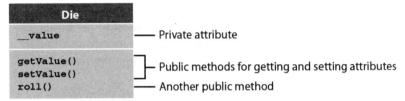

A Die class that uses properties to provide encapsulation

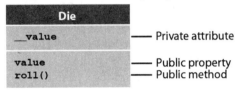

Description

- *Encapsulation* allows you to hide the data attributes of an object from other code that uses the object. This is also known as *data hiding*.
- *Public* attributes can be accessed directly by the code that uses an object.
- *Private* attributes can only be accessed indirectly through public methods or *properties*, which are a special type of method.
- An *interface* allows a programmer to use an object without understanding its internal code. If the interface of an object remains the same, a programmer can change the internal code for the object without needing to change any of the code that uses the object.

UML diagramming note

- The double underscores (__) identify the attributes that are private.

Figure 14-9   How object encapsulation works

How to hide attributes

Figure 14-10 begins by showing the Die class that's been used so far in this chapter. The constructor for this class creates a public attribute named value and sets it to 1. Then, the roll() method sets this value to a random number from 1 to 6.

This class works fine in most cases. But what happens if the calling code directly accesses the value attribute and sets it to an illegal number such as 10 or -1? In that case, the Die object doesn't work correctly.

To solve this problem, you can make the attribute private as shown in the second example. In this example, the constructor creates a private attribute named __value and sets it to 1. Then, the getValue() method provides an indirect way to get the number that's stored in the __value attribute, and the roll() method provides an indirect way to set the number that's stored in the __value attribute. Since there's no setValue() method that provides an indirect way to set the __value attribute, there's no way to set this attribute to an invalid value.

But what happens if code attempts to access the __value attribute directly? In that case, Python doesn't change the value that's stored by the __value attribute. This shows that the attribute is hidden from the calling code.

It's important to note that making an attribute private doesn't make it secure. It's possible, through programming tricks, to access private attributes directly. However, making an attribute private clearly tells other programmers that they shouldn't access or modify the variable directly because the object might not work correctly if they do.

The Die class with a public attribute named value

```
class Die:
    def __init__(self):
        self.value = 1

    def roll(self):
        self.value = random.randrange(1, 7)
```

Code that directly sets and gets the public attribute

```
die = Die()
die.value = 10      # illegal value!
print("Die:", die.value)
```

The message that's displayed on the console

```
Die: 10
```

The Die class with a private attribute named __value

```
class Die:
    def __init__(self):
        self.__value = 1

    def getValue(self):
        return self.__value

    def roll(self):
        self.__value = random.randrange(1, 7)
```

Code that attempts to directly access a private attribute

```
die = Die()
die.__value = 10
print("Die:", die.getValue())
```

The message that's displayed on the console

```
Die: 1
```

Code that indirectly sets and gets the private attribute

```
die = Die()
die.roll()
print("Die:", die.getValue())
```

Description

- To make an attribute private, prefix the name of the attribute with a double underscore (__).

- Attempting to directly access a private attribute from outside the class to set its value doesn't work. However, you can use methods to indirectly access a private attribute to get or set its values.

Figure 14-10   How to hide attributes

How to access hidden attributes with methods

Figure 14-11 begins by showing a Die class that implements the first diagram in figure 14-9. To start, the constructor defines a hidden attribute named __value and initializes it to 1. Then, the getValue(), setValue(), and roll() methods provide a way to indirectly access that attribute.

The getValue() method gets the value that's stored in the __value attribute and returns it to the calling code. As a result, it's known as a *getter method*. By convention, getter methods begin with the word get. Since a getter accesses data, it's also known as an *accessor*.

The setValue() method sets the value that's stored in the __value attribute. As a result, it's known as a *setter method*. By convention, setter methods begin with the word set. Since a setter changes data, it's also known as a *mutator*.

However, before the setValue() method changes the value that's stored in the __value attribute, it performs some data validation. To start, it checks whether the value parameter is less than 1 or greater than 6. If so, it raises a ValueError that contains a message that indicates that the value must be from 1 to 6. Otherwise, this method sets the __value attribute to the value parameter.

The roll() method also sets the value that's stored in the __value attribute. To do that, it calls the randrange() function of the random module.

As you review this code, note that there are three ways to set the __value attribute. When a programmer creates an object, the constructor sets this attribute to 1. Then, if necessary, the programmer can use the setValue() method to set this attribute to a specified value. Or, the programmer can use the roll() method to set this attribute to a random value.

At this point, you may be wondering, is the setValue() method even necessary? The answer is that it depends on how this object is going to be used. If you don't include this method in the Die class, the roll() method is the only one way to change the __value attribute. That's a simple and elegant design that's easy for other programmers to understand and use. It certainly works well enough for the Dice Roller program. But maybe that design doesn't provide enough flexibility for other programs that the Die object might be used in.

You might also be wondering whether it makes sense for the constructor to initialize the __value attribute to 1? Again, the answer depends on how this object is going to be used. Setting the __value attribute to 1 is a simple approach that's easy for other programmers to understand, and it works for the Dice Roller program. But maybe the Die object would work better for other programs if the __value attribute was initialized to a random integer from 1 to 6. Or maybe it would work better if the constructor included a named parameter for the value that specified a default value of 1.

The Die class with methods that access a private attribute

```
class Die:
    def __init__(self):
        self.__value = 1

    def getValue(self):
        return self.__value

    def setValue(self, value):
        if value < 1 or value > 6:
            raise ValueError("Die value must be from 1 to 6.")
        else:
            self.__value = value

    def roll(self):
        self.__value = random.randrange(1, 7)
```

Code that uses the getter and setter methods

```
die = Die()
die.setValue(6)
print("Die:", die.getValue())
```

The message that's displayed on the console

```
Die: 6
```

Code that attempts to use the setValue() method to set invalid data

```
die = Die()
die.setValue(-1)
```

The error message that's displayed on the console

```
ValueError: Die value must be from 1 to 6.
```

Description

- You can use public methods to get and set the value of a private attribute.
- The method that gets the value of the attribute is known as a *getter method*, and the method that sets the value of the attribute is known as a *setter method*.
- Since a getter accesses data, it's also known as an *accessor*. Since a setter changes data, it's also known as a *mutator*.
- By convention, getter and setter methods begin with get and set respectively.

Figure 14-11   How to access hidden attributes with methods

How to access hidden attributes with properties

The previous figure showed how to use methods to access hidden attributes. However, Python supports a special type of method known as a *property* that provides a more elegant way for other programmers to access hidden attributes. To create a property, you use a special language feature known as an *annotation*.

Figure14-12 begins by showing the two annotations used to specify the methods for getting or setting properties. To designate a method for getting a property, you code the @property annotation just above the method definition. To designate a method for setting a property, you code the @ sign, followed by the name of the property, followed by a period, followed by the word *setter*.

The Die class shows how this works by implementing the second diagram in figure 14-9. First, the @property is coded above the method named value. This method gets the value by returning the __value attribute. Second, the @value.setter annotation is coded above another method named value that accepts one parameter from the calling code: the value. The body of this method works like body of the setValue() method shown in the previous figure. In short, it performs some data validation and only sets the __value attribute to the value parameter if the data is valid.

Now that you've seen how to access hidden attributes with methods or properties, take a moment to consider the benefits of using properties. To start, the code for accessing a property is typically more concise than the code for accessing a method. More importantly, properties allow you to use the same interface for accessing attributes indirectly as you do for accessing attributes directly. This allows you to start coding a class by using the simplest and easiest way to access its data: public attributes.

Later, if you need more control over the access to these attributes, you can change them to private attributes and code properties to access them. And you can do that without having to change the interface. As a result, this should have a little if any impact on any code that uses these objects.

Two annotations for getting and setting properties

Annotation	Description
`@property`	Coded above the getter method for the property.
`@propertyName.setter`	Coded above the setter method for the specified property.

A Die class that uses a property to access a private attribute

```
class Die:
    def __init__(self):
        self.__value = 1

    @property
    def value(self):
        return self.__value

    @value.setter
    def value(self, value):
        if value < 1 or value > 6:
            raise ValueError("Die value must be from 1 to 6.")
        else:
            self.__value = value
```

Code that uses the value property to get and set data

```
die = Die()
die.value = 6
print("Die:", die.value)
```

The message that's displayed on the console

```
Die: 6
```

Code that attempts to use the value property to set invalid data

```
die = Die()
die.value = -1
```

The error message that's displayed on the console

```
ValueError: Die value must be from 1 to 6.
```

Description

- A *property* is a type of method that's commonly used to get and set a private attribute.

- To code a property, you must code the appropriate *annotation* above the method. In Python, an annotation begins with the @ symbol.

- The property that gets the value of the attribute is known as the *getter property*, and the property that sets the value of the attribute is known as the *setter property*.

Figure 14-12   How to access hidden attributes with properties

The Die and Dice classes with encapsulation

Figure 14-13 shows encapsulated versions of the Die and Dice classes. By now, you should be familiar with the Die class. However, this version of the class doesn't provide a setter method for the value property. In other words, the value property is a *read-only property*. That's fine because most programs will use the roll() method to set the __value attribute. As a result, the name property only needs to provide a way to get the __value attribute.

In contrast, if you only provide a setter method for a property, it becomes a *write-only property*. In this figure, though, there aren't any write-only properties.

The Dice class begins with a constructor that creates a private attribute named __list to store the list of Die objects. To get the list, this code provides a read-only property named list. However, lists are mutable. As a result, if you return this list, the calling code can change the attribute. For example, the calling code could call any of the methods of the list object to add, remove, or sort Die objects. Clearly, this would break the encapsulation of the Dice object.

To prevent direct access to this list, this code converts the list to a tuple, which is an immutable object. Then, it returns the tuple to the calling code. As a result, the calling code can use this tuple to get the Die objects. Since these Die objects are mutable, the calling code could call the roll() method to change their values. However, it can't add, remove, or replace any of the Die objects of the __list attribute. This approach implements encapsulation reasonably well. However, in the next chapter, you'll learn how to improve the encapsulation for this class even further.

Note that the Die and Dice classes in this figure use public properties that have the same names as the public attributes of the Die and Die classes in figure 14-7. In other words, these classes have the same *interface* as the Die and Dice classes that were presented earlier. As a result, you can use these encapsulated versions of the Die and Dice objects in the Dice Roller program presented in figure 14-8 without making any changes to the code in that program. All you need to do is replace the old dice module with the new one.

A UML diagram for two classes that use encapsulation

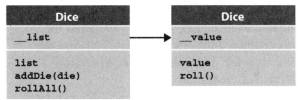

The dice module

```
import random

class Die:
    def __init__(self):
        self.__value = 1

    @property                        # read-only!
    def value(self):
        return self.__value

    def roll(self):
        self.__value = random.randrange(1, 7)

class Dice:
    def __init__(self):
        self.__list = []

    @property                        # read-only
    def list(self):
        dice_tuple = tuple(self.__list)
        return dice_tuple

    def addDie(self, die):
        self.__list.append(die)

    def rollAll(self):
        for die in self.__list:
            die.roll()
```

Description

- If you only code a getter, you create a *read-only property*. Conversely, if you only code a setter, you create a *write-only property*.

- If you return a mutable attribute (such as a list), the calling code can change the attribute directly. One way to encapsulate a mutable attribute is to convert the mutable attribute to an immutable object (such as a tuple) before returning it.

- Since the Die and Dice classes use a property to access the hidden attribute, these classes have the same interface as the Die and Dice classes presented earlier in this chapter. As a result, you can use them in the Dice Roller program without making any changes to the other code in that program.

Figure 14-13   The Die and Dice classes with encapsulation

The Product class with some encapsulation

To round out your understanding of encapsulation, figure 14-14 shows the Product class presented earlier in this chapter with some encapsulation. So far, this class only encapsulates the product's price. To do that, it uses a private attribute named __price to store the price of the product.

However, the Product class provides two ways to set a product's price. First, you can set the price by passing a price parameter to the constructor. Second, you can set the price by passing a price parameter to the price property. To make sure that the same data validation is applied to both ways of setting the price, the second statement of the constructor sets the price by passing the price parameter to the setter for the price property. Then, the price property checks the price parameter to make sure it's valid. If so, it sets the __price attribute to the price parameter.

Alternately, you could include the data validation code in the constructor like this:

```
def __init__(self, name="", price=0.0, discountPercent=0):
    self.name = name
    # same data validation code as the setter property
    if price < 0:
        raise ValueError("Price can't be less than 0")
    else:
        self.__price = price
    self.discountPercent = discountPercent
```

This might be easier to understand when you're first getting started. However, duplicating this code violates the DRY (Don't Repeat Yourself) principle, and makes this class more difficult to maintain. For example, if you later need to change the data validation code, you need to change it in two places, which is both tedious and error-prone.

Note that you could use a similar approach to provide data validation for the discount percent, which must be greater than or equal to 0 and less than or equal to 100. You could also provide data validation code for the name attribute so that it's not more than a specified number of characters. However, there's often no need to provide this kind of data validation.

When you use Python, you can wait to implement encapsulation until the need for it becomes clear. However, with other languages that don't support properties, it's more important to implement encapsulation early since implanting encapsulation in those languages typically changes the interface for the object.

A UML diagram for a Product class that uses some encapsulation

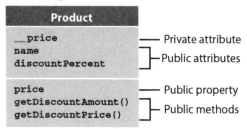

The code for the Product class

```
class Product:
    def __init__(self, name="", price=0.0, discountPercent=0):
        self.name = name
        self.price = price  # passes price param to price setter
        self.discountPercent = discountPercent

    @property
    def price(self):
        return self.__price

    @price.setter
    def price(self, price):
        if price < 0:
            raise ValueError("Price can't be less than 0")
        else:
            self.__price = price

    def getDiscountAmount(self):
        return self.price * self.discountPercent / 100

    def getDiscountPrice(self):
        return self.price - self.getDiscountAmount()
```

Code that attempts to use the price property to set invalid data

```
product = Product()
product.price = -11.50
```

Code that attempts to use the constructor to set invalid data

```
product = Product("Hammer", -11.50)
```

The error message that's displayed on the console

```
ValueError: Price can't be less than 0
```

Description

- If you want to allow the constructor to set a private attribute and you also want to provide a setter property for that attribute, you can call the setter property from the constructor. That way, the constructor and the setter perform the same processing.

Figure 14-14   The Product class with some encapsulation

The Pig Dice game

This chapter finishes by presenting a version of the Pig Dice game that uses an object to store all variables related to the state of the game. This makes it easy to pass the game state from one function to another.

In addition, this Pig Dice game uses the Die object of the dice module described in figure 14-13. This shows that the Die class can be used in multiple programs. You just import it into your program and use it as you would use any other object.

The console

Figure 14-15 begins by showing the console for the PIG game. If you read chapter 4, you should already be familiar with how this game works. As a result, you can focus on the coding changes.

The code

The game module begins by importing the Die class from the dice module. This is the Die class shown in figure 14-13. To make this class available to the Pig Dice game, the dice.py file is in the same directory as the game.py file.

After importing the Die class, the game module defines the Game class. This class only contains a constructor that doesn't accept any arguments from the calling code. Within the constructor, the code defines six public attributes to store the state of the game, and it initializes these attributes to values that are appropriate for a new game. For example, the turn attribute is set to 1, the score is set to 0, and the isGameOver attribute is set to False. In addition, this constructor creates a Die object and assigns it to the die attribute.

As a result, the calling code can get any of these attributes to check the state of the game, and it can set any of these attributes to change the state of the game. In addition, the calling code can get a Die object and call its roll() method to change the state of the Die object.

The pig_dice module begins by importing the Game class from the game module. Then, it defines a function that displays a welcome message that includes the rules of the game.

The console

```
Let's Play PIG!

* See how many turns it takes you to get to 20.
* Turn ends when you hold or roll a 1.
* If you roll a 1, you lose all points for the turn.
* If you hold, you save all points for the turn.

TURN 1
Roll or hold? (r/h): r
Die: 5
Roll or hold? (r/h): r
Die: 4
Roll or hold? (r/h): r
Die: 5
Roll or hold? (r/h): h
Score for turn: 14
Total score: 14

TURN 2
Roll or hold? (r/h): r
Die: 6
Roll or hold? (r/h): h
Score for turn: 6
Total score: 20

You finished in 2 turns!
Play again? (y/n):
```

The game module

```python
from dice import Die

class Game:
    def __init__(self):
        self.turn = 1
        self.score = 0
        self.scoreThisTurn = 0
        self.isTurnOver = False
        self.isGameOver = False
        self.die = Die()
```

The pig_dice module

```python
from game import Game

def display_welcome():
    print("Let's Play PIG!")
    print()
    print("* See how many turns it takes you to get to 20.")
    print("* Turn ends when you hold or roll a 1.")
    print("* If you roll a 1, you lose all points for the turn.")
    print("* If you hold, you save all points for the turn.")
    print()
```

Figure 14-15   The Pig Dice game (part 1)

In part 2 of figure 14-15, the play_game() function contains the code that's called when the game is started. Here, the first statement creates a Game object. Then, this code starts the main loop for the game. This loop continues until the isGameOver attribute of the Game object is set to True. Within this loop, a single statement calls the take_turn() function and passes it the Game object.

The take_turn() function begins by printing the turn number. To do that, it gets the turn from the Game object. Then, it resets the scoreThisTurn and isTurnOver attributes. This isn't necessary on the first turn but is necessary for subsequent turns. Next, it begins a while loop that continues until the isTurnOver attribute is set to True.

Within the loop, the first statement prompts the user to choose whether to roll or hold. If the user chooses to roll, this code calls the roll_dice() function and passes the Game object to it. If the user chooses to hold, this code calls the hold_turn() function and passes the Game object to it.

The roll_die() function begins by getting the Die object from the Game object. Then, it calls the roll() method of the Die object. As you should know by now, this changes the value that's stored in the Die object. Next, this code prints the value that's stored in the Die object to the conole.

After that, the roll_die() function checks whether the die is 1. If so, it changes several attributes of the Game object. More specifically, it sets the scoreThisTurn attribute to 0, it increments the turn attribute by 1, and it sets the isTurnOver attribute to True. In other words, it discards all points for this turn and ends the turn. Then, it prints a message to the console that indicates that the turn is over and that there was no score for this turn. However, if the die is not 1, this code increments the scoreThisTurn attribute by the value of the die.

The hold_turn() function begins by changing two attributes of the Game object. The first statement increments the score attribute by the scoreThisTurn attribute, and the second statement sets the isTurnOver attribute to True. In other words, this code saves the score for the turn and ends the turn. Then, the code prints the score for the turn and the total score to the console.

After that, the hold_turn() function checks whether the score is greater than or equal to 20. If so, it sets the isGameOver variable to True, and prints a message that indicates how many turns it took you to finish the game. To do that, this message accesses the turn attribute of the Game object. However, if the score is not greater than or equal to 20, this code just increments the turn attribute by 1.

The main() function calls the display_welcome() function to display the welcome message and rules for the game. Then, it calls the play_game() function from within a loop that lets the user play more than one game.

If you compare this code with the code for the Pig Dice program that's in chapter 4, you should see how creating a Game object makes it easier to work with the state of the game. For a simple program like this, you can use global variables as shown in chapter 4. But using objects to organize the data works a lot better.

The pig_dice module (continued)

```python
def play_game():
    game = Game()
    while not game.isGameOver:
        take_turn(game)

def take_turn(game):
    print("TURN", game.turn)
    game.scoreThisTurn = 0
    game.isTurnOver = False
    while not game.isTurnOver:
        choice = input("Roll or hold? (r/h): ")
        if choice == "r":
            roll_die(game)
        elif choice == "h":
            hold_turn(game)
        else:
            print("Invalid choice. Try again.")

def roll_die(game):
    game.die.roll()
    print("Die:", game.die.value)
    if game.die.value == 1:
        game.scoreThisTurn = 0
        game.turn += 1
        game.isTurnOver = True
        print("Turn over. No score.\n")
    else:
        game.scoreThisTurn += game.die.value

def hold_turn(game):
    game.score += game.scoreThisTurn
    game.isTurnOver = True
    print("Score for turn:", game.scoreThisTurn)
    print("Total score:", game.score, "\n")
    if game.score >= 20:
        game.isGameOver = True
        print("You finished in", game.turn, "turns!")
    else:
        game.turn += 1

def main():
    display_welcome()
    while True:
        play_game()
        choice = input("Play again? (y/n): ")
        print()
        if choice != "y":
            print("Bye!")
            break

# if started as the main module, call the main function
if __name__ == "__main__":
    main()
```

Figure 14-15   The Pig Dice game (part 2)

Perspective

This chapter has presented the most useful skills for working with classes and objects. In addition, it has presented two of the most important principles of object-oriented programming: object composition and encapsulation. In the next chapter, you'll learn about two more important principles of OOP: inheritance and polymorphism.

When you're first getting started with OOP, it can be hard to see its advantages over procedural programming. For now, you can focus on just two. First, dividing the code into classes often makes it easier to reuse code. For example, the Die and Dice classes presented in this chapter could possibly be reused by many programs. Second, using classes helps you separate the different layers of a program. That can simplify the development of the program and make the program easier to maintain and enhance later on. For example, one common design pattern is to use classes to structure a program so it has three layers as explained in chapter 16.

Terms

procedural programming	object composition
object-oriented programming (OOP)	encapsulation
class	public method
class diagram	public attribute
Unified Modeling Language (UML)	data hiding
attribute	private attribute
method	property
data structure	interface
object	getter method
instance of a class	accessor
instantiation	setter method
identity of an object	mutator
state of an object	annotation
behavior of an object	read-only property
constructor	write-only property

Summary

- *Object-oriented programming* (*OOP*) groups related variables and functions into *data structures* called *objects*. A *class* can be thought of as the template or blueprint from which the *objects* are made.

- *UML* (*Unified Modeling Language*) is the industry standard used to describe the classes and objects of an object-oriented application. A UML *class diagram* describes the attributes and methods of one or more classes.

- The *attributes* of a class define the data that an object can store. The *methods* of a class define the tasks that an object can perform. Often, these methods provide a way to modify the attributes of the object.

- Once you create an object from a class, the object has an *identity* (a unique address), a *state* (the data that it stores), and *behavior* (the methods that it contains). As a program runs, an object's state may change.

- An object is an *instance* of a class. In other words, you can create more than one object from a single class. The process of creating an object from a class is sometimes called *instantiation*.

- A *constructor* is a special method that defines the attributes for an object and initializes the values of those attributes.

- In Python, all methods, including constructors and properties, must take a reference to the object itself as their first parameters. By convention, this reference is named *self*.

- *Object composition* is a way to combine simple objects into more complex ones.

- *Encapsulation* allows you to hide the data attributes of an object from other code that uses the object. This is also known as *data hiding*.

- *Public* attributes can be accessed directly by the code that uses an object. *Private* attributes can only be accessed indirectly through public methods, including constructors and properties.

- A *property* is a special type of method that can be used to provide access to a hidden attribute.

- An *annotation* is a line of code that begins with the @ symbol and tells Python something about the code that follows. For example, the @property annotation tells Python that the method that follows gets the value for a property.

- An *interface* allows a programmer to use an object without understanding its internal code.

- A method that gets the value of the attribute is known as a *getter* or *accessor* method. A method that sets the value of the attribute is known as a *setter* or *mutator* method.

- When you create a property, if you only code a getter method, you create a *read-only property*. If you only code a setter method, you create a *write-only property*.

Exercise 14-1   Enhance the Dice Roller program

In this exercise, you'll enhance the Dice Roller program by making some improvements to its classes. When you're done, rolling two dice should look something like this:

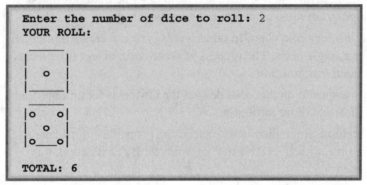

```
Enter the number of dice to roll: 2
YOUR ROLL:

 _____
|     |
|  o  |
|_____|

 _____
|o   o|
|  o  |
|o___o|

TOTAL: 6
```

Open and test the program

1. In IDLE, open the dice.py and dice_roller.py files that are in this folder:
   `python/exercises/ch14/dice_roller`

2. Review the code and run the program to make sure it works correctly. Note that it starts by displaying an image for each of the 6 possible die values.

Improve the Die class

3. In the Die class, modify the roll() method so it returns the __value attribute after it sets it to a random number from 1 to 6.

4. In the Die class, modify the constructor so it sets the __value attribute by calling the roll() method. This makes sure that the __value attribute for a new Die object stores a valid number for the die.

5. In the Die class, modify the setter for the value property so it doesn't allow a value greater than 6.

6. Run the dice module and use Python's interactive shell to make sure these changes work correctly.

7. In the Die class, add a read-only property named image that gets a string for the image that represents the die's current value.

Improve the Dice Roller program

8. Open the dice_roller.py file and run it to make sure the Dice Roller program still works correctly. Since you didn't change the interface for the Die class, it should.

9. Modify the code that displays the roll so it uses the new image property to display an image for each die instead of displaying the value.

10. At the start of the program, modify the code that displays the 6 die images so it uses a loop to create a Die object for each valid number and to display its image. This reduces code duplication since the code that defines the image is only stored in one place now, in the Die class.

Improve the Dice class

11. In the Dice class, add a method named getTotal() that gets the total value of all Die objects currently stored in the Dice object.

12. In the dice_roller.py file, add the code that displays the total each time the user rolls the dice.

Exercise 14-2   Create an object-oriented Movie List program

In this exercise, you'll convert the Movie List program presented in chapter 6 so it uses objects instead of storing the data for the movie in a list.

Open and test the program

1. In IDLE, open the movie_list.py file that's in this folder:
   `python/exercises/ch14/movies`

2. Review the code and note how it uses a list to store the data for each movie.

3. Run the code to make sure it works correctly.

Define a Movie object that can store the data for each movie

4. Add a module named objects to the program's folder.

5. In the object module, write the code for a class named Movie that defines a Movie object that stores the name and year of a movie. This class should include a getStr() method that returns the name of the movie followed by its year in parentheses.

6. Run the module. This should display the interactive shell. Then, use the shell to test the class by creating a Movie object and printing it to the console.

Modify the program so it uses the Movie object

7. Switch back to the movie_list.py file, and add a statement that imports the Movie class.

8. Modify the main() function so it creates a list of Movie objects instead of a list of lists.

9. Modify the list() function so it uses the getStr() method to display each movie. Note how this simplifies the code.

10. Modify the add() function so it creates a Movie object from the user input. Note how this simplifies the code.

11. Modify the delete() function so it uses the Movie object to display the name of the movie that's deleted. Note how this makes the code easier to read and understand.

Exercise 14-3   Create an object-oriented Temperature Converter

In this exercise, you'll modify the Temperature Converter program presented in chapter 4 so it uses object-oriented programming instead of procedural programming.

Open and test the program

1. In IDLE, open the two files stored in this folder:

   ```
   python/exercises/ch14/temperature
   ```

2. Review the code for the program and note how it uses the functions in the temperature module to convert the temperatures.

3. Run the code to make sure it works correctly.

Define a Temp object that can store a temperature

4. Switch to the temperature.py file. At the top of this module, define a class named Temp that defines two hidden attributes to store the degrees Fahrenheit and Celsius.

5. In the Temp class, define the methods that set the hidden attributes. When you set one unit of temperature, it should also calculate and set the other unit of temperature. For example, when you set degrees Fahrenheit, it should also calculate and set degrees Celsius.

6. In the Temp class, define the methods that get the hidden attributes. These methods should round the number that it returns to 2 decimal places.

7. Delete the to_fahrenheit() and to_celsius() functions.

8. In the temperature module, modify the code in the main() function so it tests the Temp class.

9. Run the temperature module. It should successfully convert the temperatures specified by the loops.

Modify the program so it uses the Temp object

10. Switch back to the convert_temperatures.py file, and modify the import statement so it imports the Temp class from the temperature module.

11. In the convert_temp() function, create a Temp object and use it to set and get the temperatures.

15

How to work with inheritance

In the previous chapter, you learned how to work with encapsulation, one of the fundamental concepts of object-oriented programming. In this chapter, you'll learn how to work with two more fundamental concepts of object-oriented programming: inheritance and its cousin, polymorphism.

Inheritance is typically used by the developers of large programs to develop a consistent set of classes. When used correctly, inheritance can simplify the design of a program and reduce code duplication. However, when used incorrectly, inheritance can violate encapsulation and create unwanted dependencies between classes.

In this chapter, you'll begin by learning *how* inheritance works. Then, at the end of this chapter, you'll learn *when* it makes sense to use inheritance.

How to work with inheritance

Inheritance allows you to create a new class that's based on an existing class. Along with encapsulation, it is a fundamental concept of object-oriented programming. This chapter starts by presenting an overview of how inheritance works. Then, it shows the coding details.

How inheritance works

When inheritance is used, a *subclass inherits* the public attributes and methods of a *superclass* as shown by the diagram in figure 15-1. Then, when you create an object from the subclass, that object can use these attributes and methods. The subclass can also add new attributes and methods to the superclass, and it can change the way the attributes and methods of the superclass work by *overriding* them and providing new code for them.

The three classes in the UML diagram in this figure show how this works. Here, the superclass is the Product class. This class has three public attributes and three public methods. The attributes and the first two methods are the same as the Product class presented in the previous chapter. However, the getDescription() method is a new method that's described in the next figure.

In this diagram, there are two subclasses: Book and Movie. These classes inherit the three attributes and the three methods from the Product superclass. Then, each subclass adds a new attribute. The Book class adds the author attribute, and the Movie class adds the year attribute. In addition, both classes change the way the getDescription() method of the Product class works by overriding it.

In this book, we use *superclass* to refer to a class that another class inherits and *subclass* to refer to a class that inherits another class. However, a superclass can also be called a *base* or *parent class*, and a subclass can also be called a *derived* or *child class*.

A UML diagram for three classes that use inheritance

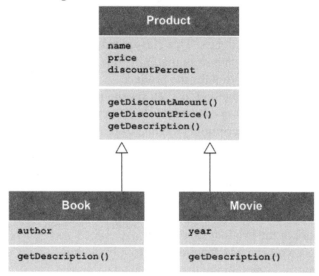

Description

- *Inheritance* lets you create a new class based on an existing class. Then, the new class *inherits* the attributes and methods of the existing class.

- A class that another class inherits is called a *base class*, *parent class*, or *superclass*.

- A class that inherits another class is called a *derived class*, *child class,* or *subclass*.

- A subclass can add new attributes and methods to the superclass. It can also *override* a method from the superclass by providing its own version of the method.

UML diagramming note

- To indicate that a class inherits another class, a UML diagram typically uses an arrow with an open (not shaded) arrowhead.

Figure 15-1   How inheritance works

How to define a subclass

Figure 15-2 shows how to define a subclass. To start, the first example shows the code for the superclass, the Product class. This class is the same as the Product class presented in the previous chapter, except that it includes a method named getDescription that returns the description for the product.

For this superclass, the getDescription() method just returns the name of the product. As a result, any subclasses of this class can use this getDescription() method too. Or, they can override the getDescription() method to provide their own code for that method.

The second example shows how to create a subclass, the Book class. To indicate that a class is a subclass, you follow the name of the class with a set of parentheses. Then, within the parentheses, you code the name of the class that you want to inherit. Here, the Book class inherits the Product class. In other words, the Book class is a subclass of the Product superclass.

After you declare the subclass, you can add functionality to it by adding attributes, constructors, and methods. For example, the Book subclass adds a new attribute and a new constructor. The Book class also overrides the getDescription() method defined by the Product class.

The constructor for the Book subclass accepts four parameters. The first three are the same as the Product class, but the fourth provides the value for the public attribute named author. Within this constructor, the first statement calls the constructor of the Product class. This initializes the name, price, and discountPercent attributes that are defined by the Product class. Then, the second statement defines and initializes the author attribute.

To override a method of the superclass, you begin by coding a method with the same name as the method in the superclass. In this case, the getDescription() method of the Book class overrides the getDescription() method of the Product class. The code within this method returns a string that's created by concatenating the string that's returned by the getDescription() method of the Product object with "by" and the author attribute of the Book object.

When you override a method, it often makes sense to begin by calling the method in the superclass as shown in this example. That way, if you change the method in the superclass later, the method in the subclass will reflect that change. However, in Python, it's legal to code the method in the subclass like this:

```
def getDescription(self):
    return self.name + " by " + self.author
```

In this case, the getDescription() method of the Book class completely overrides the getDescription() method of the Product class and no longer reflects any changes made to it. That might be what you want in some situations, but you should think twice before doing this as it could make your code harder to maintain.

The syntax for working with subclasses

To define a subclass

```
class SubClassName(SuperClassName):
```

To call a method or constructor of the superclass

```
SuperClassName.methodName(self[, argumentList])
```

The code for the Product superclass

```
class Product:
    def __init__(self, name="", price=0.0, discountPercent=0):
        self.name = name
        self.price = price
        self.discountPercent = discountPercent

    def getDiscountAmount(self):
        return self.price * self.discountPercent / 100

    def getDiscountPrice(self):
        return self.price - self.getDiscountAmount()

    def getDescription(self):
        return self.name
```

The code for the Book subclass

```
class Book(Product):
    def __init__(self, name="", price=0.0, discountPercent=0, author=""):
        # call the constructor of the superclass
        Product.__init__(self, name, price, discountPercent)

        # set the author
        self.author = author

    # override the getDescription method
    def getDescription(self):
        return Product.getDescription(self) + " by " + self.author
```

When coding a subclass...

- You can directly access public attributes of the superclass.

- You can add new attributes and methods that aren't in the superclass.

- You can call methods of the superclass (including constructors and properties) by coding the name of the superclass, the dot operator, and the name of the method.

- You can override existing methods in the superclass by coding methods that have the same name.

Figure 15-2   How to define a subclass

How polymorphism works

Polymorphism lets you treat objects of different types as if they were the same type by referring to a superclass that's common to the objects. In figure 15-3, for example, the show_products() function treats Book and Movie objects as if they were Product objects. Like encapsulation and inheritance, polymorphism is a fundamental feature of object-oriented programming.

One benefit of polymorphism is that you can write generic code that's designed to work with a superclass. Then, you can use that code with objects that are created from any class that inherits the superclass. For instance, the first example in this figure shows the getDescription() methods for the Product, Book, and Movie classes. The Book version of the getDescription() method adds the author to the end of the product's description. Similarly, the Movie version adds the year to the end of the product's description.

The second example shows how polymorphism works with these classes. This code begins by importing the Product, Book, and Movie classes from the objects module. Then, it defines two functions that show how polymorphism works.

The show_products() function accepts a list or tuple of Product objects. Within this function, the code shows the products by printing the string that's returned by the getDescription() method to the console.

The main() function shows how this works. To start, the first statement creates a tuple of three Product objects. Here, the first object is a Product object, the second is a Book object, and the third is a Movie object. Then, the second statement passes this tuple to the show_products() function.

When you run this code, Python uses polymorphism to call the correct getDescription() method from each object. The console in this figure shows that this works correctly. The key to polymorphism is that Python decides which method to call based on the inheritance hierarchy at runtime.

Three versions of the getDescription() method

In the Product superclass
```
def getDescription(self):
    return self.name
```

In the Book subclass
```
def getDescription(self):
    return Product.getDescription(self) + " by " + self.author
```

In the Movie subclass
```
def getDescription(self):
    return Product.getDescription(self) + " (" + str(self.year) + ")"
```

Code that uses the overridden methods
```
from objects import Product, Book, Movie

def show_products(products):
    print("PRODUCTS")
    for product in products:
        print(product.getDescription())
    print()

def main():
    # a tuple of Product objects
    products = (Product('Stanley 13 Ounce Wood Hammer', 12.99, 62),
                Book("The Big Short", 15.95, 34, "Michael Lewis"),
                Movie("The Holy Grail - DVD", 14.99, 68, 1975))
    show_products(products)

if __name__ == "__main__":
    main()
```

The console
```
PRODUCTS
Stanley 13 Ounce Wood Hammer
The Big Short by Michael Lewis
The Holy Grail - DVD (1975)
```

Description
- *Polymorphism* is a feature of inheritance that lets you treat objects of subclasses as if they were objects of the superclass.
- If you access a method of a superclass object and the method is overridden in the subclasses of that class, polymorphism determines which method is executed based on the object's type.

Figure 15-3   How polymorphism works

How to check an object's type

When working with objects, you sometimes need to check an object's type and perform different processing depending on the type. To do that, you can use the built-in isinstance() function as shown in figure 15-4.

The example in this figure begins by importing the Product, Book, and Movie classes from the objects module. Then, it defines a show_product() function that accepts Product, Book, or Movie objects. This function performs different processing depending on the object's type.

Within this function, the second statement prints a line to the console that displays the product's name. To do that, this code accesses the name attribute of the Product object. This works because the Book and Movie objects inherit this attribute from the Product object.

The if statement that follows checks whether the product is a Book object. If so, it prints a line to the console that displays the author's name. Since this module has imported the Book class, there's no need to prefix the Book class with the name of the module. However, if you imported the module, but not the class, you would have to prefix the name of the Book class like this:

```
isinstance(product, objects.Book)
```

The second if statement works like the first one, but it checks whether the Product object is a Movie object. If so, it prints a line to the console that displays the movie's year.

The next statement prints a line to the console that displays the product's discount price. To do that, this code calls the public getDiscountPrice() method that's defined by the Product superclass and inherited by the Book and Movie subclasses.

The main() function shows that the isinstance() functions in the show_product() function work correctly. First, the main() function creates a Product object. Then, it passes that object to the show_product() function. Since this Product object is not a Book or Movie object, this prints two lines of product data to the console.

Then, the main() function creates a Movie object and passes it to the show_product() function. Since this object is a Movie object, this prints three lines of product data to the console, including the movie's year.

A function for checking an object's type

Function	Description
isinstance(*object*, [*modName.*]*ClassName*)	Returns True if the object is an instance of the specified class. Otherwise, returns False.

Code that uses the isinstance() function

```
from objects import Product, Book, Movie

def show_product(product):
    print("PRODUCT DATA")
    print("Name:                ", product.name)
    if isinstance(product, Book):
        print("Author:             ", product.author)
    if isinstance(product, Movie):
        print("Year:               ", product.year)
    print("Discount price:    {:.2f}".format(product.getDiscountPrice()))
    print()

def main():
    product1 = Product('Stanley 13 Ounce Wood Hammer', 12.99, 62)
    show_product(product1)
    print()

    product2 = Movie("The Holy Grail - DVD", 14.99, 68, 1975)
    show_product(product2)

if __name__ == "__main__":
    main()
```

The console

```
PRODUCT DATA
Name:            Stanley 13 Ounce Wood Hammer
Discount price:  4.94

PRODUCT DATA
Name:            The Holy Grail - DVD
Year:            1975
Discount price:  4.80
```

Description

- You can use the isinstance() function to perform different processing for different types of objects.

Figure 15-4   How to check an object's type

The Product Viewer 2.0 program

To show how all of the pieces work together in a Product Viewer program, the next two figures present the objects module and product_viewer module.

The objects module

Figures 15-5 shows all the code for the Product superclass and two of its subclasses: Since you've already seen the code for the Product and Book classes you can focus on the Movie class.

The Movie class works like the Book class. To start, it inherits the Product class. Then, the constructor of the Movie class defines and initializes a public attribute named year. Next, it defines a getDescription() method that overrides the getDescription() method of the Product class. This method returns a string that includes the string that's returned by the getDescription() method of the Product class as well as the year attribute of the Movie class.

The objects module

```
class Product:
    def __init__(self, name="", price=0.0, discountPercent=0):
        self.name = name
        self.price = price
        self.discountPercent = discountPercent

    def getDiscountAmount(self):
        return self.price * self.discountPercent / 100

    def getDiscountPrice(self):
        return self.price - self.getDiscountAmount()

    def getDescription(self):
        return self.name

class Book(Product):
    def __init__(self, name="", price=0.0, discountPercent=0, author=""):
        Product.__init__(self, name, price, discountPercent)
        self.author = author

    def getDescription(self):
        return Product.getDescription(self) + " by " + self.author

class Movie(Product):
    def __init__(self, name="", price=0.0, discountPercent=0, year=0):
        Product.__init__(self, name, price, discountPercent)
        self.year = year

    def getDescription(self):
        return Product.getDescription(self) + " (" + str(self.year) + ")"
```

Figure 15-5   The Product, Book, and Movie classes in the objects module

The user interface and product_viewer module

Figure 15-6 presents the user interface and the code for the product_viewer module. In the interface, you can see the data that's displayed by the show_products() and show_product() functions.

The code in the product_viewer module uses the Product, Book, and Movie classes presented in the previous figure. Here, the show_products() function calls the getDescription() method of the current product object in the loop to print the data for the product. Thanks to polymorphism, this calls the correct getDescription() method depending on the type of the current product.

In the show_product() function, the if statements use the isintance() method to determine what type of object is being displayed. Then, the display is varied based on that object type.

Like the Product Viewer program in the previous chapter, the main() function creates a tuple of Product objects. To do that, it calls the constructor of the Product class to create each object, and it stores each object in the tuple without going through the intermediate step of creating a variable name that refers to the object.

After creating the tuple of product objects, this code passes that tuple to the show_products() function, which displays the numbered list of products. Next, this function prompts the user to enter a number that corresponds with a product. It then gets the corresponding Product object from the tuple of Product objects, and passes that Product object to the show_product() function. This displays the data for the product object, which varies based on the object type.

The user interface

```
PRODUCTS
1. Stanley 13 Ounce Wood Hammer
2. The Big Short by Michael Lewis
3. The Holy Grail - DVD (1975)

Enter product number: 2

PRODUCT DATA
Name:            The Big Short
Author:          Michael Lewis
Discount price:  10.53
```

The product_viewer module

```python
from objects import Product, Book, Movie

def show_products(products):
    print("PRODUCTS")
    for i in range(len(products)):
        product = products[i]
        print(str(i+1) + ". " + product.getDescription())
    print()

def show_product(product):
    print("PRODUCT DATA")
    print("Name:            ", product.name)
    if isinstance(product, Book):
        print("Author:          ", product.author)
    if isinstance(product, Movie):
        print("Year:            ", product.year)
    print("Discount price:   {:.2f}".format(product.getDiscountPrice()))
    print()

def main():
    print("The Product Viewer program")
    print()
    products = (Product('Stanley 13 Ounce Wood Hammer', 12.99, 62),
                Book("The Big Short", 15.95, 34, "Michael Lewis"),
                Movie("The Holy Grail - DVD", 14.99, 68, 1975))
    show_products(products)

    while True:
        number = int(input("Enter product number: "))
        print()

        product = products[number-1]
        show_product(product)

        choice = input("Continue? (y/n): ")
        print()
        if choice != "y":
            break

if __name__ == "__main__":
    main()
```

Figure 15-6   The Product Viewer 2.0 program

How to override object methods

With Python 3 and later, a class named *object* is the superclass for all classes. In other words, every class automatically inherits the object class. As a result, the methods of the object class are available from every object. Then, to get your objects to work the way you want, you sometimes need to override some of these methods.

How to define a string representation for an object

One of the most used methods of the object class is the __str__() method. That's because Python automatically calls this method when it needs a string representation of an object. For example, when you supply an object as the argument of the print method, Python calls the __str__() method of the object class.

So, when you code a class, it's generally a good practice to override the __str__() method of the object class to provide more detailed information about the object. If possible, this information should be concise, informative, and easy to read. Otherwise, the __str__() method that's provided by the object class returns a string that includes the name of the class and its identifier.

The first example in figure 15-7 shows a __str__() method for the Product class. It returns a string that includes the three public attributes of the Product class, separated by a pipe character (|). This provides all of the data that's stored in the Product object in a format that's easy to read.

The second example shows some code that automatically calls the __str__() method of the Product object. Here, the first statement creates a Product object. Then, the second statement passes the Product object to the print() function. This causes the console to display the data that's stored in the three attributes of the Product object. However, if the Product class didn't contain a __str__() method, this code would call the __str__() method from the object class. And that would cause the console to display a message that includes the Product object's class and identifier.

When you're developing an object-oriented program, it's often helpful to have a string representation like the one in the first example. That way, if you want to view the data for an object, you can print the object to the console. Alternately, you might want to provide a default string representation that's appropriate for the user interface of a program to display. In that case, the __str__() method would probably return a string more like the string that's returned by one of the getDescription() methods shown earlier in this chapter. One way to do that is to call the getDescription() method from the __str__() method like this:

```
def __str__(self):
    return self.getDescription()
```

A method of the object class

Method	Description
`__str__(self)`	Returns a string for the object that includes the name of its class and its identifier.

The syntax for overriding the __str__() method

```
def __str__(self):
    return stringForObject
```

A __str__() method in the Product class

```
def __str__(self):
    return self.name + "|"  + str(self.price) + "|" + \
           str(self.discountPercent)
```

Code that automatically calls the __str__() method

```
product = Product('Stanley 13 Ounce Wood Hammer', 12.99, 62)
print(product)
```

The console if the Product class overrides the __str__() method

```
Stanley 13 Ounce Wood Hammer|12.99|62
```

The console if the Product class doesn't override the __str__() method

```
<objects.Product object at 0x03769930>
```

Description

- The *object class* is the superclass for all classes. In other words, every class inherits the object class. As a result, the methods defined by the object class are available to all classes.

- The __str__() method is a special method that's automatically called whenever an object needs to be converted to a string such as when the print statement prints an object to the console or when the str() function attempts to convert an object to a string.

- The __str__() method in the object class returns a message that includes the name of the class for the object as well as its identifier. If that's not what you want, you can override this behavior by defining your own __str__() method.

- When coding classes, you often want to override the __str__() method so it returns a string that's concise, informative, and easy to read.

Figure 15-7   How to define a string representation for an object

How to define an iterator for an object

When you use a for loop to iterate through each object in a list of objects, Python automatically calls the __iter__() and __next__() methods to initialize the loop and to get the next object in the sequence of objects. As a result, if your object contains multiple objects and you want to use a for loop to iterate through those objects, you can override the __iter__() and __next__() methods as shown in figure 15-8.

The first example in this figure presents a constructor for a Dice class. It creates a private attribute named __list with a value of an empty list. This list will be used to hold one or more Die objects.

The second example shows one way to code the __iter__() and __next__() methods for the Dice class. To start, the __iter__() method defines a private attribute named __index and initializes that attribute to -1. Then, the second statement returns the self object to indicate that the current object is the iterator. In other words, the current Dice object contains the __next__() method that's needed to iterate through each Die object that's stored in the Dice object.

This example continues by defining the __next__() method. This method begins by checking whether the __index attribute is greater than or equal to the length of the private __list attribute that stores the list of Die objects. If so, this code raises a StopIteration exception, which causes the loop to end.

Otherwise, this code increments the __index attribute by 1. As a result, the first time through the loop this attribute is equal to 0, which is the index for the first item in the list. After incrementing the index, this code gets the Die object that's at the specified index from the list, and it returns that object to the calling code. This is how this class makes the Die objects that are stored in the private __list attribute available to the for statement in the calling code.

The third and fourth examples show how easy it is to loop through all of the Die objects in the Dice object after you've added the __iter__() and __next__() methods. Here, the third example creates a Dice object that contains five Die objects. Then, the fourth example uses a for loop to print the value of each Die object to the console with a space between each value. This works just as if the Dice object was a list or any other built-in container object that allows you to iterate over each object in the container. However, if you don't code the __iter__() and __next__() methods for the Dice class, the third and fourth examples display an error that indicates that the object is not iterable.

As you review this code, note that all methods of the class begin and end with double underscores. This clearly shows that the methods are private methods that Python can call from an object but that you can't call directly. Instead, Python calls these methods when it needs them.

The __str__(), __iter__(), and __next__() methods are just a few of the many methods available from the object class. If, for example, you want the built-in len() function to work correctly on a container object, you can override the __len__() method to return the number of objects in the container. If you want to use the + operator to add two objects together, you can override the __add__() method. And so on. This is known as operator overloading, and it provides a way to make your user-defined objects work more like built-in objects.

Two more methods of the object class

Method	Description
`__iter__(self)`	Returns the iterator for the object and initializes the index for the iterator.
`__next__(self)`	Returns the next object in the sequence of objects. If there are no more objects, this method should raise the StopIteration exception.

The constructor for a Dice class with a list for one or more Die objects

```
class Dice:
    def __init__(self):
        self.__list = []
```

Two methods that define an iterator for the Dice class

```
def __iter__(self):
    self.__index = -1    # initialize index for each iteration
    return self

def __next__(self):
    if self.__index >= len(self.__list)-1:
        raise StopIteration()
    self.__index += 1
    die = self.__list[self.__index]
    return die
```

Code that creates a Dice object that contains five Die objects

```
dice = Dice()
for i in range(5):
    die = Die()
    dice.addDie(die)
```

Code that automatically calls the __iter__() and __next__() methods

```
for die in dice:
    print(die.value, end=" ")
```

The console if the Dice class defines an iterator

```
1 1 1 1 1
```

The console if the Dice class doesn't define an iterator

```
TypeError: 'Dice' object is not iterable
```

Description

- When coding container classes, you often want to override the __iter__() and __next__() methods so you can iterate through the objects within the container. This improves the encapsulation of the object and makes it easier for other programmers to use the object.

- It's common to use an iterator to provide a public way to access the objects that are stored in a private attribute of an object.

Figure 15-8   How to define an iterator for an object

The Die and Dice classes

Figure 15-9 shows the Die and Dice classes from the previous chapter after they've been modified to override the __str__(), __iter__(), and __next__() methods. Since these classes are mostly the same as the Die and Dice classes presented in the previous chapter, this figure highlights the code that's new.

The Die class overrides the __str__() method to provide a string representation for the object. This class only defines one attribute, the value attribute. As a result, the obvious string representation for this object is to return the value attribute after it has been converted from an integer to a string. This makes it easier for other programmers to get a string representation of the value attribute.

The Dice class overrides the __iter__() and __next__() methods to make it possible to use a for loop to iterate through each Die object stored in the __list attribute. As a result, this class no longer needs a getTuple() method to provide a way to loop through the Die objects as it did in the previous chapter. Instead, you can loop through the Dice object itself. This makes it easier for other programmers to use this class.

In the previous chapter, the Dice Roller 1.0 program needed to call the getTuple() method of the Dice object to get an iterable object. It also needed to call the value method of each Die object to get the value of the object. As a result, the code that displayed the values of the dice looked like this:

```
for die in dice.getTuple():
    print(die.value, end="")
```

Now, however, with the Die and Dice classes shown in this figure, the code that displays the values of the dice can be simplified to the code at the bottom of this figure:

```
for die in dice:
    print(die, end="")
```

This isn't a huge difference if you're only going to use the Die and Dice classes for a single program. But it could be a significant difference if you reuse these classes in many programs. Also, this change makes your objects work more intuitively, which is nice for you and for other programmers who might use this class.

The dice module

```
import random

class Die:
    def __init__(self):
        self.__value = 1

    @property   # read-only!
    def value(self):
        return self.__value

    def roll(self):
        self.__value = random.randrange(1, 7)

    # make it easier to get the value
    def __str__(self):
        return str(self.__value)

class Dice:
    def __init__(self):
        self.__list = []

    def addDie(self, die):
        self.__list.append(die)

    def rollAll(self):
        for die in self.__list:
            die.roll()

    # define the Dice object as the iterator
    def __iter__(self):
        self.__index = -1   # initialize index for each iteration
        return self

    # define the method that gets the next Die object
    def __next__(self):
        if self.__index == len(self.__list)-1:
            raise StopIteration
        self.__index += 1
        die = self.__list[self.__index]
        return die
```

Code that displays the value of each die

```
for die in dice:
    print(die, end=" ")
```

Figure 15-9   The Die and Dice classes

Two more skills for the road

To develop simple programs like the ones in this book, you typically don't need to use inheritance. However, if you continue with programming, you'll eventually need to use inheritance. In addition, if you ever design a larger or more complex program, you'll need to learn when it makes sense to use inheritance and when you should use composition instead.

How to work with custom exceptions

Figure 15-10 shows how to create a custom exception. To do that, you can code a subclass that inherits one of the classes in the Exception hierarchy. This is a good example of when it makes sense to use inheritance in your programs.

To start, this figure shows the hierarchy for some common exceptions. By now, you should have a pretty good idea of how this inheritance hierarchy works. For example, it should be clear to you that the FileNotFoundError is a subclass of the OSError, which is a subclass of the Exception class.

The first example in this figure defines a class named DataAccessError that inherits the Exception class. The body of this class contains a single pass statement. As a result, the DataAccessError class works the same as the Exception class. However, it has a different name and a different position in the inheritance hierarchy. This is important because the name of the error gives the programmer information about the error. In addition, the position in the inheritance hierarchy gives the programmer the flexibility to handle a DataAccessError differently than other types of exceptions.

The second example shows how to use the DataAccessError class. Here, the first statement imports the DataAccessError class from the objects module. Then, this code attempts to read movie data from a CSV file and return a list of movie data. However, if an exception occurs, this code raises a DataAccessError with an appropriate message.

At this point, you may be wondering, why bother raising this exception? If Python encounters an error, it will raise the FileNotFoundError or the OSError. Why not just let the calling code handle those exceptions?

The problem with that approach is that it exposes the implementation details of the read_movies() function to the calling code. For example, the calling code may need to include code that handles the FileNotFoundError or the OSError exceptions. Then, if you later decide to change the implementation details of this function, the calling code will need to handle different exceptions. For example, if you change this function so it reads data from a database instead of a file, the calling code needs to handle database exceptions, not file exceptions.

The advantage of raising the DataAccessError is that it hides the implementation details of the read_movies() function from the calling code. This allows you to use the same exception regardless of the implementation details of the function. As result, changing the implementation details of the function doesn't change the type of exception that the function might raise.

The hierarchy for six common exceptions

```
Exception
    NameError
    OSError
        FileExistsError
        FileNotFoundError
    ValueError
```

The syntax for creating your own exceptions

```
class CustomErrorName(ExceptionClassName):
    pass
```

A DataAccessError class that defines a custom exception

```
class DataAccessError(Exception):
    pass
```

A module that uses the DataAccessError class

```
from objects import DataAccessError

def read_movies():
    try:
        movies = []
        with open("movies.csv", newline="") as file:
            reader = csv.reader(file)
            for row in reader:
                movies.append(row)
        return movies
    except FileNotFoundError:
        raise DataAccessError("Data source not found.")
    except Exception:
        raise DataAccessError("Error accessing data source.")
```

Code that handles a custom exception

```
from objects import DataAccessError

try:
    movies = db.read_movies()
except DataAccessError as e:
    print("DataAccessError:", e)
```

The console when the FileNotFoundError occurs

```
DataAccessError: Data source not found.
```

The console if you don't use the DataAccessError class

```
FileNotFoundError: [Errno 2] No such file or directory:
'movies.csv'
```

Description

- To define a custom exception, you can code a class that inherits one of the built-in exception classes. Then, you can use that exception as you would any other exception.

Figure 15-10   How to work with custom exceptions

When to use inheritance

Figure 15-11 begins by listing three guidelines for when it makes sense to use inheritance in your programs. First, it makes sense to use inheritance when the subclass *is a* type of the superclass. For example, this chapter has presented a Book object that *is a* type of a Product object.

Second, it makes sense to use inheritance when both classes are part of the same logical domain. For example, the Product, Book, and Movie objects shown in this chapter are all in the same domain. In other words, they're all part of a domain that's attempting to define the different types of products for a system.

Third, it makes sense to use inheritance when the subclass primarily adds features to the superclass. In other words, it makes sense when a subclass adds new attributes, properties, or methods to the superclass that are only needed in the subclass. In addition, a subclass may override some methods to change the behavior of the subclass. However, if the subclass needs to override many methods, or if you find yourself wishing that you could remove some methods from the superclass, you are probably better off using composition instead of inheritance.

To illustrate, this figure shows a Dice class that inherits the built-in list class. When coding a container class like the Dice class, this type of approach is tempting because it's so easy. You just inherit the list class, add the rollAll() method, and you can use all the features of the list class to work with a list of Die objects. However, this approach breaks several of the guidelines for when it makes sense to use inheritance and leads to several problems.

First, the Dice object presented in this figure is *not* a type of list object. A list stores an ordered list of any data type. A Dice object stores one or more Die objects and provides methods for working with them. It's more accurate to say that the Dice object *has a* list object that it uses to work with multiple Die objects. As a result, the Dice object should use composition as shown in the previous chapter, not inheritance.

Second, the Dice class is *not* part of the same logical domain as the list class. The Dice and Die objects are part of a logical domain that's used to model dice objects that programmers can use in games. The list class is an implementation class that provides core functionality for all Python programmers.

Third, the interface for the Dice object is too complex. Ideally, this object would only provide the methods necessary to use it. This helps to make the Dice object easy for other programmers to use. Instead, this object includes all of the operators and methods for working with the list class, which provides more functionality, but also makes it harder for other programmers to use it.

Fourth, it violates encapsulation. That's because it allows other programmers to directly access the list that stores the Die objects. But this is an implementation detail that should be hidden from other programmers. Instead, you should be able to change the list to another collection such as a dictionary without changing the interface of the Dice object. That way, other programmers could continue to use the Dice object without needing to modify any of their code.

It makes sense to use inheritance when...

- One object *is a* type of another object.
- Both classes are part of the same logical domain.
- The subclass primarily adds features to the superclass.

A Dice class that inherits the list class (not recommended)

```
class Dice(list):
    def rollAll(self):
        for die in self:
            die.roll()
```

Code that uses this Dice class

```
dice = Dice()
dice.append(Die())          # uses append method from list class
dice.append(Die())
dice.rollAll()
die = dice[0]               # uses operators from list class
dice.insert(0, Die())       # uses insert method from list class
dice.pop()                  # uses pop method from list class
print("Die value:", die.value)
print("Dice count:", len(dice))
```

A few of the problems with this approach

- **The Dice object *is not a* type of list object.** A list object stores any type of object and provides a wide variety of methods for working with those objects. A Dice object stores Die objects and provides specialized methods for working with them.

- **Both classes are *not* part of the same logical domain.** The list class is an implementation class that provides a general-purpose object that all Python programmers can use to work with lists of objects. The Dice class is part of a specific logical domain that creates a model that programmers can use to store and roll multiple dice.

- **The interface is too complex.** The Dice object should only provide the methods necessary to use it. This makes it easy for other programmers to use.

- **It violates encapsulation.** The Dice object allows other programmers to access the list that stores the Die objects. But the list is an implementation choice that should be hidden from other programmers in case you want or need to change the implementation later.

Description

- If an object *is a* type of another object, it typically makes sense to use inheritance to create the relationship between the two classes.

- If an object *has a* type of another object, it typically makes sense to use composition to create the relationship between the two classes.

Figure 15-11   When to use inheritance

Perspective

Conceptually, this is one of the most difficult chapters in this book. Although the basic idea of inheritance is easy enough to understand, figuring out how to use it to benefit your programs can be difficult. So if you find yourself a bit confused right now, don't be disheartened.

Fortunately, when you're getting started, you typically don't need to code classes that inherit other classes. As you learn more about programming, you'll see more examples of how to use it and your understanding of it should grow. For example, the classes in Python's Exception hierarchy might have been a bit confusing when they were first presented in chapter 7. But now, you should understand how these classes work a little better.

The good news is that you don't have to understand every nuance of how inheritance works to use it. In fact, since all classes automatically inherit the object class, you've already been using inheritance without even knowing it. If you continue with programming, you'll learn how to inherit other classes to create graphical user interfaces (GUIs), web programs, and mobile apps. For example, chapter 18 shows how you can use inheritance to create a GUI. In addition, as you learn more about object-oriented design, you'll learn more about when it makes sense to use inheritance.

Terms

inheritance	derived class
superclass	child class
subclass	override a method
base class	polymorphism
parent class	object class

Summary

- *Inheritance* lets you create a new class based on an existing class. The existing class is called the *superclass*, *base class*, or *parent class*, and the new class is called the *subclass*, *derived class*, or *child class*.

- A subclass inherits all of the public attributes and methods of its superclass. The subclass can add new attributes and methods, and it can *override* existing methods with new versions of the methods.

- In a subclass, you can use the name of the superclass to call its methods.

- *Polymorphism* lets you treat objects created from a subclass as if they were objects of the superclass.

- You can use the built-in isinstanceof() function to check if an object is an instance of a particular class.

- All classes inherit the *object class*. This class provides methods, such as the __str__() method, that are available to all classes. To get your classes to work the way you want, you sometimes need to override these methods.

- If an object *is a* type of another object, it makes sense to use inheritance to create the relationship between the two classes. If an object *has a* type of another object, it makes sense to use composition to create the relationship between the two classes.

- Encapsulation, inheritance, and polymorphism are three of the fundamental concepts of object-oriented programming (OOP).

Exercise 15-1   Enhance the Product Viewer program

In this exercise, you'll enhance the Product Viewer program shown in this chapter so it provides for one more type of product: a music album. When you enter the product number for a music album, it should print the data to the console like this:

```
Enter product number: 4

PRODUCT DATA
Name:           Rubber Soul
Artist:         The Beatles
Format:         CD
Discount price: 10.00
```

Open and test the program

1. In IDLE, open the objects.py and product_viewer.py files in this folder:

   python/exercises/ch15/product_viewer

2. Review the code and run the program to make sure it works correctly. Note that the Movie class displays the format, which is DVD, as part of the name of the product.

Improve the Movie and Book classes

3. In the Movie class, add an attribute named format that stores the format of the product. For example, the format could be DVD, streaming, and so on.

4. In the product_viewer module, modify the code that creates the Movie object so it stores "DVD" as the format attribute instead of appending this data to the end of the name attribute. Then, modify the code that displays the Movie object, so it displays the format on a separate line, after the year of the movie.

5. Repeat steps 3 and 4 for the Book class. You can use "Hardcover" as the format for the book. Or, if you prefer, you can specify a different type of book format such as "Paperback" or "ebook".

Add an Album class

6. In the objects module, add a class named Album that inherits the Product class. The Album class should add two attributes: one for storing the artist and another for storing the format.

7. In the product_viewer.py file, modify the code that creates the objects so it includes a fourth object, an Album object. This object should contain the data for a music album that you like. Then, add code that displays the Album object as shown at the beginning of this exercise.

Add a Media class

8. In the objects module, add a class named Media that inherits the Product class. This class should add a format attribute to the Product class.

9. Modify the Movie, Book, and Album classes so they inherit the Media class, not the Product class. This should create a class hierarchy that looks like this:

```
Product
    Media
        Movie
        Book
        Album
```

10. Modify the Movie, Book, and Album classes so the constructor of each class accepts a format argument and passes that argument on to the constructor of the Media class. In other words, these classes should set the format attribute by calling the constructor of the Media class. Note how this reduces code duplication.

11. In the product_viewer.py file, modify the code that displays the products so it only displays the format attribute for Media objects. Note how this reduces code duplication.

Exercise 15-2   Work with Author and Authors objects

In this exercise, you'll work with a Book object that uses an Authors object to store one or more Author objects.

Open and test the program

1. In IDLE, open the objects.py and authors_tester.py files that are in this folder:
    `python/exercises/ch15/authors`

2. Review the code and note how the Book object uses an Authors object to store one or more Authors.

3. Run the code to see how it works. At this point, it doesn't display the book or author information correctly, but you'll fix that later in this exercise.

Improve the Author, Authors, and Book classes

4. In the Author class, add a __str__() method that returns the first and last name of the author, separated by a space.

5. In the Authors class, add a __str__() method that returns the name of each author, separating multiple authors with a comma and a space.

6. In the Book class, add a __str__() method that returns the title of the book, followed by the word "by" and one or more authors, with each author separated by a comma.

7. Run the authors_tester module again. This time, it should display the correct data for the book and author information.

Make sure the program works correctly for a single author

8. In the authors_tester module, comment out the statement that adds the second author. Then, run the module again. This should work, but the last line says "Authors" where it should say "Author".

9. Modify the code so it uses the count property of the Authors object to display the correct label for the author or authors depending on the number of authors for the book.

Define and use an iterator for the Authors object

10. In the Authors class, add the __iter__() and __next__() methods that make it possible to use a for statement to loop through all Author objects stored in the Authors object.

11. In the authors_tester module, add a for statement that loops through each author in the Authors object and prints each author to the console. When you're done, running this module should display this data to the console:

```
The Authors Tester program

BOOK DATA - SINGLE LINE
The Gilded Age by Mark Twain, Charles Warner

BOOK DATA - MUTLIPLE LINES
Title:    The Gilded Age
Authors:  Mark Twain, Charles Warner

AUTHORS
Mark Twain
Charles Warner
```

16

How to design an object-oriented program

Now that you understand how to code an object-oriented program, you're ready to learn how to design one. This chapter presents some of the most useful skills for doing that. To illustrate this process, this chapter presents a console version of a Shopping Cart program. If you've ever bought something from a website, you should be familiar with how a shopping cart works, and that should make it easy for you to focus on the design techniques that are presented in this chapter.

Techniques for object-oriented design

The objects for a program are often designed by developers who specialize in object-oriented design. This is especially true for large systems that have many programmers working on them. How well this is done can directly affect your job as a programmer. In general, well-designed objects are easy to work with, while poorly-designed objects are difficult to work with. In fact, when you work with poorly-designed objects, you often need to figure out how they are designed before you can use them appropriately.

This topic starts by showing how to create a model of the objects for an object-oriented program. Then, this topic presents an architecture that's often used for object-oriented programs.

Five steps for designing an object-oriented program

In many cases, you can base the model for an object-oriented program on an existing real-world system. The illustration at the top of figure 16-1 presents a conceptual view of how this works. Here, you can see that the information about the people, documents, and facilities within a real-world system is mapped to the classes and objects of an object-oriented system.

As you design your model, each class represents one object, or *entity*, in the real-world system. Then, each object created from the class stores one *instance* of the entity, and each *attribute* of the object stores one item of information about the entity.

This figure presents five steps you can follow to design a model for your objects. Step 1 is to identify all the data attributes that need to be stored in your objects. Step 2 is to break complex attributes down into smaller attributes whenever that makes sense. Step 3 is to identify the classes of the system and determine the attributes that they define. Step 4 is to identify the methods that each class should provide. And step 5 is to refine the classes, attributes, and methods. The next few figures describe each of these steps in more detail.

An object-oriented program is modeled after a real-world system

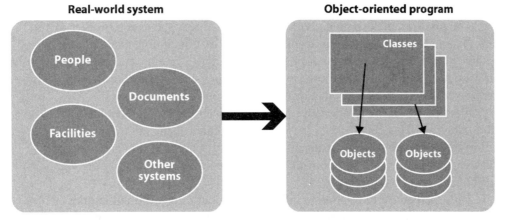

Five steps for designing an object-oriented program

Step 1:   Identify the data attributes

Step 2:   Subdivide each attribute into its smallest useful components

Step 3:   Identify the classes

Step 4:   Identify the methods

Step 5:   Refine the classes, attributes, and methods

Description

- An object-oriented program should model a real-world system. The job of the designer is to analyze the real-world system and then map it onto the object-oriented program.

- A class in an object-oriented program typically defines an object that corresponds with an object, or *entity*, in the real world.

Figure 16-1   Five steps for designing an object-oriented program

How to identify the data attributes

The first step in designing your objects is to identify the data attributes of the system. You can use several techniques to do that, including analyzing an existing system if there is one, evaluating comparable systems, and interviewing anyone who will be using the system. If an existing system uses documents, such as printed invoices or forms, that's an excellent source of information.

Figure 16-2 shows two screen captures of a website that implements a shopping cart. This chapter uses these screen captures as the main source of information for the data attributes of our Shopping Cart program. Keep in mind, though, that you should use all available resources when you identify the data attributes for a program.

These screen captures contain information about three different entities: products, line items, and shopping carts. The first screen contains information about a product such as its list price, discount percent, savings, and discount price. In addition, it allows you to specify the quantity, which is part of the line item entity.

The second screen contains some of the same information. However, it shows the data that's stored in the cart entity and the line item entity. To start, the cart displays one line for each item. This is the line item entity, and it includes the product description, discount price, and quantity. Although each line item contains the same type of information, each cart can contain multiple line items.

In addition, the second screen includes some general information about the cart that doesn't apply to a single line item. This includes the number of items in the cart and the total cost of the items in the cart.

One of the things you need to consider as you review screen captures like these is how much data your system needs to store. If, for example, you're creating a shopping cart for a company that only provides a few simple products, you might not need to store data about whether the item is in stock, the format of the product, and so on.

A screen capture that can be used to identify data attributes

Another screen capture that can be used to identify data attributes

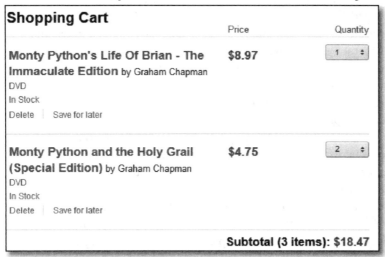

The data attributes identified from the screen captures

Product name	List price	Item count
Product creator	Discount percent	Cart total
Product format	Discount amount	Quantity
Stocking message	Discount price	

Description

- Depending on the nature of the system, you can identify data attributes in a variety of ways, including interviewing users, analyzing existing systems, and evaluating comparable systems.

Figure 16-2   How to identify the data attributes

How to subdivide the data attributes

Some of the data attributes you identify in step 1 of the design procedure may consist of multiple components. In step 2, you divide these attributes into their smallest useful values. Figure 16-3 shows how.

The first example in this figure shows how you can divide the name of a customer. Here, the name is divided into two attributes: first name and last name. When you divide a name like this, you can easily perform operations like using the first name in a salutation, such as "Dear Eric." In contrast, if the full name is stored in a single attribute, you have to use the string methods to extract the component you need. That can lead to unnecessarily complicated code. In general, then, you should separate a name like this whenever you need to use the name components separately. Later, when you need to use the full name, you can combine the first and last names using concatenation and provide a method or property that returns the full name.

The second example shows how you typically divide an address, if you need to store one for your program. In this example, the street number and street name are stored in a single attribute. Although you could store these components in separate attributes, that usually doesn't make sense since these values are typically used together. In other words, the data attributes should be divided into their smallest *useful* values.

As in the previous step, knowledge of the real-world system and of the information that's needed by the program is critical. In some circumstances, it may be okay to store data attributes with multiple components in a single attribute. That can simplify your design and reduce the overall number of attributes. In general, though, most designers divide data attributes as much as possible. That way, it's easy to access any data attribute, and you don't have to change the object design later if you find that the object would work better if you could access just part of an attribute.

A customer name that's divided into first and last name

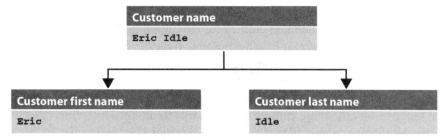

An address that's divided into street address, city, state, and zip code

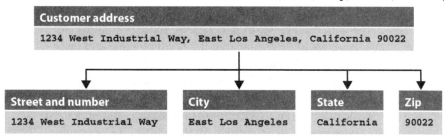

Description

- If a data attribute contains two or more components, you should consider subdividing the attribute into multiple attributes. That way, you won't need to parse the attribute each time you use it.

- The extent to which you subdivide a data attribute depends on how it will be used. Because it's difficult to predict all future uses for data, most designers subdivide data attributes as much as possible.

- When you subdivide a data attribute, you can easily rebuild it when necessary by concatenating the attributes.

Figure 16-3   How to subdivide the data attributes

How to identify the classes

Figure 16-4 presents the three main entities for the Shopping Cart program that's presented in this chapter, and it lists the possible data attributes that can be associated with each one. In most cases, you'll start to recognize the main entities that need to be included in a data structure as you identify the data attributes. For example, the data attributes identified in the two screens in figure 16-2 can be grouped into the three entities shown in this figure: product, line item, and cart. Although you may identify additional entities later on in the design process, it's sufficient to identity the main entities at this point. These entities become the classes for your programs.

After you identify the main classes, you need to determine which data attributes are associated with each class. In many cases, the associations are obvious. For example, it's easy to determine that the product name and price attributes should be stored in the Product class. It's easy to determine that the quantity attribute should be stored in the LineItem class. And it's easy to determine that the cart total attribute should be stored in the Cart class.

However, some associations aren't so obvious. In that case, you may need to list a data attribute under two or more entities. In this figure, for example, you can see that the product discount price is listed in the Product and LineItem classes. Later, as you refine your design, you may be able to remove these repeated attributes. For now, though, it's okay to include them.

As you identify the classes, you may decide that you don't need some of the data attributes you identified in previous steps. In this figure, for example, the attributes that aren't needed are crossed out.

Similarly, although you should be able to identify most of the data attributes in the first two steps of the design process, you may occasionally think of additional attributes during the third step. If that happens, you can add them in the third step. In this figure, for example, italics are used to identify the only attribute that was added in this step, the line item total attribute.

Finally, you may want to mark any data attributes that are included in two or more classes. In this figure, for example, asterisks are used to mark four of the attributes. Then, you can decide later which of the classes should be used to store these attributes.

Although you can use any notation you like for this step of the design process, it's a good practice to document your design decisions. Although you can go directly to the use of UML diagrams for this step, it often makes sense to use a simpler notation until you have identified the classes that you're going to need and have a good idea of which attributes belong to each class.

Possible classes and attributes for a Shopping Cart program

Product	LineItem	Cart
Product name*	Product name*	~~Item count~~
~~Product edition~~	Product discount price*	Cart total
~~Product creator~~	Quantity	
~~Product format~~	*Line item total*	
~~Product stocking message~~		
Product price		
Product discount percent		
Product discount amount		
Product discount price*		

Description

- After you identify and subdivide all of the data attributes for a program, you should group them by the classes with which they're associated.

- If a data attribute relates to more than one class, you can include it under all of the classes it relates to. Then, when you write the code for the classes, you may be able to remove the duplicate attributes.

- As you assign the attributes to classes, you should omit attributes that aren't needed, and you should add any additional attributes that are needed.

The notation used in this figure

- Data attributes that were identified but aren't needed are crossed out.

- Data attributes that were added are displayed in italics.

- Data attributes that are related to two or more entities are followed by an asterisk.

Description

- To identify the classes for a program, you can use notation like this or a modified version of your own.

Figure 16-4   How to identify the classes

How to identify the methods

Figure 16-5 presents a UML diagram that shows the classes and attributes that were identified in the previous figure. In addition, this UML diagram identifies some of the methods that define the behavior of each object. For example, the Product class includes attributes for name, price, and discount percent. However, it uses methods to calculate and return the attributes for the discount amount and discount price.

On the other hand, the LineItem class includes an attribute for a Product object. This provides access to all of the Product object's attributes and methods. In addition, the LineItem class includes a getTotal() method that calculates and returns the line item total. To do that, this method can get the discount price from the Product object and multiply it by the quantity.

Finally, the Cart class begins by using a private attribute to store LineItem objects. Since this attribute is private, the methods of the Cart class provide the only ways to add and remove items from this list. This is considered a good practice since it keeps the user interface for the Cart object simple and allows you to limit the behaviors that are provided by the Cart object. Besides providing methods for adding and removing LineItem objects, the Cart class provides methods for getting a count and total for all LineItem objects in the cart.

At this point, you should realize that you could use getter properties instead of the getter methods shown in this figure. In the Product class, for example, you could use a getter property named discountAmount that calculates and returns the discount amount for the product. This would make it easier for other programmers to access the discount amount.

However, all three classes in this figure use methods to get the values that are calculated from attributes. This provides a consistent user interface that clearly shows the difference between the state and behavior of an object. When you're getting started with object-oriented design, this consistency can be helpful, but you can use whichever approach makes the most sense to you.

As you work on this step, you can add methods that are necessary for the object to work correctly. For example, as you test the system, you may find that you need to provide a way to update a line item that's in the cart with a new item. In that case, you could add a method to do that.

Similarly, you can add convenience methods that make it easier for other programmers to work with the object. For example, if you find that you often need to convert the discount price from a float value to a string value that displays two decimal digits, you could add a method named getDiscountPriceStr to do that.

As you work on this step, you need to keep in mind that the public attributes, properties, and methods of your objects define the object's user interface. Remember too that you want to keep this user interface consistent, intuitive, and easy for other programmers to use. One way to do that is to limit the number of methods that are available from an object to the ones that are absolutely necessary.

The UML diagram for the classes of the Shopping Cart program

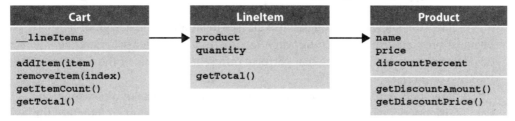

Description

- After you identify the data attributes for an object, you can attempt to identify the methods that define the behavior of an object.

- If a data attribute can be calculated from other data attributes in the class, you can add a property or method that calculates the value for that attribute.

- As you work on this step, you can add methods that are necessary for the object to work correctly or convenience methods that make it easier for other programmers to work with the object.

- Since methods perform actions, their names typically begin with a verb such as get, calculate, add, remove, and so on.

- To model the relationships between the classes in an object-oriented system, you can use *UML (Unified Modeling Language) diagrams*.

Figure 16-5   How to identify the methods

How the three-tier architecture works

Figure 16-6 shows how you can use classes to simplify the design of a business program using a *multi-tier architecture*. In a multi-tier program, the developer separates the classes that perform different functions of the program into two or more layers, or *tiers*.

A *three-tier architecture* like the one in this figure consists of a presentation tier, a business tier, and a database tier. This is the most common architecture for structuring programs.

The *presentation tier* handles the details of the program's user interface. So far, all of the programs presented in this book have been console programs. In these programs, most of the code for the presentation tier is stored in the main() function for the program and other functions that the main() function calls. In other words, the code for the presentation tier of a console application is typically procedural, not object-oriented.

In chapter 18, though, you'll learn how to create a graphical user interface (GUI) for a program. In these programs, the code for the presentation tier is typically stored in a class that defines the objects needed to display the user interface. In other words, the code for a GUI is typically object-oriented, not procedural.

The *database tier* stores the code that provides the data access that's required by the program. Typically, this requires retrieving, adding, updating, and deleting data. Although this tier typically works with data that's stored a database, it can also work with data that's stored in files or other data sources. To work with this data, the database tier can define classes and methods. With Python, though, it's also common to use functions to provide the database access.

The *business tier* provides an interface between the database tier and the presentation tier. This tier often includes classes that correspond to business entities such as products and customers. It may also include classes that implement business rules, such as discount or credit policies. The classes in this tier are often referred to as *business classes*, and the objects that are created from these classes are often called *business objects*.

One advantage of developing programs with a multi-tier architecture is that you should be able to swap out one tier without having to modify the other tiers. For example, you should be able to swap out the presentation tier so it uses a GUI instead of using the console without having to modify any classes in the business or database tiers.

A second advantage of developing programs with a multi-tier architecture is that it allows programmers to divide work among members of a development team. For example, one group of developers might work on the database tier, another group on the business tier, and still another group on the presentation tier.

A third advantage is that it allows developers of a program to share classes. In particular, developers working on different parts of a program can all use the classes that make up the business tier. That's one of the reasons that it's important to do a good job of designing the objects in the business tier.

The three-tier architecture of an application

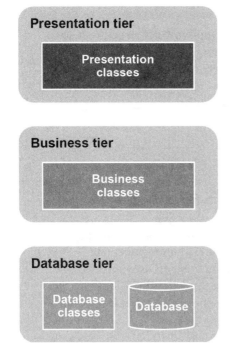

Description

- To simplify development and maintenance of large programs, many applications use a *three-tier architecture* to separate the application's user interface, business rules, and database processing. Each tier of the architecture may consist of one or more modules that contain classes or functions.

- The classes or functions in the *presentation tier* control the application's user interface. For a console application, the presentation tier typically uses a series of functions to provide console input and output. For a GUI application, the presentation tier typically consists of one class for each type of window in the GUI.

- The classes or functions in the *database tier* handle all of the application's file or database processing.

- The classes in the *business tier* define the *business objects* and rules for the application. These classes act as an interface between the classes in the presentation and database tiers.

Figure 16-6   How the three-tier architecture works

The Shopping Cart program

When you create an object-oriented program, you typically structure it so it's divided into the three tiers you just learned about. Then, you can store each tier in one or more modules. To show how this works, this chapter presents an object-oriented version of a Shopping Cart program. This program should give you a good idea of how to structure a three-tier program.

The business tier

Figure 16-7 shows the classes for the business tier. To clearly identify these classes as part of the business tier, they're stored in a file named business.py. As a result, they're available from the business module.

The code in this figure implements the UML diagram presented in figure 16-5. To start, the Product class defines three attributes (name, price, and discountPercent), two methods (getDiscountAmount and getDiscountPrice), and a constructor that initializes all three attributes. Similarly, the LineItem class defines two attributes (product and quantity), one method (getTotal), and a constructor that initializes both attributes.

The Cart class, on the other hand, is more complicated. To start, it uses a private attribute to store a list of line items. Then, it provides a constructor that initializes this attribute to an empty list. After that, this class provides methods for adding or removing items from the cart (addItem and removeItem). These methods define the interface that other programmers can use to add or remove items from the cart.

The getTotal() method returns the total of all items in the cart. To do that, this code loops through each item in the cart and adds the total for each item to the total for the cart.

The getItemCount() method returns the total number of items in the cart. To do that, this code uses the built-in len() function to return the number of items in the private line items attribute.

The __iter__() and __next__() methods provide a way for other programs to use a for loop to iterate over each item in the cart. This is a feature that most programmers would expect from an object like the Cart object.

As you review this code, you might wonder why you can't just use the built-in len() function to get the count of items in the Cart object. The answer is that you can, but first the Cart class needs to override the __len__() method of the object class. Then, other programmers could use the len() function on a Cart object to get the count of line items instead of using the getItemCount() method. Both approaches work, and the Cart class could implement both approaches.

In general, though, you can make your classes easier to maintain and use by limiting the number of ways other programmers can use your objects. That's why you should make sure a method is both helpful and needed before you add it to a class.

The business module

```
class Product:
    def __init__(self, name="", price=0.0, discountPercent=0):
        self.name = name
        self.price = price
        self.discountPercent = discountPercent

    def getDiscountAmount(self):
        discountAmount = self.price * self.discountPercent / 100
        return round(discountAmount, 2)

    def getDiscountPrice(self):
        discountPrice = self.price - self.getDiscountAmount()
        return round(discountPrice, 2)

class LineItem:
    def __init__(self, product=None, quantity=1):
        self.product = product
        self.quantity = quantity

    def getTotal(self):
        total = self.product.getDiscountPrice() * self.quantity
        return total

class Cart:
    def __init__(self):
        self.__lineItems = []

    def addItem(self, item):
        self.__lineItems.append(item)

    def removeItem(self, index):
        self.__lineItems.pop(index)

    def getTotal(self):
        total = 0.0
        for item in self.__lineItems:
            total += item.getTotal()
        return total

    def getItemCount(self):
        return len(self.__lineItems)

    def __iter__(self):
        self.__index = -1
        return self

    def __next__(self):
        if self.__index == len(self.__lineItems)-1:
            raise StopIteration
        self.__index += 1
        lineItem = self.__lineItems[self.__index]
        return lineItem
```

Figure 16-7   The business tier

The database tier

Figure 16-8 shows the database tier for the Shopping Cart program. To start, it shows a CSV file named products.csv that stores the data for the program, which in this case is the data for three products. Each product is a DVD for a movie that has a list price and a discount percent. In other word, this file stores the data for each Product object.

The db module stores the code for the database tier. This code does not define a class. Instead, it provides a single function that gets data from the CSV file. However, this class uses the Product class from the business module. This shows that some tiers of an application can define functions that work with objects that are defined by the classes and methods in other tiers.

The db module begins by importing the csv module. Then, it imports the Product class from the business module. Next, it defines a constant that stores the filename of the CSV file.

Finally, the db module defines the get_products() function that returns a list of Product objects. This function begins by opening the CSV file. Then, it loops through each row of the file. Within this loop, the first line stores the data from the current row in a Product object. The second line stores the Product object in the list of product objects.

In other words, this code maps each line of the CSV file to an object. If you store your data in a relational database instead of a file, as shown in chapter 17, the code that converts a row in the relational database to an object and vice versa is known as *object-relational mapping*, *O/R mapping*, or just *ORM*.

This figure also shows code that does some simple testing of the database and business layers. To start, this code imports the db module and all three classes of the business module. Then, the first statement calls the get_products() function of the db module to get a list of Product objects. The second statement gets the second Product object in the list. The third statement creates a LineItem object that stores this Product object with a quantity of 2. The fourth statement creates a Cart object. The fifth statement adds that LineItem object to the Cart object. And the remaining statements print some of the data that's available from these objects to the console. This testing isn't thorough, but it shows that these objects work.

For a complete Shopping Cart application, of course, the database tier would do more than provide methods for retrieving the Product objects from a file. For instance, it would provide methods for saving and retrieving Cart objects. It would also use a database instead of files. In chapter 17, you'll learn more about how that would work.

The products.csv file

```
The Holy Grail (DVD),4.75,30
Life of Brian (DVD),8.97,20
The Meaning of Life (DVD),6.50,15
```

The db module

```python
import csv
from business import Product

FILENAME = "products.csv"

def get_products():
    products = []
    with open(FILENAME, newline="") as file:
        reader = csv.reader(file)
        for row in reader:
            # convert row to Product object
            product = Product(row[0], float(row[1]), int(row[2]))
            products.append(product)
    return products
```

Code that tests the database and business layers

```python
import db
from business import Product, LineItem, Cart

products = db.get_products()
product = products[1]
lineItem = LineItem(product, 2)
cart = Cart()
cart.addItem(lineItem)
print("Product:  ", product.name)
print("Price:    ", product.getDiscountPrice())
print("Quantity: ", lineItem.quantity)
print("Total:    ", cart.getTotal())
```

The console

```
Product:   Life of Brian (DVD)
Price:     7.18
Quantity:  2
Total:     14.36
```

Description

- In a complete Shopping Cart application, the database tier would also provide for retrieving and saving Cart objects.

- If you store your data in a relational database instead of a file, the code that converts a row in the relational database to an object is known as *object-relational mapping*, *O/R mapping*, or just *ORM*.

Figure 16-8   The database tier

The presentation tier

Part 1 of figure 16-9 shows the user interface for the Shopping Cart program. This user interface is a console, and it should give you a good idea of how the presentation tier works with the business and database tiers. However, a Shopping Cart program like this would typically use a GUI interface, not a console interface.

In this interface, the program starts by displaying the program title, a command menu, and a numbered list of products. Then, it prompts the user for a command. When working with these commands, the user can select a product by entering the number that corresponds with the product.

Note, however, that to add an item to the cart, you use the number of the item in the Products list. But to delete an item from the cart, you use the number in the cart display.

The user interface

```
The Shopping Cart program

COMMAND MENU
cart - Show the cart
add  - Add an item to the cart
del  - Delete an item from cart
exit - Exit program

PRODUCTS
Item   Name                        Price    Discount   Your Price
1      The Holy Grail (DVD)        4.75       30%         3.32
2      Life of Brian (DVD)         8.97       20%         7.18
3      The Meaning of Life (DVD)   6.50       15%         5.53

Command: add
Item number: 1
Quantity: 2
Item 1 was added.

Command: add
Item number: 3
Quantity: 1
Item 2 was added.

Command: cart
Item   Name                     Your Price   Quantity    Total
1      The Holy Grail (DVD)        3.32          2         6.64
2      The Meaning of Life (DVD)   5.53          1         5.53
                                                          12.17

Command: del
Item number: 1
Item 1 was deleted.

Command: cart
Item   Name                     Your Price   Quantity    Total
1      The Meaning of Life (DVD)   5.53          1         5.53
                                                           5.53

Command: exit
Bye!
```

Description

- To implement this interface, this program uses functions as shown in parts 2 and 3 of this figure.

- Normally, however, the user interface for a Shopping Cart application would be a GUI, not a console, and it would be implemented with classes and objects as shown in chapter 18.

Figure 16-9   The presentation tier (part 1)

Parts 2 and 3 show the code for the user interface. This code is a series of functions, not a class that defines an object. However, this code imports all three objects from the business module and uses them in its functions. By now, you should be able to understand most of the code presented in this figure. However, there are a few tricky spots.

To start, the show_products() and show_cart() functions use two format strings to align columns of data on the console. In both methods, the first format string aligns the strings that provide the column names, and the second format string aligns the different types of data for each column.

The show_products() function loops through a list of Product objects and uses the attributes and methods of these objects to display the data that's available from them. Similarly, the show_cart() function loops through each LineItem object in the Cart object and uses the attributes and methods of these objects to display the data that's available from them. In this function, you can use a for loop because the Cart class overrides the __iter__() and __next__() methods of the object class.

The shopping_cart module   **Page 1**

```python
import db
from business import Product, LineItem, Cart

def show_title():
    print("The Shopping Cart program")
    print()

def show_menu():
    print("COMMAND MENU")
    print("cart - Show the cart")
    print("add  - Add an item to the cart")
    print("del  - Delete an item from cart")
    print("exit - Exit program")
    print()

def show_products(products):
    print("PRODUCTS")
    line_format1 = "{:<5s} {:<25s} {:>10s} {:>10s} {:>12s}"
    line_format2 = "{:<5d} {:<25s} {:>10.2f} {:>10s} {:>12.2f}"
    print(line_format1.format("Item", "Name", "Price",
                              "Discount", "Your Price"))
    for i in range(len(products)):
        product = products[i]
        print(line_format2.format(i+1,
                product.name,
                product.price,
                str(product.discountPercent) + "%",
                product.getDiscountPrice()))
    print()

def show_cart(cart):
    if cart.getItemCount() == 0:
        print("There are no items in your cart.\n")
    else:
        # items = cart.lineItems
        line_format1 = "{:<5s} {:<25s} {:>12s} {:>10s} {:>10s}"
        line_format2 = "{:<5d} {:<25s} {:>12.2f} {:>10d} {:>10.2f}"
        print(line_format1.format("Item", "Name", "Your Price",
                                  "Quantity", "Total"))
        i = 0
        for item in cart:
            print(line_format2.format(i+1,
                    item.product.name,
                    item.product.getDiscountPrice(),
                    item.quantity,
                    item.getTotal()))
            i += 1
        print("{:>66.2f}".format(cart.getTotal()))
        print()
```

Figure 16-9   The presentation tier (part 2)

In part 3, the add_item() function begins by getting an item number and quantity from the user. If that item number matches one of the items in the Products list that's displayed by the program, this function gets the corresponding Product object from the list of products, creates a LineItem object with the specified product and quantity, and adds that LineItem object to the Cart object that's referred to by the cart parameter.

The remove_item() function begins by getting the number of the line item to delete. If the line item number matches one of the line items in the cart, this code removes the corresponding line item from the cart.

Before the main() function enters the main loop for the program, it calls the get_products() method of the db module to get the list of Product objects for the program. In addition, it creates a Cart object that can store the LineItem objects for the program.

As you review this code, note how it uses the Product, LineItem, and Cart objects that are defined by the business tier. Also note that it contains a single line of code that accesses the database tier to return a list of Product objects. This shows how the business tier acts as the interface between the other tiers of the program.

The shopping_cart module   **Page 2**

```python
def add_item(cart, products):
    number = int(input("Item number: "))
    quantity = int(input("Quantity: "))
    if number < 1 or number > len(products):
        print("No product has that number.\n")
    else:
        # Get Product object, store in LineItem object,
        # and add to Cart object
        product = products[number-1]
        item = LineItem(product, quantity)
        cart.addItem(item)
        print("Item " + str(cart.getItemCount()) + " was added.\n")

def remove_item(cart):
    number = int(input("Item number: "))
    if number < 1 or number > cart.getItemCount():
        print("The cart does not contain an item " +
                "with that number.\n")
    else:
        # Remove LineItem object at specified index from cart
        cart.removeItem(number-1)
        print("Item " + str(number) + " was deleted.\n")

def main():
    show_title()
    show_menu()

    # get a list of Product objects and display them
    products = db.get_products()
    show_products(products)

    # create a Cart object to store LineItem objects
    cart = Cart()
    while True:
        command = input("Command: ")
        if command == "cart":
            show_cart(cart)
        elif command == "add":
            add_item(cart, products)
        elif command == "del":
            remove_item(cart)
        elif command == "exit":
            print("Bye!")
            break
        else:
            print("Not a valid command. Please try again.\n")

if __name__ == "__main__":
    main()
```

Figure 16-9   The presentation tier (part 3)

Perspective

Object-oriented design is a complicated subject. Because of that, it's impossible to teach everything you need to know in a single chapter. However, with the skills you've learned in this chapter, you should be able to design the business tier for object-oriented programs of your own. Then, in chapter 17, you'll learn how to work with databases, which should shed more light on how the database tier should work. And in chapter 18, you'll learn how to build a GUI, which should shed more light on how the presentation tier should work.

Terms

entity	database tier
instance	business tier
attribute	business class
UML (Unified Modeling Language)	business object
multi-tier architecture	object-relational mapping
three-tier architecture	O/R mapping (ORM)
presentation tier	

Summary

- You can use *UML diagrams (Unified Modeling Language diagrams)* to model the relationships between the classes in an object-oriented application.
- A *three-tier architecture* divides a program into three layers, or *tiers*.
- The *presentation tier* consists of the classes or functions for the user interface.
- The *database tier* consists of the database and the database classes that work with it.
- The *business tier* consists of the *business classes* that define the *business objects* and rules of the program.
- If you store your data in a relational database instead of a file, the code that converts a row in the relational database to an object and vice versa is known as *object-relational mapping*, *O/R mapping*, or just *ORM*.

Exercise 16-1   Design a Task List program and implement your design

In this exercise, you'll design the business objects for a program that stores one or more lists of tasks. It should be a simplified version of the following screen captures:

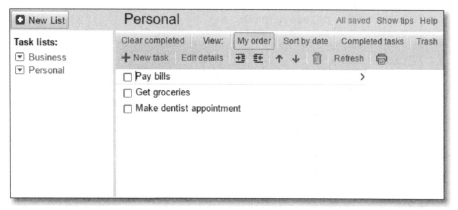

Note that this program shows two task lists (Business and Personal), but the user could add more lists, and each list can contain zero or more tasks.

For the first three steps, you can use a word processor or text editor. The only deliverable will be the UML diagram that you prepare in steps 4 and 5.

Design the business objects for the program

1. Identify the data attributes.

2. Subdivide each attribute into its smallest useful components.

3. Identify the classes by sorting the data attributes into categories.

4. Identify the methods by drawing a UML diagram for the class. To do that, you can use a software tool (many are available for free), or you can sketch the diagram on a piece of paper.

5. Refine the classes, attributes, and methods. When you're done, you should be ready to start coding and testing the business objects for the program.

Implement the business objects and test them

6. Write the code for the business objects.

7. Test the business objects. To do that, you can use the interactive shell, or you can write code that tests these objects.

8. As you work on the previous two steps, you can further refine the classes, attributes, and methods for the business objects.

Implement the user interface and test it

9. Write the code that implements the user interface. When you're done, it should look something like this:

```
COMMAND MENU
list      - List all tasks
add       - Add a task
complete  - Complete a task
delete    - Delete a task
exit      - Exit program

TASK LISTS
1. Personal
2. Business

Enter number to select task list: 1
Personal task list was selected.

Command: add
Description: Pay bills

Command: add
Description: Get groceries

Command: list
1. Pay bills
2. Get groceries

Command: complete
Number: 1

Command: list
1. Pay bills (DONE!)
2. Get groceries

Command:
```

To get this to work, you can hard code a list that stores the names of the two task lists (Personal and Business).

Implement the persistence layer and test it

10. Write the code that writes and reads the business objects to one or more files. For now, you can store the names of the task lists in one file, and you can store the data for each task list in a separate file. In the next chapter, you'll learn how to store data in a database, which has many advantages over storing it in one or more files.

Section 4

Database and GUI programming

To this point in the book, you've been developing programs that store their data in files if they store their data at all. You've also been developing programs that get data from the console and display the results on the console. In the real-world, though, most programs store their data in databases and use graphical user interfaces (GUIs) to get user entries and display results.

That's why this section shows you how to do both. In chapter 17, you'll learn how to develop programs that store their data in databases. In chapter 18, you'll learn how to develop programs that have GUIs. You can read these chapters in whichever sequence you prefer since they aren't related, and you don't have to read section 2 before you read these chapters.

However, we do recommend that you read all three chapters in section 3 on object-oriented programming before you read chapters 17 and 18. Then, in chapter 17, you'll study a program that uses business objects and has a three-tier architecture. And in chapter 18, you'll see how GUI programming depends on inheritance. In short, chapters 17 and 18 will enhance your understanding of how object-oriented programming is used in the real world.

17

How to work with a database

In chapter 7, you learned how to work with programs that store data in files. In the real world, though, most programs store data in databases. That's because storing data in a database provides many advantages over storing data in a file.

In this chapter, you'll learn how to work with a database. More specifically, you'll learn how to use Python to work with a SQLite database. Note, however, that most of these skills also apply to working with other types of databases such as MySQL, Oracle, and SQL Server databases.

An introduction to relational databases

In 1970, Dr. E. F. Codd developed a model for a new type of database called a *relational database*. This type of database eliminated some of the problems that were associated with standard files and other database designs. By using the relational model, you can reduce data redundancy, which saves disk storage and leads to efficient data retrieval. You can also view and manipulate data in a way that is both intuitive and efficient. Today, relational databases are the de facto standard for database applications.

To facilitate the use of relational databases, a *database management system (DBMS)* like MySQL or SQL Server is used. The DBMS not only lets you create and maintain databases, it also maintains the integrity of the databases and helps them run as efficiently as possible.

How a database table is organized

In a relational database, data is stored in one or more *tables* that consist of *rows* and *columns*. This is illustrated by the relational Movie table in figure 17-1. Rows and columns can also be referred to as *records* and *fields*, and a value that is stored at the intersection of each row and column is sometimes called a *cell*.

In this example, each row contains information about a single movie. Then, each column in the row provides data about that movie, including name, year, and running time in minutes. In addition, the first column in this table provides a unique ID for each movie, and the second column provides an ID that associates each movie row with a movie category. For example, the third row in this table is for a movie named Aladdin that was released in 1992 and has a running time of 90 minutes. It also has a movie ID of 3 and a category ID of 1.

Most tables in a relational database have a *primary key* column that uniquely identifies each row in the table. In this example, the movieID column is the primary key for the table. In other words, two movies in the table can't have the same ID. Often, the DBMS generates the primary keys for the records as they are added to the table, which is the case for this table. Also, the DBMS won't allow a record to be added to the table if it has the same (a duplicate) primary key.

In general, each table in a database is modeled after a real-word entity such as a product, customer, or movie. Then, if the entities for a table provide their own unique keys like product number or invoice number, those columns can be used for the primary key so they don't need to be generated. A primary key can also consist of two or more columns.

The Movie table

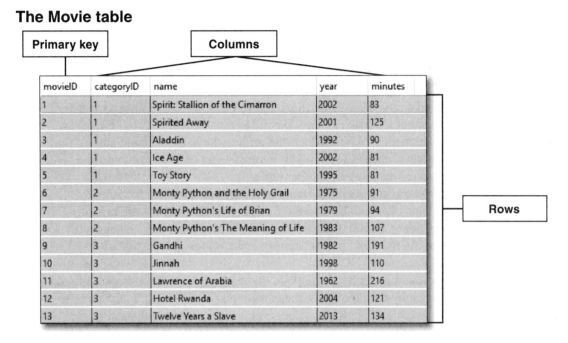

Concepts

- A *relational database* consists of *tables*. Tables consist of *rows* and *columns*, which can also be referred to as *records* and *fields*.

- A table is typically modeled after a real-world entity, such as a product or customer, but it can also be modeled after an abstract concept, such as the data for a game.

- A column represents an attribute of the entity, such as a movie's name.

- A row contains a set of values for one instance of the entity, such as one movie.

- Most tables have a *primary key* that uniquely identifies each row in the table.

- The primary key is usually a single column, but it can also consist of two or more columns.

Figure 17-1   How a database table is organized

How the tables in a database are related

The tables in a relational database can be related to other tables by values in specific columns. The two tables shown in figure 17-2 illustrate this concept. Here, each row in the Category table is related to one or more rows in the Movie table. This is called a *one-to-many relationship*. In other words, a category can have many movies, but a movie can only belong to one category.

Typically, relationships exist between the primary keys in one table and *foreign keys* in another table. A foreign key is simply one or more columns in a table that refer to a primary key in another table.

In this example, the categoryID column in the Movie table is a foreign key that refers to the categoryID column in the Category table, which is the primary key for that table. For example, the first row in the Movie table has a categoryID of 1 that relates to the first row in the Category table, which is the Animation category.

You should know that the Movie table in this figure is unrealistic because its rows are in sequence by both movieID and categoryID. As soon as records are added to the Movie table, though, the cateogeryIDs won't be in sequence. If, for example, a 14th record is added to the table with a categoryID of 2, the categoryID sequence will be broken.

Although a one-to-many relationship is the most common type of relationship, two tables can also have a one-to-one or many-to-many relationship. If a table has a *one-to-one relationship* with another table, the data in the two tables could be stored in a single table. Because of that, one-to-one relationships are used infrequently.

In contrast, a *many-to-many relationship* is usually implemented by using an intermediate table that has a one-to-many relationship with the two tables. In other words, a many-to-many relationship can usually be broken down into two or more one-to-many relationships.

The relationship between a Category table and a Movie table

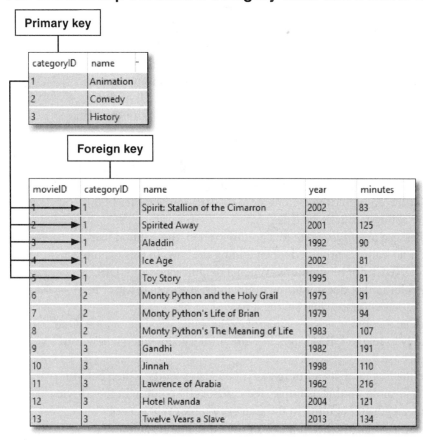

Concepts

- The tables in a relational database are related to each other through their key columns. For example, the Category and Movie tables in this figure use the categoryID column to create the relationship between the two tables.

- The categoryID column in the Movie table is called a *foreign key* because it identifies a related row in the Category table. A table may contain one or more foreign keys.

- When you define a foreign key, you can't add rows to the table with the foreign key unless there's a matching primary key in the related table.

- The relationships between the tables in a database correspond to the relationships between the entities they represent. The most common type of relationship is a *one-to-many relationship* as illustrated by the Category and Movie tables.

- A table can also have a *one-to-one relationship* or a *many-to-many relationship* with another table.

Figure 17-2   How the tables in a relational database are related

How the columns in a table are defined

When you define a column in a table, you assign properties to it as indicated by the design of the Movie table in figure 17-3. First, you need to define a name for the column, which should generally reflect the type of information that the column stores. Then, you need to define a *data type* for the column, which determines the type of data that the column stores. In this table, all of the columns use the INTEGER type to store integer numbers, except for the name column, which uses the TEXT type to store the name of the movie.

In addition to choosing a data type, you must identify whether the column can store a *null value*. The NULL keyword represents a value that's unknown, unavailable, or not applicable. If you don't allow null values, then you must provide a value for the column or you can't store the row in the table. In this figure, none of the columns can be NULL.

You can also assign a *default value* to a column. Then, the column uses the default value if no value is provided when adding the row. In this example, the default value is NULL for all columns. When a default value of NULL is combined with a column that doesn't allow null values, it forces the user to provide a value for that column when saving a row.

When you define a column as the primary key, its value must be unique. One way to assure that is to let the DBMS generate the primary key when a new row is added to the database.

When you define a column as a foreign key, you also specify which column it refers to in another table. In this example, the categoryID column in the Movie table refers to the categoryID column in the Category table. When a column is a foreign key, its value must exist in a row of the table that it references. In addition, the DBMS won't let you delete a row from a table if other tables contain foreign key values that refer to that row.

If, for example, there are any movies in the Movie table that belong to category 1, the DBMS won't let you delete the category 1 row from the Category table. If the DBMS didn't enforce this constraint, you would end up with movies that have foreign keys that refer to a category that doesn't exist. These keys can be referred to as *orphaned keys*.

The columns of the Category table

Name	Data Type	Not Null?	Default Value	Primary Key?	Foreign Key?
categoryID	INTEGER	Y	NULL	Y	N
name	TEXT	Y	NULL	N	N

The columns of the Movie table

Name	Data Type	Not Null?	Default Value	Primary Key?	Foreign Key?
movieID	INTEGER	Y	NULL	Y	N
categoryID	INTEGER	Y	NULL	N	Y
name	TEXT	Y	NULL	N	N
year	INTEGER	Y	NULL	N	N
minutes	INTEGER	Y	NULL	N	N

Common SQLite data types

Type	Description
TEXT	A variable-length Unicode string.
INTEGER	Integer values of various sizes.
REAL	Decimal values that can contain an integer portion and a decimal portion.
BLOB	The data is stored exactly as entered. Can contain binary data such as images.

Description

- The *data type* that's assigned to a column determines the type of data that can be stored in the column.

- Each column definition also indicates whether or not it can contain *null values*. The NULL keyword indicates that the value of the column is unknown.

- A column can also be defined with a *default value*. Then, that value is used if another value isn't provided when a row is added to the table.

- If a column is defined as a primary key, some databases automatically generate its value when a new row is added to the table.

- When you define a column as a foreign key, you specify the column in another table that the key refers to.

- To avoid creating *orphaned keys*, a database typically prevents you from deleting a row if one of its values is being used as a foreign key in another table.

Figure 17-3   How the columns in a table are defined

How to use the SQL statements for data manipulation

Structured Query Language, or *SQL*, is a standard language for working with databases. In conversation, SQL is pronounced "S-Q-L" or "sequel". In this book, we use "sequel" as the pronunciation so we refer to *a* SQL statement, instead of *an* SQL statement.

The SELECT, INSERT, UPDATE, and DELETE statements that you'll learn about next make up SQL's *Data Manipulation Language* (*DML*). These statements work with the data in a database, and they are the statements that programmers use every day in their programs. As a result, these are the statements that you'll learn how to use in this chapter.

In contrast, the CREATE DATABASE, DROP DATABASE, CREATE TABLE, and DROP TABLE statements are part of SQL's *Data Definition Language* (*DDL*). These statements are typically used by database administrators to create and delete databases and tables, and they aren't presented in this book.

How to select data from a single table

The *SELECT statement* is the most commonly used *SQL statement*. It is used to retrieve data from one or more tables in a database. When you run a SELECT statement, it is commonly referred to as a *query*. The result of a query is a table known as a *result set*, or *result table*.

Figure 17-4 shows the syntax for a SELECT statement that gets all of the columns of a table, and it shows the syntax for a SELECT statement that gets only selected columns. In the syntax summaries for SQL statements, the capitalized words are SQL keywords, and the lowercase words are the ones that you supply. Also, the brackets indicate optional components of a statement, and the bar (|) indicates a choice between two options.

The first example in this figure shows how to get all columns and selected rows from the Movie table. Here, the SELECT clause uses the asterisk (*) wildcard to indicate that all of the columns in the table should be retrieved, and the FROM clause specifies that these columns should be retrieved from the Movie table. Then, the WHERE clause indicates that each row should have a categoryID column that's equal to 2. As a result, this query returns three rows and five columns.

The second example shows how to get selected columns and rows from the Movie table. This time, the SELECT clause identifies the name and minutes columns, and the FROM clause identifies the Movie table. Then, the WHERE clause specifies that each row that's returned by the statement should have a running time that's less than 90 minutes.

Last, the ORDER BY clause indicates that the retrieved rows should be sorted in ascending order by the minutes column. This sorts the rows from the shortest movie to the longest movie. However, if you wanted to switch the sort order, you could use the DESC keyword instead of the ASC keyword. Then, the rows would be sorted in descending sequence instead of ascending sequence.

The syntax for a SELECT statement that gets all columns

```
SELECT *
FROM table
[WHERE selection-criteria]
[ORDER BY column-1 [ASC|DESC] [, column-2 [ASC|DESC] ...]]
```

A SELECT statement that gets all columns

```
SELECT * FROM Movie
WHERE categoryID = 2
```

movieID	categoryID	name	year	minutes
6	2	Monty Python and the Holy Grail	1975	91
7	2	Monty Python's Life of Brian	1979	94
8	2	Monty Python's The Meaning of Life	1983	107

The syntax for a SELECT statement that gets selected columns

```
SELECT column-1[, column-2] ...
FROM table
[WHERE selection-criteria]
[ORDER BY column-1 [ASC|DESC][, column-2 [ASC|DESC] ...]]
```

A SELECT statement that gets selected columns and rows

```
SELECT name, minutes
FROM Movie
WHERE minutes < 90
ORDER BY minutes ASC
```

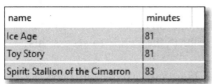

name	minutes
Ice Age	81
Toy Story	81
Spirit: Stallion of the Cimarron	83

Description

- A *SELECT statement* is a SQL statement that returns a *result set* (or *result table*) that consists of the specified rows and columns.

- To specify the columns to select, use the SELECT clause.

- To specify the table that the data should be retrieved from, use the FROM clause.

- To specify the rows to select, use the WHERE clause.

- To specify how the result set should be sorted, use the ORDER BY clause. Within this clause, use the ASC keyword to sort a column in ascending order or the DESC keyword to sort a column in descending order.

Figure 17-4   How to select data from a single table

How to select data from multiple tables

Figure 17-5 shows how to use the SELECT statement to retrieve data from two tables. This is commonly known as a *join*. The result of any join is a single result set.

An *inner join* is the most common type of join. When you use an inner join, the data from the rows in two tables are included in the result set only if their related columns match. In this figure, the SELECT statement joins the data from the rows in the Movie and Category tables, but only if the value of the categoryID column in the Movie table is equal to the categoryID column in the Category table. In other words, if there isn't any data in the Movie table for a category, that category isn't added to the result set. This join results in a user-friendly result set because the category now has a name instead of a numerical ID.

To code an inner join, you use the JOIN clause to specify the second table and the ON clause to specify the columns to be used for the join. Then, if a column in one table has the same name as a column in the other table, you must qualify the column name by coding the table name, a dot, and the column name. This is illustrated by both columns in the ON clause. This is also illustrated by the first two columns in the SELECT clause.

When a column in one table of a join has the same name as a column in the other table, you can use the AS clause to create an *alias* for the column name. In this example, an alias of categoryName is assigned to the Category table's name column. So that's the name that's displayed at the top of the column in the result set, and that's the name that you can use in your Python code to access this column.

Although there are other types of joins besides inner joins, inner joins are so common that they are the default type of join. That's why you don't have to code the INNER keyword before the JOIN keyword when you code your SQL statement.

Although this figure only shows how to join data from two tables, you can extend this syntax to join data from additional tables. If, for example, you want to create a result set that includes data from three tables named Category, Movie, and Actor, you can code the FROM clause of the SELECT statement like this:

```
FROM Movie
    JOIN Category ON Category.categoryID = Movie.categoryID
    JOIN Actor ON Actor.movieID = Movie.movieID
```

Then, you can include any of the columns from the three tables in the column list of the SELECT statement.

The syntax for a SELECT statement that joins two tables

```
SELECT column-1 [AS alias-1] [[, column-2] [AS alias-2]]...
FROM table-1
    [INNER ]JOIN table-2 ON table-1.column-1 = table-2.column-2
```

A statement that gets data from two related tables

```
SELECT Movie.name, Category.name AS categoryName, minutes
FROM Movie
    JOIN Category ON Category.categoryID = Movie.categoryID
WHERE minutes < 90
ORDER BY minutes ASC
```

name	categoryName	minutes
Ice Age	Animation	81
Toy Story	Animation	81
Spirit: Stallion of the Cimarron	Animation	83

Description

- To return a result set that contains data from two tables, you *join* the tables. To do that, you can use a JOIN clause.

- Most of the time, you'll want to code an *inner join* so that rows are only included when the key of a row in the first table is equal to (matches) the key of a row in the second table.

- If you don't specify the join type you want, an inner join is used by default.

- If the two tables you want to join contain duplicate column names, you have to qualify the column by prefixing each column name with its table name. Otherwise, the column name is ambiguous, and the database doesn't know which column to retrieve.

- When you qualify a name, you often want to provide a new name, or *alias*, for the column name so each column in the result set has a unique name. To do that, you can code the AS keyword followed by the aliases for the columns.

- When you're getting started with joins, you may want to prefix every column with its table name so it's clear which table the column is coming from. However, this is only required for the column names that are the same in both tables.

Figure 17-5   How to select data from multiple tables

How to insert, update, and delete rows

Figure 17-6 shows how to use the INSERT, UPDATE, and DELETE statements to add, update, or delete one or more rows in a database. Note that none of these statements return a result set. Instead, they change the data in the database.

The *INSERT statement* is used to add a row to a database table. As the syntax and examples show, you can do that in two ways. Here, the INTO clause in the first INSERT statement provides a list of the columns that data will be provided for. Then, the VALUES clause provides the values for those columns in the same sequence as the columns. Note here that you don't have to provide values for columns like the MovieID column that will have their values generated by the DBMS. And you don't have to provide values for columns that have default values. For the Movie table, though, none of the columns provide default values.

The second INSERT statement shows that the column list in the INTO clause is optional. In other words, you don't need to supply the list of column names after the table name. In this case, though, you must code the values in the order in which the columns are defined for the table, and you must supply a value for every column, even ones that SQLite generates automatically.

The syntax and example for the *UPDATE statement* show how to use that statement to update the data in one or more columns of one or more rows. Here, the SET clause specifies the columns and values that are to be updated, and the WHERE clause specifies which rows should be updated. In the example, the UPDATE statement updates the minutes column in the row where the movieID column is equal to 4, so only one row is updated.

Last, the syntax and examples for the *DELETE statement* show how to delete one or more rows in a table. Here, the WHERE clause identifies the row or rows to be deleted. As a result, the first DELETE statement deletes the row from the Movie table where the movieID equals 12, so only one row is deleted. But the second DELETE statement deletes all rows in the Movie table that have a year that's equal to 1979, so more than one row is deleted.

When you use DELETE statements, you need to be aware of how dangerous they can be. That's because a coding error in the WHERE clause can delete far more rows than you intended. So use DELETE statements with care, especially when you're deleting rows based on columns that don't contain unique values.

When you specify a value within a SQL statement, you must enclose string values in single quotes. However, you aren't required to enclose numeric values in single quotes. This is illustrated by the INSERT, UPDATE, and DELETE statements in this figure, but it's also true for SELECT statements.

The syntax for the INSERT statement

```
INSERT INTO table-name [(column-list)]
VALUES (value-list)
```

A statement that uses a column list to add one row

```
INSERT INTO Movie (name, year, minutes, categoryID)
VALUES ('Juno', 2007, 96, 2)
```

A statement that doesn't use a column list to add one row

```
INSERT INTO Movie
VALUES (14, 2, 'Juno', 2007, 96)
```

The syntax for the UPDATE statement

```
UPDATE table-name
SET expression-1 [, expression-2] ...
WHERE selection-criteria
```

A statement that updates a column in one row

```
UPDATE Movie
SET minutes = 84
WHERE movieID = 4
```

The syntax for the DELETE statement

```
DELETE FROM table-name
WHERE selection-criteria
```

A statement that deletes one row from a table

```
DELETE FROM Movie
WHERE movieID = 14
```

A statement that deletes multiple rows from a table

```
DELETE FROM Movie
WHERE year = 1979
```

Description

- The *INSERT, UPDATE,* and *DELETE statements* modify the data that's stored in a database. These statements don't return a result set.

- Be careful when deleting or updating based on columns that might not be unique, since you could inadvertently delete or update more rows than intended.

- When you specify a value within a SQL statement, you must enclose string values in single quotes. However, you aren't required to enclose numeric values in single quotes.

Figure 17-6   How to insert, update, and delete data

How to use *DB Browser for SQLite* to work with a database

SQLite is a popular open-source relational database that can be embedded into programs. This chapter shows how to use SQLite as your database because it's easy to set up and because Python includes built-in support for working with SQLite.

To work with a SQLite database, we recommend that you install and use *DB Browser for SQLite*. If you haven't already installed DB Browser, the appendix for your operating system will show you how.

How to use DB Browser to view and edit a table in a SQLite database

Figure 17-7 begins by showing how to open the file for the database. After the file is opened, the tree for the tables in the database is displayed in the Database Structure tab. If you expand the tables in this tree, you can see how the columns in the tables are defined.

To view the data in one of the tables, you can click on the Browse Data tab and select the table you want to view from the drop-down Table list. This displays the data in all the rows and columns of the table. In this figure, the data in the Movie table is displayed. As you view a table, you can sort it by the data in any of the columns, just by clicking on the column name.

To edit the data in the rows and columns, you can just change the data in the cells. To add or delete rows, you can click on the New Record or Delete Record button. Then, to save any changes to the table, you can click the Write Changes button. Or, to cancel the changes, you can click on the Revert Changes button.

DB Browser for SQLite while using the Browse Data tab to view a table

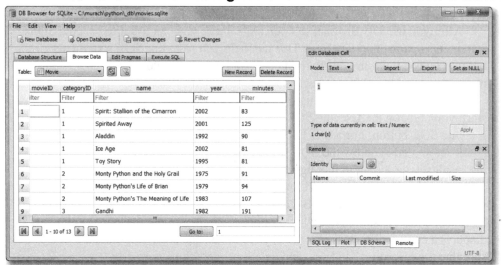

How to open a database

1. Start DB Browser for SQLite.

2. Click the Open Database button or choose the File→Open Database command. Then, use the dialog box to select the SQLite database you want to open. The database for this chapter is located here:

   `\murach\python\_db\movies.sqlite`

3. This displays the tree structure of the database in the Database Structure tab.

How to view a table

1. Click the Browse Data tab.

2. Use the drop-down Tables list to select the table that you want to view.

3. To sort the table by the values in a column, click on the column name.

How to edit a table

- To edit the data in the rows, change the data in the table.

- To add or delete rows, use the New Record or Delete Record button.

- To save the changes, click the Write Changes button.

- To cancel the changes, click the Revert Changes button.

Warning

- There may be a bug in the way the New Record button works. For instance, it works with the Category table but reports an error with the Movie table. So remember that you can also add records by using SQL INSERT statements, as in the next figure.

Figure 17-7   How to use DB Browser for SQLite to view and edit a database table

How to use DB Browser to run SQL statements

After you use DB Browser to open a database, you can use it to execute SQL statements against that database. This can help you test your SQL statements before you use them in your Python code, and it can help you debug SQL statements that aren't working correctly.

Figure 17-8 shows how to use DB Browser to execute a SQL statement. To start, you click on the Execute SQL tab, enter a SQL statement, and click the Execute SQL button. For a SELECT statement, DB Browser then displays the result set in a table below the SQL statement and a completion message below the result set, as shown in this figure.

Of course, INSERT, UPDATE, and DELETE statements don't return a result set. So, for those statements, DB Browser doesn't display a result set. However, it still executes the statement, which modifies the data in the database, and it still displays a completion message. Then, you can use the Browse Data tab to make sure that the insertions, updates, and deletions were done correctly.

This assumes that the SQL statements don't contain errors. But if they do, DB Browser displays error messages instead of completion messages. These messages will often help you find and fix the errors.

To make it easy to identify the keywords in a SQL statement, the examples in this book capitalize the keywords. You should realize, however, that this capitalization is optional. So, if you want to use lowercase letters in the keywords when you type them into DB Browser, you can do that.

The Execute SQL tab after a SQL statement has been executed

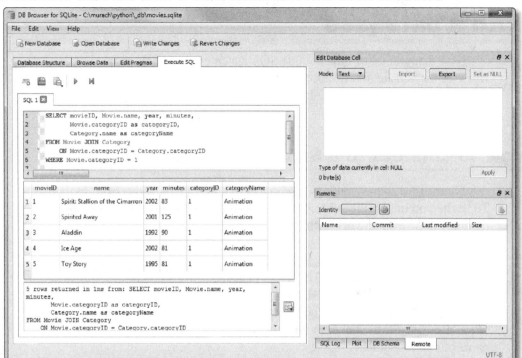

How to execute a SQL statement

- Click the Execute SQL tab.
- Enter the SQL statement.
- Click the Execute SQL button.

Description

- When a SELECT statement is run, the result set is displayed in a table below the SQL statement, and a completion message is displayed below the result set.
- When an INSERT, UPDATE, or DELETE statement is run, a result set isn't returned, but a completion message is displayed. Then, you can use the Browse Data tab to see whether the right rows have been inserted, updated, or deleted.
- If the SQL statement contains errors when it is run, an error message is displayed that can help you find the cause of the error.

Figure 17-8   How to use DB Browser for SQLite to run a SQL statement

How to use Python to work with a database

Now that you know how to code SQL statements and how to use DB Browser for SQLite to test those statements, you're ready to learn how you can use those statements in Python as you develop programs that work with a database.

How to connect to a SQLite database

Figure 17-9 shows you how to connect to a SQLite database from Python. To begin, you import the sqlite3 module as shown in the first example. This module allows you to work with SQLite databases.

Once you've imported the sqlite3 module, you need to open a connection to the database. To do that, you call the connect() method from the sqlite3 module to create a *connection object*. This method accepts an argument that specifies the path to the database file. If the database file is in the working directory, which is usually the same directory as the program file, you only need to specify the name of the database file as shown in the second example. Here, the database file has a name of movies.sqlite.

Although this technique is adequate for programs like the ones in this book, it may not be adequate for real-world programs. That's why the next example shows how to connect to a database that isn't in the working directory. To start, this example imports the sys and os modules. Then, it uses the sys module to determine whether the platform is Windows, Mac OS X, or Linux. If the platform attribute is "win32", the operating system is Windows. That's true even if you are running on a 64-bit version of Windows. If the platform attribute isn't "win32", it's safe to assume that the operating system is OS X or some variant of Linux or Unix.

On a Windows system, this example connects to the movie database that's in the _db directory by supplying a complete path to its file. However, on OS X and Linux, normal users can't store files outside of their own home directory. As a result, if you are running as a normal user (and you should be for security reasons), the database file is most likely installed in the home directory.

Then, to get the user's home directory, this code accesses the environ dictionary that's available from the os module and uses the HOME key to get the home directory of the user who is running the program. Next, it appends the path to the database file to the path to the home directory. The last statement in this example gets a connection object by passing the path to the database file to the connect() method of the sqlite module.

When your program is through with a connection object, your program should close it so its resources are returned to the system. That last example in this figure shows how to use the close() method of a connection object to do that. Here, the if statement checks whether the connection object named conn exists. If it does, the close() method is called.

How to import the module that supports SQLite databases

```
import sqlite3
```

The syntax for connecting to a database and returning a connection object

```
conn = sqlite3.connect(path_to_database_file)
```

How to connect to a database that's in the working directory

```
conn = sqlite3.connect("movies.sqlite")
```

How to connect to a database that's not in the working directory

```
import sys
import os

if sys.platform == "win32":                                    # Windows
    DB_FILE = "/murach/python/_db/movies.sqlite"
else:                                                          # Mac OS X and Linux
    HOME = os.environ["HOME"]
    DB_FILE = HOME + "/Documents/murach/python/_db/movies.sqlite"
conn = sqlite3.connect(DB_FILE)
```

How to use the close() method to close a connection object

```
if conn:
    conn.close()
```

Description

- To work with a SQLite database in Python, you need to import the sqlite3 module.

- To connect to a database, call the connect() method on the sqlite3 module with the path to the database. This returns a *connection object* that you can use to access the database.

- If the database file is in the working directory, which is usually the same directory as the program, the path to the database is just the name of the database file. Otherwise, you can specify a complete path to the database file.

- If you need to get the home directory of the current user, you can import the os module and use its environ dictionary.

- Because a SQLite database runs locally and isn't accessible over a network, you don't need a username or password to connect to it.

- When you're through with a database connection, you need to close it so it frees up the resources that it's using.

Figure 17-9   How to use Python to connect to a SQLite database

How to execute SELECT statements

Figure 17-10 shows how to execute SELECT statements with Python. But first, in order to execute any SQL statement on a database, you need to get a *cursor object* for the database. To do that, you call the cursor() method from the connection object. Then, to execute a SQL statement, you call the execute() method from the cursor object. If the method requires any values as arguments, you pass a tuple argument that supplies the values to the method.

The first example in this figure shows how to get a cursor object named c. Then, the second example shows how to execute a simple SELECT statement for the database that's represented by the cursor object. Here, the first statement creates a variable named query that stores a SELECT statement that gets all rows from the Movie table. Then, the next statement runs the query by calling the execute() method from the cursor object and passing the query variable as the first argument.

When you code a SQL statement in Python, you can enclose it in single or double quotes. However, since SQL statements often span multiple lines, it's often better to use three single quotes as shown in this example. That way, you don't have to concatenate multiple lines of code.

The third example in this figure shows how to run a query based on input provided by the user of the program. Here, the query selects all movies with a running time of less than a parameter value that will get passed to the query. In a query like this, a question mark (?) is used as a placeholder for each parameter that's needs to be supplied by the calling statement. Then, when you call the execute() method, you pass a tuple that contains the required placeholder values as the second argument for the method.

When you use this technique, remember that you must include a comma at the end of a tuple that contains only one value. In this example, the SELECT statement has only one placeholder so the tuple has a comma after the value 90. That means that the statement will return a result set that contains all movies with a running time of less than 90 minutes.

When your program is through with a cursor, it should close it so its resources are released to the system. That's why the last example in this figure shows how to do that. First, you need to import the closing() function from the Python contextlib module. Then, you need to code a with statement for the closing() function that contains the statements that use the cursor. This code will close the cursor object whether or not an exception is thrown.

The cursor() method of the connection object

Method	Description
`cursor()`	Returns a cursor object that you can use to execute SQL statements.

The execute() method of the cursor object

Method	Description
`execute(sql [params_tuple])`	Executes the SQL statement. If the statement includes question mark placeholders, you supply the values for the placeholders in a tuple parameter.

How to get a cursor object from the connection object

```
c = conn.cursor()
```

How to execute a SELECT statement that doesn't have parameters

```
query = '''SELECT * FROM Movie'''
c.execute(query)
```

How to execute a SELECT statement that has a parameter

```
query = '''SELECT * FROM Movie
           WHERE minutes < ?'''
c.execute(query, (90,))
```

How to automatically close the cursor object

The code for importing the closing() function

```
from contextlib import closing
```

The syntax for automatically closing the cursor object

```
with closing(resource) as name:
    statements
```

How to automatically close the cursor object

```
with closing(conn.cursor()) as c:
    query = '''SELECT * FROM Movie'''
    c.execute(query)
```

Description

- To execute a SELECT statement in Python, you use the cursor() method of the connection object to get a *cursor object*. Then, you use the execute() method of the cursor object to execute the SQL statement.

- To mark a variable in a SQL statement, you code a question mark (?) placeholder. Then, you provide a tuple parameter for the execute() method that provides the values for the placeholders. But remember that a tuple with only one item must end with a comma.

- When you are done with a cursor, you should close it to make sure its resources are released. To make sure that happens, even if an exception occurs, you can code the database operations in a with statement that uses the closing() function.

Figure 17-10   How to use Python to execute SELECT statements

How to get the rows in a result set

After you execute a query, the cursor object contains a result set with the rows returned by the query. Then, to access a row or rows, you can use the fetchone() or fetchall() methods of the cursor object. These methods are summarized and illustrated in figure 17-11.

The first example begins by getting a cursor and executing a query that selects the movie in the Movie table that has an ID of 5. Then, it uses the fetchone() method to get the row that's in the result set and store it in a variable named movie. Because this code is within a with statement for the closing() function, the cursor is closed after the statements are executed.

After a row is stored in the movie variable, you can access the columns of the row using an index. For instance, the second example prints the name, year, and running time for the movie by specifying indexes of 2, 3, and 4 for those columns. This works because movieID and categoryID are in the columns with the indexes 0 and 1.

Because indexes don't clearly identify the data that's stored in the columns, the third example shows how to access the columns by name. To do that, you set the row_factory attribute of the connection object to sqlite3.Row. Once that's done, you can access the columns of a row by name, which makes your code easier to read and less prone to errors. In addition, your code won't break if you add a column to the table later on that changes the indexes.

If you want to access all of the rows in a result, you can use the fetchall() method as shown in the last example. Here again, the query returns all rows in the Movie table that have a running time of less than 90 minutes. Then, the fetchall() method stores all of these rows in a list named movies. At this point, you can use a for loop to access each movie in the list. In this example, this loop prints the movie's name, year of release, and running time.

The fetchone() and fetchall() methods of the cursor object

Method	Description
`fetchone()`	Returns a tuple containing the next row from the result set. If there is no next row in the result set, this method returns None.
`fetchall()`	Returns a list containing all of the rows in the result set.

How to use the fetchone() method to get a row from of a table

```
with closing(conn.cursor()) as c:
    query = '''SELECT * FROM Movie
               WHERE movieID = ?'''
    c.execute(query, (5,)
    movie = c.fetchone()
```

How to access columns by index

```
print("Name:     " + movie[2])
print("Year:     " + str(movie[3]))
print("Minutes: " + str(movie[4]))
```

How to access columns by name

How to use the row_factory attribute to enable name access

```
conn.row_factory = sqlite3.Row      # Row is a SQLite constant
```

How to access columns by name

```
print("Name:     " + movie["name"])
print("Year:     " + str(movie["year"]))
print("Minutes: " + str(movie["minutes"]))
```

How to use the fetchall() method to retrieve all rows in the cursor

```
with closing(conn.cursor()) as c:
    query = '''SELECT * FROM Movie
               WHERE minutes < ?'''
    c.execute(query, (90,))
    movies = c.fetchall()
```

How to loop through all rows

```
for movie in movies:
    print(movie["name"], "|", movie["year"], "|", movie["minutes"])
```

The console

```
Spirit: Stallion of the Cimarron | 2002 | 83
Ice Age | 2002 | 81
Toy Story | 1995 | 81
```

Description

- If you access columns by index, your code can break if the database structure changes. When you access columns by name, your code is more durable and easier to read.

- Before you can access columns by name, you need to set the the row_factory attribute of the connection object to the SQLite constant named Row (sqllite.Row).

Figure 17-11   How to use Python to get the rows in a result set

How to execute INSERT, UPDATE, and DELETE statements

Figure 17-12 shows how to use Python to execute INSERT, UPDATE, and DELETE statements. This works much like executing a SELECT statement, but these statements don't return a result set. Instead, they modify the data in the database.

Also, when you execute one of these SQL statements, the database is changed but it isn't saved to the database. To save the changes, you must call the commit() method of the connection object. Otherwise, the changes are lost.

The first example in figure 17-12 shows how to use an INSERT statement to add a new movie to the database. First, it sets four variables to the name, year, running time, and category ID of the movie to be added to the database. Next, it uses a with statement to open a cursor object named c.

Inside the with statement, the code creates a string named sql that stores the INSERT statement. This statement uses question mark placeholders for four values. Then, the execute() method is called with a tuple argument that supplies the values for these placeholders. As a result, the INSERT statement that the database actually runs becomes:

```
INSERT INTO Movie (name, year, minutes, categoryID)
VALUES ('Juno', 2007, 96, 2)
```

After this statement is executed, the commit() method is called to save the new row to the database.

The second example shows an UPDATE statement that changes the running time to 84 minutes for the movie with an ID of 4. Here again, note the use of the parameterized SQL statement, and the tuple that supplies the values for the two placeholders in the SQL statement.

The last example shows a DELETE statement that deletes the movie with an ID of 12 from the database. This SQL statement is similar to the previous two statements, but note the comma in the tuple argument that passes just one value to the DELETE statement.

The commit() method of the connection object

Method	Description
`commit()`	Commits the changes to the database.

How to execute an INSERT statement

```
name = "Juno"
year = 2007
minutes = 96
categoryID = 2

with closing(conn.cursor()) as c:
    sql = '''INSERT INTO Movie (name, year, minutes, categoryID)
             VALUES (?, ?, ?, ?)'''
    c.execute(sql, (name, year, minutes, categoryID))
    conn.commit()
```

How to execute an UPDATE statement

```
id = 4
minutes = 84

with closing(conn.cursor()) as c:
    sql = '''UPDATE Movie
             SET minutes = ?
             WHERE movieID = ?'''
    c.execute(sql, (minutes, id))
    conn.commit()
```

How to execute a DELETE statement

```
id = 12

with closing(conn.cursor()) as c:
    sql =   '''DELETE FROM Movie
              WHERE movieID = ?'''
    c.execute(query, (id,))
    conn.commit()
```

Description

- As with the SELECT statement, you use question marks (?) to identify the parameters in the INSERT, UPDATE, and DELETE statements. Then, you use the execute() method to supply the values for those parameters.

- After you execute an INSERT, UPDATE, or DELETE statement, you need to *commit* the changes by calling the commit() method from the connection object. If you don't, the changes aren't saved in the database.

Figure 17-12   How to execute INSERT, UPDATE, and DELETE statements

How to test the database code

To give you a better idea of how the Python skills that you've just learned work, figure 17-13 presents an example that works with the movies database. To start, this code imports the sqlite3 module for working with a SQLite database. Then, it imports the closing() function that automatically closes the cursor object when you're done with it.

The next statement connects to the movies database. Here, the code only specifies the name of the file for the database, not its complete path. As a result, the database file must be in the working directory. So, if you use IDLE to open the db_tester.py file and run it, it should connect to the movies database.

This is followed by a statement that sets the row factory attribute for the connection object. As a result, the statements that follow can use names instead of indexes to refer to the columns in the result sets.

The next block of code executes a SELECT statement that gets all columns from the Movie table for all movies that are less than 90 minutes long. Then, it uses a loop to print the name, year, and minutes for these movies to the console. After the SELECT statement, this code executes an INSERT statement that adds a new movie to the database, and a DELETE statement that removes that movie from the database.

When you're new to database programming, experimenting with code like this is a good way to get started. As you experiment, you will not only see how the statements work, but also what errors can occur.

How to handle database exceptions

When you write the code that works with a database, the database may throw exceptions if it can't execute the code successfully. For example, SQLite raises an exception if you try to execute a query on a table that isn't in the database, or if you attempt to add a row to a table that has the same primary key as another row in the table.

However, unlike a traditional database like MySQL or SQL Server, SQLite doesn't raise exceptions for some types of operations that may result in bad data such as orphaned keys. For example, SQLite doesn't raise an exception if you attempt to insert a row that has an invalid foreign key value, or if you attempt to delete a row that has a foreign key value that's being used by other rows.

If you need to handle database exceptions, you can use try statements to handle the exceptions just as you would handle any other exception. In this figure, for example, the code that executes the SELECT statement may raise an OperationalError. That might happen, for example, if the connect() method doesn't find the movies.sqlite database. In that case, SQLite creates a new database that's empty and doesn't have a Movie table. Then, the except clause prints an error message and sets the movies variable to None. That way, the code that follows can check whether the SELECT statement executed successfully.

Before you add exception handling to your programs, though, you should try to write your code so it avoids the operations that could throw exceptions. That's always a good practice, and that's illustrated by the program in the next figure.

Code that tests the database

```
# import the sqlite module and closing function
import sqlite3
from contextlib import closing

# connect to the database and set the row factory
conn = sqlite3.connect("movies.sqlite")
conn.row_factory = sqlite3.Row

# execute a SELECT statement - with exception handling
try:
    with closing(conn.cursor()) as c:
        query = '''SELECT * FROM Movie
                    WHERE minutes < ?'''
        c.execute(query, (90,))
        movies = c.fetchall()
except sqlite3.OperationalError as e:
    print("Error reading database -", e)
    movies = None

# display the results
if movies != None:
    for movie in movies:
        print(movie["name"], "|", movie["year"], "|", movie["minutes"])
    print()

# execute an INSERT statement
name = "A Fish Called Wanda"
year = 1988
minutes = 108
categoryID = 1
with closing(conn.cursor()) as c:
    sql = '''INSERT INTO Movie (name, year, minutes, categoryID)
            VALUES (?, ?, ?, ?)'''
    c.execute(sql, (name, year, minutes, categoryID))
    conn.commit()
print(name, "inserted.")

# execute a DELETE statement
with closing(conn.cursor()) as c:
    sql =   '''DELETE FROM Movie
                WHERE name = ?'''
    c.execute(sql, (name,))
    conn.commit()
print(name, "deleted.")
```

The console

```
Spirit: Stallion of the Cimarron | 2002 | 83
Ice Age | 2002 | 81
Toy Story | 1995 | 81

A Fish Called Wanda inserted.
A Fish Called Wanda deleted.
```

Figure 17-13   How to test the database code

The Movie List program

In chapter 7, you learned how to code a Movie List program that stores its data in a text file. However, a real-world program would store this information in a database. That's why this chapter finishes by presenting a three-tier version of the Movie List program that stores its data in a SQLite database.

The user interface

Figure 17-14 begins with the user interface for another version of the Movie List program. In contrast to the Movie List program in chapter 7, though, this program groups movies by category and stores more data for each movie. It also stores its data in a SQLite database.

When this program starts, it displays a list of commands followed by a list of categories that includes the IDs for the categories. Then, the users have to use these IDs as they use some of the commands. For instance, the cat command requires the ID of the category so it can display just the movies in that category. And the add command requires a category ID that specifies the type of movie that's being added.

The business tier

The business tier of the Movie List program defines two business objects: a Movie object and a Category object. For simplicity, both of these objects use public attributes to store their data. These attributes correspond to the columns of the Movie and Category tables in the movies database.

The Movie class begins with a constructor that assigns default values to all of its public attributes. Here, the category attribute is assigned a default value of None. This indicates that this attribute is designed to store a Category object, not an ID for the category.

The Category class works like the Movie class. However, it only provides two public attributes: id and name.

In both classes, the constructors provide default values for all of the arguments. This isn't necessary, but this makes these classes easier to use. For example, when the code adds a movie to the database, the Movie object doesn't need to have an ID because the database generates the ID automatically. However, when the code creates a Movie object from data that it retrieves from the database, it needs to set the ID to the value that's stored in the database. By providing default values for all of the arguments, you provide for both cases.

The user interface

```
The Movie List program

COMMAND MENU
cat  - View movies by category
year - View movies by year
add  - Add a movie
del  - Delete a movie
exit - Exit program

CATEGORIES
1. Animation
2. Comedy
3. History

Command: add
Name: The Lion King
Year: 1994
Minutes: 89
Category ID: 1
The Lion King was added to database.


Command: cat
Category ID: 1

MOVIES - ANIMATION
ID   Name                                Year   Mins   Category
------------------------------------------------------------------
1    Spirit: Stallion of the Cimarron    2002   83     Animation
2    Spirited Away                       2001   125    Animation
3    Aladdin                             1992   90     Animation
4    Ice Age                             2002   81     Animation
5    Toy Story                           1995   81     Animation
14   The Lion King                       1994   89     Animation

Command: exit
Bye!
```

The objects module for the business tier

```python
class Movie:
    def __init__(self, id=0, name=None, year=0, minutes=0, category=None):
        self.id = id
        self.name = name
        self.year = year
        self.minutes = minutes
        self.category = category

class Category:
    def __init__(self, id=0, name=None):
        self.id = id
        self.name = name
```

Figure 17-14   The Movie List program (part 1)

The database tier

Part 2 of figure 17-14 presents the code for the database tier, which is stored in a module named db. To begin, this code imports the modules, functions, and classes that this code uses. This includes the Category and Movie classes from the objects module. Then, it sets a global variable for a connection object to None. This is followed by six functions.

The connect() function sets the global conn variable to the connection object. To do that, the first statement declares that the conn variable is global, which is required if this variable is going to be modified. Then, the first if statement creates a new connection object if the conn variable doesn't already contain one.

The if statement within the outer if statement is needed because the database file isn't in the same directory as the program file. As a result, the nested if statement sets a different path to the database file depending on the operating system that the program is running on. Once that's done, the connection object is created and the row factory attribute is set to allow the use of column names when accessing the result sets.

The close() function that follows closes the connection. To do that, this function first checks if the conn variable refers to a connection object. If so, it calls the close() method of the conn variable. Because this code only accesses the conn object and doesn't change it, it doesn't need to declare the conn variable as global.

The make_category() function is a utility function that accepts a row from a result set as an argument. This function contains a single line of code that creates a Category object from the data that's in the row and returns that object. This function is called by the three functions that follow

The make_movie() function works similarly, but it creates a Movie object from a row. However, the category attribute of the Movie object stores a Category object. As a result, this code calls the make_category() function to create a new Category object that's set as the category attribute of the Movie object.

The get_categories() function returns a list of all of the available categories in the database. To do that, it creates a query that selects the category ID and name from the Category table, using an alias of categoryName for the column that contains the name of the category. This is necessary because the make_category() function uses this alias to get the name of the category. After defining the query, this function executes the query and fetches all of the results. Then, it creates an empty list called categories, and loops over each row in the the result set. Within this loop, the code appends a Category object for each row to the list. To do that, it calls the make_category() function.

The get_category() function works similarly, but it only gets one Category object that corresponds with a single category ID. After this function accepts an argument for the category ID, it uses the fetchone() method to fetch the row for the specified category. Then, it calls the make_category() function to make a Category object from the row, and it returns the Category object.

The db module for the database tier

```python
import sys
import os
import sqlite3
from contextlib import closing

from objects import Category
from objects import Movie

conn = None

def connect():
    global conn
    if not conn:
        if sys.platform == "win32":
            DB_FILE = "/murach/python/_db/movies.sqlite"
        else:
            HOME = os.environ["HOME"]
            DB_FILE = HOME + "/Documents/murach/python/_db/movies.sqlite"
        conn = sqlite3.connect(DB_FILE)
        conn.row_factory = sqlite3.Row

def close():
    if conn:
        conn.close()

def make_category(row):
    return Category(row["categoryID"], row["categoryName"])

def make_movie(row):
    return Movie(row["movieID"], row["name"], row["year"], row["minutes"],
            make_category(row))

def get_categories():
    query = '''SELECT categoryID, name as categoryName
               FROM Category'''
    with closing(conn.cursor()) as c:
        c.execute(query)
        results = c.fetchall()

    categories = []
    for row in results:
        categories.append(make_category(row))
    return categories

def get_category(category_id):
    query = '''SELECT categoryID, name AS categoryName
               FROM Category WHERE categoryID = ?'''
    with closing(conn.cursor()) as c:
        c.execute(query, (category_id,))
        row = c.fetchone()

    category = make_category(row)
    return category
```

Figure 17-14   The Movie List program (part 2)

The get_movies_by_category() function accepts a category ID as an argument. Then, it creates a query that joins the Movie and Category tables on the categoryID column that's in both tables. Because both tables have a column named name, this code uses an alias of categoryName for the name column of the Category table. This prevents a name collision between the name columns that are in both the Movie and Category tables.

After defining the query, this code executes the query and fetches all of the rows in the result set. Then, it creates an empty list named movies, and loops over each row in the result set. Within the loop, the code uses the make_movie() function to create a Movie object from each row, and it appends that object to the movies list. After the loop, this function returns the list of Movie objects.

The get_movies_by_year function works similarly, except that it selects the movie by year instead of by category_id. As a result, the only difference between these two functions is the WHERE clause in the SELECT statement, and the argument that the code supplies to the execute() method of the cursor object.

The add_movie() function accepts a Movie object as an argument. Within this function, the first statement creates a parameterized SQL statement that adds a row to the Movie table. Then, this code executes the SQL statement and uses the Movie object to provide the parameters for the SQL statement. Finally, this function commits the changes to the database.

The delete_movie() function accepts a movie ID as an argument. Within this function, the first statement creates a SQL statement that deletes a row from the Movie table. Then, this code executes the SQL statement with the movie ID of the record to be deleted as the argument. This function also finishes by committing the changes to the database.

The db module for the database tier (continued)

```python
def get_movies_by_category(category_id):
    query = '''SELECT movieID, Movie.name, year, minutes,
                      Movie.categoryID as categoryID,
                      Category.name as categoryName
               FROM Movie JOIN Category
                      ON Movie.categoryID = Category.categoryID
               WHERE Movie.categoryID = ?'''
    with closing(conn.cursor()) as c:
        c.execute(query, (category_id,))
        results = c.fetchall()

    movies = []
    for row in results:
        movies.append(make_movie(row))
    return movies

def get_movies_by_year(year):
    query = '''SELECT movieID, Movie.name, year, minutes,
                      Movie.categoryID as categoryID,
                      Category.name as categoryName
               FROM Movie JOIN Category
                      ON Movie.categoryID = Category.categoryID
               WHERE year = ?'''
    with closing(conn.cursor()) as c:
        c.execute(query, (year,))
        results = c.fetchall()

    movies = []
    for row in results:
        movies.append(make_movie(row))
    return movies

def add_movie(movie):
    sql = '''INSERT INTO Movie (categoryID, name, year, minutes)
             VALUES (?, ?, ?, ?)'''
    with closing(conn.cursor()) as c:
        c.execute(sql, (movie.category.id, movie.name, movie.year,
                        movie.minutes))
        conn.commit()

def delete_movie(movie_id):
    sql = '''DELETE FROM Movie WHERE movieID = ?'''
    with closing(conn.cursor()) as c:
        c.execute(sql, (movie_id,))
        conn.commit()
```

Figure 17-14   The Movie List program (part 3)

The presentation tier

Part 4 of figure 17-14 presents the code for the presentation tier, which is stored in the ui module. This class begins by importing the db module and by importing the Movie class from the objects module. Then, the first two functions display a title and a command menu. This is followed by four more functions.

The display_categories() function prints a list of categories, along with their IDs. To do that, this function calls the get_categories() function from the db module to get a list of Category objects. Then, it loops over each Category object in the list and print its id and name to the console. Here, the str() function converts the category ID from an integer to a string.

The display_movies() function accepts an argument for a list of Movie objects and an argument for a title term. Within this function, the first statement prints a title that begins with "MOVIES -" and ends with the title term. The second statement defines a format string that's used to align the data in columns. The third statement prints the column names for the result set. And the fourth statement prints a separator line that's 64 characters long. Then, the code loops through each Movie object in the list. Within this loop, the statement aligns and prints the data that's stored in each Movie object.

The display_movies_by_category() function prompts the user to enter a category ID and converts the entry to an int value. Then, it passes the category ID to the get_category() function of the db module, which returns a Category object for the specified category. Next, an if statement checks whether a Category object has been returned. If so, it passes the category ID to the get_movies_by_category() function of the db module, which returns a list of Movie objects. Last, this code passes this list and the uppercase name of the specified category to the display_movies() function.

The display_movies_by_year() function works much like the display_movies_by_category() function. However, it accepts the movie's year as an argument instead of the category. Then, it passes this argument to the get_movies_by_year() function of the db module. This returns a list of Movie objects. Finally, this code calls the display_movies() function and passes it the list of Movie objects and the year argument after it has been converted to a string.

The ui module for the presentation tier

```python
#!/usr/bin/env/python3

import db
from objects import Movie

def display_title():
    print("The Movie List program")
    print()
    display_menu()

def display_menu():
    print("COMMAND MENU")
    print("cat  - View movies by category")
    print("year - View movies by year")
    print("add  - Add a movie")
    print("del  - Delete a movie")
    print("exit - Exit program")
    print()

def display_categories():
    print("CATEGORIES")
    categories = db.get_categories()
    for category in categories:
        print(str(category.id) + ". " + category.name)
    print()

def display_movies(movies, title_term):
    print("MOVIES - " + title_term)
    line_format = "{:3s} {:37s} {:6s} {:5s} {:10s}"
    print(line_format.format("ID", "Name", "Year", "Mins", "Category"))
    print("-" * 64)
    for movie in movies:
        print(line_format.format(str(movie.id), movie.name,
                                 str(movie.year), str(movie.minutes),
                                 movie.category.name))
    print()

def display_movies_by_category():
    category_id = int(input("Category ID: "))
    category = db.get_category(category_id)
    if category == None:
        print("There is no category with that ID.\n")
    else:
        print()
        movies = db.get_movies_by_category(category_id)
        display_movies(movies, category.name.upper())

def display_movies_by_year():
    year = int(input("Year: "))
    print()
    movies = db.get_movies_by_year(year)
    display_movies(movies, str(year))
```

Figure 17-14   The Movie List program (part 4)

The add_movie() function begins by prompting the user for the data for a new movie including its name, year, minutes, and category ID. Then, this code calls the get_category() function of the db module to get the Category object for the specified category ID. Next, an if statement checks to make sure a Category object has been returned. If it hasn't been returned, an error message is displayed to the user and the function ends.

If it has been returned, this code creates a Movie object and passes it the appropriate data, including the Category object. But note that this code doesn't assign a value to the id attribute of the Movie object. This isn't necessary since the database generates the ID value automatically when it adds the movie to the database.

After the Movie object has been created, this code calls the add_movie() function of the db module and passes it the new Movie object. Then, it displays a message that indicates that the movie was added.

The delete_movie() function is much simpler. To start, it prompts the user for a movie ID. Then, it calls the delete_movie() function of the db module with the movie ID as the argument, and it prints a message that indicates that the movie was deleted. This code could be improved by first making sure that the ID entered by the user is actually in the database table. But when you're using SQLite, if the ID isn't in the table, nothing is done.

The main() function begins by calling the connect() function in the db module to open a connection to the database. Then, it displays the title, the command menu, and a list of categories, including the category IDs.

After displaying this information, the function enters a loop where it waits for the user to enter a command. Once the user enters a command, this code calls the appropriate function depending on the command entered by the user. For example, if the user enters the cat command, the code calls the display_movies_by_category() function. But if the user enters the exit command, this code executes a break statement, which causes the loop to end. Then, this code calls the close() function of the db module to close the database connection. Last, it prints a message that indicates that the program is exiting.

The ui module for the presentation tier (continued)

```python
def add_movie():
    name        = input("Name: ")
    year        = int(input("Year: "))
    minutes     = int(input("Minutes: "))
    category_id = int(input("Category ID: "))

    category = db.get_category(category_id)
    if category == None:
        print("There is no category with that ID. Movie NOT added.\n")
    else:
        movie = Movie(name=name, year=year, minutes=minutes,
                      category=category)
        db.add_movie(movie)
        print(name + " was added to database.\n")

def delete_movie():
    movie_id = int(input("Movie ID: "))
    db.delete_movie(movie_id)
    print("Movie ID " + str(movie_id) + " was deleted from database.\n")

def main():
    db.connect()
    display_title()
    display_categories()
    while True:
        command = input("Command: ")
        if command == "cat":
            display_movies_by_category()
        elif command == "year":
            display_movies_by_year()
        elif command == "add":
            add_movie()
        elif command == "del":
            delete_movie()
        elif command == "exit":
            break
        else:
            print("Not a valid command. Please try again.\n")
            display_menu()
    db.close()
    print("Bye!")

if __name__ == "__main__":
    main()
```

Figure 17-14   The Movie List program (part 5)

Perspective

The goal of this chapter is to prepare you for developing programs that use a database. To that end, this chapter has introduced you to the SELECT, INSERT, UPDATE, and DELETE statements that you'll use in most database programs. This chapter has also shown you how to use Python to execute these SQL statements and to work with the result sets that are returned. Now, if you understand the Movie List program that's presented in this chapter, you've developed a useful set of database programming skills.

You should know, however, that there's a lot more to learn about database programming. In contrast to SQLite databases, for example, MySQL, Oracle, and SQL Server are full-blown Database Management Systems. These databases are designed to run on a server and be accessed by remote clients, so you need to provide for more types of errors. They also offer more functionality than SQLite.

When you work with one of these Database Management Systems, you're going to want to learn skills like how to use the Data Definition Language (DDL) to create your own databases; how to handle the exceptions that are thrown by these systems; how to use views, stored programs, and triggers; and much more. So when you're ready to start adding these skills to your skillset, please remember our best-selling books on MySQL, SQL Server, and Oracle.

Terms

relational database	SQL (Structured Query Language)
database management system (DBMS)	DML (Data Manipulation Language)
	DDL (Data Definition Language)
table	SQL statement
row	SELECT statement
column	query
record	result set
field	result table
cell	join
primary key	inner join
foreign key	alias
one-to-many relationship	INSERT statement
one-to-one relationship	UPDATE statement
many-to-many relationship	DELETE statement
data type	SQLite
null value	DB Browser for SQLite
default value	connection object
orphaned key	cursor object

Summary

- A *relational database* consists of *tables*. Tables consist of *rows* and *columns*, which can also be referred to as *records* and *fields*.

- A *primary key* is used to identify each row in a table.

- The tables in a relational database are related by *foreign keys* in one table that have the same values as primary keys in another table. Usually, these tables have a *one-to-many relationship*.

- Each column in a database table is defined with a *data type* that determines what type of data can be stored in that column. In addition, the column definition specifies whether the column allows *null values* or has a *default value*.

- To work with the data in a database, you use *SQL (Structured Query Language)*. To access and update the data in a database, you use *SQL statements*.

- The *SELECT statement* returns a *result set* from one or more tables. To return data from two or more tables, you *join* the tables based on the data in related columns. An *inner join* returns a result set that includes data only if the related columns match.

- To update the data in a database, you use the *INSERT, UPDATE*, and *DELETE statements*. These statements don't return a result set.

- SQLite is a popular open-source relational database that can be embedded into programs so they can use it to store their data. To review the structure and data of a SQLite database and to execute SQL statements against it, you can use a program called *DB Browser for SQLite*.

- To execute a SQL statement in Python, you use the cursor() method of a *connection object* to get a *cursor object*, and then the execute() method of the cursor object to execute the SQL statement.

- To work with the result set of a SELECT statement in Python, you use the fetchone() or fetchall() methods of the cursor object.

Exercise 17-1   Review a SQLite database and test some SQL statements

This exercise gives you a chance to use DB Browser for SQLite to review the SQLite database that's used by the Movie List program that's presented in this chapter. You will also use DB Browser to test some SQL statements against this database.

Use DB Browser for SQLite to connect to the movies database

1. If you haven't already installed DB Browser for SQLite, do that now. For instructions, please see the appendix for your operating system.

2. Start DB Browser for SQLite. Then, use DB Browser to open the database named movies.sqlite that's in this directory:

   `murach/python/_db`

Review the tables in the movies database

3. Use the Browse Data tab to review the data in the Movie table.

4. Use the Browse Data tab to review the data in Category table.

Run SQL statements against the movies database

5. Use the Execute SQL tab to enter a query that selects all columns from the Movie table where the category ID is 2, and click the Run SQL button to execute this statement. This should display a result set.

6. Modify the value for the category ID in the query so it only selects movies that have a category ID of 3. Then, run this query and view the result set.

7. Modify the query so it only returns the name and year columns. Then, run this query and view the result set.

8. Modify the query so it sorts the result set by year in descending order.

9. Enter an INSERT statement that inserts a new row into the Movie table. Then, run this SQL statement. This shouldn't display a result set, but it should add a new row to the Movie table.

10. Use the Browse Data tab to browse the Movie table and view the new row.

11. Use the Execute SQL tab to run a DELETE statement that deletes the new row.

12. Use the Browse Data tab to make sure the row was deleted.

13. Continue to experiment until you're sure that you understand the SQL statements that are used by the Movie List program in this chapter.

Exercise 17-2   Enhance the Movie List program

In this exercise, you will enhance the Movie List program by improving its delete command and by adding a min command that lets the user view movies with run times that are less than a specific number of minutes.

```
Command: del
Movie ID: 14
Are you sure you want to delete 'Juno'? (y/n): y
'Juno' was deleted from database.

Command: min
Maximum number of minutes: 100

MOVIES - LESS THAN 100 MINUTES
ID  Name                                    Year   Mins  Category
------------------------------------------------------------------
4    Ice Age                                2002   81    Animation
5    Toy Story                             1995   81    Animation
1    Spirit: Stallion of the Cimarron     2002   83    Animation
3    Aladdin                              1992   90    Animation
6    Monty Python and the Holy Grail      1975   91    Comedy
7    Monty Python's Life of Brian         1979   94    Comedy
```

Open and test the program

1.   In IDLE, open the objects.py, db.py, and ui.py files that are in this folder:

     python/exercises/ch17/movies

2.   Review the code and note how the ui module uses the db module and the Movie class from the objects module. Then, run the program. If necessary, modify the path to the database file so it's correct for your system.

Improve the del command

3.   In the db module, add a get_movie() function that gets a Movie object for the specified movie ID.

4.   In the ui module, modify the delete_movie() function so it gets a Movie object for the specified ID and asks whether you are sure you want to delete the movie as shown above. This code should only delete the movie if the user enters "y" to confirm the operation.

Add the min command

5.   In the db module, add a get_movies_by_minutes() function that gets a list of Movie objects that have a running time that's less than the number of minutes passed to it as a parameter.

6.   In the ui module, add a display_movies_by_minutes() function that prompts the user to enter the maximum number of minutes and displays all selected movies. This should sort the movies by minutes in ascending order.

7.   Modify the main() function and the display_menu() function so they provide for the min command.

18

How to build a GUI program

So far in this book, you have learned how to create a console interface for a program. However, most modern programs such as web browsers, word processors, and spreadsheets use a graphical user interface (GUI). In this chapter, you'll learn the basics of using Python to build a GUI program.

This chapter shows how to use object-oriented programming techniques to build a GUI, which is generally considered a best practice. As a result, you should be familiar with the concepts and skills presented in chapters 14 and 15 before you read this chapter. Then, the object-oriented techniques presented in this chapter will reinforce those concepts and skills.

How to create a GUI that handles an event

Most programs today use a *graphical user interface (GUI)*. To create one with Python, you use a *toolkit* that makes it easier to create the components of a GUI such as windows, buttons, and entry fields. Although many GUI toolkits are available for Python, this chapter shows how to use tkinter, which is a commonly used tookit that's included with Python.

How to display a root window

With the tkinter toolkit, a GUI begins with a component that's typically called the *root window*. Once you've created a root window, you can add *components* to it such as buttons, labels, and text entry fields. In figure 18-1, for example, the first window contains ten components: four labels, four text entry fields, and two buttons. These components can also be called *widgets*.

To create a root window, you import the tkinter module, usually into a shorter namespace such as tk as shown in the first example. Then, you can call the Tk constructor that's available from the tk namespace to create the root window and assign it to a variable as shown in the second example. By convention, this variable is named root.

After you create the variable for the root window, you can set up the window. For example, you can set its title by calling its title() method. Or, you can set its width and height by calling its geometry() method with a string argument that specifies the width and height in pixels.

After you set up the root window, you call its mainloop() method. This displays the GUI and causes the program to enter an *event processing loop* that listens for *events* such as the user clicking on a button. Later, you can write the code that responds to the events.

If you forget to call the mainloop() method, your program will never enter the event processing loop. As a result, it executes the code in the script in sequence and then exits. This is a common mistake that beginning GUI programmers make. So if you attempt to run a GUI program and the program ends right away, make sure that your code calls the mainloop() method.

You must also be sure that all the code that sets up the window comes before the call to the mainloop() method. If, for example, the call to the title() method is coded after the call to the mainloop() method, the call to the title() method will never run. This is another common mistake that beginning GUI programmers make.

A window with ten components

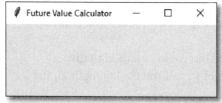

The constructor and some methods of the root window

Constructor	Description
`Tk()`	Creates a Tk object that defines the root window.
Method	**Description**
`title(title)`	Sets the title of the root window to the specified title.
`geometry(str)`	Sets the width and height of the root window to the number of pixels specified by the string.
`mainloop()`	Makes the root window visible and starts an *event processing loop* that allows a program to handle *events* that occur on the window. You need to call this method after all other code that sets up the root window.

How to import the tkinter module

```
import tkinter as tk
```

How to create an empty root window

```
root = tk.Tk()
root.title("Future Value Calculator")
root.geometry("300x200")
```

How to make the root window visible

```
root.mainloop()
```

An empty root window

Description

- The top level window of a tkinter GUI is a Tk object that's typically known as the *root window*.

- Once you've created a root window, you can add *components* to it such as buttons, labels, and text entry fields. Components can also be referred to as *widgets*.

Figure 18-1   How to display a root window

How to work with frames and buttons

Once you've created a root window, you typically add one or more frames to it. A *frame* is an invisible container that you can use to group components. Then, you add other components such as *buttons* to the frame as shown in figure 18-2.

To work with frames and buttons, you start by importing the ttk module from the tkinter module, as shown in the first example in this figure. Then, you can use the classes in the ttk module to create a frame and two buttons.

The second example creates a frame by calling the Frame constructor in the ttk module and passing it two arguments. The first argument specifies the parent component, which is the component that contains this component. In this case, the code adds the frame to the root window that was created in the previous figure.

The second argument of the Frame constructor is optional, but you'll often want to provide it. It sets the padding between the frame and the edge of the parent component. In this case, it sets 10 pixels of padding between each of the sides of the frame and the sides of the root window. If you don't set any padding, the frame and any components in the frame push up against the sides of the window.

After the first statement in the second example creates the frame, the second statement displays it by calling its pack() method. By default, the pack() method automatically sizes the frame to be just large enough to hold the components it contains. However, you can pass arguments to the pack() method to change this behavior.

In this example, the fill argument is set so it fills all of the available horizontal and vertical space in the parent container. In addition, the expand argument is set to True. This tells the frame that if the size of the parent container changes (if, for example, the user resizes the window), the frame should expand and contract so it continues to fill all of the available space.

After you create a frame, you usually add components to it. In this figure, the third example creates two Button objects and adds them to the Frame object. Like the Frame class, the Button class takes the parent component as its first argument. In this case, the parent component is the frame.

For a button, the second argument sets the text that's displayed by the button. In this example, the first button displays the text "Click me!", and the second button displays the text "No, click me!".

After you create the buttons, you need to call the pack() method to display them as shown in the fourth example. If you forget to call the pack() method, the buttons aren't displayed when you run the code.

Two constructors of the ttk module

Constructor	Description
`Frame(parent[, padding])`	Creates a Frame object and adds it to the specified parent component with the specified padding in pixels between the edge of the frame and its parent component.
`Button(parent, text)`	Creates a Button object with the specified text and adds it to the specified parent component.

A method for working with all components

Method	Description
`pack([fill][, expand])`	Makes the component visible. To make a component automatically resize itself vertically and horizontally to fill the parent component, you can set the fill argument to BOTH and the expand argument to True.

How to import the ttk module from the tkinter module

```
from tkinter import ttk
```

How to create a frame and add it to the root window

```
frame = ttk.Frame(root, padding="10 10 10 10")
frame.pack(fill=tk.BOTH, expand=True)
```

How to create two buttons and add them to the frame

```
button1 = ttk.Button(frame, text="Click me!")
button2 = ttk.Button(frame, text="No, click me!")
```

How to display the buttons

```
button1.pack()
button2.pack()
```

Two buttons in a frame

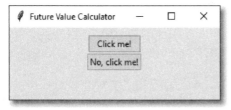

Description

- A *frame* is an invisible container that's used to group other components.
- Most tkinter components, including frames and buttons, have a constructor that accepts the parent component as its first argument.

Figure 18-2   How to work with frames and buttons

How to handle a button click event

When you click one of the buttons that are defined in the previous figure, an *event* is generated that informs the toolkit that the button has been clicked. Then, to perform an action, you need to handle this event by connecting it to a function that contains the code that should be executed when the event occurs. This function is called a *callback function* or an *event handler*.

To illustrate, figure 18-3 presents a user interface that handles two button click events. Here, clicking the first button changes the title displayed in the title bar, and clicking the second button exits the root window.

To connect the buttons to the functions that are executed when the buttons are clicked, you code the command argument of the button constructor. This is illustrated by the first example. Here, the first statement connects the button named button1 to the click_button1() function. Then, when a user clicks this button, the program calls the click_button1() function. Similarly, the second button calls the click_button2() function when it is clicked.

The second example in this figure defines the two callback functions. Here, the click_button1() function changes the title of the root window. Then, the click_button2() function calls the destroy() method of the root window. That closes the root window and causes the main loop for the GUI to end, which ends the program.

Note that you could specify the root.destroy() method instead of the click_button2() function in the command argument for the second button. In most programs, though, you would want to perform some tasks before calling the destroy() method. For example, you could display a closing message or prompt the user to save any unsaved data. In a case like that, you could add code to the click_button2() function before it calls the destroy() method.

The GUI after the user clicks the first button

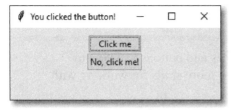

An argument of the Button constructor

Argument	Description
command	Specifies the function that's executed when a user clicks on the button.

How to create two buttons that are connected to callback functions

```
button1 = ttk.Button(frame, text="Click me", command=click_button1)
button2 = ttk.Button(frame, text="No, click me!", command=click_button2)
```

The destroy() method of the root window

Method	Description
destroy()	Closes the root window and causes its event processing loop to end, which ends the program.

The callback functions that the buttons are connected to

```
def click_button1():
    root.title("You clicked the button!")

def click_button2():
    root.destroy()
```

Description

- To make a button execute a function when a user clicks on it, you use the command argument of the Button constructor to connect it to a function. Then, when the user clicks on the button, Python calls that function.

- A function that's called by a component such as a button is commonly known as a *callback function* or an *event handler*.

Figure 18-3   How to handle a button click event

More skills for working with components

Now that you've learned how to create frames and buttons and how to handle a button click event, you're ready to learn more skills for working with components.

How to work with labels and text entry fields

Most programs get data from the user. To do that, they use components like the labels and text entry fields that are shown in figure 18-4.

As the name suggests, *labels* typically label other components to show what they do. In this figure, for example, the first label tells the user what to enter in the first entry field, and the second label describes the value that's displayed in the second entry field.

To create a label and add it to a frame, you call the Label constructor of the tkk module and pass it the parent component and the text that the label should display. This is illustrated by the first example. Then, you call the pack() method to display the label.

Unless you need to work with a label after you create it, though, you don't need to assign the label to a variable. In that case, you can use code like the second part of the first example to display a label. This code chains the creation of the label with the pack() method so the label is never assigned to a variable.

A *text entry field* is a component that allows a user to enter text. This type of component is also known as a *text box*, *text field*, or *entry field*. Before you create a text entry field, you typically create a StringVar object that you can use to get and set the text that's available in the text entry field.

To illustrate, the first statement of the next example creates a StringVar object named investmentText. Then, the second statement creates a text entry field named investmentEntry by calling the constructor of the Entry class. This sets the width of the Entry field in characters. More importantly, it uses the textvariable argument to *bind* the StringVar object to the Entry component.

When the Entry constructor binds a text entry field to a StringVar object, that object is automatically updated when the user changes the text in the entry field. As a result, you can use the get() method of a StringVar object to get the value that the user enters into the Monthly Investment field, and the set() method to set its value.

The third example in this figure shows how to create a read-only text entry field. This is similar to the previous example except the state argument is set to "readonly". ". As a result, the user can't enter a value in the text field, but the code can use the set() method of the StringVar object to set a value in the text field.

The last example shows how the get() and set() methods can be used. Here, the first statement gets the value that has been entered into the Monthly Investment field. The second statement sets the value in the Future Value field, which displays a new text value in the field.

A window that contains labels and text entry fields

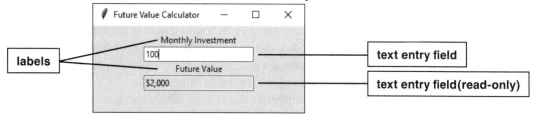

Constructors for creating labels and text entry fields

Constructor	Description
Label(*parent*, *text*)	Creates a label with the specified text and adds it to the specified parent component.
Entry(*parent*, *width*, *textvariable*[, *state*])	Creates an entry field with the width in characters, adds it to the parent component, and binds it to a StringVar object. For a read-only field, set the state argument to "readonly".

The StringVar class of the tkinter module

Constructor/Method	Description
StringVar()	Creates a StringVar object.
get()	Gets the string in the StringVar object.
set(*str*)	Sets the string in the StringVar object.

How to create a label and display it

```
investmentLabel = ttk.Label(frame, text="Monthly Investment")
investmentLabel.pack()
```

Another way to create a label and display it

```
ttk.Label(frame, text="Monthly Investment").pack()
```

How to create a text entry field and bind it to a StringVar object

```
investmentText = tk.StringVar()
investmentEntry = ttk.Entry(frame, width=25, textvariable=investmentText)
```

How to create a read-only text entry field and bind it to a StringVar object

```
fvText = tk.StringVar()
fvEntry = ttk.Entry(frame, width=25, textvariable=fvText, state="readonly")
```

How to get or set a string in a text entry field

```
investment = investmentText.get()
fvText.set("$2,000")
```

Description

- A *label* is a component that displays text. It can be used to identify another component such as an entry field.

- A *text entry field* is a component that displays text and lets the user enter text. This type of component is also known as a *text box*, *text field*, or *entry field*.

- When the state of an entry field is set to "readonly", it can only display text.

Figure 18-4   How to work with labels and text entry fields

How to lay out components in a grid

Until now, you've been using the pack() method to add components to a frame. However, the pack() method doesn't give you much control over how the components are laid out in the frame. To gain more control, you can replace the pack() method with the grid() method, as shown in figure 18-5.

To start, this figure shows a frame that aligns four labels and four text entry fields in a grid of four rows and two columns. This creates eight cells for eight components. Normally, this frame wouldn't display the grid lines, but the lines are shown in this figure so you can clearly see the rows, columns, and cells.

When you call the grid() method, the first two arguments specify the column and row for the component. In addition, you often supply other arguments.

The first example in this figure creates the layout for the first two rows shown at the top of this figure. Here, the first statement creates the first label and calls its grid() method to set its column and row arguments to 0. This displays the label in the first column of the first row. Next, it sets the sticky argument to the E constant of the tkinter module. This aligns the text within the component with the right (East) side of the cell.

The second statement creates an Entry field and calls its grid() method to specify a column of 1 and a row of 0. This displays the text entry field in the second column of the first row. Since this code doesn't set the sticky argument, it uses the default value of the W constant. This causes the component to stick to the left (West) side of the cell. The next two statements work similarly, but they add the components to the second row instead of the first row.

By default, when you lay out the components in a grid, there is no padding between the cells. Then, you can use the padx and pady arguments of the grid() method for each component to add horizontal and vertical padding. Although that gives you complete control over the formatting, that is typically tedious and often unnecessary.

Another alternative is illustrated by the second example in this figure. Here, the same padding is added to each component in the frame. To do that, the winfo_children() method of the frame is used to get all of the components in the frame. Then, a for loop is used to add the same padding to each component. Within the loop, the grid_configure() method of each component is used to apply the padding. This technique not only makes it easier to set the padding for all of the components. but it also makes it easier to change the padding if you decide that the frame would look better with more or less padding.

Note that the grid_configure() method is used in the loop instead of the grid() method. That's because the grid_configure() method lets you modify the settings for the components after you have added them to the frame and used the grid() method to format them. You should also know that the grid_configure() method accepts the same arguments as the grid() method.

Eight components in a grid of two columns and four rows

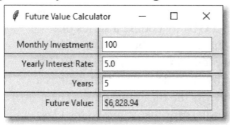

Some of the arguments of the grid() method of a component

Argument	Description
`column`	The column index where the component should be added, starting with an index of 0.
`row`	The row index where the component should be added, starting with an index of 0.
`sticky`	A value that determines which side of the container the component should stick to. Valid values are the N (North), W (West), E (East), and S (South) constants of the tkinter module. Optionally, you can specify a tuple of values for multiple directions. For example, if you specify a tuple of W and E, the component is stretched horizontally.
`padx`	Specifies the horizontal padding in pixels between this component and the next component in the grid.
`pady`	Specifies the vertical padding in pixels between this component and the next component in the grid.
`columnspan`	Specifies the number of columns the component should span.
`rowspan`	Specifies the number of rows the component should span.

How to use a grid to lay out the components in a frame

```
ttk.Label(frame, text="Monthly Investment:").grid(
    column=0, row=0, sticky=tk.E)
ttk.Entry(frame, width=25, textvariable=investmentText).grid(
    column=1, row=0)

ttk.Label(frame, text="Yearly Interest Rate:").grid(
    column=0, row=1, sticky=tk.E)
ttk.Entry(frame, width=25, textvariable=rateText).grid(
    column=1, row=1)
```

How to add padding to all components in a frame

```
for child in frame.winfo_children():        # gets all child components
    child.grid_configure(padx=5, pady=3)    # pads each child component
```

Description

- To lay out components in a grid, you use the grid() method for each component.

- To pad all of the components in frame, you can use the winfo_children method of the Frame object to get all of the child components in the frame, and the grid_configure() method of each component to add the padding.

Figure 18-5   How to lay out components in a grid

How to code a class that defines a frame

So far in this chapter, you've been building a GUI by coding a series of statements that create objects from the classes that are available from the ttk module. That's an easy way to get started. However, as your programs grow larger, you typically want to organize this code by creating a class that defines a frame. To do that, you can create a class that inherits the ttk.Frame class. Then, you can add all of the components and event handlers for that frame to the class.

Figure 18-6 starts by showing a window that contains a frame that's defined by a class. Then, it shows the code for the InvestmentFrame class that defines this frame. This class inherits the Frame class that's available from the ttk module. In other words, the InvestmentFrame class is the subclass, and the Frame class is the superclass.

After the class definition, the code defines the constructor of the subclass. In this constructor, the first line calls the constructor of the superclass, passing itself as the first argument and the parent window as the second argument. In addition, it passes a padding argument that sets the padding to 10 pixels on all four sides of the frame.

The second statement of the constructor calls the pack() method of the subclass object. That's possible because this subclass inherits the pack() method from the superclass.

The third statement of the constructor creates a StringVar object for the text entry field and stores it as a public attribute. This makes it easy to access this attribute from event handlers such as the clear() method that's defined later in the class.

After creating the StringVar object, this code creates the three components that the frame contains. All three of these components supply the self keyword as the first argument. This passes an InvestmentFrame object to the constructors for these components. As you learned in chapter 15, this works because you can use a subclass object anywhere a superclass object is required. As a result, you can use your frame subclass as the parent object for these components.

Note that the code that creates the button passes a command argument of "self.clear". As a result, clicking the Clear button executes the clear() method that's defined in this class.

This clear() method works much like the callback function described earlier in this chapter. However, since it's a method of a class, not a function of a module, it's easy to access the data that's stored in the attributes of the class. Here, the first statement uses a public attribute to get the string from the text entry field and print it to the console. Then, the second statement uses the public attribute to clear the text entry field by setting it to an empty string.

After the class, the code in the if statement starts by creating a root window and setting its title. Then, it creates an InvestmentFrame object by passing the root window as the parent argument. This adds the InvestmentFrame object to the root window. Finally, it calls the mainloop() method on the root window to display the root window and start the event processing loop.

A window that contains a frame that's defined by a class

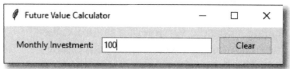

A class that defines a frame

```python
import tkinter as tk
from tkinter import ttk

class InvestmentFrame(ttk.Frame):
    def __init__(self, parent):
        ttk.Frame.__init__(self, parent, padding="10 10 10 10")
        self.pack(fill=tk.BOTH, expand=True)

        # Define string variable for the entry field
        self.monthlyInvestment = tk.StringVar()

        # Create a label, an entry field, and a button
        ttk.Label(self, text="Monthly Investment:").grid(
            column=0, row=0, sticky=tk.E)
        ttk.Entry(self, width=25, textvariable=self.monthlyInvestment).grid(
            column=1, row=0)
        ttk.Button(self, text="Clear", command=self.clear).grid(
            column=2, row=0)

        # Add padding to all child components
        for child in self.winfo_children():
            child.grid_configure(padx=5, pady=3)

    # Define the callback method for the Clear button
    def clear(self):
        print("Monthly Investment:", self.monthlyInvestment.get())
        self.monthlyInvestment.set("")

if __name__ == "__main__":
    root = tk.Tk()                     # Create the root window
    root.title("Future Value Calculator")
    InvestmentFrame(root)              # Create the frame
    root.mainloop()                    # Display the frame
```

Description

- To create a class that defines a frame, you can inherit the ttk.Frame class.
- When coding a subclass of the ttk.Frame class, the constructor of the subclass must call the constructor of the superclass and pass it a reference to the parent component. The subclass constructor can also pass other arguments to the superclass constructor.
- When coding a subclass of the ttk.Frame class, you can use the self keyword anywhere you need a reference to the current frame object. For example, you can use the self keyword as the first argument of a component's constructor.

Figure 18-6   How to code a class that defines a frame

The Future Value program

In section 1, you learned how to create a console version of a Future Value program that computes the future value of a monthly investment amount. Now, figure 18-7 presents a GUI version of this program.

The business module

The business module for this program consists of one business class named Investment. If you've read chapter 14, you shouldn't have any trouble understanding how this code works. In short, it defines three public attributes for storing the monthly investment, the yearly interest rate, and the number of years. Then, it defines a method called calculateFutureValue() that calculates the future value based on the data in the three attributes and returns that value.

The ui module

The ui module for this program starts by importing the tkinter and ttk modules. Then, it imports the locale module that's presented in chapter 9 so the values can be formatted as currency, and it imports the Investment class from the business module.

Next, this code defines a class named FutureValueFrame that inherits the ttk. Frame class. Here, the constructor for the subclass calls the constructor of the superclass to pass the parent component to the superclass and to add 10 pixels of padding to all sides of the frame.

After calling the constructor of the superclass, this code stores a reference to the parent component in a public attribute named parent. This makes it possible for the Exit button to call the destroy() method of the parent component. This works because the parent component is the root window. Then, the constructor creates a new Investment object and assigns it to the attribute named investment. If possible, it also sets the locale to the current region for the user's computer. If that isn't possible, it sets the locale to the United States.

The constructor continues by defining four StringVar objects that will store the data for the investment. After setting up the StringVar objects, the last line of the constructor calls the initComponents() method shown on the next page to initialize the components that are displayed on the frame. As part of that initialization, this method binds the four StringVar objects to the four text entry fields.

The user interface

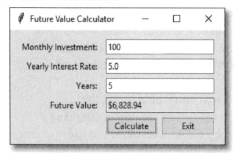

The business module

```
class Investment():
    def __init__(self):
        self.monthlyInvestment = 0
        self.yearlyInterestRate = 0
        self.years = 0

    def calculateFutureValue(self):
        monthlyInterestRate = self.yearlyInterestRate / 12 / 100
        months = self.years * 12

        futureValue = 0
        for i in range(months):
            futureValue += self.monthlyInvestment
            monthlyInterestAmount = futureValue * monthlyInterestRate
            futureValue += monthlyInterestAmount

        return futureValue
```

The ui module

```
import tkinter as tk
from tkinter import ttk
import locale

from business import Investment

class FutureValueFrame(ttk.Frame):
    def __init__(self, parent):
        ttk.Frame.__init__(self, parent, padding="10 10 10 10")
        self.parent = parent
        self.investment = Investment()
        result = locale.setlocale(locale.LC_ALL, '')
        if result == 'C':
            locale.setlocale(locale.LC_ALL, 'en_US')

        # Define string variables for text entry fields
        self.monthlyInvestment = tk.StringVar()
        self.yearlyInterestRate = tk.StringVar()
        self.years = tk.StringVar()
        self.futureValue = tk.StringVar()

        self.initComponents()
```

Figure 18-7   The Future Value program (part 1)

The initComponents() method begins by calling the pack() method of the FutureValueFrame class to add it to the parent component. Then, it displays the four labels and text entry fields in a grid. To do that, it creates a label with the text "Monthly Investment" and displays it in the first row of the first column of the grid for the frame. It also sets the sticky argument to tk.E so the labels are right-aligned.

After creating this label, this code creates a text entry field to get the monthly investment and binds that entry field to the StringVar object stored as the monthlyInvestment attribute of the current object. As a result, if the user changes the value of the text in the component, the monthlyInvestment attribute is automatically updated to the new value. The code then displays this component in the second column of the first row.

The code continues in this fashion until all labels and text entry fields have been added to the grid for the frame. The only variation is that the text entry field for the future value is in a read-only state so it can only be used to display text.

After the initComponents() method finishes adding the labels and entry fields, it calls the makeButtons() method to create and display the two buttons for the user interface. Then, it loops over of the child components of the frame and adds some padding to make the user interface visually pleasing.

The makeButtons() method begins by creating a frame for the buttons using the self keyword to specify the parent component. As a result, the button frame is a child of the future value frame. Then, this code displays the button frame in the first column of the fifth row. However, this code specifies that the frame should span both columns of the row and be aligned with the right (East) side of the row.

After creating and displaying the button frame, the makeButtons() method creates the Calculate and Exit buttons and adds them to the frame. For the Calculate button, this code sets the command argument to call the calculate() method of the current object and adds some horizontal padding between the two buttons. For the Exit button, this code sets the command argument to the destroy() method of the parent component. Since this program sets the parent component to the root window, this closes the root window and exits the program.

The calculate() method is executed when the Calculate button is clicked. This method begins by setting the attributes of the Investment object to the values stored in the text entry fields. To do that, it gets strings from the StringVar attributes and converts those strings to the appropriate numeric types. Then, this code displays the future value of the investment in the appropriate field. To do that; it uses the calculateFutureValue() method of the Investment object to calculate the future value; it formats that value as currency for the current locale; and it sets the formatted value in the appropriate StringVar attribute.

After the FutureValueFrame class, the code in the if statement creates a root window and sets its title. Then, it creates new FutureValueFrame object, passing it the root window as the parent component. Finally, it starts the program and enters the main event processing loop.

The ui module (continued)

```python
def initComponents(self):
    self.pack()
    ttk.Label(self, text="Monthly Investment:").grid(
        column=0, row=0, sticky=tk.E)
    ttk.Entry(self, width=25, textvariable=self.monthlyInvestment).grid(
        column=1, row=0)

    ttk.Label(self, text="Yearly Interest Rate:").grid(
        column=0, row=1, sticky=tk.E)
    ttk.Entry(self, width=25,
              textvariable=self.yearlyInterestRate).grid(
        column=1, row=1)

    ttk.Label(self, text="Years:").grid(
        column=0, row=2, sticky=tk.E)
    ttk.Entry(self, width=25, textvariable=self.years).grid(
        column=1, row=2)

    ttk.Label(self, text="Future Value:").grid(
        column=0, row=3, sticky=tk.E)
    ttk.Entry(self, width=25, textvariable=self.futureValue,
              state="readonly").grid(column=1, row=3)

    self.makeButtons()

    for child in self.winfo_children():
        child.grid_configure(padx=5, pady=3)

def makeButtons(self):
    # Create a frame to store the two buttons
    buttonFrame = ttk.Frame(self)
    buttonFrame.grid(column=0, row=4, columnspan=2, sticky=tk.E)

    ttk.Button(buttonFrame, text="Calculate",
               command=self.calculate).grid(column=0, row=0, padx=5)
    ttk.Button(buttonFrame, text="Exit",
               command=self.parent.destroy).grid(column=1, row=0)

def calculate(self):
    self.investment.monthlyInvestment = float(
        self.monthlyInvestment.get())
    self.investment.yearlyInterestRate = float(
        self.yearlyInterestRate.get())
    self.investment.years = int(self.years.get())

    self.futureValue.set(locale.currency(
        self.investment.calculateFutureValue(), grouping=True))

if __name__ == "__main__":
    root = tk.Tk()
    root.title("Future Value Calculator")
    FutureValueFrame(root)
    root.mainloop()
```

Figure 18-7   The Future Value program (part 2)

Perspective

In this chapter, you learned all of the skills you need to use the tkinter toolkit to create a GUI for the Future Value program. Along the way, you saw a good example of how object-oriented programming is used in the real world.

Of course, there's still plenty more to learn about creating GUIs. For example, you may want to learn how to use tkinter module to work with other types of controls such as check boxes, radio buttons, combo boxes, and lists. You may want to learn how to use tkinter to display photographs or other graphics. You may even want to learn how to use a different GUI toolkit. But whatever you decide to learn next, you'll have a skillset that you can build on.

Terms

graphical user interface (GUI)	callback function
toolkit	event handler
root window	label
component	text entry field
widget	text box
event processing loop	text field
frame	entry field
button	bind
event	

Summary

- Python programs that have *graphical user interfaces* (*GUIs*) are created by using a *toolkit* such as the tkinter toolkit that's included with Python.

- The top level window of a tkinter GUI is a Tk object that's typically known as the *root window*.

- After you create a root window, you can add *components* to it such as buttons and labels. Components can also be referred to as *widgets*.

- The mainloop() method of the root window makes the window visible and starts an *event processing loop* that lets a program handle the *events* that occur on the window and on its child components.

- A *callback function* is called when an event such as a click occurs on a component such as a button. A callback function is also known as an *event handler*.

- A *label* is a component that displays text. A *text entry field* is a component that displays text and lets the user enter text. A text entry field is also known as a *text box*, *text field*, or *entry field*.

- A *frame* is an invisible container that's used to group other components. To lay out the components within a frame in a grid pattern, you can use the grid() method of each component.

Exercise 18-1   Modify the Future Value program

In this exercise, you'll create a Future Value program that allows you to make two side-by-side calculations in the same window. When you're done, the GUI should look like this:

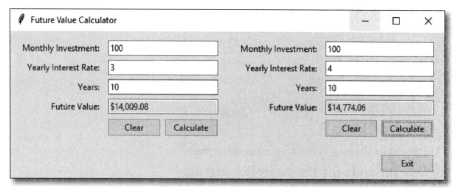

Review the code for the application

1. Open the ui.py file that's in this folder:

   ```
   python/exercises/ch18/future_value_gui
   ```

2. Review the code in this ui module. Note that the if statement at the end of this module creates one FutureValueFrame object and displays it in the root window. Then, run this module to make sure it works correctly.

Use another frame to display two FutureValueFrame objects

3. At the end of the ui module, edit the if statement so it creates two FutureValueFrame objects and adds them both to the root window.

4. Run the program. This should display two FutureValueFrame objects in the window, but they won't be side by side, and they'll both have Exit buttons.

Add and use a new class named FutureValueFramess

5. At the start of the ui module, add a new class named FutureValueFrames. This class should define a frame that displays two FutureValueFrame objects side by side with an Exit button below.

6. Since the FutureValueFrames class should use the grid() method to add the FutureValueFrame objects, you need to delete the pack() method from the initComponents() method of the FutureValueFrame class. Do that now.

7. Modify the code in the if statement at the end of the ui module so it displays a root window that contains one FutureValueFrames object. Then, test these changes.

8. Modify the code for the makeButtons() method in the FutureValueFrame class so it displays a Clear button instead of an Exit button. This function should be connected to a clear() method. Then, define a clear() method that sets all four entry fields to empty strings, and test this change.

Exercise 18-2   Develop a GUI version of the MPG program

In this exercise, you'll develop a GUI version of the MPG program that you worked with as a console program in section 1 of this book. When you're done, the GUI should look like this:

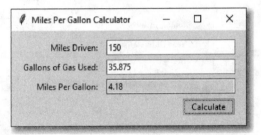

Review the code for the console program

1. Open the mpg_gui.py file that's in this folder:

    `python/exercises/ch18/mpg`

    This provides some starting code for the application.

2. Review the code and run it to see what it does. It should display a root window with one label and an empty text entry field.

Create the GUI for this program

3. Modify the code for this program so it displays the correct title for the root window.

4. Modify the code so it creates StringVar objects for all three text entry fields.

5. Modify the code so it displays all seven components as shown above.

6. Run the program. This should display a window that looks like the window above. However, if you click the Calculate button, it won't do anything.

Handle the event that occurs when the user clicks the button

7. Add a calculate() method that does the MPG calculation. It should divide the Miles Driven entry by the Gallons of Gas Used entry and round it to two decimal places. This method should also display the result of the calculation in the Miles Per Gallon field.

8. If you haven't done so already, add the code that connects the Calculate button to the calculate() method.

9. Test the program to make sure the Calculate button works.

Appendix A

How to set up Windows for this book

This appendix shows how to install and configure the software that we recommend for developing Python programs on a Windows system. For the first 16 chapters of this book, you only need to install Python and the source code for this book.

Chapter 17, however, requires the use of a SQLite database. As a result, you need to install a development tool for working with SQLite databases. For that, we show you how to install and use *DB Browser for SQLite*.

As you read this appendix, please remember that most websites change frequently. As a result, some of the procedures in this appendix may have changed since this book was published. Nevertheless, these procedures should still serve as good guides to installing the software.

How to install the source code for this book

Figure A-1 shows how to download and install the source code for this book. This includes the source code for the programs presented in this book, the starting programs for the chapter exercises, and the solutions to the exercises.

When you finish this procedure, the book programs as well as the exercise and solution files should be in the folders shown in this figure. Then, you can run the programs presented in this book, and you're ready to do the exercises for this book.

The Murach website

www.murach.com

The folders for the book programs, exercises, and solutions

```
\murach\python\book_apps
\murach\python\exercises
\murach\python\solutions
```

How to download and install the files for this book

1. Go to www.murach.com,
2. Find the page for *Murach's Python Programming*.
3. If necessary, scroll down to the FREE downloads tab.
4. Click the FREE downloads tab.
5. Click the Download Now button for the exe file, and respond to the resulting pages and dialog boxes. This should download an installer file named python_allfiles.exe to your hard drive.
6. Find the exe file on your computer and double-click on it. Then, respond to the dialog boxes that follow. This installs the files for this book in folders that start with
   ```
   \murach\python
   ```

If you prefer to use a zip file instead of the exe file...

1. Find the book and FREE downloads tab on our website as in steps 1-4 above.
2. Click the Download Now button for the zip file (python_allfiles.zip).
3. Find the zip file on your computer, and double-click on it to extract the files for this book into the \murach\python folder.

Description

- We recommend that you store the files for this book in folders that start with \murach\python. That way, you will be able to find them more easily.
- By default, the python_allfiles.exe file that you download from our website will install all of the files on your C: drive in the \murach\python folder. However, the first dialog box lets you change that before the installation takes place.
- If you change the location of the python folder, all of the programs will still work, with one exception. That is the Movie List program of chapter 17, which specifies the \murach\python path for the database file. To fix that, though, you can change the database path in the Python code.
- After you install the folders and files on your computer, you can move or copy them to another device or another location.
- You may also want to make a second copy of the exercises folder as a backup. Then, if you want to go back to the original version of the starting code for an exercise, you'll have it.

Figure A-1   How to install the source code for this book

How to install Python and IDLE

Figure A-2 shows how to install Python. To make this easy, the Python website provides an installer that installs everything you need to start developing Python programs. That includes IDLE which is an integrated development environment for editing and testing Python programs.

When you install Python, be sure to download the latest Python 3 release. Although Python 2 is still available, the programs in this book were developed with Python 3. As a result, you should use Python 3 to run these programs.

After you install Python, you can use the second procedure in this figure to make sure that you've correctly installed Python, IDLE, and the programs for this book. If you prefer to wait, though, the exercises for chapter 1 walk you through a similar procedure.

The Install Python dialog box

How to install Python and IDLE

1. Go to the download page for Python. The easiest way to find this page is to search the Internet for "Python download".

2. Click on the link for downloading the installer file for the latest version of Python 3 that's available for your system.

3. Find and double-click on the downloaded file. This file should have a name like python-3.5.2.exe.

4. In the Install Python dialog box, be sure to check the Add Python 3.5 to PATH box.

5. Click Install Now to install Python and IDLE, its integrated development environment.

How to run IDLE to make sure everything is working

1. Find and start IDLE. When IDLE starts, the window for the interactive shell is displayed.

2. Use the File→Open command to open this file:
   `\murach\python\book_apps\ch01\future_value.py`

3. Press F5 to run the program in the IDLE shell. Enter the data that you're prompted for, and enter "n" for the final prompt when you're ready to exit from the program.

4. Close both of the IDLE windows to end the program.

Description

- IDLE is the integrated development environment that gets installed with Python.

- In chapter 1, you'll learn how to use IDLE, but you can start it right after you install Python to make sure everything is working.

Figure A-2   How to install Python and IDLE

How to install DB Browser for SQLite

Remember that the only chapter that uses a SQLite database is chapter 17. So you don't need to install a development tool for working with SQLite databases if you aren't going to read that chapter or use the book programs, exercises, and solutions for that chapter.

If you are going to read that chapter, figure A-3 shows how to install the software that you'll need. Although several management tools are available for SQLite, the one we recommend is *DB Browser for SQLite*.

The download page for DB Browser for SQLite

`http://sqlitebrowser.org/`

How to install DB Browser for SQLite

1. Find the download page for DB Browser for SQLite. The easiest way to do that is to search the Internet for "DB Browser for SQLite".

2. Follow the instructions on that web page to download the installer file.

3. Find the installer file on your system and run it.

4. Accept the default options.

Description

- SQLite is used for the database that's used by the program in chapter 17.

- *DB Browser for SQLite* is the program that we recommend for viewing and editing a SQLite database as well as for running SQL statements against a SQLite database.

- If you aren't going to use the book applications, exercises, or solutions for chapter 17, you don't need to install DB Browser for SQLite.

Figure A-3   How to install *DB Browser for SQLite*

How to use DB Browser to verify or restore a database

Figure A-4 shows how to verify that the database that's used by the program in chapter 17 of this book has been installed correctly. To do that, you use DB Browser to connect to the movies database and view the Movie table as shown in the first procedure in this figure.

The only problem you're likely to have is that the database isn't in the folder that's shown in this figure. If that's the case, you can either move the database into the correct folder, or use DB Browser to select it from the folder that it's in.

If you ever need to restore the database to its original state, the second procedure in this figure shows how to do that. To start, you use DB Browser to connect to the movies database. Then, you run the SQL script named create_movie_db.sql. Of course, another alternative is make a backup copy of the original database file before you start modifying the original.

The Browse Data tab of DB Browser for SQLite

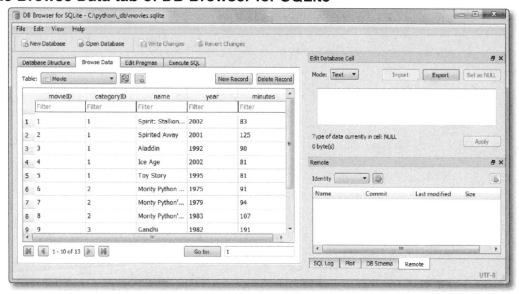

How to verify that the database is installed correctly

1. Start DB Browser for SQLite.

2. Click the Open Database button. Then, use the resulting dialog box to select the SQLite database that's located here:

   `\murach\python\_db\movies.sqlite`

3. In the main panel, click the Browse Data tab.

4. Use the drop-down Table list at the top of the tab to select the Movie table. If DB Browser displays the data for the movies, the database was installed successfully.

How to restore the database

1. Use DB Browser to open the movies database as described above.

2. Click the Execute SQL tab.

3. Click the Open SQL File button that's below the Execute SQL tab and use the resulting dialog box to select the SQL file that's located here:

   `\murach\python\_db\create_movie_db.sql`

4. Press F5 or click the Execute SQL button to execute the SQL statements and restore the database that's open.

Figure A-4   How to use DB Browser to verify or restore a database

Appendix B

How to set up Mac OS X for this book

This appendix shows how to install and configure the software that we recommend for developing Python programs on a Mac OS X system. For the first 16 chapters of this book, you only need to install Python and the source code for this book.

Chapter 17, however, requires the use of a SQLite database. As a result, you need to install a development tool for working with SQLite databases. For that, we show you how to install and use *DB Browser for SQLite*.

As you read this appendix, please remember that most websites change frequently. As a result, some of the procedures in this appendix may have changed since this book was published. Nevertheless, these procedures should still serve as good guides to installing the software.

How to install the source code for this book

Figure B-1 shows how to download and install the source code for this book. This includes the source code for the programs presented in this book, the starting programs for the chapter exercises, and the solutions to the exercises.

When you finish this procedure, the book programs as well as the exercise and solution files should be in the folders shown in this figure. Then, you can run the programs presented in this book, and you're ready to do the exercises for this book.

The Murach website

`www.murach.com`

The folders for the book programs and exercises

```
/Documents/murach/python/book_apps
/Documents/murach/python/exercises
/Documents/murach/python/solutions
```

How to download and install the files for this book

1. Go to www.murach.com.
2. Find the page for *Murach's Python Programming*.
3. If necessary, scroll down to the FREE downloads tab and click it.
4. Click the Download Now button for the zip file. This will download a file named py_allfiles.zip.
5. Move this zip file from your Downloads folder into your Documents folder.
6. Double-click on the py_allfiles.zip file to extract the book_apps, exercises, and solutions folders for this book into the /murach/python folder.

Description

- After you install the folders and files on your computer, you can move or copy them to another device or another location.

- Remember, though, that this book assumes that the book_apps, exercises, and solutions folders are in the /Documents/murach/python folder.

- If you change the location of the python folder, all of the programs will still work, with one exception. That is the Movie List program of chapter 17, which specifies the /murach/python path for the database file. To fix that, though, you can change the database path in the Python code.

- You may also want to make a backup copy of the exercises folder. Then, if you want to go back to the original version of the starting code for an exercise, you'll be able to do that.

Figure B-1   How to install the source code for this book

How to install Python and IDLE

Figure B-2 shows how to install Python. To make this easy, the Python website provides an installer that installs everything you need to start developing Python programs. That includes IDLE, which is an integrated development environment for editing and testing Python programs.

When you install Python, be sure to download the latest Python 3 release for your system. Although Python 2 is still available, the programs in this book were developed for Python 3. As a result, you should use Python 3 to run these programs.

The Install Python dialog box

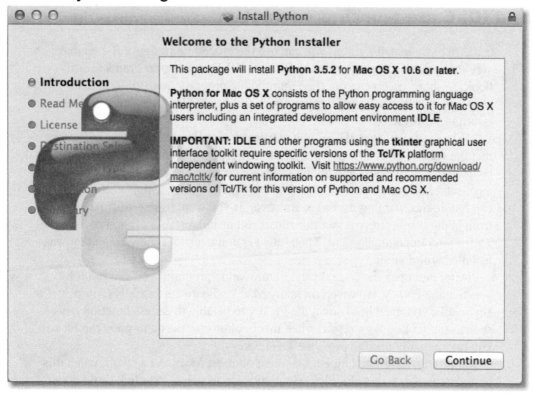

How to install Python and IDLE

1. Go to the download page for Python. The easiest way to find this page is to search the Internet for "Python download".

2. Download the installer file for the latest version of Python 3 that's available for your system.

3. Find and double-click on the downloaded file. This file should have a name like python-3.5.2-macrosx10.6.pkg. That will start the installation.

4. Continue by accepting the defaults that are offered.

Description

*   IDLE is the integrated development environment that gets installed with Python.

Figure B-2   How to install Python and IDLE

How to verify that Python and IDLE are working correctly

After you install Python, you can use the procedure in figure B-3 to make sure that you've correctly installed Python, IDLE, and the programs for this book. In short, if you can run the Future Value program that's presented in chapter 1, you're ready to get started with this book. However, there are a few issues to be aware of.

When you first start IDLE, you may get a warning message that indicates that the version of Tcl/Tk may be unstable. Fortunately, this only impacts chapter 18 of this book, and the program for chapter 18 typically runs without any problems, even with the "unstable" version of Tcl/Tk. So, if you want, you can ignore this warning message. However, if you want to stop this message from being displayed, you can download and install a stable version of Tcl/Tk for your operating system. Then, this version overrides the version that was installed with Python.

After you open the code for the Future Value program, you can run it by pressing the F5 key. However, on many Mac keyboards, especially laptop keyboards, you must hold down the Fn key to be able to access function keys such as the F5 key. As a result, when this book instructs you to press the F5 key, you may actually need to press the Fn+F5 keys.

Similarly, right-clicking isn't enabled on most Macs. As a result, when this book instructs you to right-click, you may need to press Ctrl-click (hold down the Ctrl key while you click).

For both of these issues, you can edit your system preferences if you prefer. For example, you can edit the preferences for your keyboard so you can access the function keys (F1, F2, etc.) without having to hold down the Fn key. Similarly, you can edit the preferences for your mouse to enable right-clicking.

The IDLE shell with the Tcl/Tk WARNING message

```
O O O                        Python 3.5.2 Shell
Python 3.5.2 (v3.5.2:4def2a2901a5, Jun 26 2016, 10:47:25)
[GCC 4.2.1 (Apple Inc. build 5666) (dot 3)] on darwin
Type "copyright", "credits" or "license()" for more information.
>>> WARNING: The version of Tcl/Tk (8.5.9) in use may be unstable.
Visit http://www.python.org/download/mac/tcltk/ for current information.

= RESTART: /Users/MurachMac/Documents/python/book_apps/ch01/future_value.py =
Welcome to the Future Value Calculator

Enter monthly investment:      100
Enter yearly interest rate:    12
```

How to run IDLE to make sure everything is working

1. Start IDLE. To do that, you can select Applications→Python 3.5→IDLE from Finder.

2. When IDLE starts, the window for the interactive shell is displayed. If the Tcl/Tk WARNING message is shown, you can ignore it by pressing the Enter key, or you can fix it as described below.

3. Use the File→Open command to open this file:

    /Documents/murach/python/book_apps/ch01/future_value.py

4. Press F5 or Fn+F5 to run the program in the IDLE shell. Enter the data that you're prompted for, and enter "n" for the final prompt when you're ready to exit from the program.

5. Close both of the IDLE windows to end the program.

How to fix the Tcl/Tk WARNING message

*   Go to the link in the WARNING message of the IDLE window. Then, download and install the version of Tcl/Tk that's recommended for your operating system.

*   Make sure to install the recommended version of Tcl/Tk that corresponds with the version that's already installed on your system. In this figure, for example, Tcl/Tk 8.5.9 is already installed on your system, so you should install the recommended version of Tcl/Tk 8.5, not Tcl/Tk 8.6.

A note about function keys (F1, F2, etc.)

*   This book often instructs you to press the F5 key to run the program. On most laptop keyboards, you need to hold down the Fn key to be able to access the function keys (F1, F2, etc.). So, you must press Fn+F5 to access the F5 key. However, you can change this behavior by editing the system preferences for your keyboard.

A note about right-clicking

*   This book occasionally instructs you to right-click, because that's common on Windows. On a Mac, right-clicking is not enabled by default. However, you can get the same result by Ctrl-clicking (holding down the Ctrl key and clicking). Or, you can enable right-clicking by editing the system preferences for your mouse.

Figure B-3   How to verify that Python and IDLE are working correctly

How to install DB Browser for SQLite

Remember that the only chapter that uses a SQLite database is chapter 17. So you don't need to install a development tool for working with SQLite databases if you aren't going to read that chapter or use the book programs, exercises, and solutions for that chapter.

If you are going to read that chapter, figure B-4 shows how to install the software that you'll need. Although several management tools are available for SQLite, the one we recommend is *DB Browser for SQLite*.

The download page for DB Browser for SQLite

http://sqlitebrowser.org/

How to install DB Browser for SQLite

1. Find the download page for DB Browser for SQLite. The easiest way to do that is to search the Internet for "DB Browser for SQLite".

2. Follow the instructions on that web page to download the installer file.

3. Find the installer file on your system and run it.

4. Accept the default options.

Description

- SQLite is used for the database that's used by the program in chapter 17.

- *DB Browser for SQLite* is the program that we recommend for viewing and editing a SQLite database as well as for running SQL statements against a SQLite database.

- If you aren't going to use the book applications, exercises, or solutions for chapter 17, you don't need to install DB Browser for SQLite.

Figure B-4   How to install *DB Browser for SQLite*

How to use DB Browser to verify or restore a database

Figure B-5 shows how to verify that the database that's used by the program in chapter 17 of this book has been installed correctly. To do that, you use DB Browser to connect to the movies database and view the Movie table as shown in the first procedure in this figure.

The only problem you're likely to have is that the database isn't in the folder that's shown in this figure. If that's the case, you can either move the database into the correct folder, or use DB Browser to select it from the folder that it's in.

If you ever need to restore the database to its original state, the second procedure in this figure shows how to do that. To start, you use DB Browser to connect to the movies database. Then, you run the SQL script named create_movie_db.sql. Of course, another alternative is make a backup copy of the original database file before you start modifying the original.

The Browse Data tab of DB Browser for SQLite

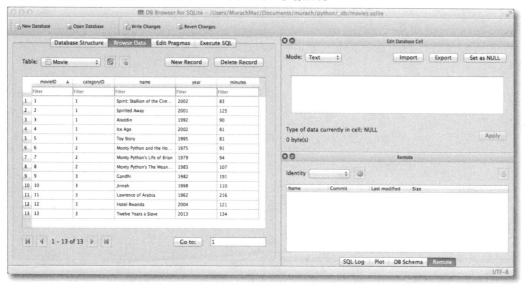

How to verify that the database is installed correctly

1. Start DB Browser for SQLite.
2. Click the Open Database button. Then, use the resulting dialog box to select the SQLite database that's located here:

   `\murach\python\_db\movies.sqlite`
3. In the main panel, click the Browse Data tab.
4. Use the drop-down Table list at the top of the tab to select the Movie table. If DB Browser displays the data for the movies, the database was installed successfully.

How to restore the database

1. Use DB Browser to open the movies database as described above.
2. Click the Execute SQL tab.
3. Click the Open SQL File button that's below the Execute SQL tab and use the resulting dialog box to select the SQL file that's located here:

   `\murach\python\_db\create_movie_db.sql`
4. Press F5 or click the Execute SQL button to execute the SQL statements and restore the database that's open.

Figure B-5   How to use DB Browser to verify or restore a database

Index

XYZ

100% Guarantee

When you order directly from us, you must be satisfied. Our books must work better than any other programming books you've ever used...both for training and reference...or you can send them back within 60 days for a prompt refund. No questions asked!

Mike Murach, Publisher

Ben Murach, President

Learn another of the top 10 languages

If you're programming for the web, you need to know JavaScript and jQuery. And our book offers you the same practical content, clarity, paired pages, and sample code that have been such a help in learning Python.

Core programming language books

Murach's Python Programming	$57.50
Murach's Beginning Java with NetBeans	57.50
Murach's Beginning Java with Eclipse	57.50
Murach's Java Programming (5th Ed.)	59.50
Murach's C# 2015	57.50
Murach's Visual Basic 2015	57.50

Web development books

Murach's HTML5 and CSS3 (3rd Ed.)	$54.50
Murach's JavaScript and jQuery (3rd Ed.)	57.50
Murach's PHP and MySQL (2nd Ed.)	54.50
Murach's Java Servlets and JSP (3rd Ed.)	57.50
Murach's ASP.NET 4.6 Web Programming with C# 2015	59.50
Murach's ASP.NET 4.5 Web Programming with VB# 2012	57.50

Database/SQL books

Murach's MySQL (2nd Ed.)	$54.50
Murach's Oracle SQL and PL/SQL for Developers (2nd Ed.)	54.50
Murach's SQL Server 2016 for Developers	57.50

Prices and availability are subject to change. Please visit our website or call for current information.

We want to hear from you

Do you have any comments, questions, or compliments to pass on to us? It would be great to hear from you! Please share your feedback in whatever way works best.

 www.murach.com

 1-800-221-5528
(Weekdays, 8 am to 4 pm Pacific Time)

 murachbooks@murach.com

 twitter.com/MurachBooks

 facebook.com/murachbooks

 linkedin.com/company/
mike-murach-&-associates

hat software you need for this book

- Python and the IDLE development environment that comes with it.
- For chapter 17, you also need to install *DB Browser for SQLite*.
- You can download this software for free and install it as described in appendix A (Windows) or appendix B (Mac OS X).

The downloadable programs and files for this book

- All of the programs that are presented in this book.
- The starting program files for the exercises in this book.
- The solutions for the exercises.

How to download the applications and files

- Go to www.murach.com, and go to the page for *Murach's Python Programming*.
- Scroll down the page until you see the "FREE downloads" tab and then click on it.
- If you're using a Windows system, click the DOWNLOAD NOW button for the exe file to download a file named python_allfiles.exe. Then, find this file in Windows Explorer and double-click on it. That will install the files for this book in this folder: \murach\python.
- If you're using a Mac, click the DOWNLOAD NOW button for the zip file to download a file named python_allfiles.zip. Then, move this file into the Documents folder of your home folder, use Finder to go to your Documents folder, and double-click on the zip file. That will create a folder named /murach/python that contains all the files for this book.
- For more information, please see appendix A (Windows) or B (Mac OS X).

www.murach.com

Core programming language books

Murach's Python Programming	$57.50
Murach's Beginning Java with NetBeans	57.50
Murach's Beginning Java with Eclipse	57.50
Murach's Java Programming (5th Ed.)	59.50
Murach's C# 2015	57.50
Murach's Visual Basic 2015	57.50

Web development books

Murach's HTML5 and CSS3 (3rd Ed.)	$54.50
Murach's JavaScript and jQuery (3rd Ed.)	57.50
Murach's PHP and MySQL (2nd Ed.)	54.50
Murach's Java Servlets and JSP (3rd Ed.)	57.50
Murach's ASP.NET 4.6 Web Programming with C# 2015	59.50
Murach's ASP.NET 4.5 Web Programming with VB# 2012	57.50

Database/SQL books

Murach's MySQL (2nd Ed.)	$54.50
Murach's Oracle SQL and PL/SQL for Developers (2nd Ed.)	54.50
Murach's SQL Server 2016 for Developers	57.50

Prices and availability are subject to change. Please visit our website or call for current information.

Learn another of the top 10 languages

If you're programming for the web, you need to know JavaScript and jQuery. And our book offers you the same practical content, clarity, paired pages, and sample code that have been such a help in learning Python.

We want to hear from you

Do you have any comments, questions, or compliments to pass on to us? It would be great to hear from you! Please share your feedback in whatever way works best.

 www.murach.com

 twitter.com/MurachBooks

 1-800-221-5528
(Weekdays, 8 am to 4 pm Pacific Time)

 facebook.com/murachbooks

 murachbooks@murach.com

 linkedin.com/company/
mike-murach-&-associates

What software you need for this book

- Python and the IDLE development environment that comes with it.
- For chapter 17, you also need to install *DB Browser for SQLite*.
- You can download this software for free and install it as described in appendix A (Windows) or appendix B (Mac OS X).

The downloadable programs and files for this book

- All of the programs that are presented in this book.
- The starting program files for the exercises in this book.
- The solutions for the exercises.

How to download the applications and files

- Go to www.murach.com, and go to the page for *Murach's Python Programming*.
- Scroll down the page until you see the "FREE downloads" tab and then click on it.
- If you're using a Windows system, click the DOWNLOAD NOW button for the exe file to download a file named python_allfiles.exe. Then, find this file in Windows Explorer and double-click on it. That will install the files for this book in this folder: \murach\python.
- If you're using a Mac, click the DOWNLOAD NOW button for the zip file to download a file named python_allfiles.zip. Then, move this file into the Documents folder of your home folder, use Finder to go to your Documents folder, and double-click on the zip file. That will create a folder named /murach/python that contains all the files for this book.
- For more information, please see appendix A (Windows) or B (Mac OS X).

www.murach.com